BETWEEN HOPES AND MEMORIES

MICHAEL JACOBS was born in Genoa, Italy, in 1952 and took a degree in History of European Art at the Courtauld Institute, Universty of London. For his Courtauld doctorate, awarded in 1982, he spent seven years travelling around northern Italy on a moped. His numerous books on art and travel include the *Phaidon Companion to the Art and Artists of the British Isles* (1980; with Malcolm Warner), *The Good and Simple Life: Artist Colonies in Europe and America* (Phaidon 1982), *A Guide to Provence* (Viking/ Penguin, 1988), and the *Blue Guide to Czechoslovakia* (1992). In 1988 he moved to Seville to research *A Guide to Andalusia* (Viking/ Penguin, 1990), and he has subsequently lived in different parts of Spain, writing books on *The Road to Santiago de Compostela* (Viking/Penguin, 1991), *Barcelona* (A. & C. Black, 1992), and *Madrid* (George Philip, 1992). His extensive travels around Spain have resulted in the Spanish newspaper *ABC* dubbing him 'the George Borrow of the High-Speed Train Era'.

BETWEEN HOPES
AND
MEMORIES

A Spanish Journey

MICHAEL JACOBS

PICADOR

First published 1994 by Picador

This edition published 1996 by Picador
an imprint of Macmillan General Books
25 Eccleston Place, London sw1w 9nf
and Basingstoke

Associated companies throughout the world

ISBN 0330 32041 6

3 5 7 9 8 6 4 2

A CIP catalogue record for this book is available from
the British Library

Typeset by CentraCet Limited, Cambridge
Printed and bound in Great Britain by
Mackays of Chatham plc, Chatham, Kent

For Jackie, again

Sobre la tierra amarga,
caminos tiene el sueño
laberínticos, sendas tortuosas,
parques en flor y en sombra y en silencio;
  criptas hondas, escalas sobre estrellas;
retablos de esperanzas y recuerdos.

Over the bitter earth,
dreams are of
labyrinthine journeys, tortuous paths,
parks in flower and in shadow and in silence;
  deep crypts, ladders to the stars;
tableaux of hopes and memories.

Antonio Machado, *Del camino* ('The Journey')

Contents

From the Escorial

THE path I followed was one that had lured generations of sentimental travellers. I had been drawn to it once before, as a teenager wandering alone for the first time around Spain, spurred on by romantic visions of a country steeped in a spiritual past. The path then was a lonely dust track along which I had hurried in a futile race against the setting sun.

Over twenty years later I found it to be asphalted for much of its length, and bordered by lamp-posts and a large white fence enclosing a smart private golf course. The tiny hermitage, heralding the wooded hill at the final stage of the journey, had once seemed lost among the trees, but now was surrounded by picnic benches and an improvised football pitch. It was a holiday afternoon in March, and the area was filled with Madrilenians taking advantage of the first warm day of the spring. Near the top of the hill, the closeness of my destination was suggested by the presence of a popular refreshments kiosk: 'La Silla de Felipe II'.

The Seat of Philip II, a landmark in the romantic topography of Spain, could be an illustration from one of those old history books for children where grimacing Moors are fighting valiant Christians, or Ferdinand and Isabella are triumphant on horseback at the gates of Granada. When the fashion for romantic historical pictures had been at its height it had, indeed, been the subject of a painting by the once renowned but now entirely forgotten artist, Luis Alvarez Catalá.

This work had been much criticized at the time on the grounds that the ill-informed spectator was likely to conclude that the 'seat' of the title referred not to the rock-hewn throne from which Philip II was shown supervising the construction of the royal palace and monastery of the Escorial, but to the prominently positioned sedan chair on which the gouty monarch had been carried up to this lofty spot. There is, of course, no sedan to confuse the visitor, but many will doubtless be as puzzled as I was to find not one but two rock-hewn thrones.

I decided that the slightly higher of the two was the authentic one and dutifully joined the queue of day-trippers, waiting to savour the brief and probably mistaken illusion of occupying the very seat where Philip II had observed the gradual realization of his obsessive dream. The view has been endlessly evoked, the emphasis being on its immensity and rugged grandeur. To my right stretched a craggy plateau of giant boulders leading the eye to the distant tower blocks of Madrid; to the left, under the shadow of grey peaks that were streaked – as in the paintings of Velázquez – by the last of the winter snow, stood that vast granite repository of hackneyed notions about Spain, the Escorial.

SPAIN IS a country continually defined and constrained by metaphors, and there are even those who have interpreted its very shape as a protruding spiritual presence thrusting out not into the Atlantic but into the mystical imagination. Few other countries have produced archetypal personalities of such resonance as Carmen, Don Juan and, above all, Don Quixote and Sancho Panza, whose names are continually invoked to describe the opposing extremes of the Spanish character. Architecture, too, has been reduced to metaphors in an attempt to explain the national mentality. Thus travellers have rarely failed to reflect on the presence right in the middle of a Spanish cathedral of an invariably poorly lit choir, or *coro*. Rather than dismissing the choir's unusual position as the consequence of a liturgical decision taken by the twelfth-century Bishop of Santiago, Diego Gelmírez, or accounting for the bad lighting as the result of stringent economy measures imposed by the Church authorities, the visitor has often found the whole phenomenon to be suggestive of the dark, forbidding, morbidly fascinating streak that has been thought to lie at the heart of Spanish culture. The analogy of the *coro* can be extended further, with the Escorial itself being seen as no less than the *coro* of Spain.

No one would suggest that all the forces that have shaped

England have been crammed into the panelled halls of Windsor Castle, but comparable claims have been made for the granite corridors of the Escorial. The autocratic placing of this palace–monastery at the very centre of Spain, combined with its megalomaniac scale and unprecedented austerity, have tempted writers to see in it a symbol of Spanishness no less potent than Don Quixote. For the nineteenth-century philosopher Miguel de Unamuno a visit to the Escorial was as essential for those 'endowed with a historical sense of their Spanishness as a pilgrimage to Mecca was for Muslims'.

It was not surprising that the style of its principal architect, Juan de Herrera, would be taken up by those rebuilding Spain in the wake of the Civil War of 1936–9. But long before the building had acquired Fascist overtones, Unamuno himself had noted how those who came there tended to bring with them prejudices that aspired to be aesthetic but that turned out to be political and religious. The architectural appreciation of the Escorial, and the ambivalent feelings towards its scale and austerity, have clearly been influenced by ambiguous and fanciful ideas about Philip II himself, a monarch 'poorly known and even less understood', according to Unamuno, and someone whose romanticized life has inspired a combination of fascination and revulsion.

The Gothic fantasist, William Beckford, felt 'a sort of shudder' on first viewing the Escorial in 1782, a shudder 'to which no doubt the vivid recollections of the black and blood-stained days of our gloomy Queen Mary's husband not slightly contributed'. But while Beckford found a morbid excitement in the Escorial, others have been able to see in it only the dark shadow of Philip's religious bigotry and the totalitarianism of Habsburg rule.

Fanaticism, repression, sobriety, cruelty, extremism, puritanism, corruption, pride, grandeur, morbid obsession, and what has been referred to as the 'profound permanence in Spain', are among the many Spanish clichés that have been heaped on the Escorial. No wonder that a building so loaded with metaphors has provided an oppressive experience for most of those who have visited it. From the time of the French Romantic traveller Théophile Gautier, visitors have felt relief on emerging afterwards into the open

3

air, H. V. Morton even describing how he and his group 'hastened with pleasure into a first-class hotel and ordered sherry and dry Martinis'.

As a representative national monument, the Escorial clearly had its limitations; fortunately Spain could boast another building as rich in metaphorical associations as the Escorial but one that offered a diametrically opposed image of the country. The Alhambra provided a necessary corrective to the funereal chill of the Escorial. It brought to the peninsula a sensuality unparalleled in architecture, and helped to ensure that the Spain of dark spirituality was balanced by a land pointedly defined by Mario Praz in 1929 as the 'last resort of the sexually repressed intellectual'.

The Escorial and the Alhambra, two sides of the traditional image of Spain, bring together many qualities travellers have pursued in their search for what is now and absurdly referred to as the 'real Spain' but which should more accurately be described as 'romantic Spain'. Certain countries, such as Italy, France and Greece, have been particularly subject to romantic distortion; Spain is unique in the extent to which its image has been moulded by a tradition of romantic travel-writing so strong that it continues to affect the expectations of those coming here.

Central to this tradition has been a belief in Spain as one of Europe's most exotic destinations, a belief that dates back at least to the seventeenth century and would be distilled into that famous tourist slogan of the 1960s, 'Spain is different'. The essence of the exotic is the unfamiliar, and by the seventeenth century, Spain had become one of the least familiar of the major European countries, deterring travellers through a reputation for bad roads and poor inns, tales of banditry and the Inquisition, and, perhaps most important of all, insufficient cultural prestige.

Voltaire, who never visited Spain, wrote in 1760 that it was 'a country which we know no better than the wildest parts of Africa and which does not merit being better known'. By this date, however, the very unfamiliarity of Spain had begun to inspire growing curiosity as well as a growing number of travel books – so much so that one visitor, Alexander Jardine, could remark in 1788 that if Spain 'is little known, this is due not to lack of writers but of readers'. Visitors to the country in Jardine's day were relatively few, but, as Jardine himself noted, there had already developed among them a compulsion to write books on their return. The books were still largely sober in tone, their pages filled with learned commentaries on Spain's Classical antiquities, as well as suggestions for the improvement of the country's industries, commerce, agriculture and government.

William Beckford, passing through Spain in 1787, took with him two characteristic examples of this literary genre, Edward Clarke's *Letters Concerning the Spanish Nation* (1763) and Major William Dalrymple's *Travels through Spain and Portugal in 1774* (1777). Beckford himself had a rather more emotional approach to places than that displayed by either of these two authors, and, in a gesture heralding the birth of the romantic travelogue, decided on his arrival in Madrid to throw the worthy but ponderous volumes into the Manzanares.

The much-abused Manzanares ('a rivulet with the reputation of a river', according to Cervantes) could have silted up almost entirely with the countless travel books foreigners came to write on Spain in Beckford's wake. Some idea of their profusion can be had from the subaqueous gloom of the London Library's lower basement, where the remote section devoted to Spanish travel literature houses row upon row of musty and barely disturbed nineteenth-century volumes. Most of these works do not merit close examination, and a quick browse through a random selection will reveal their depressing similarity.

As with the resurgence of foreign interest after the death of Franco in 1975, early nineteenth-century interest in Spain was closely connected with a programme of major social reform initiated during the enlightened reign of Charles III. The emergence of Spain into the modern world, combined with greatly improved communications, encouraged travel, though it would not be long before these new visitors would find in the country's backwardness its essential appeal. They tended to criticize Spain for the same reasons that they praised it. They decried the place for lacking England's civilized qualities at the same time as they revelled in its apparently medieval character and picturesque old traditions. They rarely failed to comment on the cruelty of the Spaniards, their religious fanaticism, and the dangers of a Spanish tour, and yet they were exhilarated by the spectacle of a bullfight, by the drama of Holy Week processions, and even by the possibility of being subjected to that ultimate of romantic thrills – an attack by bandits (a risk so slight that only one literary traveller had apparently experienced it).

Appreciation of Spain in the nineteenth century was remarkably partial, travellers tending to see in the country only those aspects of it that seemed to confirm their curious and blinkered views. The exceptional variety of the Spanish countryside, for instance, was rarely remarked on, travellers preferring instead to evoke a savage wilderness, which provided a suitable background for tales of adventure. Moreover, though many travellers confessed to having been struck by the expressive power of the wild Spanish landscape, few found therein any real beauty. Spain was not a country one visited for its scenery; for natural beauty one looked to the Arcadian lushness of Italy.

Similar prejudices affected the appreciation of Spanish culture, which, for all the exposure Spain received during the nineteenth century, would remain little known or understood. The eighteenth-century obsession with Classical antiquities had given way in the following century to a tedious passion for the monuments of Moorish Spain. Other aspects of Spanish architecture were generally judged by the extent to which they fell short of French or Italian models. In the visual arts, travellers concentrated exclusively on Goya and the great masters of the Golden Age, whose works appeared to share the emotional and technical preoccupations of the nineteenth century, and offered visual evidence of stereotypical national qualities such as mysticism, aristocratic aloofness, harsh realism and southern sweetness.

The musical life of Spain was usually condemned, travellers' enthusiasms being reserved almost entirely for the nascent flamenco tradition, which was already considered less an excuse for gypsies to make money from gullible tourists than an expression of the country's 'soul'. As for literature, the one work of universally recognized genius was Cervantes's *Don Quixote*, but few travellers bothered to read beyond its first fifty pages.

The Spain of the romantic imagination came to seem more attractive than the country itself, and lured travellers in a way that the reality of Spain could not. That this romantic image was becoming increasingly difficult to sustain as the nineteenth century wore on did nothing to stem the flow of travellers; nor did it lessen their compulsion to produce books about these journeys. Romantic adventures of a journey through Spain became ever less plausible as banditry was eradicated and an extensive network of railways reduced the length of a trip to a mere three to four weeks. The publication in 1852 of *Roget's Thesaurus* might have encouraged some travellers in their adjective-strewn descriptions of such overpraised sights as the Alhambra, but none of these writers seems to have realized that what was needed was not new words but new attitudes. The mythology of this illusory Spain was reinforced as fresh and direct observations of the country came to be replaced by the mindless and incessant repetition of ideas, images and platitudes that had been formulated in an ever more distant past.

Bizet's *Carmen* of 1875, to cite one of the most famous examples of Spanish myth-making, was noted at the time for its searing contemporary realism, and yet the work was based on a short story by Prosper Mérimée, which had brought together, some thirty years earlier, all the romantic clichés of southern Spain, from banditry to gypsies and matadors. Mario Praz, attempting in 1928 the first serious demolition of romantic Spain, delighted in pointing out how Edmondo de Amicis – the gushing Italian author of one of the most influential travel books on Spain of the late nineteenth century – had borrowed a description of a bullfight from a famous passage in Théophile Gautier's *Voyage en Espagne*, which in turn had relied heavily on one of the seventeenth-century letters of the scarcely creditable Madame d'Aulnoy, who might never have left her native France but could have derived her own passionate account of the fight from the one featured in a letter by an obscure countess.

The romantic image of Spain was a ruthless travesty of the country, but it was an image so strong that it eventually came to be adopted and perpetuated by the Spaniards themselves. The cultural phenomenon known as *costumbrismo*, which had evolved in the nineteenth century as a reaction against the false foreign image of Spain, ended up by catering to the selfsame stereotypes, forcing the artists and writers associated with this style to make a living through their sentimental portraits of bandits, *majos*, *cigarreras* and bullfighters.

Of greater significance still was the way in which the romantic image of Spain came to permeate the years of intense cultural activity between Spain's loss of Cuba, Puerto Rico and the Philippines in 1898 and the outbreak of Civil War in 1936. Unamuno, Azorín and other victims of the deep-rooted malaise engendered by 1898 scoured the harsh Castilian plateau in search not of real landscapes but of metaphors of noble suffering, solitude and spiritual redemption. Others, among them Manuel de Falla, Isaac Albéniz, Enrique Granados and Federico García Lorca, found consolation instead in that alternative side to romantic Spain, the jasmine-scented sensuality that nineteenth-century travellers had always fancifully interpreted as a legacy of the Moors.

Nostalgia of an ever growing intensity ensured the survival of romantic Spain into modern times. The object of this nostalgia would become confused in the course of the twentieth century, so that what had once been a mere yearning for a distant golden age extended into a yearning for romantic Spain itself – often little more than a yearning for lost youth. Examples can be found in three of the greatest of modern accounts, Gerald Brenan's *South from Granada* (1957), Laurie Lee's *As I Walked Out One Midsummer Morning* (1968) and Norman Lewis's *Voices from the Old Sea* (1984).

Brenan and Laurie Lee looked back respectively to the Spain they had known in the 1920s and 1930s, while Lewis described the life he had led in a Catalan fishing village in the late 1940s, before the onslaught of tourism. All three encouraged a longing for Spain's traditional rural life, a life that had only marginally interested the nineteenth-century traveller but which by now had come to be seen as the last refuge of romantic Spain. Their accounts are by no means idyllic ones, but they are informed by a belief that the Spanish past was somehow more noble and more beautiful than the Spanish present.

Brenan had become disillusioned with Spain by the time of his death outside Málaga in 1984, while Lee expressed a recent desire never to return there, believing that 'the Spaniards of today have lost their identity and been poisoned by soap, by *Dallas* and *Dynasty*.' The notion of a lost innocence was given further emphasis by Norman Lewis, who, in the foreword to *Voices from the Old Sea*, referred to the 'uncorrupted fisherfolk' of a Spain nearing the end of its 'spiritual and cultural isolation'. This was the Spain of Lewis's youth, 'a country still recognizable as that of Lorca, of Albéniz, and of Falla, still as nostalgically backward-looking as ever, still magnificent, still invested with all its ancient virtues and ancient vices'.

'Unchanged and unchangeable' was how the romantic traveller Richard Ford had described Spain in 1845, and this was exactly how many foreigners would want to remember the country right up to the last year of Franco's dictatorship. Those with nostalgic memories of Spain from as late as the 1960s will probably enjoy the odd pang of recognition on turning through a remarkable group of sepia photographs taken between 1913 and 1918 by a German called Kurt Hielscher. Published originally under the slightly misleading title of *Unknown Spain*, these photographs show remarkably comprehensively a Spain as yet barely touched by the modern world. In 1991 they were reissued by a Spanish publisher alongside photographs of the same places seen today from exactly the same angle as Hielscher had shot them. Comparison between old and new is revealing, not least because some of the places have remained virtually unaltered up to the present day, down to the same stork's nest or crack in the wall. For the most part, however, the differences are striking, and there are doubtless many who will be dismayed to find that where there were once quaintly askew tiled roofs, dusty alleys disturbed only by donkeys, or costumed women washing clothes at an ancient-looking fountain, there are now geometrical skylines of television aerials and corrugated iron, car-congested streets, and an ugly municipal swimming-pool.

The most surprising changes are those affecting the appearance of Spain's historical monuments, the very foundations of Ford's 'unchanged and unchangeable country'. The fountain of the Alhambra's famed Courtyard of the Lions has been reduced to half its height, while above this a pointed, plainly tiled roof has replaced what was once a glowing, polychromed dome; a forest has grown up behind the Escorial, and a river has been rerouted at Aranjuez. The changes multiply on closer examination of the photographs, leading perhaps to the conclusion that little in Spain is of 'profound permanence'. Many monuments have gone altogether; others are now in a terminal state of ruin, but many more have been restored in a way that goes beyond mere restoration, so that out of nothing there have suddenly appeared crenellated towers, lancet windows, drawbridges, coats of arms and other mock features that, far from reinstating the old Spain of Hielscher's photographs, have served only to reveal the extent to which the popular image of the past is little more than a pastiche.

High up in the Galician mountains, in an isolated hamlet of stone dwellings, a Spanish expert on nuclear submarines once told me of his amazement that anyone could still think of Spain in essentially romantic terms. The circumstances of our meeting – beside the fireplace of a medieval pilgrims' hostel – might not have been entirely conducive to his ridicule, but it had as its basis the incontestable statement that the Spain of the EC and 1992 could no longer be thought of as the backward, unchangeable, exotic country that had so appealed to the romantic traveller. Writers who might once have toured Spain in search of exotica for their books have now been forced further and further afield, up obscure tributaries of the Orinoco, or into war-torn zones of Papua New Guinea. Accounts of Spanish journeys, written in breathless prose, are slowly trickling out, leaving the task today of perpetuating the image of 'romantic Spain' mainly to the tourist brochures. In the serious literature on the country, an obsession with 'romantic Spain' has given way now to the 'new Spain', and there have been numerous books analysing the political, social and economic processes whereby Spain has finally come to be considered – in the words of its prime minister, Felipe González – 'a normal country with normal difficulties'.

Curiously, however, at a time when Spain's image has at last been radically altered, Spaniards themselves are becoming more aware than ever before of the romantic tradition of travel-writing about their country. Anyone who tours Spain with a book in mind is not only likely to inspire what might seem an exaggerated amount of local curiosity, but also runs the risk of being labelled a 'romantic traveller', no matter how dispassionate he or she may be. What is more, the alarming number of old accounts of Spanish journeys is being rapidly matched by the number of scholarly studies that the Spaniards are devoting to these journeys, studies that bear such titles as *The Romantic Traveller in Murcia in the Early Nineteenth Century, British Travellers and Spanish Medieval Architecture, 1780–1845,* or *Granada in the Image of the Romantic Traveller.* Spanish scholars are searching obsessively through the literary journeys of the past, driven on, it would seem, not simply by curiosity about foreigners' views of their country, but by a fascination in that mysterious force underlying Spain's perpetual appeal to the wanderer.

LAURIE LEE had set out on his famous tour of Spain in 1934 in a state of self-confessed and enviable ignorance. In the late 1960s, when I first came to Spain, I brought with me romantic preconceptions based on a youthful reading of Laurie Lee, and on a dim consciousness of a tradition of Peninsular wanderings that included those of Don Quixote, the heroes of the picaresque novel, and even the medieval pilgrim to Santiago de Compostela. I sported an old, discarded beret, slept rough, and nurtured an ambition to carry out one day a journey of many months' duration that would take me to every corner of mainland Spain.

I returned regularly to Spain after Franco's death, but the opportunity to carry out the long journey I had once envisaged did not materialize until 1991, when the country was getting ready for what was being promoted as a 'magic year' dominated by the Olympic and Fifth Centenary celebrations.

Over the two decades that separated my visits to the Seat of Philip II, my notion of a Spanish journey had significantly changed through an increasing knowledge of the country, and a growing sense of the absurd. I had previously imagined some spiritual ramble along a solitary path meandering to one of those distant Castilian horizons. Now, however, the paths had multiplied, and the country I had once perceived as a single, indivisible unity had become a patchwork of daunting complexity.

The journey I now had in mind was one that would take me into those many areas of Spain rarely explored by the foreign traveller. This was territory where the unfamiliar lay less in obscure, out-of-the-way villages than in Spanish culture itself, a culture in which the central role had always been played by literature. I wanted to search out the memories of Spain's cultural protagonists, and in so doing explore the metaphorical and mythical landscapes that the Spaniards themselves had created. But I was also interested in a Spain that contradicted and even parodied romantic images of Spanishness, an ephemeral and anarchic Spain of discothèques, pollution, unpublished poets, architectural tack, gastronomic passions, historical shams, and fantastical bad taste.

It was in these less-publicized aspects of Spain that I hoped to uncover a country that was not only more human than the one generally presented by travel writers, but also more inherently Spanish. Indeed, if I had to choose one characteristic common to the many fragments that make up Spain, it would be neither 'profound permanence' nor 'Moorish sensuality', but something Spaniards refer to as *cursi*.

Cursi – sometimes slangily translated as 'naff' – carries a wide range of nuances: 'flashy', 'genteel', 'affected', 'kitsch'. Ramón Gómez de la Serna, one of the great Spanish writers and wits of the early twentieth century, recognized its central importance in Spanish life and culture, and devoted an essay to it in which he discussed the close relationship between the *cursi* and the 'surreal'. But for a true understanding of *cursi*, one has to turn to *Chromos*, an extraordinary novel written in the 1940s by a Spanish resident in New York, Felipe Alfau. The novel deals with the lingering attachment to Spain felt by Alfau and other 'Americaniards', and alternates fantastical stories of Spanish life in New York with tales of old Spain comparable to sentimental, calendar-style pictures known as 'Chromos'. Most of these come from the demented brain of a would-be writer, and feature the rise and fall of a family of jewellers based next to Madrid's Puerta del Sol. As the scene switches from an impoverished Aragonese village to the gilded salons of the aristocracy and finally to the slums of Madrid, passion, sentimentality, cliché and melodrama rise up in a crescendo of banality and bad taste, out of which emerges a decidedly burlesque Spain.

'Bull's Eye Cursi!' interjects Felipe Alfau at one point during the telling of absurd tales of old Spanish life by one of his characters. The risk of being interrupted in this way should be a warning to anyone who resorts to sentimentality and nostalgia in their evocations of Spain, but, for the moment, I shall ignore the risk and go back to that rocky vantage point above the Escorial, looking at a Spain that had changed as much of my expectations of it, and yet that still continued to inspire in me a sense of childlike anticipation of forthcoming adventures.

In my wistful mood, a distant memory returned of the Escorial at night, the monastery's massive façade illuminated only by the light from seven small windows, a light suggestive of hidden mystery but also reassuring for the young onlooker for whom the more distant glow of Madrid carried with it all the insecurities of the unknown, of a world beyond the romantic stereotype.

PART ONE

KAFKA'S UNCLE

I

The Chasm of Unanswered Questions

'THE most difficult capital in the world to understand' was how the writer Ramón Gómez de la Serna described Madrid, a city which had earlier been likened by the nineteenth-century novelist, Benito Pérez Galdós, to a 'chasm of unanswered questions'. It was a chasm that had once opened up with spectacular suddenness. Until comparatively recent times Madrid appeared to travellers as an isolated apparition in the middle of a desert, a place apparently lacking all those suburban gradations that so drearily extended the approach to other European capitals. Arriving by train at Madrid even as late as the 1960s, I had the sensation of being plunged in a matter of moments from the near wasteland surrounding the then incomplete railway station of Chamartín into an ugly, chaotic and unfocused metropolis.

I originally came to Madrid with all the prejudices traditionally held against it by foreigners, who, according to V. S. Pritchett, have usually disliked the place for its having 'so little of old Spain'. Madrid has been repeatedly referred to as a 'city without a past', a misleading way of saying that it had been a relatively insignificant township until chosen by Philip II as capital of Spain for few better reasons than its centrality. From the seventeenth century onwards, Madrid grew at a prodigious rate, and with such seeming unconcern for the preservation of the past that by the end of the nineteenth century at least one traveller, C. Bogue Luffmann, could call it 'the most modern-looking city' that he had ever known. But whereas modernity and boldness of scale have been seen as praiseworthy qualities in cosmopolitan Barcelona, in Madrid they have often been thought of as a betrayal of true Spanishness, as a sign of pretentiousness and megalomania, and as a shield with which this city of pioneering skyscrapers has tried to hide that it has remained at heart the same small and parochial Manchegan town.

'I believe no one much likes it when they first come here,' wrote Ernest Hemingway of Madrid, a city he found the best of all Spanish cities to live in, and where he became such an ubiquitous presence in the bars and cafés that one establishment off the Puerta del Sol still makes the lone claim that 'Hemingway never came here'. Hemingway loved Madrid for being almost wholly lacking in the picturesque, and for thus containing what he saw as the unadorned 'essence of Spain'. Others have praised the raw and exceptional vitality of Madrid, a place that has also appealed to those with a perverse ability to treat as virtues what most people would regard as the drawbacks of urban life. The Madrilenians themselves, the most urban-loving of Europeans, seem always to have revelled in the noise, dirt and chaos of their city and had apparently even managed to convince themselves in the seventeenth century that pollution was necessary to counteract what was then thought to be the excessive and dangerous purity of the Madrid air. The strange and unconventional side to Madrid's appeal has been a great source of inspiration in recent years to the film director and adopted Madrilenian Pedro Almodóvar, who has claimed that his love for this city has deepened after exposure to its seamier aspects. 'Cities,' he has written, 'have suburbs and pollution, noise and poverty, but it's in these imperfections that greatness can take root.'

I once thought that the greatness of Madrid lay exclusively in the art collections of the Prado, and on my first visits to the city, rushed off immediately and unquestioningly to see them. It was perhaps symptomatic of my future attitude towards Madrid, and of the passion I would acquire for the city over subsequent visits, that I would end up by feeling not the slightest compulsion to go to the Prado at all. In the spring of 1991, at a time when the city was anticipating its forthcoming year as cultural capital of Europe, I looked for greatness in a Madrid that was by turns unfamiliar, decayed, elusive and ephemeral.

★

THE ALAMEDA DE OSUNA might not be the most promising place to begin a tour of Madrid. It lies at the end of the city, in surroundings that resemble Madrid in the wake of some urban disaster. Thousands of tourists pass by the Alameda every day, unwittingly, on their way to and from the international airport of Barajas. Not even many Madrilenians know today of its existence, though older ones may recall something of its history, and some might even remember the place as a pleasant park surrounded by what was once called the Outer Belt.

My attention was first drawn to the Alameda in an article in the British magazine *Country Life*, which described it as Spain's most important landscape garden of the romantic era. Known originally as the 'Capricho de Osuna', the park and its adjoining palace had been the creation of Doña María Josefa Alonso Pimentel y Téllez-Girón, Duchess of Osuna and Countess of Benavente. A woman rivalled only by the Queen and the Duchess of Alba as the most powerful in the Court of Charles IV, the Duchess had conceived her country estate of the Capricho as a place that would reflect not only her power and prodigious wealth but also her considerable intellectual interests. A patroness of the arts, and the subject of several portraits by Goya, she also saw herself as a true woman of the Enlightenment, and developed a close interest in literature, science and philosophy. Her vision was that of a passionate Francophile, and she invited to the Capricho a long succession of Parisian actors, musicians and academics. For the library she amassed some 6500 volumes, mainly in French, while for the design of the park she brought in a landscape gardener who had made his name at the Petit Trianon at Versailles.

The article in *Country Life* referred to a current and intensive restoration campaign at the Alameda, but also mentioned in italics that the place was open every Saturday and Sunday from 10 a.m. until sunset. The main Madrid Tourist Office was unable to confirm for me these times for the simple reason that no one there had ever heard of the Alameda. Instead of getting to the Capricho and its celebrated maze I soon found myself lost in the labyrinthine capriciousness of Madrid's bureaucracy. One office led to another until eventually I was told by the head of architectural restoration for the Comunidad de Madrid that the Alameda was now looked after by the Ayuntamiento de Madrid, which had nothing to do with the Madrid administrative body for which he himself worked. By chance, however, he happened to be a good friend of the woman now in charge of the Alameda, María Condor, who, he assured me, would be only too pleased to show me around it. Apparently she had a passion for the park, and was especially keen to promote the place among foreigners.

I emerged from the faraway metro station at Canillejas to find a dreary group of residential blocks overlooking a dual carriageway. A footbridge led across the road, and in the distance could be seen the six-lane motorway connecting the city to the dormitory town into which the birthplace of Cervantes has grown; Alcalá de Henares. Somewhere in between the two motorways, in a landscape of parched grass, telegraph wires and untidy clumps of umbrella pines, lay the former summer estate of the Duchess of Osuna. I took a wrong turning and ended up at a corrugated-iron hut marking the entrance to a desolate camping site. Two gypsy women, easily mistaken for Indian squaws, were taking water from the camp to a distant reservation – the kind surrounded by traffic – where a lone horse was grazing, and a camp fire burning. A moody man in black leather pointed me in the right direction, and soon I was following the straight, tree-lined avenue along which the Duchess and her distinguished Parisian guests had once approached the Capricho. As if to confirm the momentary pastoral mood, an old shepherd and his flock suddenly appeared to my right, but this brief illusion of eternal Spain was spoilt by a backcloth of warehouses and speeding lorries. Had any of the *Country Life* readers, I wondered, ever been to the Alameda?

María Condor, with her auburn hair, pale complexion and frilly lace sleeves, bore a superficial resemblance to the English roses traditionally pictured in *Country Life*. I was thus not entirely surprised when she began to tell me about her English ancestry, and about her preference for tea, especially Earl Grey, which she drank every day for breakfast. She had of course been delighted by the article in *Country Life* and had high hopes that it would stimulate a widespread interest in the Alameda among the English, whose love of gardens was well known. She agreed that the ring of motorways detracted somewhat from the potential tourist appeal of the park, and she also warned me that the gardens would be better seen in a few months' time when all the flowers would be out and much of the present restoration would have been completed. Apart from anything else, she added, I had chosen a particularly bad day to come here, as a coachload of teenagers on a youth employment scheme was due any moment.

She gave me a leaflet explaining that the Alameda formed part of a national network of 'Workshop Schools and Apprenticeship Centres', the intention of which was 'to employ youths "abandoned" outside the job market in restoration projects related to our no less abandoned national and cultural heritage'. The coach arrived, spilling out the noisy and abandoned youths on to this neglected corner of Madrid. María Condor bravely led us all into the gardens, but her calm and softly spoken explanations were lost or ignored amid the adolescent cacophony.

A great effort of the imagination was needed to picture what the Capricho must once have looked like. Overgrown and run to seed, the park might have been described as evocative, but in its present state, reduced to a large construction site, the place had little in the way of atmosphere. María Condor spoke to an increasingly distracted and uninterested audience about the fabulous parties and theatrical spectacles that were held there in the late nineteenth century during the tenancy of Don Mariano, the tenth Duke of Osuna, and the last direct descendant of the family. Don Mariano died bankrupt as well as heirless in 1882, shortly after which the Capricho, together with all the Duke's possessions, was sold by public auction to pay off the debts of a life of excess. The estate was acquired by a banking family, the Bauers, who, shortly before their own bankruptcy in 1940, used the park for rallies and moto-cross events. Attempts were later made by two successive building companies to convert the palace into a luxury hotel, but the incomplete work succeeded only in creating further devastation to the estate.

The municipality of Madrid was left to pick up the pieces in 1974, and was now trying with diminishing funds to restore the place to the state it was in at the turn of the century, a period well documented in sepia photographs. One of these shows women in large hats and wide skirts wandering with parasols around a maze that once rivalled Barcelona's Laberint d' Horta. Nothing remains today of the original maze, but María Condor took us to a bleak Italianate terrace where the replanted privet hedges were pushing their way through the parched earth. Above this was a French garden, where columns and occasional pieces of statuary lay around like children's building blocks, waiting to be assembled. The largest and most charming part of the Capricho was a large English garden, divided in two by the undulating lines of what had once been an artificial lake and river, the water supply for which had been cut off for years.

In happier days Watteauesque parties had embarked from a bamboo hut by the side of the lake, journeying not to Cythera, but along the river to a neo-classical ballroom, which was now entirely obscured by scaffolding. The park's follies were being painstakingly re-created, though unfortunately there were no plans to reinstate the Capricho's curious mechanical figures or automata, one of which had been of a soldier who had fired gun salutes into the air, on one occasion accidentally killing a gardener. More harmless had been the automata of knitting women who had sat in the parlour of a pseudo-rustic cottage at the remotest, most wooded end of the park. This cottage, where aristocratic illusions of the simple life had once been enacted, was now empty, but its walls still bore picturesque traces of a *trompe-l'œil* decoration of dangling onions, garlic and other homely objects that gave a faint and fleeting impression of the past springing back into life.

María Condor left the best until last, when I was finally alone with her after the teenagers had gone back to the coach, and a silence had returned to the Capricho. After a long search for the key, she opened a heavy iron door, and led me down by torchlight into what was truly the 'hidden Madrid'. Many Madrilenians will know the Capricho as the place from where General Miaja had directed the Republican defence of Madrid during the Civil War. Few will be aware that anything from this period in the Capricho's history survives; fewer still will have visited the large bunker which witnessed some of the last scenes in the Civil War, when a handful of defiant Communists eventually surrendered to the Nationalists.

In the labyrinth of mildewed white tunnels one hundred feet below the Capricho, María Condor revealed to me her dreams of transforming the bunker into a museum recording the history of the Republican defence of her city. Enlivened by wallcharts, old telephones, General Miaja's desk, and other Civil War memorabilia that had been discovered at the Capricho, the museum would function as the first memorial in Spain to the Republican war effort, and an effective complement to the gruesome study in Toledo where General Moscardó held out during the siege of the Alcázar at the beginning of the Civil War. During the positive, optimistic days that had accompanied the creation in 1986 of the 'Workshop Schools and Apprenticeship Centres', detailed plans for such a museum had been drawn up, and money and help promised by the authorities at Madrid's town hall. But, as María Condor remarked, while lowering her voice and looking down to the bunker's rutted concrete floor, all had changed with 'the arrival of Madrid's new government'.

The polite and quietly genteel manner of María Condor hid strong political passions. A woman in her early thirties, she belonged to that progressive generation of Spaniards who had experienced at a formative age the social transformation of the country after Franco, and was now witnessing the return of conservatives to power, and the emergence of a young generation to whom Franco, let alone the Civil War, meant comparatively little. The 'new government' to which she was referring was that of Madrid's fifty-three-year-old conservative mayor, Alvárez del Manzano, elected to office in the summer of 1990. Municipal elections throughout Spain were gradually ousting the socialists, and there were predictions that by 1992 every important Spanish town would be run by a conservative.

Manzano himself, a great favourite with the press, was outwardly a charming and easy-going person, but with a deeply reactionary core. An anti-abortionist who believed in virginity, praised the teaching methods of the clergy, and proudly boasted of having known no other woman than his wife, he was now attempting to tidy up Madrid through such enlightened means as handing out the same fines to those who left beer glasses in the street as to those who left syringes.

With Manzano in power, the likelihood of a Republican memorial at the Alameda de Osuna was very dim indeed. But there was also the danger that the recent efforts to restore the Capricho to its former verdant glory would be set back drastically, leaving the place in ruins indefinitely. At a time when the Capricho was being turned into one of the new attractions for the Madrid of 1992, Madrid's municipal gardeners were threatening to go on strike in protest at Manzano's policies, a move that could cause permanent damage to the city's parks. Ecologists were not complaining at the prospect of this strike, for, as Manzano noted, to do so would run counter to their own political principles. Manzano, whose name means 'apple tree', at least had a sense of humour. He was capable of appreciating the gardeners' pun that they would 'turn Madrid dry, down to the Apple Tree'.

MADRID, as it prepared itself for 1992, had much in common with the Alameda de Osuna. It too had been reduced to a construction site; everywhere there seemed to be cranes, scaffolding, barriers, buildings covered in sheets of plastic, and clouds of dust caused by the ejection of debris down giant plastic chutes. Madrid was not just building for its future, it was also showing belated signs of discovering its past. Little hesitation had been shown at the turn of the century in pulling down a large section of old Madrid to make way for the American-style blocks of the Gran Vía, but preservation societies had now been formed to protect and restore those very buildings that had once seemed to many the epitome of Madrilenian brashness and bad taste. Monuments that had been closed for years promised to reopen for 1992, and had large signs outside them indicating the amount of money that either the Comunidad de Madrid, or the Ayuntamiento de Madrid had given, or was going to give, towards their restoration. Historical and literary walks around Madrid were being planned by the municipality for 1992, and there was already in operation a scheme known as 'Memoria de Madrid', with blue-

and-white diamond-shaped plaques marking the buildings or sites where famous people had lived.

Yet this surge of interest in Madrid's past was taking place against a background of mounting cynicism and concern. There were fears about the erosion of Madrid's endearing idiosyncrasies in the wake of the city's integration within the mainstream of European life; there was also a widespread feeling that with the arrival of 1992 the remaining impetus behind the construction and reconstruction would be gone altogether. Moreover, for all the recent attempts to conserve and promote Madrid's past, much of it remained inexcusably buried and forgotten, just as in the bunker of the Capricho. How, for instance, could one explain the present state of the Plaza de la Paja, the square that had been at the centre of medieval and Renaissance Madrid, but which now lay dusty and virtually unvisited only a short walk away from the tourist crowds of the Plaza Mayor? And why, I wondered, in this city so lacking in famous monuments was nothing being done about the Plaza de la Paja's remarkable Capilla del Obispo, a perpetually closed chapel which had once guarded the relics of Madrid's patron saint, and still contained one of the most exhilarating late Gothic interiors in Castile?

The chasm of unanswered questions would grow deeper as I turned away from Madrid's artistic and architectural monuments, and began instead to explore the city's literary past, a past that had provided Madrid from the Golden Age onwards with its one consistent claim to cultural greatness.

2

The Pantheon of Illustrious Men

'IBEGIN to see clearly. The cemetery is inside Madrid. Madrid is the cemetery.' The words of the Madrilenian essayist and satirist of the romantic era, Mariano José de Larra, acquired an especial appropriateness as I pursued my literary pilgrimage against a Madrid which resembled increasingly a graveyard of monuments and memories.

Unamuno wrote that the dead in Spain are never allowed to rest – but I had never realized the truth of this statement until I began finding out about the fate of Spain's Golden Age writers. Almost all the leading literary names of this period had died in Madrid, but hardly any of their corpses remained in their original tombs, and most of them had disappeared altogether. Cervantes was among the missing, a victim of a mason's oversight during the enlargement of the church where he was buried. The playwright Lope de Vega was lost towards the end of the eighteenth century, when the rearrangement of a burial vault led to his remains being ignominiously confused with those of an obscure chaplain's sister. As for the posthumous fate of Calderón de la Barca, Spain's late-seventeenth-century dramatic master, this was so bizarre as to be almost surreal.

After his death in 1681, the dramatist's body was taken to the parish church of the Salvador, where it was placed in a modest niche while awaiting the completion of a lavish marble mausoleum. The mausoleum was ready shortly afterwards, but for some reason the body adamantly remained in its niche, and would not be budged until it was compelled to do so by the demolition in 1841 of the church itself, by then in a most delapidated condition. Thereafter Calderón's body more than made up for its previous inactivity by setting off on the first stage of a hectic afterlife involving a whole series of transferences marked by solemn processions. The most sensational of these took place in 1869, following a decision to transform the vast domed basilica of San Francisco into a national pantheon.

On 19 June, accompanied by triumphal carriages, musicians, cannon-fire, horse squadrons and a 400-voice choir, the corpse of Calderón, together with those of his fellow writers Francisco de Quevedo and Garcilaso de la Vega, and many other illustrious Spaniards, were brought to the basilica. Hardly had they recovered from their journey when the parishes from which they had been taken began reclaiming them. After several more moves, the remains of Calderón were finally carried at the outset of the Civil War to a location so secret that only one old man later knew about it. And he, of course, took the secret to his own and by now undoubtedly unknown grave.

For those wishing to pay their respects to the shrines of the famous, Spain could offer no Poets' Corner, no Panthéon, no Vysehrad. The fiasco of San Francisco had left Spain without its national pantheon, or so at first I had thought until a Madrilenian friend, talking to me once about Madrid's neglected sights, asked if I had been to the Panteón de los Hombres Ilustres. 'It's a place,' he said, 'that no one in this city knows about. *No one*,' he repeated.

The place to which he referred turned out to be not some hidden, outlying attraction, but a prominent complex of domes, towers and cypresses at the very centre of Madrid, just behind the railway station of Atocha. I had passed by it numerous times and previously assumed it to be some fantastical parish cemetery devised by an architect who had clearly seen Pisa's Campo Santo. Its medieval Italian architecture had always struck me as an unusual source of inspiration for Madrid, but it now seemed especially odd knowing that the complex had been built at the end of the last century to honour Spain's famous dead. On my friend's advice I decided to have a look round.

A young security guard smiled at me from behind a rusted, heavily padlocked gate, amused that anyone should want to visit Spain's national pantheon. He said that I would need permission from the Patrimonio Nacional, the administrative body responsible for the upkeep of Spain's royal monuments. He gave me the telephone number of the head of security at the Royal Palace, whom I later phoned only to be told that a visit to the Panteón would be impossible at the present moment. In any case, the man continued, the place was a shambles and its important sculptures

– by the likes of turn-of-the-century artists such as Agustín Querol and Mariano Benlliure – had been taken away for restoration. As far as he knew there were no writers of note buried there, indeed few Spaniards of *any* description. As a place for honouring Spain's dead the Panteón had apparently proved as much of a fiasco as the Basílica de San Francisco. Unhappy perhaps in their inappropriately Italian surroundings, most of the corpses had been brought back to their original locations after only a few years, leaving behind at the Panteón just the remains of a handful of nineteenth-century politicians.

What had happened to the rest of Spain's illustrious men and women? My search continued to the suburbs of Madrid – the impoverished suburbs where all of Madrid's important cemeteries are to be found. My former mistaking of the Panteón for a parish cemetery came now to seem an inexcusable error; I should have known that many cemeteries were on the outskirts of towns, in places inhabited – if at all – by those able to afford only the cheapest of housing. The cemeteries of Spain have none of the associations of quiet charm they so often have in England, but tend to inspire instead a strong superstitious fear among Spaniards, to many of whom the worst possible luck is accidentally to set eyes on a funeral procession.

To reach one of the most historic of Madrid's cemeteries, San Isidro, I had to head far away from the centre and embark on that literal and metaphorical descent leading south from the Royal Palace down to the humble Manzanares, and across to a landscape of pylons, smoke, polluted haze, greying apartments and a spaghetti junction.

The cemetery of San Isidro has always been a place of sentimental pilgrimage, thanks to the presence there of many of the greatest Spanish writers of the nineteenth and twentieth centuries: Gómez de la Serna, the Romantic lyric poet Gustavo Bécquer, and the dramatists Juan Eugenio Hartzenbusch and José Zorrilla. The most revered of all the graves was that of Mariano José de Larra, in front of which Azorín, Pío Baroja, Ramón del Valle-Inclán and other members of the 'Generation of '98' held in 1909 a literary gathering commemorating the first centenary of the writer's birth. Luis Buñuel paid a moonlit visit to Larra's grave in the 1920s, while Gerald Brenan braved storms of dust to come and see it in the 1950s.

For both Buñuel and Brenan, however, the actual grave of Larra came to assume a subsidiary importance in relation to the intrinsic interest of the cemetery itself. Brenan was fascinated by the graves' inscriptions, which, with their naive expressions of grief such as '¡Hija mía!', '¡Carmencita mía!' and '¡Angelita!', reminded him of the pagan tombstones of Italy. Buñuel meanwhile encountered there one of the most striking images of his lifetime, an image he would use many years later in his film *The Phantom of Liberty*. Wandering on his own around the cemetery after freeing himself from friends who had come with him, he stumbled across a broken grave, from which protruded the dirty strands of a woman's hair, eerily illuminated by a shaft of moonlight.

The state of neglect into which the cemetery had fallen by Buñuel's day did not improve over the years, and by the time of my own visit a newspaper article had appeared under the title 'The Death of a Cemetery'. I was looking above all for the graves of writers, but this was not the type of cemetery to have a layout of the plots hung in the entrance lodge, nor were there arrows directing the visitor to 'Larra's Grave'. The higher, new part of the cemetery, bursting with uncut grass and unpruned trees, dates back only to the middle of the last century. No one of special importance is buried there, as far as I know, but it has a daring and virtuoso limestone memorial executed by Agustín Querol, said sometimes to be one of the finest of Madrid's art-nouveau sculptures. I found the work to be crumbling, as if made of plaster, and with one of the arms of the carved mourners broken off and loosely resting against the base of the tomb. Only afterwards did I realize that the obscure woman Querol had tried to immortalize with this work had in fact been lucky. She could have been buried in the lower cemetery, unofficially reserved for Spain's great writers.

The lower cemetery, known as the Sacramental de San Justo, came suddenly and shockingly into view from the border of a hedge-lined terrace. The overabundance of green in the upper cemetery was balanced by the ochre devastation of the lower one, which was cut into the hill like an amphitheatre or a dustbowl. From above, the Sacramental de San Justo could have been mistaken either for an abandoned archaeological site or for the ruins of a war-stricken town. Buñuel had found the cypresses here among the most beautiful he had ever seen, but they had now been reduced to worn pipe-cleaners pathetically projecting above a litter-strewn ground where skeletal ferns grew between the cracks. I hesitated before descending, but some young children offered to accompany me. They too, they said, had once been frightened about going down there, but now they happily played among the disintegrating tombs.

'Some strange people come here,' said one of them, as I continued and then forgot my search for writers' graves. Most of the dead lay buried necropolis-like in tiers of niches, but the inscriptions were barely legible, in contrast to the strident and abundant graffiti. The names of fashionable rock groups were emblazoned everywhere, but more intriguing was the large black scrawl which read enigmatically, HERE LIES MY FATHER.

The memories of famous writers were eluding me, but a morbid taste for Madrid's cemeteries was taking hold, leading me after I had left San Isidro to places remoter and stranger still. The working-class suburb of Carabanchel lies to the south. Factories, modern housing developments and mean villas of the 1920s and 1930s have grown unplanned around the former estate of the Marquis of Salamanca. The district is infamous as the location of Spain's largest prison, but it is also remembered for its cemetery, the final resting place of the kind of functionaries who populate the novels of Pérez Galdós.

I jumped into a taxi at Carabanchel's metro station, but my driver seemed as unsure about the district as I was, and, after a quarter of an hour of wandering in circles, alarmed me by leaving the city boundaries and heading towards Toledo. He left me in the middle of a threatening wasteland, beside the enormous walls of a cemetery which I soon realized was not the one I was looking for.

The old, as opposed to the new, cemetery of Carabanchel in fact lay within minutes of the metro, but was lost in an incongruous and unexpected enclave of cultivated fields. A twelfth-century chapel, often regarded as Madrid's oldest surviving monument, stood in front of it. Entering the chapel by a door below a brickwork *mudéjar* tower, I passed through a homely white interior before coming out into the cemetery itself, an intimate space sufficiently run down to qualify for the description of 'quietly melancholic'. It might almost have appealed to the funerary tastes of the English were it not for the incessant wails from loudspeakers positioned above what seemed at first to be a distant football stadium. A closer look revealed the lookout towers and barbed wire of Carabanchel's prison, housing a high proportion of Spain's terrorists and drug-dealers.

Something nightmarish, Kafkaesque, was entering my tour of Madrid's cemeteries, and curiously it was Kafka who had helped indirectly to draw me to this particular place. Kafka, whose writings are so inextricably linked to Prague and Central Europe, could well have ended up in Madrid, had a job offer from his uncle, Alfred Löwy, materialized as he had hoped. Löwy spent the last twenty-five years of his life in Madrid, working as a functionary for Spanish railways. On his return visits to Prague, he appeared to his nephew an exotic figure whose tales of Madrid inspired in him a secret yearning for this city. Löwy was buried in Carabanchel.

Madrid's largest complex of cemeteries still awaited me, on the northern, more respectable side of the Manzanares, but relegated to the area of bleak high-rise estates that lie beyond the bullring of Las Ventas. After my experiences at Carabanchel, I felt I needed the assistance of a guide, but I knew of only one Madrilenian with any enthusiasm for or knowledge of cemeteries.

Jerónimo Hernández was an Anglophile I first met in Seville, where he had gone out of his way to confirm all the prejudices about Madrid held by the Andalusians, whom he in turn would never fail to denigrate as being lazy, inefficient and superstitious. With his calculator–address book, his English sports bike, his pride in being a *yuppi*, his boasting of influential contacts and a stream of international girlfriends, he was a potentially ridiculous figure. Yet he was saved from this fate through sheer energy, and through the uncanny way in which his most extravagant claims would be borne out: one moment you would find yourself being interviewed, thanks to him, by Spain's leading newspaper; the next you would be sitting in his flat listening to the recorded answerphone messages of Tanya from New York, Janie from London, and Marina from Milan. Here was someone you were forced, if unwillingly, to believe. When he mentioned to me that he knew the cemeteries of Madrid by heart, I was sure that a tour with him of these places would leave no gravestone unturned.

'You know about our system of *sepultura perpetua*?' Jerónimo asked me as we set off towards Madrid's eastern cemeteries. 'Only the wealthy dead can stay in their tombs for more than ten years. The bones of the others are taken out and often given to doctors or artists. There's a famous scene in Valle-Inclán's play, *Bohemian Lights*, in which the gravediggers are casually digging up the remains of a poor man. Of course,' he added, 'matters would be far simpler if we had cremation in Spain. But, as some writer said recently, ours is a country that has always preferred to burn people while they're alive.'

We were driving to the civic cemetery, which Jerónimo promised would be in a far worse state than anything I had seen so far. 'It was left completely to ruin under Franco, its occupants being mainly Communists or political prisoners, most of whom didn't have much money.' However, when we arrived at the cemetery, Jerónimo found that the whole place had been tidied up since the recent burial there of Spain's famous Communist leader, Dolores Ibarruri, known to the world as 'La Pasionaria'. Disappointed by how ordinary the place now looked, Jerónimo then went on to register shock and disbelief at the disappearance of the bramble-filled ditch where Republicans had been shot and buried at the end of the Civil War. The caretaker at the entrance lodge denied that such a communal grave had ever existed.

The Almudena cemetery was just across the road from the civic one, but Jerónimo insisted on driving there in his car, and he kept on driving as we passed first the entrance gates, then the enormous, Secession-style chapel which stood a good kilometre down the entrance drive. No one, it appears, comes on foot to the Almudena, a place that would provide what the civic cemetery had so singularly failed to do – a climax of desolation.

Jerónimo furnished me with the statistics, but the figures were barely necessary to convey the horrendous scale of this labyrinth of lanes lined with crosses. The plan of the whole was said to be inspired by the three apses of an aisled church, but for those visiting the cemetery all that could be appreciated of the overall conception was the hierarchical layout on a hill, the higher levels being reserved for the more important tombs. Manoeuvring his car with startling agility between the tombs, Jerónimo confessed that he came here often on account of his father, who lay buried at the top of the hill. Others who had relatives here often gave up coming because they could not find them, but Jerónimo was lucky because his father had been buried next to a solitary tree, which, though insignificant in itself, was one of the cemetery's few easily recognizable landmarks.

We got out of the car, and from the tree observed an extraordinary panorama of tombs sweeping down to a horizon so distant that the shabby apartment blocks at the furthest and poorest end of the cemetery merely seemed like further tombs. The view was grim, but the sight of three or four tiny cars like our own winding their way around the sepulchral labyrinth brought to the apocalyptic vision a distinct touch of the absurd. Tombs had sidetracked me from literature, but now images from Spain's seventeenth-century literature were being recalled by the scene in front of me, a scene that in its combination of grand fantastical scope and overblown realistic detail could have come straight from the pen of Quevedo, author of the satirical master-piece of Spain's Golden Age, *The Visions*.

Jerónimo, a subject ripe for caricature and yet invested with powers that somehow seemed supernatural, was the perfect guide around such a world, someone who could be compared to the eponymous lame devil in one of the most famous of all Madrilenian tales, by Quevedo's follower Vélez de Guevara, in which a benign devil carries off a student on a magical tour of Madrid, beginning at the very church where Calderón's body had begun its own, no less bizarre, journey, the church of the Salvador on the Calle Mayor.

3

Comedies of Gesture

'I F YOU desire', wrote Quevedo in one of his *Visions*, 'to see
the world, come with me to the Calle Mayor, a place where
everyone meets and where you can see in a short time that
which you would have to see separately elsewhere.'

So I followed Quevedo to the Calle Mayor. In his day the
street had pushed beyond the former eastern gate of the Puerta
del Sol and out towards what was already becoming one of the
liveliest promenades in Europe, the Paseo del Prado. Entering the
Madrid that had grown up in the course of the city's dramatic
expansion eastwards, I was drawn into the literary orbit of a
district that would always be a home to writers, including
virtually all the famous names of the Golden Age. In this city
where literature has always played a central role, I thought it
appropriate that there should lie at what is now Madrid's physical
heart a district still known as the 'Barrio de los literatos'.

The nucleus of this wedge-shaped district is the Plaza de Santa
Ana, site of a former convent. The great plays of Spain's Golden
Age were nearly all performed in this area, in two theatres that
were themselves the scene of continual drama, thanks to the
insatiable and irascible Madrilenian public, who demanded a new
play every week, rushed in early to grab the best places, often
without paying, took sides in the fights between rival dramatists,
struggled to get in to the actresses' dressing-rooms, and counted
among their ranks the paid hooligans known as 'musketeers',
whose whistles, catcalls, shouts of approval, and shaking of bells
and rattles determined the success or failure of a particular
production. It was these theatres that established the essential
character of the Barrio de los literatos. Writers and actresses took
up residence here, making the district acquire a reputation for
Bohemianism, which in turn brought in prostitutes, more writers,
and a succession of populations – bullfighters, beatniks, hippies,
drug addicts and tourists.

The Plaza de Santa Ana remains to this day the heart of Madrid's theatrical world and nightlife, and resembles a more dissolute version of Leicester Square. The newly restored Hotel Victoria, with its tiers of glazed, cream-coloured balconies that would be more at home on Spain's northern coast, crowns the square like a shining toupee, set atop an ageing body whose ill-assorted clothes, ranging from the garish to the faded, include a neo-classical theatre, a mustard-green garden perpetually under restoration, and bucolic-landscape ceramics decorating the façade of a former unbucolic flamenco club named the Villa Rosa.

The square improves at night, when its ugly and discordant features become subservient to the incessant surge of the crowds flowing in and out of the bar-lined arteries of the adjoining Calles Príncipe, Huertas and the famous Echegaray, a popular place to stay for literary travellers, who enjoyed its variety and its vitality and, in the case of the young Laurie Lee, the favours of a husky young widow whose vocabulary of seduction was limited to the word 'man'.

Further east into the Barrio de los literatos, the character of the district changes significantly, becoming quieter and more obviously haunted by the ghosts of the Golden Age. Escaping momentarily from the hectic confusion of a Madrilenian Saturday night, the young medical protagonist of Luis Martín-Santos's strange, experimental novel, *A Time of Silence* (1962), suddenly finds himself among its empty, sheltered streets: 'This is where Cervantes had lived. Or was it Lope de Vega? Or perhaps both? Yes, it was here, among these streets which had preserved so well their provincial air like a cyst in the midst of a great city.'

Martín-Santos's hero wonders how a man of such vision as Cervantes could possibly have lived in this provincial-looking place. Other, more prosaic visitors to this part of the *barrio* might ponder instead why it is that the street where Cervantes was buried is called the Calle Lope de Vega, while the street where Lope de Vega lived is known as the Calle Cervantes. The naming of these streets in this way in 1835 was much criticized at the time, particularly by the indefatigable Madrilenian writer Ramón de Mesonero Romanos, who, two years earlier, had led an unsuccessful campaign to prevent the demolition of Cervantes's house, which abutted on to the future Calle Cervantes, but had its main entrance on the Calle León. The pulling down of the house where the ill, lonely and increasingly destitute Cervantes had spent the last and most productive years of his life would later shame the authorities into putting up a plaque to record its site. But the lesson of history had still not been learned, for the birthplace of Cervantes in Alcalá de Henares was demolished in the 1940s and replaced by a modern block which was itself later destroyed – in the interests, ironically, of creating a brand new 'birthplace' far grander than the modest dwelling in which the writer had been born. Miraculously, the very house where Lope de Vega wrote most of his 1500-odd plays (while conducting a personal life of a complexity outstripping Georges Simenon's) survives intact, supposedly as a museum to him. When I went to visit it, however, I found the place to be as firmly locked as on my last attempt ten years earlier. Restoration, I was assured, was still in progress, but no one seemed to know whether or not the work would be completed in time for Madrid's year as 'cultural capital'.

Instead, I paid my respects to Quevedo, who lived halfway between Cervantes and Lope de Vega and epitomized more than either of them the spirit of the city. The sole important writer of the Golden Age actually born in Madrid, Quevedo was a cruel satirist whose black vision was summarized in a poem, 'The Stages of Life', which opens with the line, 'Life begins in tears and shit'. With his tragi-burlesque outlook, his pungent prose, his fecund and feculent imagination, his eschewal of the lyrical and the bucolic, and his wicked glee in the exposure of ironies, Quevedo was undoubtedly a writer deeply rooted in Madrid's motley, polluted environment. His works greatly influenced many later Madrid writers, such as the sarcastic and outspoken Larra, the linguistically daring Martín-Santos, and the present day cynic Francisco Umbral. But his presence was so strong and lingering in this city that I began almost to think that he himself was responsible for the enigmatic and ironic oversight that became apparent on visiting the site of his house in the Barrio de los literatos.

The plaque at this site records that Quevedo lived here from 1625 to 1634, but does not mention that the previous literary occupant was the greatest of the Golden Age poets, Luis de Góngora, who had rented a room here from 1619. The irony was that Góngora was Quevedo's principal literary and personal rival, the two of them having engaged in a vitriolic literary exchange, which climaxed in Quevedo's sonnet entitled 'Be ashamed, Don Luis, go purple', an allusion not only to Góngora's purple style and continual references to the colour purple, but also, more cruelly, to the fact that the poet suffered from arteriosclerosis, which killed him in 1627. Quevedo might himself have hastened his death after taking possession in the winter of 1625 of the house where Góngora was a tenant. The winter was a particularly harsh one for the poet, but Quevedo had no hesitation in throwing him out into the streets. In so doing he seems also to have thrown the poet's memory out of the Barrio de los literatos, for Góngora, alone of the Golden Age writers, remains uncommemorated here.

The Barrio de los literatos is special in compressing so many associations of one of the richest periods in Spanish literature into so small an area. In pursuing the literary world of Madrid beyond the Golden Age, my field of vision would grow rapidly larger. From being a passive observer looking at the façades of the city, I would be drawn into an endless series of interiors, where the sole consistent feature was the smoke of cigarettes, impregnating my clothes and producing an almost perpetual cough, blurring my focus on a literary history of ever greater complexity and unfamiliarity, and eventually wafting me into a dark world of pure pleasure.

ENRIQUE BENEDITO, the director of Madrid's Tobacco Factory, the oldest to survive in Europe, was a chain-smoker. His complexion, his moustache, his jacket and tie, and the walls of his sparsely furnished office were suffused with an overall grey-to-nicotine-coloured sheen. As he spoke, he seemed continually to be igniting and extinguishing cigarettes, his source being a large white box containing unfiltered and unlabelled *negros*, tobacco in its purest and most popular Spanish form. He was in his late fifties but looked older, and had a passion not just for tobacco, but for its history, a subject on which he had lectured, he told me, on Mexican television. He spoke rapidly, almost without pausing to draw breath, and had launched into his speech without even asking me why I had come to see him. I was there, ostensibly, for literary reasons.

The tobacco factory, which dates back to the end of the eighteenth century, is to be found in Lavapiés, a district halfway down the literal and social slope to the south of the Royal Palace. Renowned even today for its popular traditions and 'authentic' or *castizo* character, it had once been famed above all for its *manolos*, the Madrilenian equivalent of the proverbially provocative and volatile lower-class dandies known generally in Spain as *majos*. Goya had painted them, and they had inspired the work of Spain's leading eighteenth-century playwright, Ramón de la Cruz, a Spanish Goldoni who had derived his subject-matter from scenes from the everyday world, and whose humble vision had given rise to what is still one of the most popular forms of Madrilenian entertainment, the musicals known as *zarzuelas*. In the absence of a true folklore tradition, the *manolos* had provided Madrid with a colourful substitute, and had come in the late eighteenth century to be as much of a tourist attraction as spivs and punks would be in London in the 1950s and 1970s. In 1874, at a time when *manolos* lived on only in the paintings of Goya, a guidebook to Madrid reported on the number of visitors who still came to the city in the hopes of seeing one. In visiting Lavapiés in 1991, I had no such illusions, but I did hope instead to meet another social type that had featured prominently both in Spanish literature and in travel accounts of Spain. I hoped to meet a *cigarrera*.

The cigarette stubs had still to rise above the brim of Enrique Benedito's wide ashtray by the time he promised to take me on a tour of the factory and introduce me to women whose families had worked here for generations. But the word for these women, *cigarreras*, led him off again on a trail of historical anecdote. Talking about the nineteenth-century *cigarreras* with a paternal pride and affection that suggested he had known them personally, he claimed that the women of the tobacco factory had once held tremendous political power in Madrid, and had been so skilful at organizing themselves that they had even inspired the nineteenth-century socialist Pablo Iglesias to form Spain's first trade union.

Benedito's manner became particularly animated as he told me stories about these women's liberated sexual morality, which seemed to confirm the traditional view of the *cigarrera* as brazen and passionate, a view encapsulated by Mérimée's Carmen – herself responsible for the rush of romantic travellers to Seville's tobacco factory in the expectation of a seraglio of voluptuous, provocative and scantily clad women. However, when talking about literature, Enrique Benedito was highly critical of the way in which the *cigarrera* had been 'romantically distorted' by the likes of Mérimée and other foreign writers. Despite his apparent flights of fantasy, Enrique Benedito was a stickler for detail, and said how disappointed he had been when attending the première of a version of *Carmen* staged by the flamenco dancer Antonio Gades. 'A *cigarrera*', he had told Gades afterwards, 'would *never* have carried a knife.'

The ashtray was now so full that every time he put out a cigarette, clouds of ash formed around his hand, and stubs spilt over on to the desk. Still without giving any sign of an imminent departure on our factory tour, he stopped talking about *cigarreras* and pulled out a large volume on the history of tobacco by one Martín Vidal, from which he began reading with difficulty a long list of history's famous smokers, among whom were Wagner, Einstein and Caruso.

When he began talking about his enormous love of literature, I received final confirmation that Enrique Benedito was no ordinary factory director. He was fluent in five languages, including German and Arabic, and was currently trying to improve his English so as to be able to read his favourite English author, G. K. Chesterton, in the original. The complete loss of sight in one eye and the increasing blurring of vision in the other were now threatening his directorship of the factory, giving an added urgency to his literary pursuits. He was looking for Braille versions of Schopenhauer, Bergson and Nietzsche. I knew then that I would never see the factory, never meet a *cigarrera*.

OUTSIDE IN the streets of Lavapiés I took in a deep breath, but my lungs were no sooner clearing than I was back once again in the Barrio de los Literatos, this time enclosing myself within the blackened and yellowed walls of Spain's most august literary institution, the Ateneo, where I breathed in must, floor wax and a lingering odour of tobacco which seemed to trail back well into the last century. An unexpectedly grand staircase, hidden behind the Ateneo's unassuming façade, led up to a gloomy gallery crowded with portraits of most of the main figures of Spanish intellectual life from the last two centuries, their features rendered uniform by the blistering, bitumen-like deterioration caused by time and smoke.

The library above the gallery, with its wrought-iron columns, is one of the few left in Europe where smoking is permitted, an indication to some that the Ateneo is one of this continent's last remaining bastions of liberal values. These values are certainly evident in the opening hours of the library, a place where one can sit reading until one o'clock in the morning every day except Christmas Day, fuelled by occasional visits to the basement bar, where white-bearded old men sit talking among the fumes.

Extensive restoration was threatened for later in the year, and doubtless computer cataloguing would soon be installed, and the rules and hours changed in accordance with the latest European standards. For the moment, however, the Ateneo remained an enclave of the past, a place conducive to begin research on the elusive and fast disappearing history of the city's fast disappearing literary cafés.

CITIES SUCH as Vienna and Paris are weighed down by the image of their café culture; this is not the case with Madrid. Characteristically, for a place that hides so much of its history, Madrid gives little hint today that it was once the scene of a café life vital to the culture and politics of the city and, indeed of the country as a whole. The famous cafés of old had mainly gone, and, as I soon found out when hunting down material in the Ateneo, no one had bothered to produce a serious study of these places. Madrilenians with stories to tell of the last great days of the city's cafés were dying without their memories being recorded, while the published memoirs were often lightweight, unrevealing and emotionally dishonest, as Spanish autobiographical writings notoriously tend to be. The cultural foundations of modern Madrid, so it would seem, had been built on the ephemeral.

A meeting held in a Spanish café has been dignified with the word *tertulia*, a word that indicates any regular informal get-together, but which is usually applied to any gathering of people who share the same interests, political views, jobs, or even place of birth. *Tertulias* were the Spanish equivalent of the French *salons* but, though held at first mainly in the houses of the aristocracy, they found their true home in the early nineteenth century, with the burgeoning of Madrid's cafés. Café society in any city has always flourished in times of political repression, and it is no coincidence that the Madrid cafés rose to fashion during the stultifying reign of Ferdinand VII, a period that also saw the birth of the Ateneo, a centre of liberal opposition right up to the time of Franco.

The main opponents of the monarch all participated in the heated *tertulias* of the Fontana de Oro, a café that would later provide the setting and the title of a historical novel by Benito Pérez Galdós. An English traveller of the 1830s, A. de C. Brooke, described this café as a large space comprising 'some hundred lawyers, who at leisure hours, which in Spain are not very limited, are to be seen busily engaged in doing nothing, that is to say, in drinking lemonade, smoking cigars, and dabbling in politics'. Galdós saw in it rather 'the magnet for the city's ardent and clamorous youth', and brilliantly evoked a mirrored, gilded interior mellowed by cigarette smoke, the steam of coffee, and the rising vapour from the oil lamps, which, after midnight, began to flicker from side to side as if saying 'no', eventually going out altogether, 'leaving the apostles of liberty to save the fatherland in darkness'.

Contemporary with the Fontana de Oro, but completely different in character, was the Café del Príncipe, a basement café so famous for its artistic and literary *tertulias* that it acquired the nickname of the *Parnasillo* ('Little Parnassus'). Rarely has Parnassus been applied to a place quite as squalid as this, a place later described as having consisted of a dozen or so chocolate-coloured tables within a dark, poky and undecorated room frequented by retired professionals who went there out of habit and inertia, oblivious to the dirty cups and glasses in which they had drunk their chocolate and to the rats who fed off the clumps of grass growing between the cracks of the unwashed floor.

The Café del Príncipe had as its pivot the complementary personalities of the *Madrilenista* Mesonero Romanos and the essayist Mariano José de Larra. Portly, bespectacled and meticulous in his ways, Mesonero Romanos was a dispassionate observer of life who devoted his clear-headed and accessible talents to the writing of guidebooks and *costumbrista* studies relating to Madrid, a city he was the first obsessively to record, and which enthused him to such a degree that he would proudly entitle his autobiography *Memoirs of a Septuagenarian, Born and Bred in Madrid* (1881). Larra too was a recorder of Madrid, a recorder of its inefficiencies, pettiness, corruption and hopeless bureaucracy, all of which he set down with a misanthropy and linguistic verve worthy of Quevedo, but with the ulterior motive of trying to reform Spanish society. The key places in the life of this political liberal and satirical journalist were circumscribed by the area between the Café del Príncipe and the Royal Palace, and perhaps it was inevitable that he eventually came to feel constricted by Madrid, the claustrophobic size of which was suggested by the centre of his world, the *Parnasillo*. He broke out of the city, rushed to Extremadura, but, like the drinkers in Eugene O'Neill's *The Iceman Cometh*, eternally condemned to the same bar, he felt lost, a nobody outside Madrid, away from his admiring circle in the *Parnasillo*. He returned to the city, which he should never have left, for, as he wrote in one of his last and most famous articles, 'All Souls' Day', he had escaped from the 'horrible cemetery' of Madrid only to find another and far more oppressive cemetery – the cemetery of his heart.

The pair of duelling pistols with which Larra shot himself, at the age of twenty-eight, lie today like sacred relics within the sham series of late-nineteenth-century rooms constituting Madrid's Museo Romántico. But the Madrid Larra knew has largely gone, swept away during the period of spectacular urban transformation that would last from the 1850s up to the outbreak of the Civil War, and give to the centre of Madrid much of its present day appearance. At the heart of this changing city was the elliptical Puerta del Sol, which acquired its current look in the course of

mid-nineteenth-century remodelling, and began intriguing foreigners such as Borrow and de Amicis with its quality of
perpetual, sea-like movement. The square became the nucleus of
the city's cafés, which experienced the most active years in their
history at a time when Madrid was developing its infamously late
eating and sleeping hours. In the 1860s Galdós found Madrilenian
life quietening down after midnight; but early in the following
century Gómez de la Serna would be writing that the Puerta del
Sol was in full swing at two or three in the morning.

Pérez Galdós moved to Madrid from his native Canaries in
1862 and made the Café Universal in the Puerta del Sol his main
base for his increasingly obsessive exploration of a city he seemed
to love the more for being 'dilapidated, dirty, inconvenient,
disorderly and dark'. The full range of his observations on
Madrid, and all his talents as a novelist, came together in what is
one of the greatest, if least recognized, works of nineteenth-
century realist literature, *Fortunata and Jacinta* (1886–7). It uses the
story of a spoilt young man and his relationships with two
women of contrasting social backgrounds to paint a panoramic
picture of Madrid, focusing initially on the Puerta del Sol area but
then spreading outwards to embrace the scorched shrubland to
the south of the city and the burgeoning wealthy suburbs to the
north. Cafés provided Galdós with a wonderful vantage point
from which to study Madrilenian life, and yet his own presence
within these places was so silent and enigmatic that he was
sometimes thought of as a spy. Though likening cafés to great
fairs 'in which an infinite variety of human products is
exchanged', he himself would be remembered in them not for his
conversation but for his habit of constantly wrapping a foot
around the leg of a table and for making paper birds, a pastime
also adopted, curiously, by his enemy, Unamuno.

As if to compensate for Galdós's shadowy presence in the life
of Madrid, the city's fashionable literary circles came to be
dominated at the turn of the century by personalities who were at
their most resplendent in café society. Unamuno referred to the
Madrid he had known from the 1880s onwards as a place with 'a
spiritual life that revolved almost entirely around cafés and
tertulias', a conceit embodied by his playwright friend Valle-

Inclán, who turned the *tertulia* into a work of art in itself. Dressed in a cape, sporting the longest of beards, and almost delighting in having lost one of his arms in a duel, Valle-Inclán treated the café as a stage from which to mesmerize his large coterie of followers by telling outlandish and fantastical tales, and hitting anyone who dared laugh at these stories with a stick. Valle-Inclán vividly illustrated the extent to which Spain's literary culture has been one in which the written word has been superseded by the spoken word, and the spoken word by what Alfau described as 'the action with a meaning – the gesture', which for him was far more of a Spanish 'speciality' than either the word or even the thought. It is a culture where poetry has resided less in what is put on paper than in the beauty of the moment.

The strange, ephemeral history of Madrid's literary cafés climaxed before the Civil War with the *tertulias* of the Madrilenian writer, Ramón Gómez de la Serna. A genius likely to elude most foreigners, his literary achievement rests largely on a genre he invented, known as *greguerías* – witty, enigmatic and metaphor-laden aphorisms ('Humour + metaphor = *greguerías*'). On one occasion, he called them 'attempts to define the indefinable, to capture the fugitive'. As with Valle-Inclán, Gómez de la Serna was one of the presiding gods in Madrid's cafés, but, unlike the Galician writer, he evolved a literary style that could have grown only out of these establishments, a style unsuited to lengthy and carefully structured compositions, but one that was dependent instead on hasty improvisations at the café table, on sudden moments of inspiration between the smoke, the coffee and the banter.

Among his books was a work of over five hundred printed pages devoted to the so-called 'Sacred crypt of the Pombo', the café at the centre of Gómez de la Serna's universe, where every Saturday night, from about ten o'clock to dawn, a *tertulia* was held with an empty seat reserved for the ghost of Larra. Interspersed with *greguerías*, neologisms and onomatopeia, Gómez de la Serna's rambling book on the Pombo reveals the author's baffling delight in the minutiae of existence, and dwells on such outwardly insignificant details as the marble surface of his favourite table. Altogether, it is a eulogy to the ephemeral, and is particularly poignant for its recording of a café society soon to be brutally terminated by a war that would scatter most of Madrid's luminaries throughout the world.

I COMBED the centre of Madrid for cafés redolent of the great *tertulias* of old, and discovered that not a single one had survived in and around the Puerta del Sol. In the aftermath of the war so many of Madrid's cafés had either been shut down, replaced by the headquarters of banks, or else transformed into Formica-surfaced, American-style cafeterias, a fate that led one *tertuliano* of the pre-war days, Díaz-Cañabate, to exclaim, 'A *tertulia* in a cafeteria! Don't even think of it!'

I found that the Café Universal of Galdós fame had remained, since the 1940s, the Cafeteria Quick, while the Pombo, after having served for many years as a cafeteria hung with posters of Tio Sam, had now become a vacant building lot.

The handful of literary cafés still standing in Madrid were those that had borne witness to the brief but intense flowering of Madrilenian café life in the 1950s and 1960s, when a new literary generation had come to the fore, headed by such strong personalities as the journalist César González-Ruano, and the future Nobel prize-winner Camilo José Cela, whose controversial novel *The Hive* (1951) had taken for its characters the habitués of a particular café. Though I had arrived in Madrid too late to be a participant in its *tertulias*, and thus to enjoy a sense of belonging to a close-knit literary community, I could at least find consolation in hunting out those with memories of this world.

An actress friend, Maite Brik, volunteered to help me in my search. A specialist in Absurdist drama who had been praised by Samuel Beckett and Laurence Olivier, Maite was as much an actress offstage as on, and was currently perfecting the former role with such gestures as sending herself anonymous bouquets of flowers to incite the jealousy of an errant husband. I had first seen her in the mid-1970s in a controversial production of Valle-Inclán's *Divine Words*, which had climaxed in a naked Nuria Espert being swung above the audience on a crane-like organ pipe. At the time, I was a stage-struck student. She meanwhile was glowing in the dying embers of Madrid's café society, surrounded and admired by artists and writers of an older generation. Her own nostalgia for this period in her life intensified her willingness to introduce me to these former *tertulianos*, but she warned me that they would all prove elusive when it came to making appointments, for they were 'people of artistic temperament'.

'You know what they're like,' she added as we embarked, Spanish-style, on a course of action leaving everything to chance, hoping that by trawling round bars, restaurants, cafés and other haunts, these figures from her youth would re-emerge. Her energy was extraordinary, but the past remained firmly in its place until the day when, going to meet her in the most obvious literary haunt of them all, I walked through the doors of the Café Gijón.

The Night I Arrived at the Café Gijón (1977) is the title of Francisco Umbral's autobiographical memoir, in which he recalls the moment in the early 1960s when he made his tentative first entrance into an institution that had seemed to him – as a budding young author full of glamorous notions about the writer's life – a hall of literary fame, a place where he himself would have to make an impression were he ever to achieve what González-Ruano had called 'conquering the Puerta del Sol'.

The Café Gijón remains today exactly as it had been left after remodelling in 1948. The one feature which it retains from the earlier days is a turn-of-the-century clock under which Galdós had supposedly sat, and which has inspired long passages of whimsical description in the copious literature on the establishment. In addition to its decoration of gilt-frame mirrors, dark mahogany tables, and plush red-velvet seating, the place has kept over the years most of the same staff, their dignified white jackets now matched by the whiteness of their hair. Inevitably, as with many places known to have been Bohemian haunts, the café is much loved by tourists, some of whom may have heard that the place once attracted Mata Hari, Salvador Dalí and Federico García Lorca.

The café's present day clientele bears little relation to those who came here in the past, though there are still a number of elderly men who always sit in the window-seats near the entrance and stand out with their wide-brimmed hats, long, nicotine-coloured hair and silver-handled walking-sticks. I had always hoped for a vacant table in this part of the café, but the few times one had materialized I had shied away from it, fearful of committing a sacrilege. Perhaps I still suffered, as the young Umbral had done, from an overwhelming respect for the literary world of old – which is why I was so taken back by the question put to me by Maite immediately after I had entered the café to meet her.

'Michael,' she asked, looking at me directly in the eyes, 'would you like to meet Buero Vallejo?' We were standing at the bar, and I had yet to adjust to the transition between the brightness of the world outside and the smoky gloom and confusion of the interior. It was lunchtime, and businessmen and their secretaries had taken over most of the café, ousting the handful of aged regulars who congregated at the window tables. 'Would you?' she repeated before pulling me by the arm to the other side of the bar towards an elderly man whose unbuttoned, smoke-coloured raincoat opened to reveal a blue suit as frayed as those that clothed the seedy waxwork figures in the nearby (and unvisited) Museo de Cera.

The idea of meeting Buero Vallejo in the Café Gijón was tantamount in my eyes to meeting Sartre at the Closerie des Lilas. His name might mean little outside the Spanish-speaking world, but he is still regarded in Spain as the most important dramatist to have emerged since the Civil War.

He had wanted at first to be a painter, but had devoted himself to drama since 1946, achieving overnight fame three years later with *The Story of a Staircase*, a work so successful that the traditional All Souls' Day production of Zorrilla's *Don Juan* had to be held over so as not to interrupt its run. Following this production, Buero Vallejo had been the toast of the Café Gijón, his only serious rival as one of the most promising of Spain's new generation of writers being the more extrovert Camilo José Cela.

Cela and Vallejo had fought on different sides in the Civil War, Vallejo picking the losing side; he was sentenced to death in 1939. The sentence was commuted eight months later to seven years' imprisonment, an experience later distilled in his works into the expression of profound suffering. Known both for his social realism and his symbolism, Buero Vallejo wrote in the 1940s and 1950s the dramatic equivalent of episodic novels such as Cela's *The Hive*, plays that concentrated on the plight not of a single individual but of a whole community. *The Story of a Staircase*, set around the staircase of one of Madrid's working-class tenements, was a collective portrait of a social milieu to which he would return again in one of his most popular plays of the following decade, *Today's a Holiday* (1956), the story of a tenement's roof terrace on the day when the residents hear – mistakenly – that they have won a lottery. Buero Vallejo described this last play as a 'tragedy of hope', and its bitter-sweet tone is typical of his work in general. Critics in the past often attacked his plays for being negative and pessimistic, but he always replied by claiming that the suffering in a tragedy was no more indicative of pessimism than laughter in a comedy was of optimism. 'I see myself,' he once wrote, 'essentially as a man and writer of tragic tendency, which, roughly speaking, is the very opposite of being unrelievedly pessimistic.'

Francisco Umbral, in his recollections of the Café Gijón, compared Buero Vallejo's mournful face to that of a 'victim of the Inquisition'. I was now in a position to study this face at close quarters. His skull-like head could have been that of a seventeenth-century aristocrat fallen on hard times. The narrow line of a moustache was just visible; the face was taut, sallow and chiselled, with two deep hollows hiding eyes which at times seemed to disappear completely. In introducing me to Buero Vallejo, Maite had told him with characteristic exaggeration that he had been an idol of mine ever since I had studied one of his plays at school. By way of reply, a hoarse, pained sound, barely audible above the noise of our corner, was slowly emitted from the narrow slit of his mouth, forcing me to move only a few inches from his face, which revealed in close-up the yellowing stumps of teeth. 'Which play?' he asked. When I told him that it had been *Today's a Holiday*, he smiled in a way that could have denoted either pleasure or wistful resignation to the fact that I had not mentioned a slightly less obvious work. 'I have written many more plays,' he said ambiguously.

He had experienced the fate of many contemporary dramatists, acquiring the status of a classic author at an early age, and
then spending the rest of his life writing plays that no one
remembered as well as the earlier ones. Embitterment had set in,
and only a few months after our meeting he was to write an open
letter to the Spanish press denouncing the Spanish government
for not including him among the Spanish writers promoted at the
1991 Frankfurt Book Fair. His personal life had suffered recently
too, and Maite would later tell me that he had never been the
same after the death of his son in a motorcycle accident.

Having succeeded in pinning down this important literary
specimen, Maite was reluctant to let him go. He showed no
impatience with us, and said that he had nothing else to do but
wait around for a 'couple of silly women' to move away from his
favourite table. His creaking voice, like an ancient mechanism in
need of oil, became smoother as Maite lubricated it with prompt-
ings about the past. 'He loves talking to people', she whispered to
me, as he launched into an account of the Café Gijón in the 1950s,
an account whose very quietness added to its dramatic intensity.

'Over there, in the middle of the café, that was where Cela
used to sit, together with the other novelists of the *juventud
creadora*. The theatre people were further down, just in front of
the tables where the lawyers had their *tertulia*. The medical *tertulia*
was at the far left, in between that of the poets and the politicians.
The painters were near the bar, next to González-Ruano and his
writer friends. Then of course González-Ruano had that famous
quarrel with the owner, something to do with his not being
treated with sufficient respect, no one knows quite why they fell
out, nor I think did he. He took his friends to the Café Teide next
door, and I believe a taxidermist *tertulia* replaced them . . .'

I wondered if there had been any tables left over for the casual
visitor to the café, but I asked instead about the window tables
that had always intrigued me. 'Those were for the *tertulia* of the
army officers,' Buero Vallejo said, making both Maite and me
recoil at the thought of an official Francoist enclave in the midst
of a café known for harbouring Bohemian dissidents, including
Cela, who was at heart an anarchist.

'The strange and wonderful thing about this café,' Buero

Vallejo continued, 'was that it was politically neutral territory. There were people like myself who had spent years in prison, or who had had most of their family wiped out, who happily sat at tables next to those who had perpetrated these crimes. The army officers took an interest in literature; they even liked my work, though they did not agree with its politics. Of course there were personal quarrels, but generally there was an extraordinary sense of harmony in the Gijón. We all had different backgrounds, different viewpoints, but when we were in the café it was as if we were all working towards the same goal.'

Nostalgia, in the listener as well as in the speaker, came inevitably to accompany this vivid recollection, and led me to ask as my final question what had happened to this life, and whether *tertulias* were still possible in the cafés of today.

'The moment,' he said, 'they started putting music and televisions in the bars and cafés, they put an end to the *tertulia*.' He paused, and then qualified this statement. 'The *tertulia* died with Franco.'

LITERATURE, which had done so much to sustain Madrid during the worst of the Franco years, lost its central position in the life of the city as social conditions became freer and easier, and as café *tertulias* slowly disappeared. If I had missed out on the *tertulias*, in compensation I had witnessed the new and often absurd social and cultural phenomena that came to supersede them in post-Franco, post-modern Madrid.

Sex rather than literature was the most blatant feature of the first years of Madrid's new-found freedom, and I can remember from the late 1970s the naked, moaning couples half-hidden in the Fascist, de Chirico-like arcades of Franco's new ministry buildings. Nudity had come to be the inevitable feature of all cultural activities, even making its way into a production of *Madame Butterfly*, the plump and ageing bodies of the singers in the roles of Pinkerton and his beloved becoming ridiculously lithe and beautiful in the bedroom.

The aura of late-Roman orgy that had entered into Madrilenian life reached its apogee in the early 1980s at the luxuriant pool and Astroturf terraces of El Lago, a substitute for the sandy public beach that had once been squeezed along the slopes of the Manzanares, and where Martín-Santos had recalled the 'empty ghosts of Ramón Gómez de la Serna's *greguerías* flowing from homosexual actors in the urinal'. Umbral remembered a day on the beach when two foreign women had been thrown out for wearing bikinis revealing only the narrowest strip of midriff. In El Lago, however, the standard costume was an obscenely small piece of material scarcely covering the genitals. *Tanga* was the Spanish word for this garment, but the English term 'posing-pouch' best indicated the behaviour of those who wore it. Taut bodies were poised interminably on the edge of diving-boards, while others on the Astroturf, reclining with gins and tonics or indulging in the slow-motion contortions of t'ai chi, were posed so that everyone would notice every detail of musculature. Colloquially the place was referred to as 'the pool of the *maricones* [homosexuals]', but single women also liked the place as they were unlikely to be irritated by the advances of men or the shrieks of children.

The special character of El Lago was the presence of a third sex, at times indistinguishable from the female sex, but recognizable on a closer look by the size of the feet, and by the way that perfectly formed breasts shot upright even when the bodies were lying flat out on the ground. El Lago was the main meeting-place for Madrid's tranvestite prostitutes, who came here during their daytime leisure hours, and provided the pool with some of its scenes of Quevedo-like comedy and nightmare as they strutted up and down in imitation of bad 1950s actresses, pausing occasionally to study the latest progress of hormone injections in their colleagues, and displaying bodies often in a halfway or bungled stage of transformation, so that the outline of a penis was often visible below a full-breasted torso, and buttocks were revealed to be as lumpy as an Archimboldo face.

A name, the *movida* (the 'movement'), was coined to describe those restless, trend-obsessed individuals who relentlessly flaunted sexuality, narcissism, outrageous fashion and all the other youthful excesses that appeared in Madrid in the late 1970s and early 1980s. The *movida* had its own philosophy, defined by the vague term *posmodernismo*; its basis was the outright celebration of the tacky and the ephemeral. The intellectual organ of the movement was the magazine called *La Luna*, which delighted in its self-consciously informal layout and badly printed cartoon-style graphics.

Its editor was Borja Casani, a handsome young man indulged by wealthy middle-class parents. Other *Luna* associates included the waif-like Sybilla, a fashion designer who had been allowed as a child to express her creativity by scrawling lipstick on the walls of her house. The star of the movement, and perhaps the only member whose reputation would prove less ephemeral than his interests, was the film director Pedro Almodóvar. His intentionally roughshod and luridly coloured works provided welcome if childish relief from the ponderous, heavily symbolic Spanish films where political repression had always been represented by the tricorns of the Guardia Civil.

All these figures came together as an ostentatious pack seen at every fashionable cultural function, one of which I remember for a rat-like Englishman who stood around proffering boxes of Rothmans cigarettes, ignored by all the pack until they discovered who he was – a man who raised industrial sponsorship for the arts. It was on the pavements of the Castellana, on summer nights, that the pack ruled Madrid, regally acknowledging their many friends and admirers among the incessant, all-night throng prowling up and down a row of open-air bars or *terrazas* stretching much of the way from Atocha to Chamartín. Mysterious laws governed the rise to fashion of a particular *terraza*; it was at the *terraza* momentarily most favoured by these laws that I was seated once when a taxi pulled up, disgorging some minor members of the *movida*, one of whom was a peroxide blonde actress, dangerously old at the age of nearly twenty-eight. They did not talk, try to find a seat, order a drink, or even seem to enjoy themselves. A teenager in a dinner-jacket accompanied the actress, and the two of them stood immobile for about ten minutes under the yellow glow of a street light, the boy staring fixedly at her while she looked up towards the sky, dressed in a swathe of shocking-green velour, a single breast exposed, like an

Amazon. A photographer was conveniently there to record the moment – their moment.

By 1991 the *movida* was an established feature in the tourist literature on Madrid. Young and not so young visitors were coming to the city with glamorous expectations of this by now mythical phenomenon, just as in another age they would have come with romantic preconceptions of *manolos* and *majas*. They tended to think of Madrid's insistent nocturnal pulse – the *marcha*, the Spaniards liked to call it – as being synonymous with the *movida*, a phenomenon long dead, according to its former apologists. No one spoke any more of *posmodernismo*, nor did Borja Casani speak to any journalists about the *movida*. Sybilla had opened an international fashion store in the elegant heart of Madrid, while Pedro Almodóvar was being wooed by Hollywood. The *terrazas* had drastically shrunk in number as a result of new municipal regulations concerning the level of night-time noise, and the necessity for adequate toilet and washroom facilities. AIDS scares and property speculation had led to the closure of El Lago, which was now a building site awaiting the creation of a large residential block.

Other institutions from an earlier age had also been threatened, and it is partly through the intercession of the Irish Hispanist and Lorca biographer, Ian Gibson, that the Café Gijón has managed to survive, despite a lucrative offer to purchase it for conversion into a luxury hotel. Around what, you might ask, does the spiritual life of Madrid now revolve? The answer seems to be suggested by a newspaper article in March 1991 claiming that the Spaniards spend five times less on culture than they do on food and drink.

4

Sybaritic Games

'FOOD,' wrote the great aphorist Georg Christoph Lichtenberg, 'probably has a very great influence on the condition of men . . . Who knows if a well-prepared soup was not responsible for the pneumatic pump or a poor one for war?'

Pablo Iglesias might have been inspired by a meeting of Madrid's *cigarreras* to form Spain's first Socialist Workers' Party, but he drafted its constitution after a plate of succulent breaded cod at Madrid's Casa Labra, a restaurant still renowned for this speciality. The idea that the Spaniards might regard food as something other than necessary subsistence, let alone as a profound source of inspiration, would have greatly amused romantic travellers to Spain, and is still unacceptable to many tourists, to whom Spanish food is essentially a vegetarian's nightmare and a cuisine of such monotonous, unimaginative simplicity as not to be a cuisine at all.

Foreigners have not only underestimated the enormous regional variety of Spanish food; they have also failed to accept that the Spaniards are one of the most food-obsessed of all Western nations. It is an obsession that unites the many different peoples of Spain, and one that is not just a consequence of recent affluence. One of the characters of Pérez de Ayala's novel, *Belarmino and Apolonio* (1921), trying to list Spain's main contributions to the Western world, rubs his hand against his belly, and comes out with 'Galician stew, Asturian pork and beans, codfish *a la vizcaina*, Valencian *paella*, Mallorcan baked sausage, not to mention *chorizo* and the Jesuits. And, of course, we can't leave out the discovery of the New World.'

To acquire a true appreciation of Spanish food it is not simply a question of going to the right places, being adventurous, or adapting to late eating hours. It is also a question of eating in company, preferably with lots of people: the most ordinary of Spanish meals can be transformed and made special both by the enthusiasm with which the Spaniards tend to eat – an enthusiasm expressed in continual cries of '¡Que rico!' ('How tasty!') – and by their love of sharing, a love that can bring to the meal an element of informality, munificence and abandon. Sharing is inherent in what is said to be the most popular of current Spanish pastimes, the *tapeo*, the eating of bar snacks either as a prelude to a meal or – at supper time – as a meal in itself. No idea of this most idiosyncratic of Spanish eating habits can be gleaned from the ridiculous *tapas* bars that have now become fashionable in Britain, where everyone sits down in twos or fours to eat their own carefully regulated, individual portions ordered from a menu. Whether accompanying a drink with a tiny individual morsel (a true *tapa*) or sharing a plate of food (a *ración*), there is always a feeling in a *tapeo* of participating in a latently anarchic group event in which gastronomic variety is complemented by chance encounters made standing at the bar or walking in the streets between bars.

'The art of the *tapeo*,' wrote Alicia Ríos, 'is like a baroque, sybaritic game . . . which pleases the fine senses by means of the multifarious smells, the friendly pats on the back, the sight of beauty on the streets.' Alicia Ríos, *consultadora gastronómica* and a Madrilenian of the more *castizo* kind, is the only Spaniard I know who has attempted to find philosophical principles in the ephemeral pleasures of eating and drinking. Her background is in philosophy, and it shows in her writings on food, many of which – such as the article on the *tapeo* – appeared in a specialist Oxford journal devoured by England's leading 'foodies'.

In print, and particularly in English, the views of Alicia might be difficult to take seriously, but all misgivings disappear completely when one meets her in person. She is the Gómez de la Serna of the kitchen, a woman who has maintained into middle age a childlike delight in everything, together with an engaging sense of fantasy, which has led her to make 'edible hats' or give talks on olive culture in specially made olive-patterned dresses. Without knowing Alicia, or without having had any experience of going out with Spaniards on a *tapeo*, what is one to make of her lengthy digressions on the 'eroticism' of the *tapeo*? Or on such minutiae of the phenomenon as the *tapa* napkin (with its 'cheeky red or blue border')? Or on the unspoken laws that prohibit the use of a knife when consuming a *tapa*? Or on the way in which discarded prawn heads or shells accumulate on bar floors 'like the fruit of the impeccable toil of the eternal *tapeador*'?

As with the mounting debris in Alicia's bars, the whole process of eating and drinking in Spain has a tendency to escalate, often alarmingly, so that a drink with friends can rarely be a single drink, and a meal can be considered complete only if it proceeds to a *copa*. A *copa*, as opposed to wine and beer, is a real drink, often a *gintonic*, a *cuba libre*, or the fashionable whisky of the moment. There are *bares de tapas* and *bares de copas*, and whereas the former are traditionally informal, inelegant, and open for much of the day, the latter are late-night bars that have become, since Franco's death, places of increasing stylishness.

Madrid's *bares de copa* deserve to be included in any cultural or social history of the city, but they are even less likely to find their serious chronicler than the literary cafés. Every time I visited Madrid in the 1980s, I was fascinated to discover which of these bars had become fashionable, and which had fallen out of favour, the one consistent feature being the ubiquitous presence of Almodóvar in the former and the write-up of the latter in the style pages of *El País*.

My favourite was the Bar Universal, which had its moment at the beginning of the decade, and truly lived up to its name, being as much the haunt of the *movida* as of the scruffier Bohemians and alcoholics of an older generation. The success and ultimate failure of the place were due to its being run by a family of writers, the Paneros, whose principal star at the time was the brilliant and wayward young poet Leopoldo, who alternated between alcoholic binges and periods in mental homes. Whenever the diminutive Leopoldo managed surreptitiously to secure a bottle of whisky from the bar's store, he would disappear without warning for days on end, chased round Madrid by his large and formidable mother. The original clientele of the Universal disappeared as quickly as he did, but would not return, the empty space being filled up with pinball machines. Later these too were taken away and the premises turned into a shop selling office equipment.

As the 1980s wore on, a host of fashionable new bars sprang up to replace the Universal, most of them priding themselves on their self-consciously tacky looks, one of them even calling itself El Cutre Inglés ('English Tack'), a pun on the name of Spain's leading department store, El Corte Inglés. Most of them came and went at lightning speed, the moment of glory for El Cutre Inglés lasting as long as it took for fashionable Madrid to laugh at its name.

At this time of greatest fickleness, around the middle of the 1980s, the fashion conscious rediscovered one of the classic institutions of the Gran Vía, the Museo Chicote, an Art Deco jewel which Laurie Lee remembered for having had an 'atmosphere of weary eroticism'. Elderly men, reading the reactionary newspaper *ABC*, frequented the place at lunchtime, but at around midnight the bar experienced an extraordinary metamorphosis, when it was invaded by the young, glamorous and famous, most of whom would drift on afterwards to other places, such as Cock or Stella, where doormen checked to see if the guests looked sufficiently interesting to be allowed inside. It was at Chicote's that I was first introduced to the producer brother of Almodóvar; it was at Cock that I first shook hands with Almodóvar himself; and it was at Stella that Almodóvar first spoke to me, saying only, 'I'm sorry, I have to go now.'

With the demise of the *movida*, the increasing slickness of Almodóvar's films and the rising number of *yuppis*, the fashionable bars became ever more chic, louder, and more restrictive in their admission policy. Crowds of hopefuls queued endlessly outside the doors of Archy – a *yuppi* temple of Babylonian scale – or gathered even more hopelessly in front of the tiny Hanoi, a black marble tomb where black-dressed poseurs would slip into the toilets in search of drugs, sex and peace. A cold postmodernism, constructed of marble and banks of video screens, had become the dominating style, though all the fashionable places of the late 1980s, however design-conscious, still managed to retain a certain anarchic exuberance, and had yet to go the way of Barcelona's *bares de diseño*, where design had come even to regulate the enjoyment and behaviour of those who went to them. In the summer of 1980 this situation was remedied by the opening of Teatriz, an old theatre transformed by the fashionable French designer Philippe Starck, into a luxurious bar and restaurant for *yuppis* and their parents.

People seemed to come to Teatriz not to look at the famous and fashionable nor to be looked at themselves. They came simply to look, and even the stylish washroom area swarmed with people watching each other manipulate with a mere touch of the foot the taps of basins resembling curiously tilted marble billard tables. Everything about Teatriz was intended as grand spectacle, the main part of the building featuring a giant swathe of red drapery covering what had once been the dress and upper circles. The drapery was parted in the middle to reveal a glimpse of the circle balcony, where people from an upper bar gazed down at those eating at tables arranged around the former auditorium. The greatest spectacle was reserved, naturally, for the stage area itself, which had been left with its original mechanism of dangling chains and bare brick wall. All Starck had done was to add a giant mirror set at an expressionistic angle, and a central rectangular bar which radiated an eerie light from its opaque surfaces. Hovering like phantom flies in the glow, the drinkers participated in an absurd metaphorical drama which had placed the bar at the centre stage of Spanish life.

ESPERANZA FLORES, a Sevillian friend, would have had little patience with Teatriz, or indeed with most of the more recent fashionable bars of Madrid. As with many Sevillians, she criticized Madrid for the same reasons that the Madrilenians criticize the inhabitants of Barcelona. When it came to bars, all she wanted was a place with friendly people. She had no interest in the stylishness of the setting, nor in what a person did or looked like, and even less in whether or not this person was famous. 'In Seville,' she kept on saying, 'no one is impressed by a person's fame, because everyone will always tell you that they know somebody who is more famous.'

Nuria Espert had encouraged her many years ago to come to Madrid to help her start up a special bar for theatre people, but she had arrived with her three children only to find a Nuria who had lost interest in the project. 'You can't play around with the livelihood of my children,' she had told the Catalan actress-director before finding employment in other bars, including the Universal, where she had designed the waiters' outfits. She was back now in Seville, but every so often would return to Madrid, to see family and friends, and to visit her favourite haunts. In the spring of 1991, shortly before I left this city to continue my tour of Spain, I spent the night with her and her friends wandering through her old stamping ground, the district now popularly known after the name of one of its streets, Malasaña.

The name Malasaña refers to a working-class patriot who played an important role in the popular uprising sparked off in this district on that fateful day made so famous by Goya: 2 May 1808. This was the date on which French troops first arrived in Madrid. The district's inhabitants would later forget Malasaña himself, but protest strongly about the use of his name, which in Spanish has an especially insalubrious ring to it, a suggestion of fetid drains and urban decay. To many of those who visit Malasaña today, the name seems appropriate to this traditionally working-class district which has preserved intact its densely packed grid of narrow streets lined with greying tenements straight from a Galdós novel. Drug addicts and alcoholics have now joined company with the ageing Bohemians who in the late 1960s had helped turn this diurnally quiet district into one of the livelier centres of Madrilenian night life.

Many people see Malasaña as threatening, but, as Esperanza discovered when she lived and worked here in the early 1980s, there are few other districts in central Madrid that still have such a reassuring intimacy. Repeated visits to establishments such as Archy, Hanoi and Teatriz were not sufficient to break through the barrier of anonymity, but a single visit to a Malasaña bar is enough for a landlord to recognize you and tell you that the friends you are looking for have moved on to a neighbouring establishment. Much has survived here of the old Madrid, the small-town Madrid eulogized by *castizos* such as Gómez de la Serna and Díaz-Cañabate. At times Malasaña has almost an element of magic, and it is on these occasions that I prefer to think of the district by its traditional name, which was used by Rosa Chacel as the title of her compelling autobiographical novel about life here in the 1930s: *El Barrio de las Maravillas* (*The District of Marvels*).

WE MET up at around ten o'clock at night at the Café Comercial, a mirrored, gilded cavern of a place overlooking the busy Glorieta de Bilbao. This had once been the scene of journalist *tertulias* and, in the 1960s and early 1970s, had witnessed a number of violent confrontations between political dissidents and the police. Though solitary pairs of old men playing cards now made up a significant section of the café's daytime clientele, the Comercial still remains one of Madrid's most popular meeting-places for visiting Andalusians and other transient members of the city's population.

The largely middle-aged group of friends whom Esperanza had gathered here had a dominant Andalusian element, but among the company was one of the best-loved personalities of Malasaña, María José, a native of the nearby Castilian town of Aranda del Duero. She was in her early forties, but with her long and thick jet-black hair, her taste for exotic old clothes bought in jumble sales and her bubbling vitality, she had a spirit younger than that of her teenage daughter. Together with Esperanza and Maite Brik, she belonged to a Spanish generation endowed with far greater energy or *marcha* than most of the emergent youth from the new and supposedly more vital Spain. To the outsider theirs was an energy that seemed at moments to verge on the self-destructive.

Numerous beers and a growing pile of shrimp debris increased the general desire to eat something more substantial, and soon we were heading south into the dark labyrinth of Malasaña, beginning our descent down a long and narrow street named after the great satirist Larra. Almost directly in front of the bizarre, turn-of-the-century headquarters of the Journalists' Union, we all slipped into a small, gloomy restaurant, which proved to be one of those modest places where the best simple Madrilenian food is to be found. Cries of '¡Qué rico!' from our long and noisy table were shouted in polyphonic harmony as we tucked into succulent morsels of raw ham; cubes of freshly made *tortilla*; Parmesan-like slices of mature, tawny-coloured Manchego cheese; blistered, nut-filled rings of deep-fried black pudding from Burgos; tiny river crabs basking in a boiling sauce speckled red with paprika; cuttlefish oozing black ink on to a virginal bed of rice; potato croquettes with a brittle coating of garlic-flavoured breadcrumbs cracking in the mouth to reveal a sensual creamy core; and plates piled high with lentils and tripe, and covered in sauce made from wine, onions, garlic, coriander, and what seemed like a complete inventory of porcine products. Everything was shared, except for the enormous bill, which Esperanza, with characteristic Sevillian grandeur, insisted on settling. The whole occasion had been, after all, her *invitación*, and the rules of this tradition had to be respected by those of her generation who had resisted the more common Spanish practice today of 'going Dutch' – or, as they say in Spain, 'going Catalan'.

These rules, however, allow others to invite those at the table to the obligatory post-prandial *copas*. The first of these was enjoyed at the restaurant itself, where we fuelled outselves for our imminent departure into the outside world with whisky, gin, Gran Duque de Alba brandy, the sloeberry liquor known as *pacharán*, homemade cherry *aguardiente*, and 'Irish Coffee' of a strength and creaminess incompatible with the statutory measures of Britain's Trust House Forte. We were just on the point of leaving when Alicia Ríos made an unexpected appearance, carrying, even more unexpectedly, a huge bunch of carnations which were then distributed to the assembled company after the drinking of further *copas* to celebrate Alicia's arrival. The spirit of the Seville Feria took us over as we emerged from the restaurant shortly before two in the morning, red or white carnations adorning the hair of the women and the lapels of the men. Other friends and acquaintances encountered in the streets were gripped by the same mood, as we continued, to the accelerating rhythm of handclaps and snatches of song, our Orpheus-like descent into the heart of Malasaña.

The heart of Malasaña is the Plaza Dos de Mayo, a traffic-free square marking the site of the barracks where guns were distributed to the rebelling Madrilenian populace on 2 May 1808. The main entrance to the barracks has been reconstructed in the middle of the square as a monument commemorating the two chief heroes of that day, the young artillery officer Pedro Velarde and the commander of the barracks, Captain Daoiz. Sculptures of the two men in naked, heroic, neo-classical guise stand beneath the former entrance arch, surrounded by rubbish, cracked paving stones, discarded syringes, and a continual guard of sallow, shrunken-faced youths with regulation black leather jackets. As so often in Madrid, the square's worst defects are hidden by the night, when the terrace façades acquire a dark grey harmony that complements the warm orange glow flickering from bars like beacons in a wilderness. Home to María José and her friends was the bar cryptically referred to as the Dos De, a small corner bar with spindly Corinthian columns, and a baroque mirror which María José herself used to embellish with paper and floral garlands. Mirrored, mahogany shelving adorned the crowded wall behind the counter, while, secreted carefully among all the old bottles and glasses, were photographs of some of the livelier moments in the bar's recent history.

One of these photographs is so grey and poorly fixed that it might have been taken over fifty years ago. We are all there, María José and Esperanza appropriately in the middle, the former holding on to the bar's central column, the latter smiling as she looks to her left at the buffoon-like pose of an ageing bullfighter called El Novillo. Alicia, her child-like innocence warped somewhat by the effects of drink, stands at the far left, next to an angular-faced gypsy woman with the penetrating glare of a Goya grotesque. I am at the very back of the picture, looking like a demented, close-cropped Hemingway, and smiling because I've just been accused by María José's boyfriend of being a spy.

The boyfriend, himself an enigma for appearing to have no life beyond the Malasaña bars, rests his arm on the shoulders of an even greater enigma, Luis Gallo, a man whom a delighted Alicia Ríos had identified for me as being one of the most *castizo* Madrilenians that I would ever be likely to meet. A wealthy, fifty-year-old Francoist with friends among the Madrilenian aristocracy, Luis Gallo was not a personality who normally associated with the *lumpen* of Malasaña, and yet in the photograph, dressed in jacket and tie, with a neatly cut moustache and a wave of brilliantined hair, he still manages to seem completely at ease in his surroundings. He could well be mistaken for one of the *señoritos* who in the old days would have toured the seedy gypsy bars of Seville and Madrid, and paid for the impromptu flamenco performance that all of us in the photograph are in fact about to witness. Luis Gallo provides the final touch to a photograph that brings together in abbreviated fashion many of the hackneyed attributes of romantic Spain – the hidden flamenco performer, the gypsy woman, the impetuous Sevillian, the bullfighter, the *señorito*, and, in the background, a foreign writer.

When the amateur photographer had moved on, the wails of flamenco filled the air. They were not ordinary Spanish wails, but those of a blond-haired Californian whose features had been prematurely aged by rough living and psoriasis. On a teenage visit to Spain, he had run off to live with the gypsies of Granada, but had been living in Malasaña for the last few years, surviving from a combination of playing in the bars, and relying on the hospitality of others. Stephen Walsh was his real name, but everyone called him El Pollo Colorado ('The flushed chicken'), a nickname derived from the vivid flush that suffused his face whenever he sang. His performance took many of us by surprise, for it seemed at first a parody of flamenco, violent and abrupt bursts of song followed by hysterical twists and turns of his guitar and epileptic seizures of his feet. Tears of laughter from the audience turned later into tears of emotion, for this expressive distortion of flamenco was intended seriously, and finally succeeded in moving us. The bathos and ultimate catharsis of the performance stimulated our group into action, forcing us, with El Pollo in tow, back into the streets of Malasaña, continuing to pursue our by now unstoppable course of squeezing every drop of pleasure from the night. Esperanza went arm in arm with Luis Gallo, while I myself was pinned between the swaying buttresses of María José and the deep-throated landlady of the Dos De; El Pollo trailed far behind, solitary and unsmiling as always. Passing the famous Laboratorio Juanse, where turn-of-the-century ceramics promoted cures for diarrhoea and other ailments, we entered the nocturnal thoroughfare of the Calle San Vicente Ferrer, stopping off to do an imitation of *salsa* in Habana, entering the bleak Manuela to interrupt a gathering of psychiatrists, wandering from bar to bar, but no longer knowing what to drink, and experiencing that early-hours-of-the-morning cocktail of emotions veering from elation and a sense of the unreal to moments of lucidity and anxiety.

El Clint, our penultimate port of call (no one in Spain ever says *último*), was a newly opened Country and Western establishment with swing doors and décor that deliberately set out to evoke the tackiness of the *movida* days, when third-rate imitators of Jackson Pollock threw large cans of paint on walls, ceilings and floors. In a dark, crammed corner, behind a group of denim-jacketed men playing billiards, I danced *sevillanas* with Esperanza to the sounds of Tammy Wynette, before slumping semi-conscious on to a bench where the grotesque gypsy woman with the terrifying stare stuck her talon-like fingers into my back and asked me if I would be hers that night.

My last memory of the bar was the sight of the seated Esperanza talking with Luis Gallo, the two of them as elegant and unruffled as ever, archetypal figures of romantic Spain oblivious to surroundings that somehow represented the distorted antithesis of this mythical land.

THERE IS a long tradition in the literature on Madrid of drinkers describing that critical moment when they come face to face with the early riser setting off to work. It is a moment that can catch the reveller offguard, but, having stayed up for so long, there can be no question of going to bed, for, as Díaz-Cañabate wrote, one of the greatest pleasures of the nocturnalist is to witness a Madrilenian dawn. The true nocturnalist has to follow the example of Quevedo, who, according to an early biographer, was someone who 'stayed out at night by day' ('*trasnocheaba de dia*'). A protracted breakfast, accompanied perhaps by brandy or *aguardiente*, is the usual way of prolonging the night, and Umbral recalled how it was customary in the 1960s and 1970s to go at dawn to eat deep-fried fish in one of the '*freidurías*' around Atocha railway station.

These days, anyone ending a night in one of the smarter districts of Madrid is likely to be sipping gin and tonic in the company of early-morning joggers drinking freshly squeezed orange juice. To avoid such an embarrassing confrontation, a number of fashionable bars have recently been opened to cater exclusively for nocturnalists looking for somewhere to go in between five o'clock in the morning and midday. However, traditionalists will finish a nocturnal spree in a *churrería*, eating *churros* (doughnut fritters) dipped into a hot cup of molten, cinnamon-flavoured chocolate. The *churrería*, another symbol of old Spain, is a dying institution in the more health-conscious Spain of today, but a characteristic example of one can still be found in Malasaña, in the street grandly named the Calle del Escorial.

This impoverished street of ruinous nineteenth-century terraces seems almost a mockery of all that its distinguished namesake has come to represent. We had seen our first early-morning workers, but the day had yet to break when we reached the street and entered the Finca de los Churros, a twilit hole of a place with an unwashed linoleum floor, a large motorbike in the corner, and, behind the simple counter, a huge, smoking vat of boiling oil in which large rings of *churros* were sizzling. A group of plump, aproned women sat gossiping at one table, while at another two emaciated youths with needle-marked arms stared vacuously about them.

The place was not licensed, but, after we had drunk our chocolate, the owner surreptitiously filled our cups with home-made *aguardiente*. Esperanza rapped her hand on the table, and, under a sign that read 'No Singing', began a *sevillana*, assisted by a raucous chorus. The owner told us to lower our voices, but to no avail. Eventually his wife appeared from the kitchen to tell us to have more respect for others. 'There's an old man dying upstairs,' she shouted.

The break of dawn after a descent into the urban hell of Madrid is the setting of a key scene in Valle-Inclán's *Bohemian Lights*, one of the most important and original Spanish dramas of this century. In a complete break from his earlier plays, in which he had expressed his continual search for eternal values through myth, legend and a stylized vision of the past, Valle-Inclán confronted contemporary urban reality, a world that for him signified flux, transience and confusion. This rambling, episodic work has as its hero a blind and neglected poet, Max Estrella, whose journey through a philistine, bureaucratic, repressive

Madrid culminates in a nocturnal bar-crawl with his ignoble sidekick, Don Latino. The scene at dawn is one the theatre director Lluis Pascual has described as 'infumable', a word that translates literally as 'unsmokable' but in theatre jargon means 'unplayable'. Enormous skill on the part of director and actors is required to achieve the right balance between tragedy and black farce in a scene in which Valle-Inclán – through the mouth of Max Estrella – first puts forward his theory of the *esperpento*, a word he was to use frequently in relation to his works.

The *esperpento*, according to Estrella, is reality seen through the concave mirrors that decorate, to this day, the exterior of a bar on the Callejón del Alvarez Gato, just off the Plaza de Santa Ana. Valle-Inclán saw Spanish reality as a grotesque deformation of European tradition, but he also believed that the only way of capturing Spanish life was to employ a systematically deformed aesthetic. There is an element of the *esperpento* in the fact that the bar that has these mirrors is known today not for having supplied one of the most eloquent metaphors in Spanish literature but for inventing the popular Spanish *tapa* of *patatas bravas*, a potato dish covered in a spicy mayonnaise sauce which oozes out, like a pink flow of lava, from a long metallic tube. But a better example of the *esperpento* is the dawn scene itself from *Bohemian Lights*, a scene in which Max Estrella dies in circumstances that are the very opposite of heroic. Valle-Inclán had no interest in psychological verisimilitude, and the death scene is typical of his drama as a whole in anticipating the Theatre of the Absurd.

The poet is shivering, but Don Latino refuses to give him his overcoat. The only reaction of Don Latino after the poet's death is to take his wallet and lottery ticket, just as the main concern of a laundry woman who later comes across the corpse is to be worried about being late for work. Stage directions indicate that a dog should be pissing in the background. The last words of the poet are suitably anti-climactic: 'Good night.'

IN MADRID dawn is traditionally the hour not only of the drinker but also of the departing traveller. As my night in Malasaña drew slowly to its close, and as I began to feel the accumulated effects of weeks of exposure to the anarchic, unusual, and at times grotesque delights of this city of transience, I had a sudden longing for the archetypal landscapes of Don Quixote and the Romantics. Dawn was well advanced as we left the Finca de los Churros. With the increasing light, and with my heart and lungs congested by smoke and alcohol, the streaks of dirt on the tenements took on the quality of a scream. Between the tall rows of houses, a narrow band of sky was turning from a dark, greyish silver to a faint, creamy blue, as if a great weight were being lifted, and a vision revealed of wide, open spaces.

PART TWO

THE TRAVELLER RISES AT DAWN

5

In the Footsteps of Don Camilo

LITERARY accounts of departures from Madrid have often taken place against a background of penumbral stillness. Azorín, setting off in 1907 on a voyage in the footsteps of Don Quixote, described the Madrilenian dawn as 'the hour in which a modern metropolis reveals all its strangeness, its abnormality, and perhaps even its inhumanity'.

Camilo José Cela was also in a pensive mood as he walked with his rucksack through the empty and sinister streets of a crepuscular Madrid at the outset of a famous journey undertaken in 1946 to the nearby region of the Alcarria. The locked houses, with their drawn blinds, led him to reflect on whether the people who lived within them were happy or unfortunate; he concluded that the former often had balconies adorned with the merest sprig of mint or marjoram, while the latter would smother their sadness and desperation with balconies bursting with geraniums and carnations. Already he was exercising what he believed to be the special gift of the traveller, a remarkable intuition and prescience in relation to everyone and everything he encounters on his journey, an ability to look through walls and into souls.

Cela's destination, like Azorín's, was the old railway station of Atocha. With its turn-of-the-century frontage crowned by gigantic bronze griffins flanking a gilded globe, Atocha belongs to what some would call the great days of Spanish rail travel, before the advent of videos and the abolition of a third class, where peasants and vagrants sat on wooden benches alongside writers in search of experience. Dawn in a station such as this had had its own seedy evocativeness. Shabbily dressed travellers formed what looked like soup queues in a ticket hall of Piranesi-like proportions, where the air was heavy with smoke and the smell of bodies that had slept rough. The daily awakening of a large city always began in a railway station, according to Azorín. The city slowly sprang to life as porters shouted and rushed by; as the first screeches of whistles and shunting trains were heard; as the lottery-ticket salesmen peddled dreams with shouts of '¡Para hoy!' ('Tickets for today!'); and as harsh and isolated beams of electric light were switched off to reveal at the end of the platforms a horizon streaked, in the words of Azorín, with 'the pinkish, pearly, violet, golden glow of dawn'.

'It was around the hour of dawn,' wrote Cela at the beginning of his journey to the Alcarria, echoing the line from Cervantes's *Don Quixote* which describes the moment when the eponymous fantasist sets off on his adventures from the inn where he has just been 'knighted'. The wanderings of both Don Quixote and the itinerant delinquent known as the *pícaro* have been a great influence on Cela, one of the surprisingly few Spanish writers to have dedicated much time to travel literature.

Up till the end of the nineteenth century, the principal travel books on Spain by Spaniards had been limited largely to factual academic works of the Enlightenment, most notably Antonio Ponz's multi-volumed *Spanish Journey*, which describes Spain's monuments with a dry thoroughness comparable to Pevsner's *Buildings of England*. More literary travel books had evolved only with the Generation of '98, whose associates such as Unamuno and Azorín had developed an obsessive interest in the landscapes of old Spain at a time when the motor car was making the Spanish countryside more accessible than ever before.

Unamuno, while praising the way in which the motor car was leading to the discovery of 'delightful corners of the country . . . hidden architectural jewels', warned of the spiritual losses occasioned when travelling became too easy. 'Nothing,' he wrote, 'reveals the ordinariness of the spirit, the coarseness and plebeian nature of the soul, more than a fondness for comfort. The person who does not know how to travel without a pillow and bathroom is an idiot.'

There was little danger of enjoying too much comfort for those who travelled around Spain by third-class rail, or even by local bus. However, any form of transport has seemed too luxurious to many of the better-known wanderers around Spain in modern times. Cela, once he had reached Guadalajara – less than an hour's train journey from Madrid – continued his journey on foot, the manner in which he would carry out all his later Spanish travels.

To walk when there is absolutely no need to do so, and in the blinding sun at that, is decidedly foreign to Spaniards. Indeed, it is a peculiarly English form of masochism, and it is not for nothing that Cela has English blood, his full name being Cela y Trulock. A significant number of English literary travellers to Spain this century have journeyed by foot, and only occasionally through necessity. Gerald Brenan, making his way to and around the Andalusian region of the Alpujarra in the 1920s, was forced by mountainous terrain and lack of roads to use his feet and a donkey. Lack of funds, combined with youthful romanticism, impelled Laurie Lee to wander on foot all the way from Vigo to the Granada coast. Pure romanticism and a magazine assignment were the reasons why the young V. S. Pritchett undertook the gruelling walk from Badajoz to Vigo, the subject of his first travel book, *Marching Spain* (1928).

Nostalgia for romantic Spain and a haughty, almost colonial attitude towards the country have inspired other British wanderers, including Lord Kilmarnock, Penelope Chetwode, and Robin Hanbury-Tenison, to journey on horseback. The eccentric Count Tschiffely, who had made a famous journey on horse from Tierra del Fuego to California in the 1920s, seemed to me to have made an eminently sensible choice when he decided in 1949 to tour Spain not on horse but on a motor cycle. But, for sheer originality, full praise must be given to Norman Lewis, who as a young man in the 1930s contemplated touring Spain by canoe.

Whether or not Cela himself would have approved of this is of course another matter. Cela, despite the element of English masochism inherent in his mode of travel, expressed – in an edition of *Journey to the Alcarria* intended for English school-children – his concern that the young English reader would have a sporting outlook on life and would confuse the 'art of wandering [*el vagabundeo*] with anything which gave exercise to the heart and limbs'. 'To wander', he continued, 'has nothing to do with sport, but is a state of mind and even a way of being, an inescapable way of understanding all that happens to you.' In his own travel books he dignified the wanderer's role by dropping the personal pronoun altogether and giving himself the near-mythical status of 'the traveller'.

I LEFT MADRID in untraditional and unromantic style, not by the dawn train, but at six o'clock on a wet afternoon, driven by a friend. Esperanza Flores had once called me a *pícaro*, which, favourably interpreted, meant that I was a person of stoic flexibility, happy to travel by whatever means possible and to accept all the hardship and hospitality which came my way. William Chislett, a journalist from Madrid, had offered to start me off on my journey by driving me to Guadalajara, where I had been granted a surprise audience with Camilo José Cela, whose footsteps I had intended to follow in fulfilment of an adolescent ambition.

To be stuck in heavy traffic and a steady drizzle in the characterless outskirts that stretch much of the way from Madrid to Guadalajara did not seem the ideal way to begin my intended reconstruction of Cela's journey through the Alcarria. I was following less in the footsteps of the Cela of 1946 than in those of the Cela of forty years later who had set off again to the Alcarria to retrace his own footsteps. The difference was that whereas I was travelling in a homely Seat Ibiza driven by the burly William, Cela had done his *New Journey to the Alcarria* in a white air-conditioned Rolls-Royce driven by a tall, sleek and glamorous young black woman whom the author had christened 'Otelina', a female diminutive of Othello.

The *cursi* spirit of Cela's return to the Alcarria is indicative of what has happened to the author in his later years. The rebelliousness of the former *enfant terrible* of Spanish literature has been succeeded by pure self-indulgence. That this writer should have been awarded the 1989 Nobel Prize for Literature seemed to many Spaniards as great an injustice as when Pérez Galdós had been passed over for this award in 1912 in favour of the mediocre Echegaray, a man remembered today largely for the bar-lined street named after him in the Barrio de los Literatos.

The winning of the prize has driven the *macho* and not exactly immodest Cela to new heights of arrogance, and has also led to much gossip after he went to Stockholm to collect it in the company not of his wife but of a young blonde whom he was later to marry. Shortly after the marriage, a journalist who had insulted Cela over the affair turned up at a party in Marbella at which the writer was present. 'This is going to be interesting,' Cela said to his friends before getting up from his chair, going over to the journalist, and, after a ferocious argument, throwing a violent punch that sent the man into the swimming-pool.

I felt a mounting fear as William and I neared Guadalajara, unsure as to whether I should be checking details of Cela's literary career or developing boxing skills. We came at last to the Guadalajara turning, and made our way to the outlying railway station from where I had been told to ask directions. The group of men in the tiny bar adjoining the station referred to Cela variously as 'Don Camilo', and 'El Nobel', and instructed us to head off along the road where I had least expected a celebrated writer to live. Guadalajara, a town heavily damaged during the Civil War, is not a place of great beauty, but immediately to the east are pleasant, hilly surroundings in which a number of expensive modern villas have been built. Cela does not live there, as I had imagined, but in flat agricultural land just to the north of the railway station, almost within sight both of the railway line and an extensive group of industrial warehouses.

A tall white wall marks the boundary of his estate, at the entrance to which was a uniformed security guard. After searching for our names on a sheet of paper, he directed our car to a yellow Portacabin in the middle of grounds which, in the rain, had as much charm as a prison exercise yard. Worse than the overall bleakness of the place were the attempts at embellishment, which included a modern imitation of one of the menhirs of Cela's native Galicia, and a series of pretentious Victorian-style lamps contrasting markedly in their fussiness with the house itself, a modern, unremarkable block. Cela and his new wife had moved here recently, after, unknown to them, a Madrilenian psychiatrist friend of mine had rejected it as being unsuitable for conversion into a mental home.

The guard led us from the Portacabin to the front door, where we were met by a maid. Her services were replaced at the end of a corridor by a man who told us to follow him into what looked like the inner sanctum of a temple. The room was dominated by an enormous, sunken recess with seating on three of its sides, and a great table in the middle. A chimneypiece, formed by a tapering stack of slates, rose like a Mayan pyramid up to a ceiling of staggering height. A profusion of books and paintings surrounded the walls, while directly above the recess, illuminated by the sharp light from the window, was a writing desk at which the author of *Journey to the Alcarria* was seated.

Cela stood up to greet us, and as he shook my hand I realized that my chances of winning a fight with this seventy-six-year-old were not good. He had a most commanding physical presence, with a large powerful body supporting a tall head with heavy features that might have been carved in granite by some Galician sculptor. Baldness fully revealed an enormous forehead which rose over penetrating, deep-set eyes framed by heavy glasses.

We took our places at the opposite ends of the recess, Cela initiating the conversation with the words, 'Well, here we are.' Indeed there I was, intimidated by his reputation and appearance, and by the great distance between us. The fact that William and I were English was very much to our advantage; Cela was an Anglophile who was only too pleased at the opportunity to talk about his English grandfather who had settled in Spain while supervising the construction of Galicia's first railway. Showing no hint of any latent irritability, Cela revealed instead a calm, understated manner, and treated us with the utmost courtesy, although he never broke into a warm smile which might have relaxed us more. The occasion was rather like a meeting with a formidable headmaster. After ten minutes, I welcomed the break provided by the arrival of his friendly young wife to ask him to sign some papers. In the meantime, I studied the surroundings more closely, examining in detail a collection of paintings that would have not looked out of place on the railings at Hyde Park Corner. His house at Mallorca had been known for its exquisite taste, but this taste was often said to have been the legacy of his first wife, an elegant, aristocratic woman. I found myself staring at a painting of two naked women, between one of whose legs was a bubble distorting a part of the anatomy for which many synonyms can be found in a dictionary of sexual terminology that Cela had recently compiled.

The conversation, so far, had not touched on literature, apart from the odd reference on Cela's part to one of his own writings. 'I once wrote this book on the Alcarria,' he said near the beginning of our meeting, clearly having judged us from the outset as benign but intellectually lightweight. This assumption that we knew nothing about his work made a refreshing contrast to the attitudes of other famous people I had met, but it hardly augured well for any future discussion on the travel literature of Spain, which was what interested me. I tried to introduce the subject by asking him if he had any intention of writing other travel books on the country.

'My reply is the one I always give to people who ask me if I'm working on any particular project. In literature, there are no projects. Books exist only when they are written, printed and bound.'

It was a reply that perhaps unwittingly explained the poorly planned, rambling and self-indulgent nature of much of Cela's recent literary output. I made no attempt to challenge it, but returned to the theme of travel, pressing him this time on the influence in Spain of his own books in this genre, and how they seemed to have inspired a recent revival in travel literature. I mentioned a fashionable young writer called Julio Llamazares, who wrote about Castile, and always referred to himself as 'the traveller'. Cela looked at me impassively.

'We had,' he said, 'a great tradition of travel-writing at the turn of the century. But nowadays one can no longer write travel books about Spain. The country has changed too much, places can be reached too easily, towns and villages have been too modernized, too overrun by tourism.'

Cela spoke in statements uttered as if they were incontrovertible truths. His views on how travel books should be written were reminiscent of the comment he had once made on the episodic style of *The Hive*: 'Novels today cannot be written in any other way.'

I suggested timidly that any aspect of a country is of potential interest to the travel writer; surely a place does not have to be old and unspoilt to be written about? He ignored me, and offered instead a reason as to why he personally had given up travel-writing.

'I stopped writing up my journeys when I was no longer able to carry them out on foot. Walking between places is the best way of learning and understanding.'

Opinions were later exchanged about what, if any, were the remaining 'unusual' places in Spain, but the subject of travel was soon abandoned. Cela stood up, not to see us to the door, as I had thought, but to take us into a tiny and discreetly hidden corner of the room. Momentarily, he became endearingly human: he was showing us the corner of his house reserved for his Nobel Prize. The heavy silver medal from the Swedish Academy hung by the window, in front of a selection of envelopes that had enclosed some of the thousands of letters of congratulation Cela had received from all over the world. The envelopes on display indicated a high level of literary intelligence among Spain's postal workers, for the only address which they bore was 'Don Camilo, Spain', or, in one case, just 'C. J. C.'

Back in our seats the conversation resumed its earlier stiff yet meandering course. We got on to recent changes in Spanish and British society. 'The British were once so well dressed,' said Cela as I shuffled nervously in my torn and mud-splattered jeans, and remembered the stained overcoat in which I had arrived. Perhaps my appearance would at least make Cela recognize in me a fellow man of the road, but even in that capacity I was not convincing. I explained that William was returning afterwards to Madrid, but that I was going to continue into the Alcarria. 'And where,' he asked, 'will you be spending the night?' I avoided the question by mumbling something about being in Brihuega the next day, but it was clear that I had not given any serious thought as to where exactly I was going or how I was to get there. Out of politeness, Cela assumed I would be reaching my destination on foot.

'Brihuega,' he said, 'is a long way from here, about 35 kilometres. You'd be hard pressed to get there in a day. It's a charming place, though, I have a particular fondness for it. The people are friendly, and there is excellent food and lodging.'

William drove me to Guadalajara bus station at around nine o'clock that evening. There was a bus, the last of the day, leaving for Brihuega in five minutes' time. I said goodbye and jumped on to the bus, carrying with me a rucksack that seemed barely sufficient to contain a day's picnic. The bus was cold, damp, and nearly empty, and its few passengers soon became involved in a heated discussion with the driver as to whether or not there would be a bus to take me away from Brihuega the following morning. The light faded, the bus left the main road, and I lost my sense of direction in the course of bumpy detours to places where no one got on or got off. The traveller took out his battered old copy of *Journey to the Alcarria*, its frontispiece now inscribed in an elaborate hand, 'A Michael Jacobs, cordialmente su amigo, Camilo José Cela.'

'THE ALCARRIA', Cela wrote in a preface to his book, 'is a beautiful region which people apparently have no desire to visit.' Antonio Ponz, writing over 150 years earlier, described a wild underpopulated region which insufficiently exploited its wealth of natural resources. This situation had changed little by the time of Cela's first visit here, and remains to a certain extent true of the region today. One of the principal changes is that the place no one wanted to visit has come to attract, thanks to Cela, generations of readers who have studied Spanish at school. I was certainly not alone in imagining the Alcarria in the same romantic light in which I had viewed the part of France where Henri Alain-Fournier had set that other perennial adolescent favourite, *Le Grand Meaulnes*. Places such as Brihuega had a magical quality for me long before I actually saw them.

The bus left me at the entrance to the old town of Brihuega, on the square where Cela had talked to a stuttering imbecile too embarrassed to tell him that a nearby fountain was popularly known as Shit Fountain. Overlooking the square today is the Hostal Torreón, a recent remodelling of the old inn where Cela had stayed in 1946.

I went inside the building to discover immediately that my visit to the Alcarria had coincided with the annual spring-cleaning of the district's nuclear power station. 'Are you an engineer?' the owner asked me before spotting in my overcoat pocket my guiltily and unsuccessfully hidden copy of Cela's *Journey to the Alcarria*. 'Ah, you're interested in Cela,' he said as he showed me upstairs to my room. 'Well, you've come to the right place.' He tried to humour me further. 'I'm putting you in the very room where Cela stayed in 1986,' he claimed, unlocking the door to what was in fact the *hostal*'s only room not occupied that night by nuclear engineers.

In the privacy of my bedroom, 'Cela's room', I looked up the Hostal Torreón in the *New Journey to the Alcarria*, and came across a dialogue the writer had had with the present owner. The owner had been under the impression that Cela was someone who would not like modern hotels, and would be disappointed by the renovations carried out to the old inn. But Cela had surprised him by replying that though modern places such as the Hotel Torreón might be lacking in the picturesque, they had the advantages of hygiene and private bathrooms.

Such unhygienic details as a caged canary and two prowling cats had featured in the modest dining-room where Cela had dined in 1946. The room where I had supper, however, was a place that cheaply parodied the pretensions of the Cela who had returned to Brihuega in grand old age. Absurdly large in scale, the room had a ceiling hung with gilded plastic chandeliers, walls painted in salmon pink, and windows covered in matching curtains arranged in baroque fashion with tassels and a fussy valance.

The old town of Brihuega seemed to have changed less than the inn, at least by night, when the impressive remains of its medieval past were given an added mystery by the growing darkness that accompanied my descent down to a large and isolated Gothic church at the edge of the town's lower and extensively preserved ramparts.

Cela had painstakingly recorded a medieval inscription above the town's twelfth-century gate; now he himself was commemorated in Brihuega by one of the many ceramic plaques that were put up in the Alcarria in 1972 to mark the twenty-fifth anniversary of the publication of his book. 'In this house,' the plaque recorded, 'C. J. C. spoke on many subjects with his friend, the owner. "*My name is Julio Vacas but they call me Portillo [Littlegate].*".' Julio Vacas was typical of the sort of eccentric who takes on the unofficial role of town cicerone, usually writes poetry, and makes up for being barely tolerated by his fellow townspeople by latching on, leech-like, to any passing stranger. Vacas told Cela how the King of France, travelling incognito, had been guided by him around Brihuega. To these and other absurdities uttered by his so-called 'friend', Cela replied with terse comments, the irony of which was apparently lost on Vacas. Irony tends also to be lost on plaques. Through being made an object of fun, Vacas had now earned himself a respectable place in the modern history of Brihuega.

A PERSISTENT mist hung over Brihuega the next morning, shrouding the town with the same mysterious beauty I had perceived at night. I was encouraged in the hope that I would not be disappointed by the local sight that had most impressed me from my early reading of Cela.

'The Factory Garden,' wrote Cela, 'is a romantic garden, a garden to die in when very young, of love or desperation, or consumption and nostalgia.' The notion of a 'factory garden' does not sound romantic; but the factory to which Cela referred was an abandoned textile factory founded by Charles III in 1787 and resembling an elegant bullring rising above the town among almond trees, chestnut blossom, and cypresses. A large eighteenth-century door led into a long, narrow and heavily decayed forecourt, at the end of which was the huge, circular structure comprising the main bulk of the factory. A further door, standing half open, revealed a glimpse of massive, dangling beams, broken carts, and piles of straw and rubble. Timidly I entered the building, and left the moment I saw the words 'Beware of the Dog' which someone had appended by hand to a notice reading, 'Private Property: Keep Out'. I did not mind dying of nostalgia, but I was not going to be savaged by some rabid Alsatian.

In a modern textile workshop, installed in one of the former stable blocks flanking the forecourt, an amused group of young women workers tried to reassure me that the dangerous dog was usually tied up. I failed to look convinced, and one of them offered to accompany me and find the gardener. We crossed the neo-classical rotunda of the old factory, which in its rustic and overgrown state could well have been one of the fantastical, overblown structures that Piranesi had depicted along the Appian Way. 'NICO! *NICO!*' the woman shouted, until finally the nearby barking of a dog was heard, followed by the appearance of a small, squat man in blue overalls. A friendly poodle rushed to lick my feet.

To visit a place that had captured my imagination over twenty years before seemed bound to lead to disappointment. But the Factory Garden of Brihuega was exactly as Cela had described it, and is one of the most beautiful Spanish gardens I have ever seen. Alain-Fournier would probably have appreciated it too, for there was something of the magical spirit of *Le Grand Meaulnes* in the way in which one suddenly emerged from the factory's ruins into a luxuriant terraced garden redolent of the last century, with box hedges, palm trees, rows of cypresses, a goldfish pond, beds of rhododendrons and honeysuckle, and such poignant details of the past as a rusted pergola and a domed birdhouse with peeling dark green paint.

The garden, Nico explained to me, had been created in 1819, when the factory had lost its royal patent and been bought by a Madrilenian family who turned the outbuildings into a summer residence. An old woman, the last direct descendant of the original owners, had died only a few months before my visit, but the place had been taken over by her nephew. There was talk now of Mozart concerts being given in the garden in the summer, and of a more ominous project – selling off the ruined rotunda for conversion into a summer school for Alcalá University. Nico's whole life had been centred around the garden, where he had worked for over twenty years, and where his father had worked before him. I put to him the inevitable question.

'Yes,' he replied, 'I was the gardener who showed Cela around in 1986, and my father is the one mentioned in the original *Journey to the Alcarria*.' He paused before saying in a low but firm voice, 'We don't have much fondness for Cela in these parts.'

Nico had the makings of a perceptive literary critic. In a single sentence he pinpointed the failings of Cela's method as a travel-writer, failings common to anyone who hopes to capture the character of a particular place on the basis of transient meetings with picturesque types: 'Cela would just spend a night in a village, go into a shop or bar, meet up with the village idiot or some deformed unfortunate, and – there you have it, the whole village summed up. Look at how he describes Brihuega. Who are the people he meets here? Why, there's that imbecile Julio Vacas. And then there's that stutterer who can't tell him the name of the fountain.'

The sun was beginning to emerge, and I was feeling generous. I told him that if it had not been for Cela, I would never have seen the Factory Garden.

FROM THE balcony of the garden the sun could be seen burning through the mist to reveal the beautiful Tajuña valley. Cela had written how at Brihuega the scenery suddenly changes, as if someone has pulled back a curtain. In place of the flat and dreary agricultural land surrounding the main road north of Guadalajara, there was now a river enclosed by hills with ochre crests peering above a dense carpet of oaks, elms and chestnut trees.

A mid-morning bus, the only one to leave Brihuega that day, drove me and a couple of other passengers the whole length of the almost deserted valley, eventually turning off on to an even smaller road, where we followed a fast-flowing stream until it climaxed in a cascade falling into the famous river Tagus. At the meeting of the waters was the village of Trillo.

A modern building at the entrance to the village bore a plaque that read: 'C. J. C. slept in this inn on 8 June 1946: "*Outside, in the midst of a haunting silence, the cascade of Cifuentes rumbles monotonously*".' The former inn had been rendered in concrete, and the wooden door to the courtyard had been replaced by a brown metal gate, like that of a garage. An old man, passing by, confirmed that the inn had been different in Cela's time. 'Everything changes in life,' he observed.

But Trillo had outwardly changed little. A restaurant and beer garden had taken the place of the village wash-house, but these too had been abandoned, and in their decayed state blended into the gentle pastoral environment as unobtrusively as the neighbouring medieval bridge, which crossed the cascade almost at the point where it joined the Tagus. On the other side of the bridge was a tree-lined, turn-of-the-century promenade, while above this projected an outcrop of rock supporting a medieval parish church and a seventeenth-century town hall. A latter-day Claude Lorraine would have had problems only with the horizon, where instead of hazy blue mountains or the columns of a distant classical temple, there rose, in massive disproportion to the actual village, the cylinders of Spain's largest nuclear power station.

'Cela gave absolutely no idea of what Trillo was like,' a librarian told me in the Town Hall, while strongly recommending that I should pay a visit not to the power station but to Trillo's former spa.

The eighteenth-century spa, still known as 'The Baths of Charles III', was referred to by Cela in 1946, but though he passed right next to it on leaving the village he made no mention of the unusual use to which it had been put the previous year. The place lies 3 kilometres upstream from the village, in idyllic surroundings. This stretch of the Tagus valley has many of the qualities of the Tajuña valley, but on a more spectacular scale; the river is wider, the banks are more densely wooded, and the hills higher, steeper, and picturesquely scarred with crevices and cliff-faces. No more perfect spot could be imagined for a family outing were it not for the spa's present associations. Since 1945 the place has served as Spain's one and only National Leprosy Institute.

The sunny spring morning helped to buoy my spirits as I walked along the Tagus in the direction of the lepers' colony. A sense of unease was also inevitable, particularly on arrival at the old-fashioned entrance lodge, which was obviously in need of repair, and apparently deserted. An old man responded to the shaking of a bell, and I was told to make my way to the Institute's administrative block, a good half-hour's uphill walk through grounds which enjoyed dramatic views of a bend in the Tagus. A group of doctors' residences, resembling colonial bungalows, stood halfway along the path, and, in the distance, there could also be seen what seemed like the bell tower of a convent. Otherwise there were few signs of life, and not much more when I reached the main part of the Institute, a group of drab Francoist blocks of the 1940s, most of which were boarded up.

Eusebio Moreno, the Institute's administrator, was fat, cheerful and down to earth. He assumed that I had heard of Dr Stanforth, the 'well-known English expert on leprosy', and an occasional visitor to the Institute. No, I did not know him, nor did I know anything about leprosy, apart from its reputation. He tried to put my mind at rest. The disease, though classified as contagious by the World Health Organization, was generally thought today to be so only if one is genetically disposed to it. In any case, he reassured me, if I were to catch it, I would probably not be aware of having it for at least twenty years.

Leprosy is rife in the Third World, and in the Philippines there is a lepers' island with a population of 315,000. Spain has one of the highest numbers of leprosy cases in Europe, but this number is still extremely small, and virtually all the cases are from the south, in particular from the provinces of Málaga, Jaén and Almería, where there are large concentrations of gypsies. Yes, he admitted, many of the locals had been anxious when the Leprosy Institute had been established, just as there had been many complaints a few years back when a centre for heroin addicts had been briefly set up in the nearby abandoned hamlet of Hontanilla. Getting local people to work at the Institute had been especially difficult at first, and Eusebio's own post had been advertised several times, his immediate predecessor having lasted barely a week. But this had been over fifteen years before, and the Institute had now become completely accepted in the community, which provided almost all the place's cleaning, maintenance and administrative staff, as well as most of the nuns who worked there as nurses.

'And what about the nuclear power station?' I asked. That had been different, he said, for the locals had immediately recognized the job potential of the place, and it had been only the 'greens' from Madrid who had protested. The working population of Trillo, so it seemed, was now equally divided between those who worked with nuclear energy and those who worked with lepers.

The National Leprosy Institute at Trillo was no ordinary leprosy institute. It was a dying one. The actual research part of the Institute no longer functioned, while the hospital was admitting no more patients, the fifty-five left being elderly terminal cases who had been rejected by their families, or had no homes to go back to. Most of the Institute's buildings had been closed down, including one containing a bakery and another with isolation cells for criminal lepers; the cinema, with its projectors from the 1940s, remained exactly the same as before, but films were no longer shown there. The future of the Institute and its seventy-five remaining staff was uncertain. Eusebio offered to drive me around the grounds and show me what was left of the former spa. A leper couple cheerfully waved at us as we drove down towards the Tagus.

The spa had functioned as such up to 1940, but the eighteenth-century buildings had survived only as ruins that had remained hidden until 1981. The extant fragments of the original spa comprised the odd marble basin, one of which had been reputedly used by Charles III. They had now been incorporated into a landscaped terrace surrounded by massive dead elms threatening to fall down at any moment. The nineteenth-century buildings behind were empty but in good condition, and Eusebio asked me my opinion of his plan to encourage British and American universities to use them for summer schools. I thought that the idea of a university summer school in the grounds of a lepers' hospital might not go down so well.

He continued to talk about his fears for the future and for his own job as we walked along the banks of the Tagus, his favourite morning stroll. We passed a ramshackle riverside cottage where a countess had once lived, and which was now crammed higgledy-piggledy with ironwork columns, metal baths and other recently dug-up spa memorabilia.

'What a wonderful spa museum we could make!' sighed Eusebio. Shortly afterwards, in a hidden and especially wooded corner of the grounds, we came to his own bungalow, where an excited labrador greeted him. 'As you can see,' he said, 'we live here in paradise.'

In the sultry heat of the late morning, we talked about Viana's Tits. 'Las Tetas de Viana', to use their official name, vie with the cylinders of the power plant as this district's most prominent landmark. They are a pair of rounded hills, at the top of which are nipple-like outcrops of rock which stand bare and erect above the green slopes below.

On his first journey to the Alcarria, Cela had taken the overgrown footpath between them; on his second, he had decided to scale the gap by balloon. The very mention of Cela made Eusebio angry.

'He treated this region very badly,' he said, 'just like Sampedro did in *The River Which Carries Us*' – a reference to a popular novel about foresters transporting timber down the Tagus. 'As for his journey by balloon . . . What a lot of trouble that caused!' The account given by Cela suggests another of the writer's victorious exploits, but the reality, according to Eusebio, was very different. The balloon had got caught in the trees, and a party had to be sent out to rescue the man. A second attempt was made, but this too had ended in fiasco. Viana's Tits had ultimately defeated the great *macho*.

I steered well clear of them, contenting myself with distant views of the mammary mounds from the main road heading south from Trillo towards Sacedón. Eusebio and others had assured me that I would have no problems in hitchhiking along this road and that many of the workers from the power station passed frequently along here.

The first car to pass did indeed stop to pick me up, but only after I had walked for four hours through a landscape that showed no signs of habitation other than a single distant goatherd whom Cela would doubtless have engaged in conversation. Rolling expanses of forests and craggy distant hills comprised at first the vista, which was later enhanced by a series of enormous reservoirs covering much of the southern half of the Alcarria. They were the last and most controversial of the many reservoirs that had been built during the Franco period. The Alcarria might have lost its vineyards, but has gained in exchange numerous potential bathing sites for Madrilenian visitors.

The young driver who had stopped to give me a lift wanted to show me a particularly good place to swim, but when we arrived there, we found that we would have had to walk over at least a kilometre of desiccated mud before reaching the water. Rain had been scant over the last two years, and the level of water in the reservoirs was now exceptionally low. We could just make out the ruins of a once wholly submerged village.

The driver was an engineer from Madrid involved in the spring-cleaning of the nuclear plant. I had asked to be dropped at Sacedón, but the car was comfortable, the man friendly, and my doubts about Cela growing. When he offered to take me all the way to Pastrana, the last stop on Cela's tour of the Alcarria, I greatly welcomed the opportunity of being able to complete in little more than a day the retracing of the most famous journey in modern Spanish literature. After all, Cela himself had taken barely a week to do the journey, and about the same amount of time to write the book.

'Have you read Camilo José Cela's *Journey to the Alcarria*?' the driver asked me as we neared our destination, having left behind the reservoirs and forested hills, and entered a cultivated and sharply undulating landscape crisscrossed with wheatfields and studded with olive trees. 'There's something,' he added, 'I've always wanted to ask a literary type such as yourself' – a flattering allusion, I believed, to the fact that I wore glasses. 'How can anyone who uses such coarse language win the Nobel Prize for Literature?'

Pastrana, a small medieval town tucked into the fold of a valley, was certainly the most attractive place Cela could have chosen to spend his final night in the Alcarria. It is the picturesque and architectural jewel of the region, with narrow streets, balconied stone houses, and such austere monuments as the imposing Renaissance Ducal Palace, famous as the place where the one-eyed

Princess of Eboli was held under house arrest as a result of her affair with Philip II's secretary, Antonio Pérez. Pastrana is the foreigner's dream of old Spain, and has, in its parish church, tapestries that are possibly the greatest works of art to be seen in any small Spanish town.

The parish priest said that he had little time to show them to me but this did not prevent him from giving me an introductory impromptu lecture on the history of Pastrana, fully supported by obscure and pedantic bibliographic references. I was left with about five minutes to see the tapestries, magnificent late-fifteenth-century Flemish works designed, according to the priest, by Portugal's most famous painter, Nuño Gonçalves.

On Cela's first visit to Pastrana, at a time when the Ducal Palace was in ruins and was being used as a store by the National Wheat Service, the tapestries were in Madrid. Cela, though he believed it was not the business of the traveller to interfere in local quarrels, had supported the townspeople in their desire to have the works returned to Pastrana. The priest asked me if I had heard of Cela. I said I had. For the first time in our meeting, and for the first time in my whole stay in the Alcarria, I heard someone say something complimentary about Cela: 'He's a great writer, a bit too strong in his language perhaps, but a great writer.'

At the end of the day, sipping a glass of wine in a Pastrana bar, I discovered that the priest, Don Licinio, had been referred to in Cela's later book on the Alcarria as the person responsible for putting up the ceramic plaques to him in 1976. He was, in Cela's words, 'a learned man who had read widely and with admirable discrimination'.

'It was about the hour of dawn . . . No, it wasn't even the hour of dawn,' Cela had corrected himself at the outset of his first journey to the Alcarria. 'It was earlier than that.' It was about 5.30 a.m. and still dark when the only bus of the day heading south from Pastrana was due to leave. I was taking it, wherever it was going, happy simply to exchange the narrow confines of the land of Don Camilo for the broader territory of Don Quixote.

6

Landscapes and Illusions

THE image of Don Quixote setting off on his wanderings around the vast plains of La Mancha is of perennial appeal to the traveller who journeys without the constraints of time or of an ultimate destination. The traveller to Spain, heading slowly south towards the promised sensuality of Andalusia, is likely to experience in La Mancha a sense of a journey truly begun, and to find that the horizons have broadened metaphorically as well as literally.

August Jacacci, an American writer retracing Don Quixote's footsteps in 1897, began his tour of La Mancha in the town of Ciudad Real, a place that struck him as the sleepy antithesis 'to the bustling New York I had left but twelve days before'. Yet, unvisited by him, and on the eastern side of the region, lay a town rapidly developing at that time into a metropolis later promoted by a desperate tourist industry as 'the New York of La Mancha'.

Albacete is an unloved town in the middle of a region owing its tourist appeal largely to Don Quixote. The Moors, bluntly but tellingly, referred to the insignificant township out of which the future Albacete would grow as Albasit ('The Plain'). A landscape of wheatfields and monotonous flatness encircles the town, offering protection neither from the intense summer sun nor from the biting winds that make the winters here reputedly among the harshest in Spain. Apart from its long-standing fame as a centre for knife-making, Albacete is renowned for its awfulness, a reputation dating back at least to the eighteenth century, when travellers coined a saying automatically quoted to me whenever I spoke of my intention of visiting the town. 'Albacete,' the saying goes, 'caga y vete', which can loosely be translated as 'Albacete, shit and run.' The many people who tried to put me off visiting Albacete only made me want to go there, particularly as none of these people had actually visited the place. I saw the town as a perfect starting-point for a tour of La Mancha, for it seemed to embody the quintessential spirit of the region chosen by Cervantes as a testing ground for the transforming powers of the imagination.

Albacete, like Madrid, is a town that has grown to great size and importance as if out of nothing while still betraying signs of its small-town origins. Avenues of smart residential blocks, suggestive of the suburbs of a prosperous metropolis, lead from the railway station to the centre of the town, where the streets lie under the shadow of pompous and eclectic buildings similar to those erected in Madrid in the early years of the century. A very different perspective on the town, however, was to be had from the place where I chose to stay, a modest *pensión* or *fonda* situated in a grimy block a few minutes' walk away from the cathedral.

The place, of a kind fast disappearing in Spain, was taken over almost entirely by the family who ran it. There was a grandmother dressed in black, a prematurely aged mother with a baby whose pram blocked the corridor, and a husband, fat and sultry, sitting around in a string vest smoking cigarettes.

My room was greyish green and windowless, and from my creaking, iron-framed bed I could hear the family's incessant quarrelling interspersed with conversations with the *fonda*'s few clients, among whom were a pale-faced young couple who seemed to be eloping, and an ageing commercial salesman with a faded, dark-brown suit that merged imperceptibly with the colour of the rotten floorboards.

But the distinguishing characteristic of this relic of old Spain – where the clamour of voices mingled with the constant sounds of coughing and the grotesque clearing of an old man's throat – was the view from the corridor window. Here I was in the very heart of a large, bustling town, and yet I was looking out on to a sunny, whitewashed courtyard which could have belonged to a traditional country inn. Chickens ran around among rubble and discarded farmyard equipment, scurrying between a ruined old cart and a large patch of earth where beans and cabbages were grown. I was reminded of the first place I had ever stayed in Spain, an urban *fonda* like this one, but even more run down, and with a pig that had escaped into the living-room.

In a new town for the first time, the immediate instinct is to go and see the 'sights', but Albacete has no obvious ones apart from a Renaissance cathedral so over-restored as to appear modern, and a modern regional museum so spacious as to reveal the shallowness of the collections. In the hope of discovering other attractions, I went to the Albacete 'Regional Promotional Office', an institution I assumed would be only too willing to provide a foreigner with literature and information about the town. However, all I could gather here was that Albacete had a tourist office, and that I should go and speak to its director.

The tourist office was in another part of the town, and so hidden away and unpromoted that only the most determined tourist with time to spare would ever manage to find it. The place was staffed by an unsmiling young couple who epitomized the Castilian character at its most notoriously closed.

'I've come to see the director.'

'He's not in.'

'Will he be in later today?'

'I don't know.'

'Does he usually work here in the mornings?'

'Sometimes.'

'Do you have any brochures on Albacete?'

'We've run out.'

'Could you tell me how I'd get from here to Ruidera?'

'No.'

'But isn't this a tourist information office?'

'Yes, but it's not a bus station.'

'Thank you, you've been very helpful.'

The director appeared as I was leaving, and looked at me in a bewildered way, surprised perhaps to find a tourist in the tourist office. His bewilderment turned to pleasure, and we went off to have a talk over a cup of coffee. I asked him if he had been the person responsible for dubbing the town 'the New York of La Mancha', but he revealed that the inventor of this ludicrous phrase had in fact been Azorín. He confessed that he had had a difficult time in making Albacete itself beguiling to tourists, but he believed that the province had considerable potential. I thought of the miles of featureless plain surrounding the town, and wondered how much Cervantes and Don Quixote were used in the promotion of this countryside. He shook his head, and said that the days of the cultured tourist travelling through Spain were over. Albacete's tourist campaigns, he said, were directed today entirely towards nature and outdoor activities rather than literature. 'Literature,' he added, 'is no longer in fashion.'

I pursued, against fashion, the subject of Albacete and literature and was recommended to go to the Instituto de Estudios Albacetenses, where the librarian spoke to me of the Marquis of Molins, a name I could associate then only with Albacete's busiest shopping street. I now learned that he was the town's 'most famous writer', and was handed a recent reissue of his 'masterpiece', *La Manchega* (1882), a work that came complete with an intriguing biographical introduction relating how the Marquis had been born in 1812, two days after his mother had been thrown out on to the streets of Albacete by her husband, the mayor. Despite such an unpromising start in life, the Marquis had gone on to evolve a wholly sentimental view of his native region, as was revealed in *La Manchega*. La Mancha, according to this book, was the most beautiful region in the world; this was due, above all, to its women, who reflected the noble simplicity of local village life and had remained, like the villages themselves, so unchanged over the centuries that Cervantes would have recognized in them his Dulcinea.

The manner in which La Mancha has been perceived by writers and travellers has a special relevance to a region that, thanks to Cervantes, is likely to encourage thoughts on reality and illusion. The traditional reputation of La Mancha, from at least the sixteenth century, is as a bleak, inhospitable expanse populated by boorish, violent people: Jacacci was advised to take a knife on his travels here, while Azorín, ten years later, was given a gun on being commissioned to write about the place. Those who have defended the landscape of La Mancha have usually done so by finding in its flat emptiness a strong metaphysical power, a view apparently espoused by the local tourist board, which refers, in rather curious English, to the way in which 'Man takes on here his real dimensions, extracted from a framework of other natural references and projected against a sky of overwhelming presence.'

An entirely different view of La Mancha is that held by the film director Almodóvar, the most infamous Manchegan of today. Far from defining the influence of his native region in spiritual terms, Almodóvar has claimed instead that La Mancha has informed his anti-heroic, anti-metaphysical outlook on Spain, an outlook which dwells on the ugly, tasteless, and surreal twists of the contemporary world.

Cervantes's own attitude towards La Mancha and the extent of his knowledge of the region are not easy to assess. The author's numerous but notoriously unreliable biographers have suggested how his imaginative development was profoundly influenced by having travelled across La Mancha at the age of six, when his father, an impoverished surgeon, took the family from Alcalá de Henares to Córdoba. Of surely greater significance, however, was his journey to Seville in 1587 to purchase and requisition wheat for the Spanish Armada. At the time he had been leading a quiet domestic life in a dreary village near Toledo, and was only too pleased to abandon his family and home and take off again on the road. New adventures awaited him in Andalusia, his requisitioning of wheat from influential landlords leading both to excommunication and to two long spells in prison, in Seville and Castro del Río.

The first part of *Don Quixote* was presented by Cervantes not as an original work but as a translation of an Arabic account written by the wise Cidi Hamete Benengeli. A line in the prologue seems also to hint that the book was begun or at least first conceived in prison. Most probably the prison referred to was neither Seville's nor Castro del Río's but rather a purely metaphorical one, perhaps even that of Cervantes's marriage. There is none the less a widespread and wholly unfounded belief, originating in the Romantic era, that the prison in question was one that still survives in the Manchegan town of Argamasilla de Alba. The dramatist Juan Eugenio Hartzenbusch, the first Director of Spain's National Library, reinforced this belief by setting up a printing press in the building to bring out a special edition of *Don Quixote*; by Jacacci's day visitors to the town were being told that the whole of Cervantes's book was written there. Argamasilla Prison, now a small Cervantine museum, continues clumsily to be referred to as 'The Cradle of the Knight of the Sad Countenance'.

Fact and fiction become increasingly muddled the further you look into the story of Cervantes and Don Quixote. Alonso Quixano, the humble citizen who had himself knighted Don Quixote, was said by Cervantes to have come 'from a certain village in La Mancha which I do not wish to name'. Others, however, have named the village as Criptana del Campo, where baptism records have unearthed a real Quixano. Meanwhile, in the parish church of Argamasilla, there has hung for many centuries a portrait of Don Rodrigo de Pacheco that has always been known as the 'portrait of the Knight of the Sad Countenance'. Then, in El Toboso, you will find the 'House of Dulcinea', in fact the house of a minor noblewoman with whom Cervantes is reputed, on no evidence whatsoever, to have been in love. Pedantic scholars have frequently tried to sort out this confusion between history and legend, but in so doing would have angered Unamuno, who identified himself so closely with Cervantes's fictional hero that he embarked on a Quixotic crusade 'to redeem the Sepulchre of the Knight of Madness from the power of the Champions of Reason'.

'Be honest. Isn't there a bit of Quixote in all of us?' asked a recent travel journalist, echoing a sentiment that has led to numerous journeys of embarrassing self-discovery through La Mancha. Of all the travellers who have followed in the footsteps of Don Quixote, the only one to have written a memorable account of the journey was Azorín. His book – published to coincide with the Cervantes celebrations of 1905 – might offer little insight into Cervantes, but it is one of the most delightful works of Spanish travel literature, fresh, ironical, and with a poignant evocation of gentle decay. More than any other of the descriptive writings on La Mancha, it also arouses in the reader an enthusiasm for the landscape, the monotony of which is lessened by observations of subtle differences in colour and contour, and by its conjuring up, in the middle of all the flatness, of pockets of pure magic.

To FOLLOW in the footsteps of Azorín rather than in those of Don Quixote himself was my principal objective on setting off one afternoon on the bus from Albacete to the fabled nearby lakes of Ruidera.

Only a few miles outside Albacete, I became fully aware of how wrong I had once been to judge La Mancha purely from what can be seen from railway lines and motorways. The silence of the little-used road from Albacete to Ruidera enhanced the haunting emptiness of the landscape, an emptiness that became ever more acute as the solitary bus manoeuvred slowly through a patchwork of pastel purples, greens, ochres and yellows, in which every furrow, spring flower, and distant line of poplars stood out in the mid-afternoon sun with heightened clarity. Travelling across such a landscape makes one susceptible to the slightest of changes. Though I had not spent the greater part of a day reaching Ruidera by horse and cart, as Azorín had done, I still experienced on nearing my destination a comparable sense of satisfaction as the horizons gradually drew in, becoming increasingly broken by trees and contours, so that eventually the landscape could almost be described as hilly and wooded.

Ruidera itself is a typical and unexceptional Manchegan village with a scattering of whitewashed roadside buildings, mainly bars and inns. The owner of one of these happened also to be the local taxi-driver. I woke him from his afternoon siesta, and arranged a price for taking me to the cave that Azorín and many others had identified as the one where Don Quixote had been transported back to the world of Carolingian romance.

Whether or not the Ruidera cave had served as Cervantes's model for the 'Cave of Montesinos' – and recent scholars favour instead a cave near the Andalusian town of Cabra – the drive there from the village passed through scenery that was so unexpected that it almost convinced me I was experiencing a vision. Suddenly

I was in an enchanting oasis of waterfalls and reedy lakes slumbering within a sensually contoured landscape of oaks, shrubs and aromatics.

I was held in an almost magical spell broken only on arrival at the cave itself. Its effect on me was exactly the opposite of that experienced by Don Quixote. The cave, situated on high ground out of sight of the lakes, occupied a dusty clearing where picnic benches had been set out, and cars could be parked. In high season, a local guide conducts regular tours of the cave, but no one was around when I was there, and I was grateful to my driver for having brought with him a powerful torch. He had no desire to come with me, however, and waited patiently in the car as I embarked on my solitary, Quixotic quest.

Don Quixote, invoking the name of Dulcinea, hacked with his sword at the briars that guarded the cave's entrance, dislodging an infernal colony of crows and jackdaws who swept the valiant knight off his feet. I was attacked instead by hundreds of persistent flies who swarmed around the rubbish that had been thrown into the cave by tourists deficient in chivalric sensibility. I resurfaced, plucked up courage, and went down again, this time covering my face with my left hand and holding my nose with my right, vainly trying to protect myself from an overpowering smell of urine and excrement. After a few minutes of slow descent, punctuated by the distant sounds of dripping water, I reached the wide chamber marking the bottom of the cave; its underground stream murmurs in a way that had conveyed to Azorín both a 'warning and a lament'. Azorín had heaped on this sorry trickle of water such adjectives as 'mysterious', 'millennial', and 'blind', and had found in it 'all the disquieting poetry of this cave of Montesinos . . .' All that I felt was an unpleasant dampness.

IN ONE of the roadside inns in the village of Ruidera I waited for the 6.30 p.m. bus to Argamasilla, preparing myself for that moment when all lingering traces of magic would vanish once I had left the area far behind. But, as anyone who has read Cervantes knows, the inns of La Mancha are strange places, where coincidences are rife and encounters fantastical. The Mesón de Juan, though recently redecorated in a pseudo-traditional style, was the oldest inn in Ruidera and had been known to Azorín.

'Lodged in the Mesón de Juan writing up these notes . . .' is a line from Azorín's *The Route of Don Quixote* and had been reproduced on a ceramic tile attached to the back wall of the inn. I sat at the bar staring at it, nibbling a slice of Manchego cheese and sipping a glass of dark red Valdepeñas wine. The room was empty, but every so often the friendly owner would come out from the kitchen to speak to me.

'If I were you, I'd keep my eyes open for that bus. Sometimes, if the driver doesn't see anyone waiting, he won't even stop.'

I stood up to go and wait outside, but the owner waved me back immediately. I still had plenty of time to spare, he said, as he poured out another glass of the strong wine. I took out my copy of Azorín, and began reading the enthusiastic descriptions of Argamasilla that take up at least half the book. The door opened and a young, blond-haired man walked in, his forehead beaded with sweat, and his skin the colour and appearance of the imitation parchment scrolls that hung on the walls, inscribed in Gothic lettering with primeval jokes. He ordered a beer and looked at me with a dazed, haunted expression, as if he were about to introduce himself as a long-lost relative of mine. Turning to a Spanish phrase book, he then asked me in a heavy German accent if I was from the region.

'He's English, of course!' the owner said, before replenishing our glasses and toasting us both, as if this chance meeting between two foreigners in an obscure Manchegan inn was a worthy cause for celebration. The German now spoke to me in English, and told me that he was cycling on his own all the way from Barcelona to Seville. His fiancée was to have come with him, but they had broken off their engagement the night before their planned trip together. He was lonely and suffering from the heat and flatness of La Mancha, but his whole journey seemed to have been undertaken in a spirit of pure masochism.

Suddenly looking at his watch, he announced that he had spent longer than the ten minutes he had allowed himself for refreshments. A further 18 kilometres of cycling were required to fulfil his daily quota of 120 kilometres, and on no account could he arrive at his final destination later than 7.45 p.m. A look of happiness came over his features as he got up to leave. 'Thank you,' he said. 'This is the first conversation I've had in ten days.'

The Argamasilla bus had still not arrived, and the bar owner was offering me another drink, 'on the house'. I reckoned that I had time to make a quick phonecall to a friend in Andalusia, and I was speaking to her when I noticed two new men in the room, staring at me no less intently than the German had done. One of them came up to me after I had put down the phone.

'Excuse me,' he said. 'I couldn't help overhearing your conversation. You're a traveller, aren't you?' I looked perplexed. 'I mean, you're a foreigner, but you're not a tourist. And to judge from what you were saying on the phone you seem to know Spain quite well.' He paused. 'But what exactly are you?'

I did not know how to reply, and was worried about the bus, which I said was due to arrive any minute. He ignored this and placed a glass of beer in my hand.

'I thought as much, it's just what I was saying to my friend. You *are* a traveller.' He smiled with immense satisfaction, and rested an arm on his friend's shoulder. 'Nacho and I, we are also travellers.'

His name was Óscar ('My mother was a great admirer of your Wilde'), and he was a gaunt and distinguished-looking man in his mid-forties, elegantly dressed in well-cut denims, and a dark-green Lacoste T-shirt. Nacho, a good twenty years younger, was wearing fashionable Bermuda shorts, and had a kind, pretty face. He was Óscar's assistant, perhaps his boyfriend, though the exact nature of their relationship was unclear.

Both, apparently, were photographers, carrying out a commission from the regional government of La Mancha. They had been asked, as far as I could understand, to record traditional Manchegan life and crafts.

The bar owner rushed in to tell me that the Argamasilla bus had arrived. Óscar insisted on giving me his address in Madrid. The owner came back to say that the bus had left.

Óscar's and Nacho's van was crammed with photographic equipment, but they cleared some room for me in the back and hoped that I would be comfortable and was not in too great a hurry. They intended being in Argamasilla by nightfall, but probably would be making various stops along the way. The early evening was the best hour for photography, and indeed the unrelievedly flat, bare landscape we entered only a few kilometres north of Ruidera had a glowing magnificence. The ochres and browns had shaken off their dusty, pastel sheen to become golden and russet; deepening shadows were cutting like acid into the earth, and the ever more distant line of the horizon sharpened to a cheese-wire fineness under a vast sky as vivid as a fresh coat of paint.

Óscar used Azorín's word, 'millennial', to describe the countryside, our narrow, empty road being the only obvious sign of the modern world. Our first stop was at a crude stone hut with a conical roof painted white, an architecture of prehistoric inspiration, exactly like one of the *trulli* of southern Italy. Its function, Óscar said, could hardly be simpler, but nothing remained simple after Óscar had explained it.

Though he proudly claimed to have learned everything about life 'from the gutter', he had a tendency in his speech to become incomprehensibly abstract and philosophical, and to return, whatever the subject, to his real hobby-horse – the evils of modern technology. In moments such as these I depended on Nacho, whose quiet, relaxed and straightforward manner was the diametric opposite of Óscar's. The stone huts, he told me, were used for storing equipment to prune the surrounding vines.

Back in the van, Óscar was railing against the iniquity of the video in modern life when he brought the van to a sudden halt, a few feet away from a dead dog. The tripod and the two cameras were brought out from the back of the van. The dog's paws were clenched in the direction of the now setting sun; steam rose from the oozing blood, and a cloud of insects hovered over the exposed entrails. Óscar knelt as closely as he could to the body, and used a Leica 80 mm. close-up lens to take shots of it.

'Everything is material to a photographer,' he said.

'I won't be showing this to my mother,' interjected Nacho, photographing the body from the same angle as his master had done.

'I don't think it'd go down too well in England, either,' I added.

'Why?' asked Óscar, surprised. '*This* is reality.'

If the dead dog was reality, illusion loomed up on the other side of the road in the form of an enormous, crenellated fantasy, tinged red by the evening sun, and poised over a large and ghostly reservoir.

'The castle of Peñarroya,' said Óscar. 'Let's go and have a drink there.' Was Óscar tilting at windmills, or did this apparently abandoned medieval ruin in the middle of an empty countryside really contain a bar? He read my thoughts and smiled. 'It's the most hidden bar in La Mancha. You might almost call it a magical bar.'

Don Quixote never went to the castle of Peñarroya, but Azorín, who did, suggested that the place must surely have been an inspiration to Alonso Quixano. Since Azorín's day the castle has been extensively restored, and though very alluring from a distance comes to seem at close quarters like a Disneyland cut-out. On the other side of the Gothic entrance gate we reached a part of the building that had been reconstructed to serve as a home to the caretaker and his family. The 'magical bar' was a large fridge in which cans of beer and Coca-Cola were kept, to be sold to passing tourists.

We continued our journey towards Argamasilla, and, as darkness fell and Óscar placed his foot on the accelerator, I discovered that the man who was driving me was none other than the Spanish photographer who had achieved notoriety a few years back for having desecrated the tomb of the German poet Rainer Maria Rilke. He had done so, he now claimed, to redeem the tomb of his 'pagan hero' from the clutches of 'Catholic bigots', but the exact details of his escapade were lost on me, and in any case the lights of Argamasilla were finally coming into view. I felt quite relieved. I was looking forward to finding a homely, rural *fonda* of the type described by Azorín. I would have a short walk through the village, a simple supper and an early night. The next day I would get up early to wander over to Cervantes's so-called 'prison', where English visitors were always said, in Azorín's day, to spend a long time lost in contemplation, one of them having even been seen to fall on his knees and kiss the ground while shouting ecstatically. This hardly seemed to me to be English behaviour, but Azorín had quoted it as an illustration of the great cult that 'the most idealistic nation of the earth' professed for 'the loftiest and most famous of all idealists'.

The strength of my own admiration for Don Quixote would not be put to the test. The van bypassed Argamasilla at about 120 kilometres an hour, and Nacho was opening three more cans of beer.

'You'd be crazy to spend the night there,' Óscar told me. 'If you find anywhere to stay, there'll be flies in the room and God knows what else.'

Óscar proposed that I should stay with them if I wanted a comfortable night. They were heading for the luxury *parador* at Manzanares, and Óscar could not comprehend how anyone could want to stay anywhere else. I had lingering qualms about missing Argamasilla, and Óscar tried to pinpoint exactly what it was that interested me in that town. I felt too embarrassed to say anything about Don Quixote, and mentioned Azorín instead.

'An Englishman and Azorín!' Óscar jeered. 'If you don't mind me saying so, that sounds rather frivolous.'

The *parador* stood on the outskirts of Manzanares, and served as an overnight stop to those plying the NIV between Madrid and the south. It was full. But Óscar was an incorrigible optimist who believed that rooms would miraculously be found for us if we waited around in the hotel bar, drinking and 'philosophizing'.

Nacho longed to find a place for the night and have a shower, but Óscar was more interested in the fate of the universe. A meeting the next day of the Manchegan farmers' lobby, which Óscar urged me to attend, was seen by him as symptomatic of a sinister conspiracy on the part of the technocrats. Radical reforms were going to be introduced that would destroy, insidiously but irreversibly, the whole traditional rural structure of La Mancha, and, by extension, that of Spain, of Europe and of the world. The next moment Óscar had leapt on to the subject of nuclear catastrophe, and was himself building up to some emotional climax, the consequences of which, in the placid hotel bar, with its quiet background music and even blander guests, were frightening to contemplate. The inevitable explosion eventually came, prompted by the closure of the bar and the temporary inability of the hotel computer to furnish us with our bill. I distractedly feigned interest in a brochure on the Spanish *parador* system as a violent Óscar waged war on the technocrats for having invented a machine that did not serve humanity so much as dominate it.

At one o'clock in the morning the three travellers found themselves at a motorway hotel called The Three Magi. Expensive, pretentious and yet of Formica tackiness, this was the type of hotel Óscar had said earlier he would never set foot in, but he was now a cowed and contrite person, led around by Nacho. In his new-found sobriety, he had appeared even to have forgotten about the next day's epoch-making meeting; as we went off to our separate rooms, he wished me luck for my journey, 'just in case we don't see each other in the morning'.

THE SOUNDS of passing lorries woke me early, and I opened the dark-green velvet curtains to see a bleak and ugly La Mancha. Oscar and Nacho were still in their rooms, the receptionist told me, but by the time I had had my breakfast their van had mysteriously gone, taking with it a catalogue I had been presented with describing Óscar as one of Spain's leading avant-garde photographers. Later, and to no avail, I would scour through books on Spanish photography in search of his name, and ask my more knowledgeable Spanish friends if they had heard of him. Once, I even tried to phone him at the Madrid number he had given me at Ruidera, but the line was dead, and his name was not listed in the directory.

The Three Magi Hotel was not an ideal location for the traveller without a car. I took my life in my hands as I crossed the motorway on foot, judging with split-second timing the brief gaps between the speeding traffic. The sense of a return to reality stayed with me on the other side of the road, where I walked for over half an hour through the dusty confusion of warehouses, garages, small factories, and patchily whitewashed modern residences that made up the outskirts of Manzanares, one of the largest of La Mancha's towns. An old woman showed me a short cut to the railway station over a fence marked 'Danger' and through a labyrinth of tracks. She told me to stay with her and keep a lookout for the luxury Talgo train, but she walked at a snail's pace, and the sounds of a train were getting closer. All she could do was smile when we reached the station platform only a few seconds before the Talgo did. I climbed aboard and slumped with relief into my seat. A young woman in uniform woke me up after a few minutes to ask me if I wanted to borrow some headphones to watch the video.

The impact of videos on Spanish coach and train travel was an aspect of the video phenomenon that had not been touched on by Óscar, whose madness I would almost have welcomed in the antiseptic setting of a Talgo, where Muzak, air-conditioning and videos, and the consequent shutting of windows and blinds, combine to give a sameness to all journeys, and to cocoon the traveller almost entirely from the environment through which he passes. Refusing the offer of the headphones, I tried instead to contemplate the landscape outside, but the images of Don Quix-ote country passing in front of my slumbering head were not those of an actual landscape but of a short video on Don Quixote and La Mancha prepared by the Spanish Tourist Board.

'Eternal Spain' reasserted itself on my alighting at Alcázar de San Juan, the Spanish town – or rather station – I had visited almost more than any other, together with the equally unappeal-ing Bobadilla and Linares-Baeza. Memories of Spanish rail tours in the pre-video days of travelling seemed to include countless changes of train at all three of these places, places that owed their importance to the whims of railways engineers in the last century, and that appear to have little life other than as junctions. A nostalgia for those days made me almost pleased to find that. Alcázar de San Juan had remained as grim as ever, a sort of Spanish El Paso where desperate-looking men milled around the pinball machines in bars that lay along the spindly arcades leading to the decayed turn-of-the-century station. The main change was that the adjoining bus station had gone; a new one had been built a good 4 kilometres away, in a clean and innocuous modern suburb.

I had time to spare, time slowly to inspect the ubiquitous statue of Don Quixote and Sancho Panza marking the intersection of the town's main streets, time to continue the sobering process of adjusting to reality after what now seemed to be an illusory previous day. Wandering leisurely towards the bus station, I confronted the dreadful possibility that Cervantes might have been born in Alcázar de San Juan had a widespread popular belief been proved correct, and had not those pedantic academics intervened and dealt an irreparable blow to Manchegan pride by finding documents that showed incontestably that the author of *Don Quixote* was from Alcalá de Henares.

The bus left for El Toboso at the end of the morning, passing through Criptana del Campo, a town scarcely more appealing than Alcázar de San Juan, but distinguished by its famous windmills lined menacingly along a ridge above the town's thinning outskirts. Jacacci had found these structures fantastical, and had quite understood how Don Quixote had mistaken them for giants. A more fantastical sight for the modern traveller, however, could be seen on the ugly main road to the west of the town, where the land of Don Quixote gave way to that of Pedro Almodóvar, and where there stood – between the garden statuary belonging to an antiques emporium and a trestle table where gypsy boys were selling melons – three beautifully repaired London telephone boxes. A kilometre or so further on the bus swerved off on to a side road, bringing me back to a more traditional and isolated La Mancha, in the middle of which was the small town of El Toboso.

IN A crowded restaurant at the entrance to the town, I sat eating lunch, the waiter bringing me a portable telephone with my third course. I made a call to Seville to say that I was in El Toboso and searching for my Dulcinea, to which my friend replied that I should come quickly to the south, where many more Dulcineas were to be found. I was waiting for the worst of the afternoon heat to pass before wandering around the town, but impatience got the better of me and I set off into El Toboso's empty, sleeping streets.

'And they entered El Toboso', read one of the town's several enigmatic signs bearing quotations from *Don Quixote*. El Toboso has usually been described as the highpoint of a Cervantine tour of La Mancha, and I could see why after a preliminary ramble around its tiny centre. The place had beautifully maintained the appearance of a quiet, sixteenth-century village, but was mercifully free of the museum-like character and expensively restored weekend homes it probably would have displayed had it been situated anywhere other than in the scorched plains of La Mancha. Its old stone monuments and simple whitewashed houses cast their shadows over dusty streets smelling of cow dung, rutted by cart wheels, and brushed by strands of escaping hay.

Azorín called El Toboso a 'stupendous' village, but also perceived an atmosphere of decay and abandon symptomatic for him of the underlying tragedy of rural Castile in the twentieth century. El Toboso has become smarter and more prosperous than when visited by Azorín, but there is no mistaking the sense of a traditional, friendly but still anachronistic community on the verge of a somnolent oblivion. On its deserted main square, with its view of a fenced-off bandstand and the rough-hewn block of the Herreran Convent of the Trinitarians, I found a shaded bench and fell asleep.

An old man was hovering over me when I woke up, addressing me in a formal, antiquated Spanish.

'Am I asking you a great impertinence,' he said, 'but where do you come from?' He told me he had been born in 1916, and had served as a choirboy in the parish church. His memories of the old El Toboso were very different from the impressions of Azorín. He remembered a lively, bustling community, 'completely unlike the village of today'. The population had now dropped from 4000 to 2400, and most of the young people had gone off to Alicante, Valencia, and, above all, Madrid. 'Madrid absorbs everything,' he sighed before saying goodbye and shuffling away, leaving me to doze off once more.

But he was back a few minutes later, asking me if I knew that the Trinitarian Convent was currently celebrating its 400th anniversary. 'I remember when Mussolini's niece Giuseffina was a nun there,' he said, succeeding in shaking off my remaining drowsiness. This time it was me who began asking the questions, anxious to learn more about the connection between the village and the dictator's niece.

Her passion for *Don Quixote*, he said, was what had first aroused her interest in Spain and had led to her transference from an Italian convent to El Toboso. She had gone back to Italy at the outset of the Civil War, when the village had fallen just within the boundaries of Republican Spain, and had been the scene of heavy fighting. The old man concluded by supplying me with a useful historical footnote. 'In the end,' he said, 'the war was won by this man called Franco. He died a few years ago, you may have heard of him.'

For Giuseffina Mussolini and other devotees of *Don Quixote*, El Toboso must have seemed the answer to their dreams, a place halfway between fact and fiction, an encapsulation of the confusion between the real and legendary Cervantes, between the author and his creation. She was one of several enthusiasts and scholars of Cervantes who had actually settled in El Toboso, sharing the place with the village's own self-styled *Cervantistas* or *Miguelistas*, as Azorín had preferred to call them. To the villagers of Azorín's day, Cervantes was always known familiarly as 'Miguel', and though none of them would claim him as a native of the place (they still persisted in the belief that he was from Alcázar de San Juan), they all were adamant that the grandfather of Cervantes was from there, and that descendants of his had remained in the village for at least two centuries. To commemorate Cervantes in a more scholarly way, one of these *Miguelistas* established a 'Cervantine Library' there at the beginning of the century, and it survives to this day, a few minutes' walk from the House of Dulcinea.

I went first to pay my respects to Dulcinea. It was now five o'clock in the afternoon, and the lady was ready to receive visitors, the elderly keeper of her house having been roused by the bell chain pulled by a prim mother and daughter from Madrid. Graham Greene may, in his novel about an unorthodox priest, *Monsignor Quixote* (1982), have labelled the house a 'trap for tourists', but the place had been considered as Dulcinea's long before tourism had come to the village. In the 1960s, the keeper informed me, the house had been turned into a museum, but almost nothing had been done to the interior, where even the original sixteenth-century furnishings had remained. For a house that had belonged to a fictional character, its interior seemed remarkably real, more real in fact than those in Spain purporting to be the actual and authentically preserved domestic surroundings of real historical personages such as Charles V, El Greco, and, of course, Cervantes. The whitewashed rooms, with their plain beams and simple furniture, had a lived-in quality which was enhanced by the absence of pseudo-antiques and information panels, and by such details as a broom casually left out. The cheese mould in the kitchen was still used for making cheese, according to the keeper, who apologized for not having any to sell to me that day. 'Have you tried Señora Blanca?' he suggested.

The Cervantine Library was closed, but a passer-by directed me instead to the home of the village's leading Cervantist, the retired parish priest, Don Nicolás. Don Nicolás, the author of a lengthy history of his village, was a frail and charming man who welcomed me warmly as a fellow Cervantist and potential settler in El Toboso, 'an ideal place for study and contemplation'. He advised me to go off and look for the village's two policemen, Antonio and Paco, to whom he had recently relinquished the keys to the library.

In searching for the policemen, I enjoyed pleasant conversations with their parents, children, wives and grandparents, before finally tracking Antonio down to the local men's club or *casino*, on the door of which was a notice announcing a raffle organized by the Society of the Sweet Name of Jesus. The first prize was a video machine and the booby prize was a 'Picture of Our Lord'. Antonio was playing cards with a large group of friends, but stood up to greet me as soon as he had finished his turn. I felt guilty that his game should be interrupted for so frivolous a reason as accompanying an Englishman to the Cervantine Library, but he said that he had only been passing the time and that his duty was to help the public.

Inside the library, Antonio explained to me how its founder, Don Jaime, had been killed during the Civil War, when the institution itself had been gutted by fire. Many of the books had been burned, but not, miraculously, the most important ones, which form today the major part of a collection of 203 editions of *Don Quixote* in 32 languages. The statistic gave Antonio evident satisfaction, as did the newly built room in which the famous 'signed editions' I had come to see were displayed. These editions had been mentioned both by Unamuno and Graham Greene and included those with the signatures of Mussolini, Thomas Masaryk, Ramsay Macdonald, Eamon De Valera, Hindenburg and Hitler, the latter's tiny, cramped scrawl being likened by Monsignor Quixote to a 'fly's mess'. To this list of figures, there had been added such recent names as François Mitterand and Margaret Thatcher. Someone in the library had either a sense of humour or else an unwholesome sense of historical perspective. Mrs Thatcher's signed copy had been placed in between Hitler's and Mussolini's.

'A tiny alley leading nowhere,' said the plaque misleadingly of an alley that led in fact to the narrow, hidden square where I saw the last of El Toboso's monuments. Beds of carnations and rows of citrus trees paid homage here to one Federico García Sánchiz, whose life-sized bronze was flanked by mourners. Who was this obscure figure to whom the grandest monument in a village resonant of Cervantes and Dulcinea had been dedicated? A Cervantist, of course, but what contribution had he made to Cervantine studies great enough to merit such an honour? His name did not feature in any Cervantine bibliography I knew of, nor had I been able to find it in the index of the Cervantine Library. Both Don Nicolás and Antonio had brought him up in conversation, but all that they could say of this supposedly renowned scholar was that he had given lectures and had coined the untranslatable and virtually unused word 'hispañolear', which means roughly to 'go around pontificating on Hispanic topics'. The plaque on his monument added that he had been born in Valencia, had gone *hispañoleando* around South America, and had returned to Spain to die in El Toboso, where his body lay in the village's civic cemetery. The inscription on his tomb was repeated on the monument and gave me an idea for my own in the eventuality of not finding a human Dulcinea on my travels. 'Here lie,' it read, 'Federico García Sánchiz and the Spain which was his Dulcinea.'

THE BUS journey from Quintanilla to Toledo approached the spiritual capital of Spain in an especially dramatic way. The roads were narrow, empty and pitted, and a sense of adventure was heightened by the bus driver getting lost in one of the largest of the desolate-looking communities that we passed through. We were aiming roughly towards the deep red disk of the low, evening sun, whose rays cast a lurid light over a landscape that in the early 1900s reminded the English authors of *Unexplored Spain* of the Athi Plains near Nairobi. Pale yellow shrubland stretching for miles was followed by fields of calcinous earth stubbled with cropped wheat; a notion of scale was provided by the odd row of telegraph poles receding sharply into nothing.

As the journey neared its end, there were rolling expanses of olive trees, and a growing profile of high, purple-brown hills. Two old men, among the few survivors of the journey, gaped with naive incredulity at the technological marvel of the as yet incomplete high-speed-train link between Madrid and Seville, an anachronism in this millennial landscape.

It was around the hour of dusk when the traveller arrived in Toledo.

7

A Toledan Night

A YOUNG Toledan taxi-driver, engaged to the twice-crowned Miss Castilla-La Mancha, had offered to show me an 'unknown', 'hidden' and 'magical' Toledo. His fiancée was known simply as 'Chus', but he had the more sonorous, biblical name of Jesús del Pozo – 'Jesus of the Well'. I had met them both at a party in Madrid, and had promised to give them a ring when next in Toledo. I did so immediately after my arrival from La Mancha, and was told by Jesús that he would take me the next day deep inside the rock on which the town was built. Tantalizing me further, he mentioned also something about the 'magical way', which he described as a 'Masonic itinerary leading from the chamber of spiritual darkness to the pyramid of enlightenment'. Outside, as we spoke, the last of the day's coach parties were setting off, and the town was preparing itself for what was traditionally its most mysterious hour. I put down the phone, and walked out into the Toledan night.

A NIGHT without sleep is known in Spanish as a 'Toledan night'. The phrase has its prosaic origins in the sleep-disturbing activities of the town's once notorious mosquitoes. But the words 'Toledan night' also have a poetic resonance, a suggestion of secretiveness and spirituality to counter the balmy sensuality implied by the notion of a 'Sevillian night'.

A 'Toledan night' expresses the traditional essence of Toledo, a town that has been thought of as a spiritual fortress akin to such diverse places as Rome, Alexandria, Durham, Lhasa and Fez. Writers have repeatedly referred to Toledo as the heart or soul of Spain, and Pérez Galdós echoed the views of many when he also called the town 'a complete history of Spain', meaning by this that its own history was a distillation of all the early forces that have shaped the country.

The rocky outcrop on which Toledo was founded hides a labyrinth of caves that have encouraged stories about the mythical origins of the town but that bear, as well, traces of a rich neolithic culture. The Romans, following the Iberians, built a citadel at the summit of the rock, a rock whose four hummocks were later dignified by scholars as seven hills so as to match those of Rome. Then came the Visigoths from their obscure Central European homeland, turning Toledo into their capital and the focus of Spain's burgeoning Christianity, and establishing the town's reputation as one of Spain's most important centres of learning. To the Moors, Toledo owes the baffling souk-like layout of its streets, the predominance here of brick over stone, the strong craft tradition, and the idea of a place where the monuments, from the cathedral onwards, concentrate their richness on the interior.

The so-called 'reconquering' Christians took the town in 1085, the horse of Alfonso XI stopping resolutely in front of what is now the intriguing palimpsest of the Cristo de la Luz, where a Visigothic chapel with a burning candle was uncovered under a mosque, which would later be turned back into a chapel by the Moors working under Christians known as *Mudéjars*. *Mudéjar* craftsmen constructed Christian Toledo, a town that prospered in the late Middle Ages under the rule of powerful dynasties of cardinals who provided Spain with the closest equivalent to the Medici family of Florence. But Toledo would soon be constrained by its past, its myths, and, not least, by its site, the town's rocky outcrop being held in the noose of a loop of river cut deep into a craggy, barren amphitheatre of hills. At the end of the fifteenth century a halt had to be called to the construction of the closed-order convents that had come by now to occupy over half of Toledo's surface area and would in later years succeed in draining away much of the town's life.

After Madrid was made capital of Spain in 1561, Toledo retained its symbolic and ecclesiastical role, but lost for ever its political and economic importance, and its vitality. El Greco, dreaming of international fame as a painter at the court of Philip II, resigned himself to a life of provincial obscurity by deciding to remain in Toledo after his rejection at the court. Pérez Galdós, writing in the 1860s, referred to Toledo as a town with a great history but only a history, a dead town with no hope of resurrection. A Sevillian night suggests the intense pleasure of the moment, but a Toledan night denotes a necrophiliac contemplation of the past.

It was as a dead town that Toledo first began to inspire in travellers an obsessive and widespread passion, aided by the late-Romantic decadence and mysticism of the last decade of the nineteenth century. Peréz Galdós, one of the earliest of the town's great nineteenth-century enthusiasts, used Toledo as the setting of *Angel Guerra* (1890–91), the first of his series of novels of atonement and redemption. Described shortly after it was written as 'the novel of Spanish mysticism', it tells the story of a dissolute Madrilenian who comes to Toledo in pursuit of a woman, but ends up there as a mystic and ascetic founding a lay confraternity and devoting himself to charity. The enormous popular success of this novel coincided, significantly, with the 'rediscovery' of El Greco, an artist who had once been regarded as a mere curiosity but was now being hailed as one of the great geniuses of Western art. His works soon came to be identified with Toledo itself to such a degree that the Greek writer Kazantzakis was disappointed to discover that the inhabitants were prosperous, well-fed bourgeois rather than the lean ascetic types he had imagined from the works of El Greco. Only after the ravages of the Civil War did the hungry townspeople acquire for him the prerequisite noble and mystical look El Greco had depicted.

Whereas foreigners perceived Toledo essentially through the paintings of El Greco, Spanish visitors took a rather broader view of Toledan culture, and developed at the beginning of the century a curious love of the town by night. In his memoirs, *Automoribundia* (1948), Gómez de la Serna recalled a visit he had made to Toledo one January night in the company of thirty writers and artists. They had wandered until dawn through the empty streets of the town, thinking not so much of El Greco as of 'Lope de Vega, Moreto, Tirso de Molina and many other of the great literary figures who had been there before us, writing in the light of a frozen candle'. Gómez de la Serna described the whole occasion as having been a 'true Toledan night', the ultimate of

Toledan experiences. The prospect of nights of this sort gave rise in the 1920s to the 'Order of Toledo', the Grand Master of which was the future film director Luis Buñuel, who found Toledo a 'magical city' that filled him with wonder, 'more because of its indefinable atmosphere than for its touristic attractions'. The qualifications for advancing to the rank of Knight in the Order were, in Buñuel's words, 'to adore Toledo without reservation, drink for at least an entire night, and wander aimlessly through the streets of the city'. The members of the Order put up at an ancient and primitive inn luridly named the Posada de la Sangre ('the Inn of Blood') and counted among their adventures a visit to the house of a blind family, where they discovered on the walls pictures of cemeteries made from human hair.

'What are these Madrileños doing in Toledo?' asks Mary McCarthy in her afterword to Felipe Alfau's *Locos: A Comedy of Gestures* (1928), one of the more bizarre and original Spanish novels of this century. The 'characters' who people this book are resident in Madrid but get together in the opening chapter in a Toledan café called the Café de los Locos, a place where 'bad writers were in the habit of coming . . . in quest of characters'. The fact that the chapter takes place at night must surely reflect the tradition of the nocturnal escapade to Toledo; but the choice of Toledo had also a metaphorical significance, for Alfau clearly had the whole of Spain in mind when he described the town as both 'a petrified forest of centuries' and 'a hostile city that died in the Renaissance and yet lived the strangest, posthumous life'. The book is written in that characteristic Spanish mixture of parody and expressiveness, and can also be seen to anticipate many of the directions taken after the war by Latin American and other experimental writers.

Alfau himself is as much of a mystery as the Toledo he describes. Born in the Basque country in 1902, he has lived in New York since 1914 and has spent his entire working life as a translator for a bank. *Locos*, which was written in English, took eight years to find a publisher, and then was almost instantly forgotten, only to be rediscovered over fifty years later. Its belated success led to the publication in 1990 of his only other novel, *Chromos*, which had been written for his own pleasure back in

1948 and now came to be shortlisted for the American National Book Award. In the spring of 1991, a journalist from *El País* finally succeeded in being granted a telephone interview with the then eighty-eight-year-old Alfau.

He found a man with a longing for death and a complete indifference to a world that had taken so long to recognize him. Alfau told the reporter that he had never had any interest in contemporary fiction, and that his knowledge of Spanish literature was based almost entirely on a schoolboy reading of classic authors such as Cervantes, Calderón and Galdós. He claimed that he had never had any literary aspirations and that he had written largely as a hobby, the idea of publishing *Locos* first coming to him when he was unemployed and short of cash. Asked whether he had returned to Spain since his childhood, he replied that he had done so in 1959, but had not enjoyed his visit, finding the place very 'changed'.

Luis Buñuel, exiled to France and Mexico after the Civil War, paid long and regular return visits to Spain from the late 1950s onwards. He had vowed never to go back to Toledo following the destruction in 1936 of the Posada de la Sangre, but he did in fact return to the town in the 1960s to film *Tristana*, the first work he had made in Spain since the war. Based on a novel by Galdós, *Tristana* had Catherine Deneuve as the eponymous heroine whose beauty becomes ever greater following the amputation first of one and then of the other leg. Much of the action takes place at night, and there is also a scene showing Catherine Deneuve with a deathmask modelled on the effigy of Berruguete in the Hospital of Tavera, one of Buñuel's former favourite nocturnal haunts.

I saw the film at its Toledan première in 1969, and then went to visit the unchanged, turn-of-the-century café that had featured in it. Later that night I wandered off with a sense of wonder and excitement into the silent moonlit streets, but came subsequently to confuse my memories of the nocturnal town with the powerful images of the film, so that the two finally coalesced to become as indistinguishable to me as Toledo and El Greco were in the minds of others.

*

THE CAFÉ of Buñuel's film, on the Plaza del Zocodover, had been replaced by 1991 by a McDonald's. I sat down near by after a brief and dispiriting stroll through a town that appeared, even in the darkness, to have acquired a phoney and smugly conservative air since my first visit. Preservation laws stricter than those of any other Spanish town had insisted that all new building work should be in accordance with the old, with the result that the whole place had developed the look of a large, redbrick sham, a sort of Spanish Nuremberg.

At the same time the wares in the town's souvenir shops indicated that the town's reputation as a tourist centre continued to rest heavily on an artist whose work had been interpreted in such a distorted way by critics that he himself had become more of a myth than a real figure, a sham of a different kind. Ever since the 'rediscovery' of El Greco, tourists have been coming to Toledo with the expectation that his works would provide some mystical experience. They have rarely considered him as an artist who was forced to make a living largely by churning out devotional pictures for provincial churches, pictures that exist in numerous versions of variable quality, and that were painted in a style that lent itself well to imitators and forgers.

As I sat in the Plaza de Zocodover, I planned a 'Toledan night' that left little room for what would normally be defined as the 'spiritual'. I was in the spiritual capital of Spain, but all I could think of was food, specifically the food served in the Asador Adolfo, an externally modern and unenticing restaurant hidden a few steps away from the cathedral.

Now that Toledo is no longer ruled by its cardinals, their role has been taken over by Adolfo, whose power and influence are steadily increasing every year. He was standing, as I came in, with a group of local dignitaries, whose conversation soon turned after my entry to an important literary prize he had recently endowed. Adolfo announced that he would waive the rules of the competition so that I could enter it myself with a piece in English to be handed in over four weeks late. The director of tourism for Castilla-La Mancha whispered to me that with Adolfo's support I would be almost certain to win the prize. In the meantime the unctuous high-pitched head waiter had made an appearance, and was asking Adolfo if I was going to be 'invited' to supper. The night was looking up.

The head waiter, like an over-enthusiastic child, pulled me by the arm into the main dining-room, where I had to feign delight and astonishment at the sight of the new décor. The plain, modern exterior of the Asador Adolfo fronted a medieval palace decorated inside by a fourteenth-century frieze, but in the newly refurbished dining-room these genuinely old elements shared the space with fake El Grecos and expensive reproduction antiques. The whole effect now formed a monument to the *cursi*. Reflections on the real and the sham were soon forgotten, however, as waiters pampered me with food and wine, lulling me into a sensual trance that left me only dimly aware of the cook's arrival at the end of the meal to serve me himself with his famous marzipan, a speciality introduced to Toledo by the Moors, perpetuated by the town's nuns, and perfected in the wood-fired oven of the Asador Adolfo. Biting into the marzipan I bit into a piece of Toledo's history, my teeth penetrating a severe outer layer coloured like scorched brick before reaching a smooth pale centre whose taste of sweetened almonds brought with it a slight flavour of the Orient.

IN MY DREAMS that night I was crawling on my hands and knees through the tunnels that led to the centre of Toledo's hidden labyrinth. But when I woke up the next morning I had a disappointing call from Jesús. Nothing, he apologized, could be arranged for me for that day. The woman whose cellar opened into the town's caves could not be found, while the 'magical way' would best be left for a later occasion, when I had more time to spare.

I left Toledo, carrying with me little more than an aftertaste of the food in the Asador Adolfo. The town that had been a beacon for the mystical traveller in Spain had become for me the place Alfau's Don Fulano describes as he prepares to jump into the Tagus and turn himself into a 'non-character': 'Toledo was a myth,' he says. 'Toledo did not exist.'

PART THREE

SWEET VENGEANCE

8

Hailing Progress

THE AVE could be perceived as a marvel of modern technology sweeping the traveller off into a land rich in myth and poetry. Its name sounds like a truncated incantation to the virgin, and is also a pun on the Spanish word for bird; it is in fact the acronym for *Alta Velocidad Española*, the new high-speed-train service linking Madrid with the Andalusian capital of Seville.

The AVE was planned to reduce the journey between the two cities from six hours to two and a half hours, and to form part of a new national network that would bring Spain closer to the rest of Europe. European-gauge lines were used instead of the wider, nineteenth-century ones designed to protect Spain from invasion by rail. The white carriages, of dove-like sleekness, incorporate the ultimate in conceptual and avant-garde design, with the letters 'AVE' written in staggered sequence so that they form the word 'AVE' only when the train is travelling at maximum velocity.

The AVE is a fitting symbol of the new Spain, of a country rushing towards a designer future with new-found optimism and energy, while in fact running dangerously near to disaster and ridicule. The inauguration of the new railway was not due until the spring of the magical 1992, but in the previous year the AVE had gathered mounting antagonism and prognoses of gloom. The laying of new tracks and the digging of tunnels had left a trail of devastation, burying vast areas of arable land under rubble, obliterating major neolithic remains, cutting a great swathe through a forest of ancient oaks, driving away eagles, deer and black vultures, and, near Toledo, destroying one of Europe's most important habitats for lynx. The conservationists had remained sceptical about all the government talk of reforestation, under-passes for animals, acoustic screens, and other schemes for repairing the irreparable. In the meantime the AVE was coming to seem an increasingly absurd, short-term and financially ruinous prospect.

Gradually it dawned on the Spanish public that the Madrid–Seville line would not be extended to Barcelona and the French frontier, that the line would never be of use to the vast majority of Spain's rolling stock, that the high-speed capacity of its trains might not be fully operational until the next millennium, and that the whole project provided an ideal potential target for the terrorist bombs of ETA.

The train, defying the more sensational of these fears, did in fact run almost as scheduled during the inaugural week, at the promised extraordinary speed, without protests, and with no problems other than the petty ones that beset ordinary rail travel, problems that would furnish the AVE with a new nickname: 'AVERIA' ('Breakdown').

Blame for the construction of this high-speed folly serving only Seville has of course fallen heavily on the shoulders of Spain's Sevillian Prime Minister, Felipe González, who stands accused like the Italian minister of the 1960s who reputedly sponsored one of Italy's costliest and least used *autostrade* for the simple reason that he wished to travel more quickly between his home in Rome and his mistress in Ancona. The AVE, like the Seville EXPO of 1992, is a symptom of the present craze for Andalusia, a region that in recent years has received what many would regard as a disproportionate amount of attention in relation to the rest of Spain. From the Romantic period onwards Andalusia has always been Spain's favourite tourist destination, but the image of the region the present Seville-dominated Spanish government has been so anxious to promote has been that of a place epitomizing more than any other the emergence of Spain into the modern world, following centuries of conservatism, isolation and repression.

Whether or not this image will end up as tarnished as that of the AVE remains to be seen, but it is unlikely to throw off the deep-seated preconceptions about the region held by generations of travellers. The AVE may have defiled the natural boundary of

the Sierra Morena, but for years to come Andalusia will still
probably be thought of as 'the land below Despeñaperros', a land
that exists as much in fiction as in reality.

The pass of Despeñaperros represents the main natural break
in a near-continuous mountain wall which joins up with the sea
to the south to cut off Andalusia from the rest of the peninsula,
and to form what the Moors referred to as the Yesira Andalus
('the island of Andalusia'). The elusive Tartesians, with their
gold-laden ships of biblical fame, gave this region a reputation
comparable to that of El Dorado, while the Greeks, Romans and
Moors helped in turn to build up its image as a natural paradise.
Romantic travellers such as Chateaubriand came to define Andalusia in terms simply of 'happiness', a metaphor used also by the
twentieth-century Sevillian poet Luis Cernuda, who, on another
occasion, called his native region 'a dream the Andalusians carry
within them'. But this image of Andalusia as a smiling, fertile,
dreamlike and fabulously wealthy region has as its obverse an
image of a desperately poor place whose undeniably impressive
natural resources have been dissipated through corruption and
incompetent government, and have largely benefited only such
privileged minorities as the absentee landlords of the vast estates
known as *latifundios*.

Bernardo de Quirós, an economic historian, wrote in 1981,
'Few travellers have been through Despeñaperros without taking
with them spectacles that have been tinted either black or rose.'
The perceptions of travellers coming to Andalusia have certainly
been blurred by the haze of *tópicos* or clichés that hangs more
persistently over Andalusia than over any other Spanish region.
Many of these travellers have suffered from the immediate
delusion of having left Europe behind and entered a land impreg-
nated with Moorish sensuality, one of them even going so far as
to perceive 'a mysterious . . . oriental character' in a town built in
the late eighteenth century for German colonists.

The most sober of heads have been turned at Despeñaperros,
and it has been common for first-time visitors to react in the same
way that Washington Irving's Russian travelling companion had
done on a journey to Andalusia in 1828: Irving observed how
his friend had behaved as if 'intoxicated . . . and in continual

transport with the luxurious indications of a southern climate'. 'Andalusia', as Cernuda put it, 'intoxicates like alcohol or opium.' But, as with all forms of intoxication, rapturous delirium with the region is liable to be followed by bitter confrontation with reality.

Azorín, in a famous essay of 1905 entitled 'Tragic Andalusia', described the overnight train journey from Madrid to Seville, and how he had woken up early in the morning in a landscape of 'indescribable sweetness'. Soothed by the sensual embrace of the Guadalquivir valley, he had later been stimulated into a state of ecstatic excitement through walking around the jasmine-scented streets of Seville. Withdrawal symptoms had occurred shortly afterwards in nearby Lebrija, where he had found himself in a place so impoverished that the local doctor had told him that its inhabitants were 'not living but dying'.

RELISHING the last year before the inauguration of the AVE, I travelled south on the same train that Azorín had taken, joining it at Aranjuez and waking up in the Guadalquivir valley on a bright morning in late May. I was not going directly to Seville, but was breaking my journey for a day or so in the province of Córdoba.

The part of the province through which the train passed had once included an area so bare and empty that an enlightened minister of Charles III had lured in northern settlers with the promise of free land and exemption from taxes; the settlers had not lasted long, being defeated both by the heat and by what one English traveller had described as the effects of 'eating unwhole-some herbs, and drinking too much wine and brandy'. Elsewhere in the province was the Communist village of Marinaleda, whose charismatic and leonine mayor had organized in 1980 a 'hunger strike against hunger' and he had been occupying since 1988 an estate belonging to the wealthy Duke of Infantado.

Neither the presence of the wild areas known as *despoblados* nor the underlying social realities of the province found any place in the work of the seventeenth-century poet Luis de Góngora, whose vision of the Cordoban countryside was purely bucolic. Following his ill-treatment in Madrid at the hands of enemies such as Quevedo, Góngora cut himself off from the world and retired to a small country property outside his native Córdoba, where he composed one of the most famous works of Spanish pastoral verse, *The Solitudes*.

But the greatest mythologizer of the Cordoban countryside was the so-called realist novelist of the late nineteenth century, Juan Valera, who, while living far away from his native Andalusia, dreamed up an arcadian landscape with which to offset his seamy tales of Andalusian village life. It was to Valera's childhood domain that I immediately headed after alighting from the train at Córdoba.

THE IDEALIZED, classically inspired countryside of Valera's fictional imagination was not dissimilar to the late-afternoon landscape that stretched in front of me. Piping goatherds would not have looked out of place among these great rolling expanses of vines, olive trees and wheatfields, with their lush, grassy enclaves and sparkling, jewel-like encrustations of spring flowers. In the shimmering haze of the far distance, geometrical clusters of cubic white buildings could just about be made out at the foot of fantastical outcrops of pale rock. I identified one of the clusters as Cabra, and turned for confirmation to my new companion, Magdalena. At the mere mention of Cabra she put her finger to her lips and with a teasing smile told me never to repeat that name again.

The inhabitants of Lucena, so I discovered, never talk about the neighbouring town of Cabra. Magdalena was from Lucena, and had collected me at Córdoba to take me on a tour of her native town and its surroundings. Only after we reached the area did I realize that neither she nor her parents had been back to the town for several years, but had merely reaped the diminishing profits from their greatly reduced estate there.

The view towards the unmentionable Cabra was from the *finca* of the family's estate manager, the vines in front of me being the main source of the family's income. Jokingly, I began referring to Magdalena as the *señorita* and she responded by assuming an exaggerated proprietorial air as she continued to lead me around her domain. We paid our respects to the estate manager, whom we found sitting under a palm in the cluttered old patio of his *finca*. A dark Filipino maid, with a coloured head scarf, curtsied in front of us and brought us glasses of cold water and Montilla wine. Later we entered an enormous musty complex of warehouses where huge wine presses lay abandoned, victims of modernization. Magdalena's family had been the last in the area to continue producing wine by traditional methods; but for several years now, the old presses had been left to rot away in the company of similarly unwieldy pieces of household furniture the family no longer had room for. Out of this accumulated junk Magdalena was hoping to find the odd piece for her home in Seville, but each object she caught sight of merely weakened her with nostalgia.

Our tour was becoming increasingly sentimental, taking us back into Magdalena's childhood. A long and gently ascending track through fields led to the family's principal country home, a rambling mansion of the early nineteenth century where Magdalena had spent her summers right up to the end of her teens. The main door had warped and could not be budged, so we stayed outside, observing the panoramic view of fields from underneath the sorry skeleton of a pergola. A Spanish Chekhov would have relished the scene, which indeed took on an absurdly nineteenth-century character when Magdalena began telling me that she had been sitting in this very spot when her future husband proposed to her.

She had been eighteen at the time, and he nearly forty, an age difference typical of several of the relationships in the novels of Valera, who himself had married a woman half his age. Magdalena's marriage had turned out to be as unhappy as Valera's, and she was now a single mother in her thirties who had walked out on her husband a few years ago, taking with her their only child. Such behaviour in Seville would scarcely have been commented on today, but in Lucena at the time it constituted a major scandal, the wronged party being, of course, the husband. Magdalena had not been back in Lucena since her separation, and she seemed to be delaying the moment when she would have to take me into the centre of the town, where she would be obliged to make lengthy detours to avoid places associated with her husband's family.

We bided our time by driving up towards evening to the Sanctuary of the Virgin of Araceli, which stands on top of the tallest and most dramatic of the rock pinnacles that rise above the town. Gerald Brenan came here in 1949, making the climb on foot during the worst heat of the afternoon simply to get away for a few hours from Lucena, a place which he found 'unendurable'. He and his wife were enchanted by the beauty and cheerfulness of the neighbouring towns of Cabra and Priego de Córdoba, but had encountered in Lucena not only a place of exceptional ugliness but also a 'Belsen atmosphere'. The poverty here was the worst they had seen in Spain, the whole town being full of emaciated bodies dressed in immodest rags tied together with safety pins. 'Were these Spaniards?' we asked. 'Were these members of that proud and modest race for whom twelve years ago even a stockingless leg was regarded as an iniquity?' They belonged in fact to what Brenan described as the 'pariah class' of day labourers, dependent on seasonal employment from the likes of large estate owners such as Magdalena's family, who must then have been at the height of their fortunes.

We entered Lucena under the cover of night; but as it was a Saturday night, we could not have chosen a time with more people out on the streets. I walked self-consciously from the car, half expecting hostile, suspicious glances in our direction, but soon realized that no one was taking the slightest interest in us. Lucena had grown from a small, gossip-ridden *pueblo* into a large and impersonal modern town. Even Magdalena was surprised for, after an absence of only a few years, she could no longer recognize any of the people, and scarcely any of the buildings. Were the respectable and wealthy-looking people parading up and down the rebuilt streets of Lucena really the descendants of the bedraggled workers Brenan had seen?

Lucena has become one of the wealthiest towns *per capita* in the whole of Andalusia, a middle-class bastion in a rural world which for centuries had known only day labourers and absentee landlords. The Jews, who brought great prosperity to the town in the Middle Ages, were now held responsible for having turned the town into a thriving centre of small businesses. The shops sold expensive knick-knacks in execrable taste, and there were many showrooms proudly displaying kitchen units with rococo trimmings, or shocking pink bathrooms with shag-pile carpets and heart-shaped baths.

Magdalena took me on a short detour to visit a family friend of hers, an elderly potter whom she said was the only Lucenan still working in the traditional style. The potter, a tall man with an enormous moustache, had a sharp wit and an eccentric personality. He also had an acute business sense, and told us that he had recently stopped producing the characteristic ochre and green Lucena ware of old in favour of the blue and white ceramics typical of the Sevillian district of Triana. This was the type of pottery that sold these days, he explained, and indeed he had recently been asked to supply hundreds of vases and plates for the official souvenir shops of the Seville EXPO. Mass-production methods now prevailed in his workshop, and it had been over a year since he had stopped using his old clay kiln, the last surviving one in the province. The enormous domed kiln lay abandoned in his courtyard, and he invited us to walk inside it. We could have been entering a paleolithic tomb.

Magdalena had always told me that she had been brought up in a palace. What she had not said was that this was the only palace in Lucena, in fact the only remaining civic monument of note in the whole town. An eighteenth-century building imposingly arranged along the town's main street, it was dominated by an elaborately sculpted frontispiece framed by dynamically twisted columns. It was the work of Lucena's most famous son, Hurtado Izquierdo, whose church at Priego de Córdoba and presbytery in Granada's Charterhouse are among the most exuberantly ornamental achievements of the Spanish Baroque. Needless to say, the palace was now boarded up, the masonry crumbling, and the upper windows broken. Magdalena's family had sold the building a few years ago to the municipality, who planned one day to convert it into a cultural centre, an increasingly common fate in today's Spain. The family had moved many of their belongings from the palace into a nearby modern flat, where

Magdalena and I were going to stay. The flat was luxurious but tiny, and the huge wooden wardrobes, ornate chandeliers, heavily gilded family portraits, and other objects that had once decorated the palace looked ludicrously cramped and incongruous in their new surroundings. We hastily left our luggage and went outside to enjoy what was left of Saturday night.

Magdalena planned to take me to a number of old-fashioned bars she was sure that I would enjoy. But every place we tried to find had been turned into either a pretentious modern establishment or a building site. 'It's been taken down' became the catchphrase of the night. Some of our discoveries, had they been made in other, less frivolous circumstances, would not have been so funny – particularly not for Magdalena, whose job was to list Andalusian buildings in need of preservation. She had spent the last three years cataloguing the region's public granaries, of which one of the oldest and finest was supposed to be in Lucena, alongside what had once been her favourite bar. We arrived, however, to find out that the whole block had disappeared, its owners having paid no regard whatsoever to the granary's protected status. Nothing surprised Magdalena any more, and she told me how in the early 1980s the municipal authorities of Lucena had even demolished the sixteenth-century town hall to make way for the present pseudo-Renaissance structure.

If most vestiges of Lucena's past had been eradicated, at least one 'historical monument' had been 'improved' and augmented in recent years: the medieval castle where Granada's last Moorish ruler, Boabdil, was briefly imprisoned, had been a sorry heap of stones during Magdalena's childhood, but now it had blossomed into a veritable fortress, complete with crenellations and a row of cubic watchtowers. Magdalena stood unbelievingly for a few moments in front of the castle, but then rushed us on to the open side door of the adjoining parish church of San Mateo, where the presence of a solitary man practising the organ enabled us to have a midnight glimpse of one of the famed baroque monuments of Andalusia.

The Sagrario Chapel, with its writhing stucco, had also been sensationally restored, but its garish freshness was at least in keeping with the architecture's joyously ornamental character.

We should have ended our tour of Lucena on this high note, but were drawn irresistibly to an open-air discotheque, luxuriant with palms, speckled with paper chains and lanterns, and enlivened by agitated, multi-coloured shafts of lighting – a modern version of the gaudy, festive chapel we had just visited. Above the entrance, letters in red, green and yellow beckoned us in with the flickering, brazen command: ELÍGEME ('CHOOSE ME').

9

Between Two Worlds

THE PLACE was unquestionably Spain, and almost certainly the south. The coffin-like room overlooked the interior courtyard of a modern apartment block, the walls of which magnified and distorted a growing cacophony of sounds – shouts, the rattling of plates, toilet flushings, the sizzling of oil, and the strident voice of María del Monte singing *Sevillanas* on the radio. A ray of intense sunlight, cutting through the shutters like a blade, forced my eyes open, waking me up at midday in a city where the transition between dreams and reality is disturbingly sharp. I was in Seville.

For two weeks, since my arrival from Lucena, I had been in a state of perpetual disorientation. I had arrived at a time when Seville was still in party season, the season when the city lives up to its traditional image by indulging in a near continual holiday. This begins with the spectacular processions of Holy Week, continues with the polka-dotted, sherry-fuelled chaos of the Feria, and culminates in that ultimate blend of the sacred and the secular: the Whitsun pilgrimage to the isolated shrine of the Virgin of the Rocío.

But the Seville to which I had returned was also being transformed into the showpiece of the New Spain, busily preparing to host in 1992 a world exhibition envisaged by its promoters as a means of returning the city to a commercial Golden Age.

The Seville of the romantic imagination, the city many of its inhabitants considered the most beautiful in the world, incapable of improvement, had been rotting away for years. Beyond the pristinely white, tourist-loved alleys of the Barrio de Santa Cruz, there lay a Moorish labyrinth of greying, dilapidated plaster and noisy, traffic-choked streets, the whole encased within the unplanned urban sprawl initiated by the Ibero-American

Exhibition of 1929, when workers poured into the city in search
of jobs.

The EXPO of 1992 was providing the perfect opportunity to
tidy up the city centre and radically to alter the urban infrastruc-
ture. I came back at a time when all this work in progress made
the city far dirtier and more chaotic than ever, and when doubts
were growing as to whether all the promised reforms would be
ready in time for the celebrations the following year. But, despite
these misgivings, a vast amount had already been achieved,
enough to unsettle me at times.

I found out that familiar features of old, such as the city's
homely airport, its neo-Moorish railway station, and the poky
garage that had functioned as the bus terminal serving Huelva
province, had been replaced by bold modern structures on a scale
that suggested that the inherently provincial Seville had become
one of the largest of the world's capitals. The most unsettling
changes of all were those affecting Seville's riverfront, which had
once looked out on to an enclosed, stagnant branch of the
Guadalquivir, and had come to a sorry end in a part of the city
where a long stretch of defaced wall had separated railway sidings
from the haunts of prostitutes and drug dealers. The city's malign
odours had now been neutralized; the water ran cleanly and freely;
an avenue of designer elegance had appeared, and sensational new
bridges connected the city with a former overgrown wasteland in
which a giant pyramid was being built as the centre of the EXPO.

In the face of all the grand schemes for the future, I was
reassured to discover that the Sevillians had at least retained intact
their famed sense of humour. The monuments of the new city had
already received nicknames, the name Paquillo ('Little Francis'),
for instance, being given to a bridge resembling a miniature
version of San Francisco's Golden Gate. Citizens of other cities
would have been busy praising or criticizing such dramatic urban
changes; the Sevillians seemed more concerned with making jokes
about what was happening, particularly if there were mishaps.

The EXPO was a rich source of jokes, and became even more
of one after the destruction by fire of the pyramid-shaped building
intended as the 'Pavilion of Discoveries'. ('The first discovery was
fire,' everyone quipped.) I had the impression that the Sevillians

were trying to reconcile the conflicting images of a fun-loving and progressive-minded city by treating the EXPO simply as a huge party of six months' duration. Indeed, the scenes within the EXPO's construction site, where magnificently stylish canvas awnings were being erected, brought to mind the preparations for both the Feria and the Rocío, and emphasized the Sevillian genius for organizing festivities and creating architecture of a purely ephemeral kind.

In anticipation of the great party, most Sevillians were already predicting what they called 'the hangover of 1992', the result of government corruption, and the closure of the many small businesses that had been born of the optimism of Spain's 'magic year'. However, by the end of May 1991, there were other, more pressing hangovers to think about.

Waking up at midday in the Sevillian flat of my friend Esperanza Flores, the remembered sounds of the Rocío pilgrimage added to my general sense of confusion. The hangover from which I was suffering was the result not so much of sherry and sleepless nights, but of having lost all sense of reality in the course of the mounting chaos of dust, fireworks and *Sevillanas* that had accompanied a dazzling, costumed procession through pines, sand dunes and marshland to a sanctuary where scenes of hysterical pagan fervour had broken out in the early hours of Whitsun morning.

'This is reality, everything else is a lie!', a by now hoarse friend of mine had shouted out at the end of the Rocío. But it was in an attempt to regain a sense of what would normally be called 'reality' that I rose from my bed in Esperanza's flat and went off to a part of Seville far away from both the modern and traditional images of the city. I went to the Parque Alcosa.

10

Unwritten Poetry

THE PARQUE ALCOSA is Seville's most outlying district. A symmetrical group of uninspired apartment blocks, a low row of shops and bars, and a dusty, arid setting disturbed by the continual sounds of planes from the neighbouring airport, the Parque Alcosa seemed a world away from the optimism of the EXPO and the haunting beauty of the Rocío. There are far worse districts of Seville, notably Tres Mil Viviendas, where sensation-seeking journalists go in search of the 'other Seville' of soaring unemployment, seedy drug pushers and gangland violence. I went there once myself with a Sevillian friend, only to be told that we were not welcome, and that we had better get out as fast as possible.

Vicarious excitements such as these are unlikely to be experienced in the Parque Alcosa, which is distinguished by its ordinariness, by the way it fails to fulfil not only the traditional image of Seville as glamorous and voluptuous, but also – as advocated by the detractors of 1992 – as violent and decaying. After the strange, chaotic days spent at the Rocío, the prospect of a return to normality was not without its appeal, and I was pleased to be invited to a family lunch in one of the 1950s apartment blocks of the Parque Alcosa.

But Paco, the coach driver who had invited me, was not entirely normal, even in Sevillian terms. No other Sevillian whom I knew had quite so many of the attributes and eccentricities of the stereotypical Sevillian as he had. A fervent hedonist who believed in spending instantly the little money he possessed, Paco was passionate about food and wine, and would eulogize the simplest and most unremarkable of dishes, such as a plate of clams from a tin. He was similarly enthusiastic about bullfighting, but, like a true Sevillian, thought the only matador of any greatness today was the ageing Curro Romero, a man notorious for doing nothing in almost all of his fights, but then redeeming himself every five years or so with a few passes of breathtaking artistry. Inevitably, for a *currista*, Paco was a devotee of all of Seville's religious festivities, and would certainly have participated when younger in the Rocío, had his poor salary and inflexible schedule as a bus driver allowed him.

His special love was Semana Santa, and he had often spoken to me about the deep emotion he had felt while working as a *costalero* – a man who carries with a dozen or so others one of the cripplingly heavy Holy Week *pasos*, or processional floats. He had once had the honour of carrying the most venerated Sevillian image of them all, the Virgin of the Macarena, the devotion to which was a *sine qua non* of all *curristas*. So it was too of anyone who wished to marry Esperanza Flores, who claimed that she could not imagine living with someone who professed allegiance to the rival Virgin of Triana.

While working as a *costalero*, Paco had caused his back permanent damage, and had been forced eventually by recurring pains to retire early on a negligible salary. I had been with him as a courier on his last coach tour, which had ended with a group of family and neighbours forming a welcoming party outside his home in the Parque Alcosa. There and then he had sold the battered wreck of his beloved old bus to a local scrap merchant. He had always refused to exchange this vehicle for any other, despite the fact that its seats were hard and falling to pieces, and that it leaked so badly that on one occasion the luggage of most of the tourists had been covered in water and mud. The old bus was Paco's hallmark, and one of the reasons why some of his colleagues considered him to be odd, an oddness compounded – in their eyes – by his overriding obsession with poetry.

In Spain, and particularly in Seville, there is nothing unusual, or to be ashamed of, about loving poetry. But Paco's poetic sensibility was so extreme that it distanced him from his colleagues, with whom he would sometimes refuse to go out drinking on the grounds that he wanted to stay in and listen to a poetry recital on the radio. Paco's poetic cast of mind was manifest in many other ways, not least in his preference for avoiding main roads and following instead winding country tracks that enabled him, in his own words, to have a 'closer contact with nature'.

Poetry was one of the reasons why Paco was so keen to invite me to lunch in his house. There were other reasons, such as the goat's cheese he wanted me to try, and his wife's delicious wild-asparagus omelette. But he wanted above all to show me his extensive library of verse, and to introduce me to his eldest son, whom he proudly considered to have the makings of a major poet. The son was a shy and awkward student of engineering who seemed to be more interested in repairing his motor cycle than in letting me have a look at his poetry. But a severe paternal reprimand eventually induced him to bring out a slim, photo-copied volume entitled *Heartache in the Night*. It had, apparently, been awarded third prize in an annual competition organized by the neighbours' association of Parque Alcosa. Paco beamed as I tried, with a feigned expression of rapture, to hide my embarrass-ment as I read through his son's verse. Afterwards he decided that the whole poetic experience I had just gone through should be rounded off with a visit to what he described as a site associated with 'Seville's greatest poet'.

Paco drove me to a Sevillian district even uglier than Parque Alcosa, situated halfway between the city's main hospital and the enormous cemetery of San Fernando. I thought I had seen every important site in Seville but had no idea where I was being taken by Paco, who insisted on keeping it a surprise. The place we finally ended up in was somewhere I thought had been pulled down long ago, and indeed I could not understand why it had not been. Dwarfed by high-rise apartments and cowering from the rush of traffic, the place was a humble, single-storey structure, with whitewashed walls and a straw roof. Still known as the Venta de los Gatos ('Inn of the Cats'), this nineteenth-century establishment on the old Carmona road had once been a popular haunt of both travellers and revellers. It had recently been restored as a modest bar, but for many years it had been an abandoned ruin, inspiring some nostalgic lines from the Sevillian writer and academic, Julio M. de la Rosa:

Everything seems dead now in the long forgotten Venta de los Gatos . . . No one sings while rolling their eyes; there are no longer those poor but happy young girls with their multi-coloured headscarves; nor the rocking-chair; nor the furtive, enamoured couples; nor the busy waiters serving their festive customers with *manzanilla* and plates of olives.

Julio M. de la Rosa was paraphrasing a description written by the famous poet to whom Paco had referred and whose name was perennially linked with the inn – Gustavo Adolfo Bécquer. The bar that had now replaced the inn was hung with Bécquer memorabilia, and was one of Paco's favourite Sevillian bars for the simple reason that Bécquer was one of his favourite poets. In guiding me here Paco was leading me to the man whose life and work have been seen to embody the poetic essence of Seville.

THE SPLENDID monument to Bécquer in the María Luisa Park is reproduced, significantly, in all the tourist brochures on Seville, and has become as identified with Seville as has the Manekin Pis with Brussels. Centred around a water cypress planted in the year of Bécquer's death, the monument is not just a glorification of the poet but also a meditation on love. Its most memorable image is a huddled group of three women in contemporary costume, their expressions of wistfulness, rapture and sadness being respectively indicative of Hopeful Love, Consummated Love and Lost Love. Despite the monument's fame and its reputation as one of the most outstanding of Spain's public memorials, the sculptor who created it – Lorenzo Coulaut Varela – is barely remembered, while the work itself receives scarcely more visitors than the Venta de los Gatos. It stands awaiting restoration in the middle of an anarchically luxuriant park where the threat of mugging has succeeded in deterring the solitary visitor from wandering off too far into its wilder areas. On one of the monument's marble surfaces someone has mysteriously scrawled, 'Here lies oblivion.'

The sweetly melancholic character of the monument and the added poignancy of its present state are richly suggestive of Bécquer's life, which in turn reflected the spirit of a city where so much talent has been squandered, devoted to the ephemeral, or gone unrecognized. Unhappy in love, disastrously married, often ill and impecunious, Bécquer published virtually nothing in his short life and might have been forgotten entirely had it not been for the attentions of a small, dedicated group of admirers who published a posthumous edition of his sole and slender collection of poems, *Las rimas*. Written with an emotional honesty and economy of expression recalling the Andalusian folk poems known as *coplas*, *Las rimas* became the most popular volume of Spanish verse until the publication in 1928 of García Lorca's *Romancero gitano*.

Love, in particular frustrated love, is the principal theme of Bécquer's work, but it is expressed in poems that are abstract and elusive, and that can be related to Seville only in the vague sense that they capture the ambivalent mood of the city, a mood in which an ineffable sweetness and sensuality belie a no less affecting and indefinable sadness. Throughout *Las rimas*, the reader is confronted by an image of a poet who is constantly struggling, not only to cope with the difficulties of his own life, but also to express the most intangible areas of human experience and feeling.

A GREAT MANY I got to know in Seville were said to be writing poetry. Some were even known as 'poets'; but few published anything, and many more were in fact writing nothing.

The most prolific were in many ways the least creative, those whose universe was centred on Seville, who pontificated on everything, incessantly told jokes, sold flowery articles on Seville to local newspapers, penned poems on every festive occasion, and were always winning poetry competitions adjudicated by friends with whom they were constantly to be seen eating, drinking, pontificating and sharing jokes.

Other 'poets' were no less prominent or modest than these 'parochials', but they did not have the same trappings of success, and tended to carry the same worn poem in their pockets from bar to bar, producing new works in the throes of alcoholic inspiration, improvising them out loud and forgetting them the next morning. Alcohol, exacerbated by eccentricity and latent madness, seems to have been an essential ingredient for most Sevillians with outstanding poetic potential, or at least for those who projected an aura of having it. The fact that their poetic output was minimal or even non-existent was in itself seen by admirers as a sign of greatness, and something that could be related to the same Sevillian tradition of genius that had produced the bullfighter Curro Romero and the Betis football team, which had not won a match for years, had sunk almost to the bottom of the third division, and yet still had a fervent crowd of supporters. The handful of 'true poets' I made friends with were, it must be said, a dying and a doomed breed, and could scarcely be called 'typical Sevillians', even though they could hardly be imagined anywhere else but Seville.

One was Antonio Luque, who once wrote a love poem punningly dedicated to Esperanza Flores:

> Cook by day
> Flower by night
> And Hope always.

These were the only words by which I could judge Antonio's supposed greatness, but, over the years, I had had plenty of opportunities to study his verbal skills in action.

A tall, pale man with taut skin and a mop of grey hair, he claimed to have aristocratic blood and to have been one of the most brilliant students in the recorded history of Seville's conservatory of music. His dubious pretensions to nobility, his reputed talents as a poet and musician and the unquestionable breadth of his learning had earned him, in his early fifties, only a humble job in charge of a students' bar and canteen. Few of his friends and acquaintances, however, had any idea of what he did for a living, or cared, for that matter, Seville being still a city where the façade one presents to the world is far more important than the reality.

Antonio's façade was wholly whimsical and had won him both detractors and admirers, the latter including the high-flying flamenco singer, José de la Tomasa. His audience listened with either irritation or delight as Antonio delivered short, frenetic speeches accompanied by extravagant gestures of hand and body. These texts were interlarded with an amazing range of cultural cross-references, together with a more limited number of superlatives such as 'genius', 'magnificent', 'sublime' and 'cretin'.

Drink pushed this loquacious man's barrage of words beyond acceptable limits, resulting in noisy bars being sometimes reduced to an eerie silence after he had risen from his seat to insult or praise someone with repeated shouts of 'Cretin!' or 'Genius!' One such outburst had been directed against Curro Romero, and though intended as an expression of Antonio's undying admiration of the man, had led to the two of us being thrown out of one of the Feria's more snobbish *casetas*.

Antonio was unstoppably provocative and argumentative and, when drunk, would generally end up by mounting one of his many hobby-horses such as his hatred of the countryside and his absolute need to be surrounded by 'asphalt, dirt and pollution'. Inspired perhaps by the flow of his argument, I would often agree with him on this point, but our stated belief in the virtue of never leaving cities was once severely put to the test when we found ourselves face to face in the Rocío: both of us had to justify our presence by insisting that the Rocío pilgrimage was an occasion on which the countryside was dignified by having the city brought to it. Only once did I attempt to contradict Antonio, an action quite justified by the seriousness of the matter under discussion. At seven o'clock in the morning, after a night of drinking, Antonio was trying to convince me that the personality of Julien Sorel in Stendhal's *Scarlet and Black* was identical to that of the whale in *Moby Dick*.

In their extreme moments of drunkenness, Esperanza tried to help alcoholic friends of hers, such as Antonio, by spoonfeeding them *tapas*. Absolutely nothing could be done, however, about the drunken fits of Fernando Ortiz, a swarthy and bespectacled man whom I first set eyes on in the ramshackle bar known as the Carbonería.

Before it was taken over by young Americans searching for 'real flamenco' and its socialist customers became prominent figures in Andalusia's corrupt regional government, the Carbonería had been Seville's principal Bohemian and intellectual haunt. It had attracted a most impressive clientèle, ranging from most of Spain's leading flamenco performers to such distinguished visitors as the poet Rafael Alberti and the Catalan novelist Vázquez Montalbán. Even in such celebrated company, Fernando Ortiz had apparently shone as a writer, and was talked about as one of the most interesting Andalusian poets to have emerged in recent years. But on the night I first saw him, I was aware only of a diminutive, Bruegel-like grotesque bawling his lungs out while walking up and down the bar with wine pouring down his open shirt.

Esperanza explained that Fernando's alcoholic problems had reached such a point that every so often a capsule had to be implanted in his stomach making him vomit every time he drank alcohol. The drunken fit I witnessed took place on the day between the expiry of the old capsule and the insertion of the new one. Before this regime, he was inebriated nearly all the time, and was one of those drinkers who manage to embroil many other people in their binges. Fernando was renowned for ringing on friends' doors in the early hours of the morning and insisting that they get up and join him in the bars.

Fernando's attempts to curtail his alcoholic intake was not helped by his belief, shared by his friends, that he was a far more interesting and inspired person when drunk than when sober. During periods of abstinence, he was reputed to be quiet and dull, and his productivity as a writer, slim at the best of times, dwindled almost to nothing. He was not short of commissions, but few were fulfilled, and deadlines were never respected. His day-to-day miseries included a dreary job in Seville's town hall and a disintegrating marriage.

Several years after encountering the drunken Fernando in the Carbonería, I finally met, in Esperanza's flat, the sober Fernando. I found a man who was gentle, sensitive and obliging. He rushed off back to his home to fetch a book of his poems called *Message of Writing*, and a selection of his beautifully written works of literary criticism. One was a prize-winning essay on Gerald Brenan, whose perceptiveness as a writer on Spain was interpreted by Fernando as the result of his having distanced himself from Spanish society. I read the Brenan essay immediately, but consigned the poetry book to a rapidly growing and chaotic pile of verse collections written by the likes of Paco's son, and printed either privately or under the auspices of obscure Andalusian town halls, local poetry societies, or village-festival magazines.

I forgot about the book until some two years later, when I was clearing out some rubbish from my room in Esperanza's flat and suffering once again from that sense of dislocation induced by a mid-morning awakening. The poems had a striking immediacy and special relevance to my particular mood at that time. Drily humorous and mordant, but reminiscent of Bécquer in both their simplicity of form and intimate, confessional tone, they dealt above all with wasted, solitary lives. One poem referred to the great literary alcoholic Malcolm Lowry and to his idea of paradise as a bar with unlimited credit. 'How close is hell to paradise,' Fernando concludes. Elsewhere, waking up with a hangover to see the 'ashes of dawn', he misquotes a famous line from Eliot's *The Waste Land*. The line, recalled as he lies in bed smoking, shaking off nightmarish visions of death and destruction, is one that sums up the lives of many of the more talented personalities to be found in Sevillian bars: 'Upon a pile of ashes I have built my ruins'.

The very fact that Fernando had managed, in between bouts of drinking and depression, to write and publish his poetry of course disqualified him from achieving true poetic greatness, as defined by Lamartine: that the best poetry is that which remains unwritten. José Luis Ortiz Nuevo, on the other hand, had perfect credentials, and indeed enjoyed a reputation as the uncrowned poet laureate of Seville. Born in the town of Archidona, he began his life inauspiciously having downed a bottle of methylated spirits at the age of two: in thanksgiving for his survival his mother fulfilled her promise to bear the child on her shoulders while climbing on her knees all the way up the steep path to the Archidonan Sanctuary of Our Lady of the Virgin of Grace. Ortiz went on to become Seville's *concejal de cultura* (arts and leisure officer), a job for which he was ideally suited, and which had as its principal duty the organization of the Feria: his popularity in the city reached new heights after he extended the Feria by instituting the *lunes de la resaca*, or 'hangover Monday'.

As he approached his late forties, Ortiz Nuevo gradually assumed the obscenely sensual look of a decadent Roman emperor, complete with beard, curly black hair, ample stomach, and – during his days at our house in the Rocío – a toga-like dressing-gown through which his large genitals could be seen swirling as he improvised an idiosyncratic *sevillana* outside the bathroom. On a different plane from ordinary mortals, incapable of normal conversation, and enigmatically silent for much of the time, he none the less had an extraordinary charisma, and held people under a strange spell as he suddenly launched into great streams of poetic prose.

His gifts were entirely verbal, for his written works – slight books on flamenco and the Feria – gave little hint of his way with the spoken word. He had, as far as I know, not produced a single poem. And yet everyone, without exception, referred to him as *el poeta*, and there were even those who greeted him as such as he walked through the streets of Seville. '¡Poeta!' they would shout, to which he would respond with a regal smile and wave, before continuing his slow and stately walk, oblivious of the real world.

A holder of high public office, and a man of great popularity, Ortiz Nuevo could enjoy the status of a star while maintaining a life-style that entirely contradicted the anodine and shallow values of the 'new Spain'. In a country that admitted less and less criticism and unorthodoxy, and placed growing emphasis on conventional notions of success and achievement, Ortiz Nuevo was refreshingly different. However, there was another Sevillian of this generation who took idiosyncrasy one stage further. He was a man who made failure seem more noble than success, and gave dignity to the idea of thwarted achievement. The ideal antidote to the Spain of '92 was Ángel Díaz.

Ángel Díaz was not a poet, but an architect, and it was architects rather than poets who were the protagonists of the 'new Seville'. But a catalogue of all the wonderful new architecture of 1992 Seville would be unlikely to feature the name of Ángel Díaz, who was potentially the most remarkable Sevillian architect of them all.

His career began with spectacular promise, and could easily have turned into a story of rapid, spiralling success. While still an architectural student he sketched out plans for a contemporary art museum in Madrid that were enthusiastically adopted by his teacher, Jaime López de Asiain. The building went on to win the National Prize for Architecture in 1969, and was a key work in the architectural history of the Francoist period, being one of the first of the many uncompromisingly modernist high-rise buildings that would become such a feature of the Madrid skyline.

By the early 1980s, architectural tastes had changed and critics were likening Madrid's Museum of Contemporary Art to a multi-storey car park; after 1989, the museum's future became exceedingly insecure when its collections were transferred to the newly completed Centro de Arte Reina Sofía. None of Ángel's commissions had the same prestige as his first, and, in the meantime, sadness entered his personal life. He soon succumbed to the 'Sevillian vice' of drinking, and was regularly to be seen in Sevillian bars with a glass of neat whisky in his hand, muttering constantly the lyrics of a once famous *sevillana*, which had personal relevance to his own feelings towards a woman he had wanted to marry.

Shortly before being introduced to Ángel for the first time, I had heard several of his drinking companions refer to him as a 'genius', praise that was not based on any knowledge of Ángel's work as an architect. The word 'genius' is so bandied about in Seville that it has become virtually meaningless, but my misgivings about its use in Ángel's case were partially dispelled after a night spent in his company.

His manner was unusually reserved for a Sevillian, and he seemed almost to squirm at the effusive and very physical way in which Sevillians tend to greet each other. To anyone approaching him, he directed a severe and penetrating glance, as if looking through people, assessing, in an instant, their mannerisms, faults and imbecilities. Clearly Ángel was not someone one wished to antagonize, for then he would mock unremittingly, brilliantly mimicking weaknesses, and haranguing with a stream of cruel wit. The more he drank, the crueller and wittier he became, but he also acted as a stage drunk, slurring his words, mumbling and repeating his speech, and staggering so much that finding a taxi could be an interminably protracted undertaking. Remarkably, even in such a state, his observations about other people remained as sharp as ever.

Ángel had the moustached, Brylcreamed appearance of an American gangster of the 1950s, and often highlighted this image by speaking English with a Chicago drawl. He had never been to Britain or to America, but had acquired both perfect English and an ability to imitate every type of British and American accent simply through his obsession with old films.

Such was Ángel's command of English that it almost led to what could have been one of the more bizarre encounters in recent Sevillian history when he was asked to act as an interpreter for Queen Elizabeth II on her visit to Seville in the autumn of 1988. Ángel's reputation as a drinker was unfortunately no less great than his fame as a speaker of English, and his services were not, in the end, called upon, thus saving potential embarrassment to Her Majesty. His drinking habits were by then getting rapidly out of hand, and, by 1990, were beginning seriously to affect his work prospects. At an international conference organized that year with the cheerful theme of 'The Architecture of Death', Ángel turned up inebriated and nearly collapsed at the podium.

In the summer of 1991 I was relieved to discover that Ángel was beginning again to receive important commissions after a long fallow period. One was to remodel the Sevillian home of the man who owned the Bar Giralda, the city's most successful bar and a place where Ángel had spent a considerable part of his life and income. Ángel's work on the house, though still incomplete, was already receiving considerable praise from architectural critics. Ángel invited me to come and see what he had done.

I knocked at the old door of a modest nineteenth-century mansion, the façade of which turned out to be all that was left of the original structure. The brilliant white interior Ángel had devised was centred around a patio, but he had resisted the temptation to create an arcaded pastiche of the sort of patio one would normally expect in an Andalusian mansion. Ángel's patio was unusually high, and had details inspired by the architecture of an ocean liner, such as port-holes and chrome railings. The sheer scale and ambition of the work were as riveting as the design itself, and certainly revealed the vast amount of money that could be made from owning a bar in Seville.

The bar owner's wife and mother-in-law hovered in the background as Ángel guided me around the house and explained the philosophy behind the architecture. The two women had little interest in the conceptual aspects of their future home, and were naturally more concerned about how they would decorate it and where they would place favourite items of furniture. From the catalogues and photographs they had brought to show Ángel, it was evident that the clarity and lightness of Ángel's vision would eventually be obscured by elaborate door handles and light switches, hideous ceramic and mosaic fittings, and a nineteenth-century clutter of heavy armchairs and furnishings.

Afterwards, when I was having a drink with Ángel in a nearby bar, I asked him if he minded about his magnificent building being tarnished by such questionable taste.

'No,' he replied. 'If my patrons decide that they want to ruin what I've done, it's up to them. I make suggestions, of course, but, after all, it's their house, and they're the ones who are going to live there. In any case,' he added, ordering another whisky, 'none of my works has ever remained as I intended. Some have been destroyed completely.'

He spoke about a beautiful riverside park of his that had recently been dug up to make way for a bridge jokingly known as the 'Puente del Lepero' (a reference to the Spanish Neasden). I mentioned instead the Museum of Contemporary Art in Madrid, which had now stood half abandoned for over two years. He showed only the mildest interest when I had to explain to him that of the original museum only the cafeteria and bookshop remained, and that the ground floor had temporarily and inappropriately been taken over by a collection of plaster casts after the antique.

'I always believe,' he responded, 'that a building reflects the character of the architect. You have only to look at my museum building in Madrid. It's sober, elegant and utterly useless.'

By now the effects of the whisky were becoming apparent, and what had begun as a short late-afternoon drink was threatening to turn into nocturnal alcoholic oblivion. He started talking about failure and frustration, and, after a couple more whiskies, kept on repeating his rightful conviction that he had 'a touch of genius'. He denigrated the successful but – in his view – talentless architects who had been taken up by the Junta de Andalucía. None of the many government-sponsored projects for the new Seville had come his way, and, only a year or so back, he had resigned himself to spending the rest of his life devising projects that would never be executed.

'That's not such a bad fate,' he said unconvincingly. 'I almost prefer to plan a building than to build one. The excitement's in the mind, not in the execution.'

Ángel had been saved from this fate not only by his friend the bar owner but also by the mayor of the nearby coastal town of Puerto Real. This mayor, Juan Barroso, had entrusted Ángel with both the construction of a huge new cemetery for Puerto Real and the remodelling of the town's splendid eighteenth-century theatre.

Barroso's choice of such a wayward figure as Ángel as one of his principal architects was typical of this unorthodox and enlightened man, who was also one of the main Spanish spokesmen against the 1992 celebrations. The President of the 'Anti-1992 Committee', Barroso had planned for the town centre a massive commemorative monument recording the terrible consequences of the so-called 'Discovery of America'. A leading Mexican artist had volunteered his services free, and a number of major writers, such as Carlos Fuentes and Anthony Burgess, had said that they would be present at the inauguration of the monument planned for autumn 1992. I wondered what Ángel thought of all this, especially in view of the enormous respect Barroso held for him, a respect that had survived Ángel's reported attempt to seduce the Mexican artist's wife in the course of an official lunch given at Puerto Real.

Ángel looked at me wearily and made it clear that he thought that the anti-1992 activities were no less absurd than the EXPO itself. Barroso's proposed monument was just another hollow gesture, and one that was unlikely to produce any major work of art.

'No great artist', he explained, 'was ever political.'

We moved away from art and politics, and I became merely a listener as an ever drunker Ángel returned to his more habitual themes, such as the films of Michael Powell, whose *A Matter of Life and Death* was a familiar element in Ángel's more rambling monologues. In earlier days he would probably have begun reciting the lyrics of his favourite *sevillana*, but a more recently acquired habit was to show his listeners a handwritten poem he always carried with him. A rumour was spreading that Ángel had suddenly emerged as a magnificent poet, but in fact the poem of which he was so proud was a Shakespeare sonnet in translation. It could almost have been his testament – the testament of a cynic tired of a world where 'needy nothing' is 'trimmed with jollity' . . .

> And gilded honour shamefully misplaced
> And maiden virtue rudely strumpeted
> And right perfection wrongfully disgraced
> And art made tongue-tied by authority . . .

I I

The Second Invasion

SEVILLE does more than intoxicate. It can have the effect of the most powerful of drugs, diminishing one's rational capacities and sense of perspective, and eventually revealing why so many of its inhabitants feel no need for that world beyond. I had been there only three weeks, but July was approaching, and with it the fear that I would end up like an ancient American woman called Lucy, who had come to Seville in the 1930s with the vague intention of writing about flamenco, and was now firmly ensconced in a Santa Cruz bar whiling away her remaining days like a junkie in the terminal stages of drug addiction. I thought of Lucy and then tore myself away from what now seemed like an eternity of low life and high living. I caught the bus for Río Tinto.

The bus sped through a short final stretch of dusty, cultivated plain before climbing into the hills of Huelva province. Within little more than an hour of my leaving Seville, the landscape had turned into a billowing dark green mantle of pines, cork trees, orchards and oaks. Andalusia is a land so thick with clichés that it merits the greatest of them all: 'land of contrasts'.

The changes in the landscape and architecture of the different parts of Andalusia complement changes in the people, changes that might sometimes seem to exist less in reality than in the minds of Andalusians. In travelling from the province of Seville to Huelva province, I had crossed a mysterious frontier separating a people who are proverbially witty and stylish from a people whose wit is supposedly infantile and whose style reportedly slovenly. On the way I had almost certainly missed out on numerous local variations of these two types, and unknowingly had gone through villages whose inhabitants were defined as 'fair-haired', 'homosexual', 'exceptionally intelligent', 'cretinous', and 'slurred in speech'.

The specific reputation attached to each Andalusian town and village is generally ridiculous, but the racial diversity of Andalusia is none the less undeniable, and stems from a particularly complex history involving the influx of Phoenicians, Romans, Greeks, Celts, Arabs, gypsies, Jews, Valencians, Galicians, the Irish, Asturians, Castilians, Germans, the British and others. While it might be far-fetched to think that the Almonteños – with their predominance of northern features and boorish behaviour – are the offshoot of a band of Vikings who got lost in the Guadalquivir swamps, one would not be too wrong in identifying the many blond-haired and blue-eyed inhabitants of Córdoba province as being descended from the German settlers of the Sierra Morena. Nor would it be fanciful to find wholly Moorish types in once isolated places such as Ronda and the Alpujarra, where many Moors lived for centuries undisturbed.

But I was heading now towards a former enclave of Britain, and thinking above all about the British impact on Andalusia. British merchants settled in Andalusia from at least the sixteenth century, and provided models of social behaviour for the Spanish aristocracy, who responded by making many of these merchants aristocrats themselves. Some of the more élitist aspects of Andalusian life have a residual British influence, such as the Ferias of Seville and Jerez de la Frontera, which take place within marquees that could have been spirited away from some English garden party, and are essentially closed, exclusive occasions at which the true *señorito* traditionally arrived on horseback. But the British impact on Andalusia was particularly strong in Huelva province, where British mining engineers appear fundamentally to have changed local life – and not simply through the introduction of football.

The emotions of an Englishman travelling to Río Tinto in the early years of the century would not have been dissimilar to those of one making his way to a remote station in colonial India. The British involvement in the copper and sulphur mines of Río Tinto dated back only to 1873, but within a period of thirty years the British had made their presence felt in a spectacular way. The mines – sometimes identified with those of King Solomon – are the oldest in the world, but their vast, hidden wealth had been virtually undisturbed since ancient times, and was successfully exploited again only with the arrival of the British. The British, though employing an entirely Spanish mining force, had an engineering and managerial staff that by 1901 had a British to Spanish ratio of sixty-four to five. By this date the British had started calling the locals 'natives' and were living in an enclosed and guarded colony where Spaniards were not allowed, the penalty for marrying one being ostracism from the community.

The story of Río Tinto under the British, like that of India under the Raj, carries nostalgia for some but shame for others. Such amusing antics of the British colony as the annual egg-and-spoon race have to be set against the dangerous and poorly rewarded conditions of the Spanish miners, whose frequent strikes were repressed with considerable cruelty, and who voiced opinions about the British that would certainly not have been held by the Andalusian aristocracy: 'Death to the British! Death to the British!' was a chant that went round the village following one of the worst accidents in the mines' history.

Henry Clay, an English globetrotter, found himself by chance in 1953 in a printer's shop in Mexico City, and was struck by an illustration showing a monocled Englishman disdainfully supervising a struggling miner pushing a coal trolley. The illustration turned out to be for the jacket of a Spanish book entitled *Under the Open Sky: From Río Tinto to North America*. Clay became absorbed in the proof copies of this book, which was an autobiographical novel by one Félix Lunar, a former miner and union leader whose strike activities had forced him to abandon his family in Río Tinto in the 1920s and to spend the rest of his life in Ohio. After reading this book Clay felt a revulsion for his English compatriots, and in particular for one 'Mr Borrow', an especially unpleasant mining director whom Lunar described as having probably been brought to Río Tinto 'from some colony in Africa'. Clay, trying to recover some of his hurt English pride, attempted to excuse the behaviour of the British on the grounds of the 'biological laws of humanity', whereby 'the Borrows of this world' were merely doing to the Spanish miners what 'the ancestors of these miners had done to the Indians of Latin America'.

'The Borrows', under the aegis of the Río Tinto Zinc

Company, would later perpetuate this 'biological cycle' by acquiring tin mines in Bolivia, where they continue to this day to impose on the impoverished and short-lived Bolivian miners conditions of near slavery. The mines at Río Tinto itself have recently reverted to Spanish ownership, but are almost certain to close down within a few years. The seams will finally have been exhausted, and the mines will be left as an infernal cavity slashed in two by the blood-coloured stream that gives the area its name.

THE VILLAGE of Río Tinto lies out of sight of the mines, in a forest clearing heavily scented with aromatics. Built at the turn of the century to replace a nearby village which was pulled down to make way for the expanding mines, it is an undistinguished place, with parallel rows of simple white houses ascending a steep hill. At the bottom of the hill stands a reminder of greater days in the form of a grand town hall, while looming in the far distance, against a background of Mediterranean pines, are the enormous modern blocks of a general hospital, the largest in Huelva province outside the capital.

The octagenarian John Hill, Río Tinto's last remaining Englishman, had gone away on holiday. He had gone, so I was told, to the coastal resort at Punta Umbría, where his British predecessors always stayed, in half-timbered Edwardian bungalows built especially by the Río Tinto Company. The present whereabouts of Mr Hunt was all the information I was able to glean in over an hour of walking through the streets of a half-empty village where everyone I hoped to see had disappeared, and where everyone else seemed – for an Andalusian community – unusually suspicious, unfriendly and unhelpful. The unwelcoming mood, and the presence in the village square of a monument commemorating the oppressed miners, made me think that the long years of British rule at Río Tinto might have created here a lasting legacy of Anglophobia. The conclusion was confirmed later in the day, after I had begun to make headway in the village, and located and made friends with the director of the newly founded Río Tinto Foundation.

Ricardo, as this man was called, was the very opposite of an

Anglophobe, and proudly showed me a British passport within minutes of our meeting. He was Spanish by blood but had acquired dual nationality, through having been born in Oxford, where his parents lived after the Civil War. The family came back to Río Tinto in the early 1960s. A baby-faced man with the look of a scruffy and intense student, Ricardo was very enthusiastic about his new job, and spoke about his future plans for the Foundation with the same earnest idealism with which a student might once have spoken about the forthcoming social revolution.

I had tracked him down to a group of isolated and semi-abandoned industrial warehouses that contained the Foundation's library and archives and would one day form part of a museum devoted to the history of Río Tinto. The very existence of the Foundation suggested the ending of an era and reflected the village's fears for the future, now that its mining industry was coming to a halt. Apart from its academic responsibility to record the past, the Foundation was contemplating turning the whole area into a mining theme park, a tourist attraction to rival any in Seville, Córdoba or Granada.

The Foundation's funds, Ricardo admitted, were at present wholly inadequate for its aims. A short tour of some of the properties belonging to the Foundation provided sorry evidence of how much needed to be done, and how much capital would be required. Ricardo led me first of all to the former headquarters of the mining company, a large and elegant Edwardian building which looked as if a bomb had dropped on it. The future tourist potential of the building lay principally in its back façade, where the historically minded visitor would be doubtless delighted by the row of ticket windows at which the miners' wages had once been handed out. There was the added appeal of a picturesque anecdote: thanks to a regulation imposed by the more temperate of the British employers, the wages had always been collected by the wives, the idea being to prevent the husbands from taking their wages direct to the bar.

Another telling but more endearing relic of Río Tinto was the British-style railway station, which stood decayed and boarded up along an abandoned, weed-ridden track on the outskirts of the village. Ricardo had dreams of retaining not only this but also a section of the British-built railway line that had led all the way to Huelva, and had bewildered past generations of Andalusian travellers by never being operational on Queen Victoria's birthday. A vision of Río Tinto's future was suddenly presented to me as Ricardo began describing visitors being huddled into Edwardian steam trains, then alighting at the mines, donning pit helmets and overalls, and being taken deep down into a reconstruction of a pit shaft.

Nothing that the Foundation was planning to create, however, promised to have the curiosity value of 'Bella Vista', the place that had drawn me in particular to this part of Andalusia. 'Bella Vista', an outlying residential community, had been the home of the former British colony, and was described to me by Ricardo as 'a living testimony to the old days of Río Tinto'. Ricardo decided to take me there himself, which gave him further opportunity to talk about Anglo-Spanish relations in Río Tinto, a subject of special interest to someone whose parents were brought up at a time when the ban on Spaniards entering the colony was still in force. I found out that the ban was officially lifted in the 1920s, but that colonial attitudes had remained almost as strong as before. 'Spanish women could now marry into the community, but they had to adapt to British ways rather than vice versa. British connections increased one's social standing.'

I asked Ricardo about his own memories of Río Tinto in the 1960s and 1970s.

'As someone born in England,' he reminisced, 'I was expected to interpret British idiosyncrasies for my classmates. One thing I remember clearly was how everyone was always intrigued by Father Christmas, a figure who was completely unheard of at that time in rural Spain. British behaviour and traditions have always fascinated me,' he continued, 'but there were many in my class who had heard terrible stories about the British from their fathers and found it difficult to forgive them. I think there was a general sense of relief when the British eventually pulled out of Río Tinto.'

I told Ricardo about the lingering feelings of hostility towards the British that I had sensed on my arrival here.

'Let me tell you a story,' he said. 'Just a few months ago I moved to a small house on a nearby modern estate. I decided to throw a party, and invited a number of friends from Seville, several of whom were British. The numbering of the houses on the estate was complex, so I thought I'd help my friends by putting an English flag above the door as a joke. The flag was torn down almost immediately. The next day I went into a local bar, and a group of elderly men came up to me. "Never," they said, "never, never put up that flag again."'

A Union Jack would not have seemed too out of place above the entrance to 'Bella Vista'. The gates to the colony might not have been guarded as they had been in the past, but nothing else seemed to have changed since Edwardian days. The colony remained as incongruous a presence in the Andalusian countryside as a white Andalusian hill village would have been in the middle of Surrey. The homely scene immediately brought to mind one of Britain's early garden suburbs, where tidy gabled houses with hedged-in gardens surround a lush and shaded communal lawn. The excellently maintained architecture was wholly British, the one concession to local taste being the use of stone rather than brick.

'Who lives in these houses today?' I wondered, my curiosity aroused above all by the evident signs of great wealth.

'Well, there's the director of the company, and a few of his engineers,' Ricardo answered. 'But the residents are mainly doctors from the general hospital. Most of them are from Madrid and northern Spain, and I think there are even a few Catalans. But you won't find many from Río Tinto here.'

We stopped to look inside the colony's Scottish-style neo-Gothic chapel, which had an interior of presbyterian simplicity. Services were no longer held here, but the building reputedly served as a popular backcloth for wedding photographs. Ricardo had a theory that a British setting was thought to enhance the importance of the occasion, at least in the eyes of those who lived in the colony. This theory was part of a much more comprehensive one he was hoping to enlarge on once we had entered what had always been the colony's social and spiritual centre – the former British Club.

The clubhouse had not opened when we arrived, so we sat

outside on a sedan chair, watching a foursome of smart young men playing tennis on a lawn court. Ricardo handed me his visiting card, which described him, to my surprise, as an 'Anthropologist'. He went on to explain that he had studied anthropology in Seville, and had been attracted to his present job through a thesis he had begun on the influence of the British on Río Tinto. Naively, I had always assumed that anthropology was essentially a study of traditional rural communities, preferably in a jungle or desert setting. For a 'native' of Río Tinto to make a formal study of his former masters seemed less like anthropology than presumptuous sociology. But Ricardo showed no flippancy in his work.

'Of course, I'm only in an early stage of my research,' he said. 'But I'm slowly evolving this theory which I think might interest you. Putting it crudely, the departure of the British in the 1970s left a social vacuum in the village which I believe is now being filled by the doctors of the newly built general hospital. The doctors and their families, united by their professional status and the fact that they are nearly all from outside the province, have formed their own tightly knit social grouping. To most of the native inhabitants these doctors are no less foreign than the British were. But what is more curious – and I can see you're unconvinced – is that they have begun aping British traditions. I'm thinking of calling my thesis, "The Second Invasion".'

The doors of the clubhouse were open now. Ricardo led me inside a large panelled room where the walls were decorated with old topographical prints and the furniture covered with Laura Ashley fabrics. We were in the lounge, and Ricardo was telling me that the women residents of 'Bella Vista' had recently reinstated the British tradition of holding an 'afternoon tea' there every Wednesday. This 'Ladies Only' occasion appeared to be a retaliation for women not being allowed into the adjoining bar, a regulation pinned on to the bar's door. As we walked through the door into this exclusively male preserve, Ricardo informed me that the penalty for breaking the rule was for the woman to purchase a bottle of vintage whisky, a tradition that had of course been instituted by the British.

The bar had an appropriately more manly décor than the

lounge, and had heavily worn leather armchairs and sofas, and a profusion of hunting and sporting trophies. A white-haired barman eyed us severely as we came into the room, making us feel that our unexpected intrusion and rather untidy appearance had somehow disturbed an age-old harmony. This was the famous 'Mr Green', of whom I had already heard numerous stories from Ricardo. His real name was Pablo Verde, but it was as 'Mr Green' that he had always been known to the British, in whose club he had worked since the 1940s. There was no one else left in Río Tinto with such an intimate knowledge of the British community as his. Unfortunately, in Ricardo's opinion, he was also an unusual and temperamental person whose years in the service of the British had left in him an unquestioning respect for authority, together with a reticence that bordered at times on the aggressive.

'The bar's not yet open,' Mr Green snapped as we approached.

'We've not come for a drink but to see you,' Ricardo retorted.

'I'm busy.'

'The friend I've brought,' Ricardo persisted, 'is an Englishman who's very interested in the history of the British in Río Tinto.'

Mr Green was not impressed.

'You've come at a bad time.'

I suggested to Ricardo that we should leave, but he decided to change tack with Mr Green.

'My friend, Dr Jacobs, is a guest of the company.'

Now that my visit had taken on an official status, Mr Green became a different person. He offered us a drink, and then willingly took us on a tour of the rest of the building. He was smiling as he showed us a large storage room once used for concerts and amateur theatricals. The stage was still there and, amid all the debris and furniture that covered it, Mr Green found a top hat that had been used in a production of a Gilbert and Sullivan operetta. He laughed as he put it on his head, then took us into the billiard room, where a game was in progress. Mr Green was now in an expansive mood, and enlisted the young billiard-players in what was going to be a revealing demonstration of British social etiquette of old.

'Never in the past,' he said, 'would I have entered this room in the way that we've done now.' He went outside again, and waited there until he heard the click of one of the billiard cues hitting the ball. Pretending that he was carrying a tray of drinks, he re-entered the room, saying as he did so that he would have lost his job in the past had he not timed his entrances so as not to disturb the players' concentration.

We ended the tour in the toilets. Mr Green was displaying a puckish sense of humour as he opened one of the cubicles to reveal a toilet that might have inspired a poem from John Betjeman or, at the very least, a nostalgic tribute from Lucinda Lambton. The seat was of the finest mahogany, and had a ceramic basin emblazoned with a delicate design of an English cottage together with the words, 'J. F. Hutton & Co., Purveyors of Luxury Sanitary Furnishings to the Late Queen Victoria'.

'The British think of everything,' said Mr Green as we found ourselves contemplating the urinal. Mr Green was pointing to a silver disk above the splash pan, and shaking with laughter so much that he could hardly explain himself. The disk, I gathered, was a directional aid for the blind drunk.

A FRIDAY NIGHT in Río Tinto was not an exciting prospect, despite the japes and jollity evinced by Mr Green. Ricardo described his home village as the dullest in the whole of Huelva, and told me how at weekends everyone went elsewhere in search of night-time fun. Once again he blamed the British, whose obsession with night-time levels of noise had apparently been inherited by their successors at Río Tinto. It was an obsession that generally had a deadening effect on villages.

Everyone that night was going to Zalamea, where the annual village festival was nearing its climax. I arrived early, at an hour when the revellers were recovering from the drawn-out festivities of the afternoon and taking stock before the night to come. It was a quiet hour in one of the quieter areas of Andalusia; but the *casetas* in the tiny hilltop square below the ruined castle, the shouts of old women gossiping across narrow streets, and the smells of a multitude of *tapas* being prepared in a correspondingly wide range of bars, were all in welcome contrast to the suburban morgue of 'Bella Vista', and signalled my return to a more familiar Andalusia.

Zalamea is not the most beautiful village in the Sierra de Huelva, and is famed less for its monuments than for being often wrongly identified as the setting of Calderón's play, *The Mayor of Zalamea*. But, from its upper square, there is an attractive view looking down over russet-coloured tiles, wooden balconies, and the receding silhouettes of row on row of forested hills. I sat on a bench to enjoy the view in the clarity of the evening light. Then I walked down to the lower and emptier part of the village, where a decayed bullring stood in an abandoned square, surrounded by dusty lanes used by donkeys. The severely pockmarked walls of the building were plastered with posters announcing the coming night's main attraction: a concert given by the Sevillian rock band, Dulce Venganza ('Sweet Vengeance').

I had given up my status as official guest of the Río Tinto mining company, and would shortly become a rock band groupie. Nicolás, a friend from Seville, was arriving by van and had arranged to meet me outside the bullring. I had been told to bring my luggage, but had little idea of what would be happening to me. All that I knew was that Nicolás was on a weekend tour with Dulce Venganza, and that he had come along with them because they were performing in his native village of Zalamea.

The large van arrived. Within minutes the square was brought to life by the witty banter and incessant pranks of Dulce Venganza. They wore dark glasses and inverted caps, and were six in number, ranging from a lithe, eighteen-year-old gypsy woman to a plump, middle-aged drummer. I was introduced to each of them in turn by their manager, Paco Carrión, a Jekyll-and-Hyde figure who spent half his life as a respectable, besuited employee in a bank, and the other half as a wild and irresponsible hedonist, given to drink, drugs, sex and every other cliché of the rock-music scene. Later that night Paco was sure to be in a dissipated state, but for the moment he had not wholly emerged from his banker persona, and began directing the laying out of the equipment and the setting up of the stage with exemplary efficiency. I lent a helping hand myself, and served cool cans of beer and Coca Cola to the sweating technicians. Dulce Venganza fooled around with their instruments and smoked dope.

By sunset preparations for the night's concert were nearing completion, and stray inhabitants of the village were wandering in to see what was happening. Nicolás found himself meeting up with friends whom he had not seen since childhood, one of whom was a tattooed old hippy who wore beads and bracelets, and took great pleasure in showing me the dark, dank cell where panic-stricken bulls were kept prior to a fight. Childhood memories were exchanged between Nicolás and his friends and, as the night set in, the bullring was crowned by a vivid dome of stars, giving it the look of some magical planetarium. A group of us walked around the very top of the ring, a by now nostalgic Nicolás pointing out to me the distant house where his first girlfriend had lived.

Paco Carrión, meanwhile, talked excitedly about the future of Dulce Venganza, who at last were beginning to be known outside Andalusia, and had even been asked to give a concert in Bordeaux in the autumn. The gypsy woman, he said, was bound to go down well in France, where an 'ethnic element' in music was always appreciated. The only problem, he continued, was her possessive, psychopathic, heroin-addicted boyfriend, whom they had shaken off only with difficulty in the course of their present tour.

The presence of the woman in the band intrigued me. I still had no idea of what sort of music I would be listening to. Paco put my mind at rest. 'It's a mixture, let's say, of acid house and flamenco.'

THE CORPULENT drummer, all fat and perspiration, was building up to a virtuoso solo climax, driven on by a swaying crowd larger than could ever have been anticipated. The guitars returned, and so did the band's charismatic singer and leader, the handsome Benito, who had now stripped down to a black string vest, and was gyrating energetically with an open can of beer in one hand

and the microphone in the other. The young and the not so young, from every nearby village, were shouting and dancing in the middle of the sand-filled arena, their movements co-ordinated by a band member tapping out an insistent reggae-style rhythm on a moving disc whose amplified sounds rose sharply above the mounting discord of the drums, the guitars, the keyboard, and the orgasmic wails of Benito.

The moment came for the gypsy woman's return. She re-entered to the accompaniment of strobe lights and dry ice, wearing a polka-dotted flamenco costume made up of a mini-skirt and a navel-hugging top. The electronic guitars changed to a flamenco rhythm, and the woman slowly raised her leg while drawing a hand up her naked thigh. The drums stood in for castanets; the band was shouting '¡Olé!', and the woman broke into an erotically charged display of footstamping that turned into a Madonna-style jive.

'This is the future of flamenco!' shouted a drunken Paco Carrión, whose family had been impresarios to flamenco's greatest and 'purest' performers. Flamenco, the guidebooks tell you, expresses the 'soul' of Andalusia. But if such a soul exists, and if music can be said to express it, it was surely present here, in this concert where the cultural barriers had broken down in the creation of a musical hotchpotch as absurd as it was powerful.

The euphoric crowds were trying to break into the improvised changing-room set up in the area reserved for the doctors and nurses attendant on a bullfight. A beaming Paco was making lines of coke with a razor, and the gypsy woman was sitting quietly polishing her nails. Benito, laughing hysterically, lay flat out on his back on a table, simulating masturbation with a beer bottle which he shook violently before opening, spraying everyone with an ejaculation of white froth. The technicians were packing up the van, and Nicolás was pushing me into it.

They were abducting me, and for a moment I thought that they were taking me back to Seville. I was past caring. It was six o'clock in the morning, and I was at the back of the van squeezed in between Paco and the gypsy woman, and waiting for her jealous boyfriend to make a Batman-like appearance and pull me outside. Only the driver was sober, but then sobriety had been a clause in his contract. We were driving on side roads illuminated by the light of the rising sun. Sweet Vengeance was on the loose and was heading towards Granada.

12

Boabdil's Return

I RECOGNIZED him by the bloated tips of his fingers, an abnormality that brought to mind the bulbous, diseased swellings of a tree. We were having our first conversation outside Granada's Casa de Vinos, but we both had the sensation of having seen each other before, perhaps in the basement of a London jazz club, in a seedy *trattoria* in Rome, or in a café in the Transylvanian town of Cluj.

The haunts we had in common multiplied as we sat talking for the first time, trying to establish where our paths might have crossed, and in the process building up a range of international coincidences as improbable-sounding as George Borrow's encounters with the Baron Taylor, a man whom he was continually running into in 'the street or the desert, the brilliant hall or amongst Bedouin haimas, at Novgorod or Stambul'. I had always assumed that this passage from Borrow's *The Bible in Spain* was a characteristically Borrovian flight of fantasy, but nothing seemed too far-fetched after I had met up in Granada with Pepe Weiss Chiozzo.

Pepe's very name confirmed the impression of confused roots given by his difficult-to-place accent and appearance. His broad, sarcastic smile, generous moustache and greased-back black hair reminded one of a Sicilian *mafioso*, but his accent was South American with a hint of German. He was in fact the son of European emigrants to Uruguay, and was born and brought up in Montevideo. His mother was Italian, and his father came from a part of Romania that until 1919 had formed the most eastern enclave of the Austro-Hungarian empire. The region was one of those forgotten lands that might have featured in a novel by Joseph Roth. It was called the Bukovina, and is memorably evoked in the opening section of Gregor van Rezzori's *Memoirs of an Anti-Semite*. Pepe's father was a Jew.

His father died in Montevideo in 1971, believing in his

confused state of mind that the shouts of the passers-by along the Avenida 18 de Julio had been those from a Balkan-looking area of old Bucharest later to be demolished by Ceauşescu. A year after his father's death, Pepe set off for Europe, where he searched to begin with for the scattered members of his family. Funding himself with a succession of short-term jobs, he spent ten years almost continually on the move, living for short periods in London, Paris, Rome, Budapest, Bucharest, Athens and Tel Aviv.

He had hoped eventually to find a place where he would have no hesitation in settling down on a more permanent basis. But the hope faded over the years, and he was on the point of returning to Uruguay when, as a final resort, he decided to give Spain a try. His only link with this country, as far as he knew at the time, was the language, but the moment he arrived he had a curious sense of homecoming. When, finally, he reached Granada, he lost all desire to travel further. He found a job there as a book representative, and was still working with this company eight years later. He lived alone on the hill of the Albaicín, in one of the beautiful, small villas with gardens that in Granada are known romantically as *carmens*.

His house was situated in what was first the commercial heart of Moorish Granada and then the main residential district for those Moors – known as Moriscos – who became token converts to Christianity so as to be able to stay on in the town after 1492. With its famously picturesque views towards the Alhambra, and its labyrinth of white alleys and cypress-shaded gardens, the Albaicín conveys more than any other surviving area of Granada the appearance of the town in its Moorish heyday.

Pepe's choice of home was not accidental, or at least not according to him. He had developed in recent years a conviction that his ancestors on his mother's side had come from Granada and had shared the fate of the Moors. His mother's family, though Catholic, had distant relatives with Jewish names such as Agar and Davide. Italian Jews were nearly all of Spanish origin, and were among the last Jews to have stayed on in Spain, where they had taken refuge in an increasingly isolated Granada. Then they too had been expelled from Paradise.

In modern times Granada has become a Mecca for romantics and dreamers. The English began the trend in the late eighteenth century, scrawling their names on the neglected walls of an Alhambra to which the traditionally philistine Granadines – the descendants, for the most part, of settlers from Castile and northern Spain – had been notoriously indifferent. For these early English travellers, with their strong anti-Catholic prejudices, the Alhambra became the supreme symbol of a civilization far superior to that which replaced it. Nostalgia for this golden age of Spanish history intensified in the following century and came to form part of a widespread 'neo-Moorish' movement promoted by the likes of Chateaubriand and Victor Hugo, both of whom were enthusiastic visitors to Granada. All lingering traces of a scholarly and archaeological approach to Spain's Moorish legacy evaporated under an overwhelmingly sensual vision of an oriental world where veiled, dark-skinned women with enticing bellies danced Salome-like in honeycombed halls. The publication in 1829 of Washington Irving's *Chronicle of the Conquest of Granada* consolidated the mythology of Granada and hastened the transition between romantic orientalism and a Cecil B. de Mille vulgarity that would result in music-halls throughout the world being given the name 'Alhambra'.

Mario Praz's *Unromantic Spain* attempted to put a stop to all the sentimental gush on this now over-restored plasterwork monument, but simultaneously García Lorca, Manuel de Falla, and other members of their Granadine intellectual circle found in the Alhambra the essence of Spanish genius and poetry, and saw in it the germ of a national renaissance. Moreover, in the absence of Moors to animate the halls of the Alhambra and the alleys of the Albaicín, they turned for cultural guidance to the gypsies, who, from the time of Gautier, had been regarded almost as successors to the Moors, thanks to their dark and sultry looks, their outcast status, their picturesque costumes and the fact that many of them had set up as blacksmiths in the very forges of the Albaicín that the Moors and then the Moriscos had had to abandon.

Romantic attitudes to Granada, the Albaicín and the Granadine gypsies are no less prevalent today, even if over-familiarity with the place has lessened potential intimations of the sublime. The desire of élitist travellers in the past to follow the example of Irving and Ford and stay within the hallowed walls of the Nasrid palaces has been succeeded by an insistence on booking a room months in advance at the Alhambra's Parador de San Francisco. A continuing fascination with gypsies, meanwhile, has led to coach outings to 'gypsy caves', where tourists watch a sorry display of flamenco and drink an insipid glass of *sangría*. To complete the whole 'romantic experience' of a visit to Granada, there is the obligatory evening trudge to the Albaicín church of San Nicolás, where row on row of video cameras wait poised to catch the setting sun as it suffuses the Alhambra's russet-red turrets with a golden glow, a performance that sometimes inspires a spontaneous round of applause.

There are few people today who would dare challenge the Alhambra's reputation as one of the great wonders of the world, least of all the Granadines, who sometimes affect an aesthetic and poetic superiority over others for the very fact of having been brought up in its shadow. Though their ancestors might well have let the whole complex fall to the ground had it not been for the attention paid to it by foreigners, they are often dismissive of the foreign hordes who descend on the place today: there are even those among them who will say that no one can truly appreciate the beauty of the Alhambra unless they happen to have visited it on one of the two or three days a decade when the Nasrid palaces are covered in snow. Yet for all their new show of sensibility, the Granadines have done little to shake off their image as philistines. The path of destruction initiated in the 1890s with the creation of the Gran Vía de Colón continues unchecked, with new outrages perpetrated every year. Beautiful old palaces and gardens are still being demolished, while around the periphery of Granada has grown up one of the ugliest ring roads in Europe. The enchanting orchard surrounding García Lorca's miraculously surviving family home is now being dug up to make way for a 'García Lorca Memorial Park'.

★

PEPE WEISS CHIOZZO had a healthy cynicism, and did not exaggerate the glamour of Granada. Nor did he endorse the customary mindless enthusiasm whenever the word 'Alhambra' is mentioned; he enjoyed shocking people by describing the Alhambra as a stranded aircraft carrier. But this cynicism had not diminished his persistent belief in the mysterious force that lured him to the town. For all his wit, sarcasm and dynamic, down-to-earth manner, he had much in common with the many young dreamers who have come to Granada with the illusion that their stay there is an integral stage in a journey towards some ultimate goal. Presentday Granada might have fallen victim to the worst extremes of tourism and commercial greed, but it has also become a refuge for the mystical and anti-materialistic ideals of the 1960s.

Granada, characterized by Lorca as having 'the worst bourgeoisie in the world' is also a close-knit university town animated not just by students but by hippies, drop-outs, and other non-conformists who go round in ponchos, long flowery dresses, and billowing white cotton robes. Granada's relatively low cost of living – much lower than that of western Andalusia – enables them to get by through busking, giving the odd class in yoga or English, and selling jewellery, leatherwork and ceramics. For many of them Granada is just a staging post *en route* for the adjoining Alpujarra, a district with its own tradition of exiles, dreamers and mystics.

The Moriscos, increasingly repressed in the early fifteenth century, gathered in growing numbers in what Gerald Brenan described as the 'broad, hollow and very broken' country which lies beyond the snowy peaks that are shown in endless postcards rising above the Alhambra and the Generalife. There, in the Alpujarra, the new settlers continued the work of their Moorish predecessors, and created orchards, lush fields and terraces of vines that survive today principally on the district's north-western slopes, clinging above an undulating and encroaching barrenness reminiscent of a papier-mâché relief map left to gather dust and cracks in some forgotten basement.

Within this isolated and mountain-enclosed land, the Moriscos organized two uprisings that spread throughout Andalusia and led to their expulsion from Spain at the beginning of the seventeenth century. Undoubtedly many of them stayed on in Spain, finding hiding-places in the Alpujarra, a land that would remain almost unvisited until over two centuries later. Pedro de Alarcón – the Guadix-born author of *The Three-Cornered Hat* – inspired interest in the area by publishing an account of a journey he had made there in 1873. He gave romantic emphasis to the wildness of the place, and also wrote about the strong Moorish presence he felt in 'every crag and crevice'.

But the writer who did most to promote the Alpujarra was Gerald Brenan. Like Pepe Weiss Chiozzo and other idealists, he found himself in this part of Spain in the course of a wildly ambitious journey of self-discovery. When he first came to Spain in 1919, this future Hispanist lacked any knowledge of the country and its culture, and intended the visit to be a continuation of a walk towards Jerusalem he had embarked on as a sixteen year old. In the end, Brenan's Spanish hiatus turned into an initial three-year stay at Yegen, a small, ugly village in the eastern half of the Alpujarra, within sight of the desert expanses of Almería.

Apart from a sexual relationship with a local woman, Brenan lived at Yegen in a self-contained world of his own, dominated by the reading of books and the writing of letters to his almost exclusively English friends. Within the confines of his wooden-beamed and white-walled Yegen home, he created a fantastical domain in which his passionate love affair with Dora Carrington could blossom, an affair which was largely platonic and epistolary. His later account of his Yegen experiences (the basis of *South from Granada*) not only encouraged the myth of the *pueblo* as the repository of 'true' Spanish values, but came also to be considered almost as an anthropological bible.

Recent research on Brenan has confirmed the suspicions of the more critical Hispanists that his travel-writings on Spain, just like the tales of his great sexual potency, have a strong element of make-believe, an example of this being his description of a visit to a ruined farm near Córdoba he claimed as having belonged to Góngora. His account of Yegen, though not at all sentimental, was perhaps as much of a distortion of the real place as was the vision of the Alpujarra embraced by the hippies who would be lured here in his wake from the late 1960s onwards.

Many of these hippies settled at first in Trevélez, a village of North African appearance renowned for its hams and for being one of the highest communities in Europe. They began taking over the local weaving industry, and also set up stalls selling exotic bracelets and ear-rings. Some made enough money from the Alpujarra's burgeoning tourism to open up their own shops, while others opted for lives of semi-self-sufficiency on the properties that could still be bought cheaply at the time.

Now, ageing hippies, ex-hippies, and new-generation hippies have encouraged the establishment in the Alpujarra of alternative religious communities, and have latterly competed in the property market with English couples who have eagerly read Brenan and despaired of finding holiday homes in Provence. Buddhism has found its way into the Alpujarra, where its largest Spanish community is to be found, housed in a domed, oriental-style building at the bottom of the steep, lush valley of the Poqueira. But the majority of today's Alpujarran inhabitants who espouse an alternative life-style and run the district's craft shops are not Buddhists but associates of the mystical Islamic sect of Sufism, a sect spreading rapidly throughout Spain, and gaining in Granada itself what some might consider an alarming stronghold.

STRANGE PHENOMENA have been observed in Granada in recent years. As I sat drinking with Pepe outside the student haunt of the Casa de Vinos, veiled women could be seen scurrying by, heading towards the Plaza Nueva, where the busy modern city of Granada comes to an abrupt end, at the entrance to the narrow verdant hollow in between the hills of the Alhambra and the Albaicín.

Pepe referred to these women as 'Sufis', though he admitted that the word is applied indiscriminately to all those of Islamic faith who now live in Granada. Often, he said, little distinction was made between Granada's recent Moroccan immigrants and the numerous European converts to Islam, who, from the early

1980s onwards, have been choosing to settle there. Many of these converts are people who flirted in the 1960s and 1970s with anarchism, Zen Buddhism, Hare Krisna, and various other hippy and alternative cults. Whatever their background, Muslims are once again gravitating towards Granada, and buying up houses and shops in what Moroccans and converts alike regard as their former home – the Albaicín.

It was Pepe who told me that Boabdil had returned – not the Moorish king himself, but a man who claimed him as a direct ancestor, and who thought the former kingdom of Granada rightfully his.

Boabdil made his return in the February of 1991, at the height of the Gulf War, when Granada's normally quiet and pacifist Islamic community joined forces with a number of university lecturers and other intellectuals to protest against the Spanish government's uncritical stance towards NATO. Some of the more extreme members of the community took to wearing armbands in the streets, waved fists in the air, and acted as if the Holy War for which they had all been prepared was finally on them. Others, more moderately, organized a day of lectures, recitals and dancing intended to draw attention to the Arab plight, to celebrate Arab genius, and to raise money for Arabs who had suffered under rampant Western imperialism.

The day, dominated by the spectre of Boabdil, culminated in unexpected fashion. The inhabitants of the Albaicín, though accustomed by then to the recorded sounds of a *muezzin* calling the faithful to prayer, were none the less surprised when, shortly after midnight, a turbaned *muezzin* was sighted profiled against the moonlight on top of the highest of the Alhambra's battlements. His wails were heard throughout the city and convinced many that the Islamic presence in the Albaicín was now more than just a passing, picturesque phenomenon. It was not only Boabdil who had come back, but the Moors themselves.

Their return to the city from which they had been expelled encouraged fears that they might soon be exacting a subtle vengeance. There were rumours that Spain's secret service and even the CIA had begun monitoring their activities in Granada.

Matters were clearly getting out of hand. Nostalgia for the lost world of Moorish Granada was taking a sinister turn.

Long before hearing about Boabdil's return I had been observing the way the Albaicín had changed over the years that I had known it. The once run-down district animated by pestering gypsy children had gradually been transformed into a Granadine Hampstead which was now being invaded, on its lower slopes, by Moroccan tea rooms, butchers selling *halal* meat, and small shops with frontages and merchandise marked with Arabic lettering.

The growth of Granada's Islamic community fascinated me, but Pepe warned me of the difficulties that I would certainly encounter in trying to find a way into this community without myself undergoing spiritual conversion. He confessed that his own status as a long-term resident in the Albaicín and someone with a great interest in the esoteric had not helped him to get any nearer to this community, which was notoriously closed to outsiders, particularly to journalists, who were thought to form part of a great American and Jewish world conspiracy.

I began to question my own motives for wanting to make contact with the 'Sufis', and wondered if my curiosity in them went deeper than a mere historical and anthropological one. Had I been infected by some modern strain of that Moorish romanticism from which so many early travellers to Andalusia had suffered? Or had I begun to feel a genuine and growing spiritual need in a Spain that had become so blatantly materialistic? My possible motives, however, would soon become lost in the course of the actual search, a search in which I was joined by the one person who Pepe thought might be able to help me. Her name was Carmen, and she was a student of Arabic at the university.

Carmen was one of those Andalusians who provide living proof that either large numbers of Moors secretly stayed on in Andalusia, or else that Andalusia had originally been North African in its make-up, and that the idea of a 'Moorish conquest' was just a fiction put about by Christian historians.

Our first meeting took place in the Arabic faculty of the university, where she presented me to the librarian and one of her teachers, both of whom confirmed the great problems in investigating Granada's Islamic community.

On Sufism itself, a remarkably large number of books had recently begun to appear in Spanish, a testimony to the growing interest in the mystical essence of Islam. But as yet no one had produced a serious study on the so-called 'Sufis' of Granada, and most of what was written was widely dispersed throughout obscure periodicals.

One of the difficulties in studying the subject was that no one was exactly sure how many different groupings there were within the city's Islamic community, the complex make-up of which was comparable apparently to that of tenth-century Córdoba or present day Beirut. The principal division was between the converts and the Moroccan immigrants, the latter worshipping exclusively in the mosque of Al-Taqua, which lay at the foot of the Albaicín and was nominally under the jurisdiction of the United Arab Emirates. Among the converts, the most genuinely 'Sufi' appeared to be the bearded, turbaned followers of a certain Umar. They gathered every evening in one of the caves of the Albaicín, where they squatted in circles by candlelight to chant in unison the ninety-nine names of Allah, so experiencing the Sufi mystical ritual of communicating with God through hypnotic trances.

Then there were the Shiites, who found inspiration in the Islamic revolution of Iran, and hung pictures in their houses of the Ayatollah Khomeini; they probably received funding from Iran too, just as other of the more politically minded Muslims of Granada were reputedly financed by Saddam Hussein and Colonel Quadaffi.

More specifically Andalusian was the convert group headed by a professor of Semitic languages known as Jaber; apart from campaigning for the legislation of polygamy in Spain and practising martial arts in order to extend his spiritual capacities, Jaber envisaged an Andalusia of the future based on the Caliphate of Córdoba, with the difference that its emir would be someone freely elected by the people.

A rival group with similar aims was Al-Andalus, which had six centres throughout Andalusia, brought out journals dealing with the region's Moorish past, and hoped that Andalusia would break away from Spain and become an independent Islamic state;

its leader, Abderraman Medina, was based in Córdoba, and had been a mentor to Jaber before the latter distanced himself from him.

Granada's numerous female converts to Islam had formed two Islamic women's organizations, a leading member of which was Sakina, who ran a women's ceramic co-operative, and was very active on behalf of the Moroccan freedom-fighters of the Polisario. But repressive Islamic attitudes towards women had led several of the converts to forsake their chosen religion. They lived now in fear of reprisals, for the convert groups to which they belonged were said to be more fanatical than most Muslim sects, and did not take kindly to those who had severed their links with the 'family'.

Of the spiritual leaders of Granada's Islamic community, the most feared, important and dictatorial appeared to be the emir of the group known as the Murabitun. The Murabitun, who accounted for by far the greatest number of Granada's converts, was a worldwide movement founded in Norwich, England, with the aim 'to confront the many and urgent economic, ecological and social problems facing the world today and to find solutions for them'.

I was assured by the Islamic experts at Granada's university that the Murabitun would welcome me with open arms should I show any interest in becoming a convert. Otherwise, it discouraged idle observers more forcefully than any of the other Islamic groups in Granada. As for the emir, he was a secretive man who was now rarely to be seen in public, and never spoke to anyone outside the community.

Carmen herself had not had any personal dealings with the Sufi community, as Pepe led me to believe, but her interest was roused by the information that we gleaned from the faculty library, and she insisted on acting as my guide through the labyrinth of Islamic Granada. Over the days following our first meeting, I would find out little about the Sufis, but much about Carmen, who could easily have been described as 'a child of the 1960s' – and not simply because of her taste in beads, bracelets, and elaborate silver jewellery of oriental inspiration. She disliked formality of any kind, was happy squatting on the ground, and was gently critical of those who showed inhibitions or who were troubled by complexes of any sort.

The friendship I developed with her had a strange element of mutual teasing and self-parody. This happened the moment she realized that I was not the totally dedicated Sufi scholar she had imagined before meeting me. The quest for the Sufis acquired the quality of a game, with both of us pretending that we were the main players in some elaborate detective story, involving the CIA, arms dealers and turbaned spies, the whole being played out under the shadow of an imminent *jihad*.

This drama of suspense and intrigue took us to every corner of the Albaicín, where Carmen revived my interest in Granada by showing me an Islamic world of hidden surprises, a world of Alhambras in miniature that lay behind plain wooden doors and simple white façades, inspiring a sense of wonder I could no longer feel in the Alhambra itself. One day, as we were standing alone in the dark, enclosed ruins of the Albaicín's Moorish baths, our game took on another dimension: Carmen became a genie employed by mysterious higher forces to lure me I knew not where.

A more practical direction to our wanderings was provided by Carmen's father, who suggested we contact a local journalist called Fefe, with whom he had collaborated on a book of words and pictures about the Polisario. Fefe, he warned us, was something of a fantasist whose state of mind had not been helped by a recent and serious blow to the head in a motor-cycle accident; none the less he was a reliable journalist, open with his information, and obsessed by Islam.

The search for Fefe began unpromisingly, as Fefe had changed his Albaicín address repeatedly in recent years, and there were rumours that he had left Granada for good and had settled in Paris. Through the newspaper to which he submitted freelance articles, we were given what we were assured was his present address. We went there and found what looked like an abandoned house, directly in front of the first mosque in Granada to have been turned into a church after 1492. We knocked, but got no answer. The neighbours did not know if anyone was living in the house at the moment, though a young Moroccan raised our hopes by remembering that he had seen there a day or so earlier a bearded man who drove around the Albaicín on a motor-bike. We decided to leave a note on the door: if this was Fefe's house, and if he happened to be in Granada at the time, could he contact us immediately at the home of Carmen's parents? Two hours later the note had gone.

As soon as he had seen the note, Fefe had rushed to Carmen's family home on the upper slopes of the Alhambra hill. When we walked in he was sitting on the sofa waiting for us impatiently and refusing offers of a glass of beer from Carmen's father. His inability to drink alcohol, he claimed, stemmed from physical complications resulting from his accident. We interpreted it as a sign of his rumoured conversion to Islam.

Fefe talked as if he had not spoken to anyone for many months. He had a smiling, giggly manner, and interweaved boyish jokes into his ceaseless, rambling narrative. He spoke about his delight in receiving a note from Carmen's family, and about how glad he was to be sharing his interest in Islam with us. This interest had grown while travelling through the Sahara desert, a landscape he had found the most beautiful in the world, but where he had also experienced the greatest solitude he had ever known. A year or so earlier in Granada he had befriended a Moroccan petrol-station attendant who had taught him Arabic. The language had come in useful a bit later when he was researching an article he had hoped to write on Granada's Sufi community. It seemed to lend credence to his professed desire to become a Muslim. He proposed that I should adopt a similar journalistic ruse if I wished to make any headway with the Murabitun and the Shiites, who had recently developed a paranoia about being spied on, and now had time only for converts. In the end, he confessed, he had decided to abandon his article. He hinted that a feigned desire to convert to Islam had turned into a genuine one. Furthermore, he had established trust and friend-ships that he did not wish to betray.

'The Muslims I've known,' he said, 'are the kindest people imaginable. They will do anything for you, and are as pleased as children if you show any interest in their culture or faith. But you don't play around with them. Two years ago,' he continued, 'the Muslims planned to put up another monument in Granada, and were sold a central site by a local property speculator. The man had sold it to them in the knowledge that planning permission would never be granted. They had effectively bought a useless site. Later, when I spoke to them about it, they showed no resentment towards this man. "He got his just deserts," they said. "He died of cancer one year later."'

Fefe, clearly not used to addressing such an interested audience as ourselves, was now greatly enjoying himself. However, his energetic enthusiasm was gradually being countered by the lingering physical effects of his accident, and he ended up in evident pain, and his speech became confused. As if by way of an apology, he explained that a metal pin had been fixed through his brain, and he parted his thinning hair in two to show a tiny hole in the skull through which it had been inserted. He agreed to the suggestion that he should go home and get some rest. He promised, though, that on some future occasion he would tell us all about the spiritual leader of Granada's Murabitun. He believed himself to be the only journalist to have met him in the last ten years. 'A whole novel could be written about the man,' Fefe said excitedly, as Carmen's father accompanied him to the door.

Two days later we took Fefe to lunch at a curious restaurant 30 kilometres to the south of Granada, near the western entrance of the Alpujarra. The restaurant was situated in a lone, converted mill standing within the green, wooded oasis lining the bottom of an otherwise arid, sun-scorched valley. It was both the headquarters of Granada's Gastronomic Society, and a place where young waiters were trained.

Our meal was preceded by a tour of a 'culinary museum' featuring a traditional Alpujarran kitchen. We were the only visitors that day, and were obsequiously looked after by three young waiters who were dressed as if for some grand, old-fashioned restaurant: one of them was a dwarf-like figure who wore a black toupee and moved like an automaton. The food was intended as a re-creation of a typical Hispano-Moorish meal from the time of the great Ziryab, a thirteenth-century lutenist, hairdresser and pioneering cook who had been summoned to Granada from his native Baghdad. Rich and heavy dishes of skate covered in almonds and raisins, and lamb smothered in honey, left Carmen and me in a somnolent mood – though not Fefe, who became more talkative than ever. I struggled to keep my eyes open as Fefe launched into the extraordinary story of Sheikh Abdalqadir, emir to the Murabitun of Granada.

IN THE LATE 1960s a stern, charismatic man calling himself Abdalqadir, recently converted to Sufism, came to Spain and began praying in secret in the former mosque at Córdoba. His subsequent arrival in Granada in 1969 galvanized the city's Islamic community, then in its infancy. Sufism had reached Granada from the Alpujarra, its message spread by a group of leather workers who had come to the city from Trevélez, and who had succeeded immediately in converting a handful of their colleagues here.

Abdalqadir made his appearance shortly afterwards and, within the context of provincial Granada, impressed people through his international vision, the apparent breadth of his learning, the range of his contacts, his abilities as a fund-raiser, and the mystery of his background. He was a born leader who gathered around him a group of converts whose number soon increased from 7 to over 300. At the top of the Albaicín he acquired a large, 400-year-old *carmen* for use both as his home and as his community's school, or *madrassah*. Every Friday evening, religious meetings were held there, reputedly involving hashish, the induction of euphoria through the repeated incantation of the mystical sound *om*, and jumping up and down in the air dressed in long silk tunics.

Increasingly dictatorial in his methods, Abdalqadir issued ever more bizarre rules and spiritual instructions. At first his followers were made to pray in public, and go around in Moorish robes, but later they were forced to adopt clandestine habits and anonymous clothes. He ordained initially that music would play a large part in his community's activities, and encouraged the Granadine authorities to allow the orchestra of Tetuan to play Arabic music within the Alhambra's Courtyard of the Lions. No sooner had the concert finished, however, than he declared that all music was atheist, and banned it entirely. Later he decreed, against all historical evidence, that cypresses were Christian trees, and was on the point of pulling down the magnificent and ancient specimens that shaded the garden of his *carmen*. More recently, influenced by German authors such as Nietzsche, he has tried to instil in his followers Teutonic ideals of strength and valour. The smoking of cigarettes has been condemned as feminine and bullfighting has been encouraged.

Not all is harmony among Abdalqadir's followers, nor has his domination of Granada's Islamic community gone unopposed. Bitter divisions within the community were exposed in 1986 when the Murabitun seized and held the city's only mosque, until eventually the Spanish courts intervened and ordered them to relinquish it. Among the Murabitun themselves evidence of a ferocious power struggle came to light a short time later with an internecine *coup d'état* in which rival factions climbed over the walls of the *madrassah* one night and kept Abdalqadir hostage.

Abdalqadir is known today in full as Sheikh Abdalqadir al-Murabit. Previously he was Sheikh Abdalqadir al-Darkawi, and before that Sheikh Abdalqadir al-Sufi. Further back still – over fifty years ago in Scotland – he was given the less sonorous name of Ian Dallas. Knowledgeable fans of the Beatles will remember Ian Dallas as the group's Scottish manager who co-wrote the screenplay of *Yellow Submarine*. Experts on the history of espionage might also know of him as the secret agent reputed to have interceded at one time between the American and Mauritanian secret services. His Murabitun admirers think of him as a great political, economic and spiritual thinker, a novelist, and a scholarly author on the relationship between Wagner and Islam.

'THE BEATLES, the Mauritanian secret service, Wagner – that says it all,' concluded Fefe, as the diminutive trainee waiter with the toupee pirouetted around him in a white jacket and tie, unsuccessfully trying to remove the crumbs left by our Moorish pastries.

'And what was he like when you met him?' I asked.

'Very British – or should I say, very Scottish. Rather Presbyterian, unsmiling, a man of few words.'

The image I was beginning to form of Abdalqadir was now so exotic that any encounter with the real person was bound to be disappointing. In any case, such an encounter would be out of the question, for the man had not been sighted for ages. I began almost to doubt his existence.

Instead of me wasting my time hunting down Abdalqadir, Fefe suggested that I should try to arrange an interview with Sidi Karim, a knowledgeable, enlightened person who had recently been made right-hand man to Abdalqadir in succession to a leading psychiatrist who had moved to Córdoba. I could ask for him in one of the leather stores of the Plaza Nueva.

The following morning I made my way to the Plaza Nueva. Carmen did not come with me, preferring at this point not to involve herself too deeply in a situation that might have unpleasant repercussions. I could always move away from Granada, she said, but she had to live here.

The staff in the leather store were charming, open and helpful. They did not know the present whereabouts of Sidi Karim, but a young, bearded man promised to find someone who probably did. We crossed the square and walked into a small, smart bookshop in one of the narrow streets at the entrance to the Albaicín. The bookshop was run by the Murabitun and was looked after by a couple of young men, looking like *yuppi* converts to Islam. We were directed to a nearby barber's shop, where a tall, thin man with a pointed beard was sitting contemplatively, while his hair was being clipped. Like a monarch holding an audience during his morning ablutions, he calmly turned his head towards us and asked me what it was that I wanted of him. My guide interceded on my behalf, and explained enthusiastically that I was someone interested in finding out more about 'our community'. The man in the chair introduced himself to me as Rafi and said that he would join us for a drink shortly in the Plaza Nueva.

My guide was called Shuayb. He had an engaging naivety, and spoke to me about the Murabitun in the same way that a foreigner might have explained his country to an inexperienced traveller with a poor command of the language. I was grateful for this, for I was able to find out that the Murabitun lived in Granada according to the principles of a commune, with everyone pooling their resources and receiving equal pay. Money and work were provided largely by a series of craft shops and engineering workshops owned by the Murabitun. Emotional problems were shared, and marital difficulties communally resolved. Shuayb seemed a happy man, and was determined that I should be so as well. He was keen that I should join him and his friends that night for a meeting in the *madrassah*.

With the arrival of Rafi, the mood at the café table changed utterly. Rafi had a soft-spoken, severe and distant manner, and did not give the impression of having a great sense of humour. His opening line made me uneasy.

'Are you looking for enlightenment?'

I stuttered, mumbled for a few moments, and revealed a nervous condition that probably indicated to him an answer in the affirmative. In fact what I said was that I was looking for Sidi Karim. Sidi Karim was ignored, and Rafi continued the conversation on a purely abstract and metaphysical level offering none of the insights into Murabitun life that Shuayb had given me. Rafi was quietly dismissive of my more specific questions relating to the Murabitun in Granada, and showed extreme reluctance to reveal any details of his own history. Largely through inference, I was able to make out that he was originally from Barcelona, and had picked up his excellent English while working in India and the Far East.

'Is there anyone in your community from North Africa?' I asked. 'Or are you all European converts?'

'We were all born Muslims,' Rafi replied. 'But we did not realize this until much later in our lives.' I suggested that an element of historical romanticism had brought them all to Granada. 'We can hardly ignore Granada's glorious past,' Rafi retorted, 'and we are all conscious of Andalusia's appropriateness as a base for the reaffirmation of Islam in the world today. But the Murabitun are to be found in many cities and in many countries. The actual places are of no importance to us.'

Shuayb seemed blissfully unaware that between Rafi and myself existed a divergence of personality and opinion that was unlikely ever to be reconciled.

'Don't you think,' he butted in excitedly, 'that Michael would enjoy coming to our meeting tonight?'

Rafi looked less convinced, and told me that he would have to make some inquiries beforehand. He asked if I had a telephone number in Granada where he could contact me.

Later that day I received a message from Rafi. No mention was made about the night's meeting in the *madrassah*, but an appointment to see Rafi again had been fixed for 12.30 p.m. the next day in the Murabitun bookshop. He was looking forward, apparently, to continuing 'our lesson'. Carmen said that if I had not returned by the late afternoon, she would assume that I had been brainwashed, and would send out a search party.

When I walked into the bookshop, Rafi was reading a Sufi parable to a young group of followers. He gestured to me to wait for him, and I took the opportunity to look more closely at the books around me. They consisted mainly of copies of the works of Ian Dallas and his Sufi *alter ego*.

Rafi apologized for keeping me waiting, and for once displayed a human side of his personality by saying that before he did anything else he quickly had to return to his home. He was worried that he had left the oven on. Perhaps, he suggested, I would like to accompany him, as we could talk to each other while walking.

Conversation hardly flowed, but I was beginning to warm more to Rafi, and to discover more about his life. We found that we shared a love of travelling, and that we could not imagine a wholly sedentary working existence. Rafi's job within the community was to negotiate the import of craftwork from Islamic countries. His home was a simple, white flat, with incense-burners, wall-hangings and a much-loved white cat.

Only when we were sitting once more at a café table in the Plaza Nueva did Rafi resume the offputting didactic manner of the previous day. Today's lesson was devoted largely to the economic views of the Murabitun, in particular to their campaign against the international banking system, and their belief that interest loans ran contrary to the precepts of the Koran, which condemns usury. I was wholly in agreement with these views, given that practical considerations did not seem to enter into them. But I unwisely extended the discussion to bring in first the economic and then the political structure of Granada's own Islamic community. I said I was under the impression that this community was dominated by a rigid political hierarchy headed by an autocrat.

'Who told you that?' Rafi asked sharply.

My potential as a convert was diminishing; I was revealing myself instead as an amateurish journalist. With persistence I succeeded in finding out that Sidi Karim was now in Murcia. But all my inquiries about Sheikh Abdalqadir were met with persistent evasion. All that Rafi could tell me was that, 'We have an emir, like all Islamic communities.'

By the time I got round to asking if there was any chance of my attending one of the *madrassah* meetings, I could only expect a negative response.

In principle, Rafi said, there was no problem. But there was no point in attending if I was only to observe and not to participate. Rafi found an analogy in food: 'Let us imagine that you are presented with an appetizing sweet, coated with honey and almonds. There's no point in just staring at it, relishing its enticing surface. You must also taste the sweet.'

I left Granada with the sweet untasted, emulating those romantic travellers who had gaped at Andalusia's sensually alluring façade without ever having risked a confrontation between image and reality, appearance and substance. Moving on before my vision of Granada's Islamic community had been wholly cleared of Moorish exoticism, I headed towards a land where sweetness had turned to bitterness and ideals had foundered.

PART FOUR

FABLED SHORE

13

Welcome to the Twilight Zone

A SHORT strip of asphalt road came to an abrupt end outside the sinister coastal hamlet of Las Negras, where a straggling band of Germans lived, on drugs and dreams. We were at the eastern end of Andalusia, but could have been at the end of the world.

The road became a rutted, stony track which plunged into a ravine filled with rubbish and prickly pears. On the other side it ascended sharply, hugging the edge of a reddish volcanic land-scape which fell into a sea so clear that even from a great height the grottoes, colourful encrustations and strange maritime life of the submerged slopes could be made out. Our Land-Rover jolted its way to the top of the hill before reaching a point where it could go no further. An abandoned lorry, with its two front wheels leaping in the air towards the sea, blocked the track in front of us. The vehicle had a Freiburg registration plate and had clearly been driven to this near-inaccessible spot by someone high either on optimism or on something more toxic.

We found the lights in its dashboard still working, and reckoned that the lorry had been left like this for a month at the most, in any case several years less than the car standing a few yards further up the track. The car was a rusted shell as ominous as an ox skull in the middle of the desert. Its body bore faint traces of psychedelic paint and a message that could have served as a latterday introduction to Dante's *Inferno*. Scratched in the rust were the words, 'Welcome to the Twilight Zone'.

We wondered what strange beings we would encounter as we continued our journey on foot, following for over an hour a vertiginous path that descended slowly towards a small bay. Behind us the indented coastline stretched in its red barrenness all the way to the mineral-studded and now protected promontory the Moors had named the 'Agate Cape'. In front of us, set back from the sea in scrubland spiked with cacti and withered palms, were the ruins of the former *finca* of San Pablo.

The *finca* had been left by its owners over seventy years earlier, and since then successive generations of hippies and idealistic vagrants had tried to set up home there. No one had stayed long, but sufficient time had been spent there for all principles and sunny visions of the simple life to have been lost. Ecologically minded Germans who had been reared in the clean environment of places such as Freiburg had ended up surrounding themselves with the detritus of the civilization they had rejected. They had gone past caring and had forsaken their vision of paradise for an arid landscape filled with rusted tins, plastic bottles, desiccated faeces, and the wispy shreds of carrier bags.

Clothes had been abandoned along with everything else. A naked blonde stood washing herself at a spring at the entrance to the *finca* while, beyond her, on the beach, two young men enhanced the primeval aspect of the place and its community by tying esparto grass around their naked thighs and using bamboo sticks in a game of spears. When the worst of the afternoon sun had gone, an even stranger sight was created by the emergence from behind the scraggy bushes of a nude procession – surely from a circus? – formed by an African woman with a box on her head, a pregnant Filipino, and two heavily tattooed German men, with their blond hair tied in pony-tails, and a rhesus monkey on one of their shoulders.

We tried as best we could to adjust ourselves to our new surroundings; but our own nakedness somehow reinforced our air of displaced city-dwellers. Carmen's boyfriend, Pablo, took his white body behind a rock and read a book on medieval Spanish history. The flabby and equally pale Javier Landa, a *bon viveur* friend from the north, slowly dragged his feet along the beach, inspecting the well-polished stones and pebbles as if they were objects in one of his beloved antique shops. Only Carmen, wearing nothing but black flippers, a mask and a snorkel, seemed a true child of nature, and explored her bizarre new environment without the slightest trace of self-consciousness. She lent me a spare mask and beckoned me into the water, where we dived down into a world where mermaids were a possibility.

Two days earlier the Pope had spoken out against the morally lax inhabitants of the new Spain, and had amused many of my friends by referring to today's Spaniards as 'neo-pagans'. 'Neo-paganism' became the catchphrase of the four of us who had set off from Granada in the direction of a barren no man's land which had the promise of raw experience and the lure of the unfamiliar.

THE VAST area stretching from the Alpujarra to the Catalan-speaking lands of the Levante could be described as a 'twilight zone', not only because of its strangeness and shadowy, indeterminate position between the Spain of the Romantics and the designer Spain of today, but also because of its overwhelming atmosphere of decay. The ruins of its past are echoed in the crumpled, eroded landscape, where dying oases of palms and citrus trees cling pathetically to the beds of struggling, dried-up rivers. Entering this land from the province of Granada, one is also struck by the ugliness of so much of the architecture, the tasteful and cheerful white simplicity of the typical Andalusian village being transformed here into sprawling groups of dirty ochre cubes to which has been added the occasional strident ceramic patchwork, or a coat of paint in lurid green, orange or red.

The tackiness of this part of Spain is quite exceptional, and has been exacerbated in its western half by the growing of fruit and vegetables under great sheets of plastic which create permanent condensation. From the Granada coastline right up to the remote coastal town of Almería, the traveller might think that the American conceptual artist Christo has been at work, wrapping up in plastic all the available land lying between the sea and the bare mountains. This so-called 'plastic culture' has been hailed as an 'economic miracle', but the strain of the additional workload has proved too much for many of the farmers. Large pockets of this 'culture' have already been abandoned, leaving the plastic sheets as tattered, greying fragments that rustle in the wind above parched parcels of earth.

A 'shithole' was how someone from Almería province described his native land to me. But 'shitholes' have a perennial fascination for writers, including Gerald Brenan, who loved to escape from his Alpujarran refuge, and plunge himself into the squalor of Almería, a town that would remain until the 1960s more accessible by sea than by land. A mountain pockmarked by the inhabited caves of the impoverished suburban district of La Chanca hides Almería from the 'plastic culture'. Brenan would probably not be disappointed today with Almería, the old and seedy heart of which continues to decay in the shadow of its imposing Moorish fortress, or *alcazaba*. Within the old town centre, with its ageing prostitutes, he would still be able to find a *fonda* as sordid as the one where he stayed in the 1920s, smelling of 'drains and stale urine'.

Describing his affection for this establishment, Brenan wrote of the 'pleasure to be found in the descent into poverty and in the contrasts it offered'. A similar attitude, though differently expressed, is apparent in the writings of Juan Goytisolo, an author who has developed a passion for Almería comparable to the passion of other travellers for the Alhambra.

Goytisolo is not Almerian but Catalan, and, like Brenan, was very conscious as a young man of his privileged, middle-class background. Piqued by having been accused by Jean Genet of being a wimp, the young Goytisolo tried to shake off the trappings of his genteel, cosseted upbringing by experiencing the absinthe, cheap sex and rough living of the port areas of his native Barcelona. Contact with working-class Barcelona also brought him into contact with the city's numerous Almerian immigrants, whose tales of their native province inspired him with an intense desire to go himself to this land that embodied the social and geographical antithesis of his original milieu.

Goytisolo first came to Almería in the early 1950s, and immediately fell in love with the landscape, in particular with the agitated, pinnacled forms of the so-called 'Almerian desert', which occupies much of the eastern half of the province. He expressed his enthusiasm to a bar-keeper at Sorbas, who sharply retorted, 'For us, sir, it is an accursed landscape.' A developing social conscience, itself the product of middle-class guilt, would later become integral to his interest in Almería, but would be confused with an inherently romantic fascination with the region's Moorish past.

Goytisolo looked back at Almería's brief period of splendour and commercial prosperity under the caliphate of Abd al-Rahman III and suggested that the expulsion of the Moors and the neglect of their brilliant systems of irrigation could be held entirely responsible for the devastated appearance of the contemporary Almerian countryside. As with many of the romantic travellers to Granada, Goytisolo's sentimental attitude towards the Moors accentuated his strong antipathy to Catholic Spain, an antipathy that would lead in his case to a rejection of his native country and a move to Marrakesh.

Goytisolo's experiences in Almería were greatly to influence his *Juan the Landless* trilogy, a fictional work about immigrant life that established him as one of Spain's most innovative writers of the post-war years. Two earlier and more accessible works were his study of the gypsy district of *La Chanca* (1954) and his travelogue *Campos de Níjar* (1956), an account of a short journey by bus and foot through the flat stretch of land between the Cabo de Gata and the equally denuded Sierra de Alhamilla. The latter work, one of the greatest of Spanish travel books, is far less polemical in tone than *La Chanca*, and is written in a laconic, objective style which brings out more effectively the author's anger with the social conditions of the area and with the authorities who were doing so little to improve them. Goytisolo, who has rarely been seen to smile in public, is not a writer known for his humour, but there is an amusing passage in *Campos de Níjar* in which he describes an encounter with a couple of French tourists, whose smart car has broken down in the middle of nowhere: 'This'll teach you to take me to poor places,' the wife angrily tells her husband.

The Almería described in Goytisolo's book is a province where tourism is in its infancy. 'Mini-Hollywood' – a Wild West sham indistinguishable today in its sinister decrepitude from many of the real-life communities of Almería – had yet to be built, while the future tourist resort of Mojácar, in the province's easternmost corner, was still a picturesque hill village described by a Belgian traveller of the time as 'this jewel of unknown Spain'.

We stayed near Mojácar, in the fishing port of La Garrucha, which was where Carmen's parents came from. Her father had been apprenticed to a local photographer whose invaluable documentary record of the town at the beginning of the century had been entirely destroyed in the Civil War. La Garrucha, a place rapidly developing into a popular resort, is currently being given an entirely bogus past, its unpretentious seafront having acquired a set of 'nineteenth-century' street-lamps and a baroque-style marble balustrade. Mojácar, meanwhile, has been changed from a quiet and authentically Moorish village into a noisy, neo-Moorish honeycomb of bars, restaurants, hotels and craft shops. That this plaster sham should be 'The Birthplace of Disney' (according to a recently removed road sign) is singularly appropriate, though sadly, this too is false. A Chicago birth certificate quashes once and for all the bizarre local tradition that the American cartoonist was born illegitimately in Mojácar to a woman called Consuelo Suarez.

Camilo José Cela had argued with me in Guadalajara that one of the few parts of Spain to remain relatively unchanged and unknown was the Almerian interior. One night, as I walked through the streets of Mojácar with my friends, Carmen pointed out the lights of the distant hill village of Serena. She had been there a few years before and remembered the place as being so primitive as to be beyond 'even the frontiers of neo-paganism'. We decided to go there the next day, but found, after a promisingly difficult drive along a winding, unsurfaced road, that the tourism of the coast had reached even here. A notice in English pinned to one of the bars was advertising an evening of 'champagne and *tapas*'.

Following our disappointment with Serena, our hopes of discovering a truly 'hidden' Spain in Almería province began slowly to vanish. We concentrated instead on the pursuit of neo-paganism, a pursuit greatly encouraged by Javier, a sybarite who refused to be hurried in anything and believed that few things in life were more important than eating and drinking. Thanks to

Javier, and to his subtle powers of persuasion, our primary concern became the search for a good place to have lunch, our most rewarding find being a restaurant in the nearby town of Vera where the owner was attempting to revive traditional Almerian specialities in danger of dying out. Our visit there coincided, surrealistically, with an outing of geriatric marathon runners, who, having risked their lives earlier in the day through racing, were trying to ensure a complete collapse through gorging on such unusual but heavy local specialities as the pasta-based *gorullos*.

A discovery of Javier's from the year before was a bar lost in the olive-covered slopes to the north of Mojácar. It was called the Delfos, and seemed from Javier's description an essential port-of-call for neo-pagans. We went there on what was intended as the last night before my friends returned to Granada.

The Delfos had grown out of an old farm, but in the course of its growth had lost most points of contact with tangible reality. It was the creation of an ageing artist with flowing white hair who had begun his career making sculptural assemblages, but who was now interested in only one of these – the bar itself. He scoured the local antique shops, accumulating old gramophones, bird cages, Empire furniture, Turkish hangings, garden statuary, and other miscellanea to put beside works of art donated by friends and clients, along with all manner of junk acquired from rubbish tips, roadside warehouses and the surrounding fields. The predominance of white plaster columns, Corinthian capitals, cherubs and Classical nudes achieved a decadent late-Roman look, but the place was too chaotic and confusing to warrant close stylistic analysis. Inspiration had got out of control, and the 'installation' was now expanding into more and more rooms, and even spilling outside into a garden cluttered with ponds, box hedges and pergolas. The objects took precedence over the select and beautiful clientèle, who sat in quiet, cowed groups, kissed silently below statues of Cupid, or else disappeared completely, as they did in a dining-room that seemed to have been set for a great baroque banquet which had never taken place.

Could the Delfos be described as truly stylish, or did it represent kitsch on a quite breathtaking scale? The question was partially answered by Javier, who described it as being in 'Murcian taste', a reference to the adjoining region to the east. This in turn made Carmen and Pablo recall an article they had read on 'La Granja', an even more curious bar in the middle of the Murcian *huerta*. I questioned Javier about 'Murcian taste', and found that his conception of it had been formed more through the imagination than through any close contact with Murcia itself. Carmen's and Pablo's own knowledge of Murcia was equally indirect, though both of them agreed with Javier in conceiving of Murcia as an Almería writ large, a region with an appeal lying somewhere between the sordid and the pretentious.

A magazine survey carried out in the late 1970s revealed that the Spanish region least popular among Spaniards themselves was Murcia. Yet few Spaniards have penetrated further than Murcia's coastal resorts. The ignorance as to what Murcia was really like, the possibility of discovering places even stranger than the Delfos, and my continuing search for the *cursi* only increased my desire to get to this region as soon as possible. In the general mood of excitement induced by the Delfos, I tried to encourage my friends to come with me. Carmen said that she was anxious about some exams she was studying for, while Pablo pointed out that our intended 'long weekend' at La Garrucha had already turned into an eight-day trip. Javier was the most amenable of the three, and, as always, would have the final say. The prospect of Murcia appalled him, but he had an irrepressible curiosity in new people and new places, and was in no hurry to get back.

The four of us set off the next day, after a characteristically late start that had merged into the obligatory lunch and afternoon *siesta*. A fanciful sense of impending doom affected us after we had passed a sign marked 'Palomares', the site of what could have been the world's greatest catastrophe: in 1966, three American nuclear warheads had accidentally fallen here but had mysteriously failed to explode. A stretch of bleak, rocky coast separates Palomares from the Murcian border, on the other side of which we immediately entered the port of Aguilas, where a handful of grand turn-of-the-century monuments survive alongside ugly apartment blocks radiating outwards from an uninviting bay.

We arrived at sunset, and made our way in the dusk to a small industrial suburb where a gypsy antiques dealer kept his warehouse. The owner of the Delfos was a frequent visitor here, and his own bar seemed less remarkable as we stared like children at the gypsy's fantastical bric-à-brac and resplendent *objets d'art*, so unexpected in this dusty, out-of-the-way location.

I was attracted above all to a life-sized and faintly coloured *papier-mâché* king wearing an expression both intensely sad and alarmingly human. The king was one of the Magi, and had a letterbox below his neck where children could post their requests for Epiphany. I bought the king, and, as we headed off by night towards the interior town of Lorca, he sat on the back seat of the Land-Rover like some strange passenger in fancy dress. In the course of our Murcian journey, the paint would begin flaking from his face, his features would become ever sadder, and his presence more and more extraordinary, mirroring the character of the region we had entered.

At Lorca I began seriously to wonder if the impressions formed of places by travel-writers in the course of casual visits have any validity whatsoever. Lorca is a decayed market town which had known great prosperity in the early Middle Ages and again in the baroque period. It still has one of the largest *comarcas*, or municipal districts, in the whole of Spain, but has yet to recover from its dramatic economic decline of the middle years of this century, when it acquired a ditty of the 'shit-and-run' variety: 'De Lorca, ni el polvo' – 'Not even its dust loves Lorca.'

At the nadir of the town's post-war poverty, the English writer Rose Macaulay spent a night here, and was enchanted. A long, glowing description of Lorca features in *Fabled Shore* (1949), her famous and learned account of a journey from the Pyrenees to southern Portugal. She could not understand how romantic travellers such as Richard Ford and Henry Swinburne were both so negative about Lorca, the former finding it a 'dull, unsocial place', the latter seeing in it 'nothing . . . to make a note of but the dress of a gypsy, the daughter of the inn-keeper'. Macaulay herself, in the course of only two pages, writes of Lorca as being 'an infinitely agreeable town', 'an enchanting town', and 'truly lovely, with the rare, blanched pastel beauty of a Wedgwood vase'.

None of Macaulay's terms of praise sprang to mind as we

entered Lorca at around ten o'clock that night. The town had admittedly changed considerably since her day and its old centre had been neglected in favour of the chaotic modern town below it. Our nocturnal impression of the old town was not of a place of delicate Wedgwood beauty but of somewhere coated with cracked and disintegrating clay. We climbed up there to look for somewhere to stay, hoping perhaps to come across somewhere as picturesque as Macaulay's Fonda Comercio, a 'very pleasant . . . seventeenth-century inn', where she had been well looked after by a 'pleasant' proprietor. We had to make do in the end with an unfriendly and sordid hotel in the modern quarter.

Lorca was in *fiesta*, but the animation was almost entirely concentrated on the town's lower slopes. At around two o'clock in the morning we followed a festive stream of people towards the *feria* ground, at the very bottom of the town. In the last stages of our descent, beyond an unguarded single-track railway line, we came across a part of town so strange as to compound our most bizarre ideas of what Murcia was like.

It was a rectangular district resembling a cross between a garden suburb and a city park. It had been laid out around the turn of the century as a residential district for Lorca's dozen or so rich families. Art-nouveau and art-deco villas, together with recent buildings in a modernist and post-modernist style, were arranged along shaded pedestrian avenues illuminated by wrought-iron lamps elaborately fashioned with Classical detailing. Some of the villas, freshly painted, still exuded great wealth, but others showed signs of having fallen on hard times. Near the entrance was a fine art-nouveau structure protected by rusted, bedraggled coils of barbed wire, and divided into two by unsubtle means: a solid wall of grey concrete led from the middle of the entrance gate to the exact centre of the house itself, where it cut in two not only the front door but also the central balcony above. Further on, we stood equally amazed ouside the gardens of a grand 1920s villa with blinds in vivid blue plastic and a surrounding row of Classical-style busts, including one of Cervantes, and another of a toga-clad figure wearing spectacles. 'Murcian taste, Murcian taste,' muttered Javier, as other such villas came into view, revealing a side of Lorca that had apparently passed Rose Macaulay by.

In the adjoining *feria* ground, drunken youths staggered in menacing groups around stalls that were the antithesis of the elegant *casetas* of Seville. Intimidated by a succession of young men indulging in macho camaraderie and displays of strength, we moved on to a stall run by the 'Peña de los Ecólogos de Lorca', where we expected to find a more sensitive type of person, perhaps even someone who was concerned about the terrible pollution of the Murcian environment. But the Lorcan ecologists were not typical of 'greens', and proved to be leather-jacketed hooligans crushing cans into the ground, and throwing beer and wine at anyone who approached them. We would cross their paths a few hours later, in a nearby discotheque unecologically called La Gasolinera, which gathered together on a dance floor, damp with drink and urine, the dregs of a Lorcan night.

Rose Macaulay rose fresh and early on her first and only morning in Lorca, and was pleased to find the place as delightful and friendly as she had the evening before. We rose not so early and saw the harsh midday sun highlight the dirt, rubble and collapsing masonry of the old town. Numerous cranes and signs reading 'Obras de Emergencia de Restauración' indicated that drastic efforts were being made to save the place, but the sheer size and quantity of the monuments made one wonder how long it would be before the money ran out.

The restoration campaign was being directed largely at the old town's main square, which had been greatly admired by Macaulay and has the makings of one of the great baroque squares of Spain, with its arcaded town hall, its richly ornamental seventeenth- and eighteenth-century palaces, and its enormous cathedral, rising high above its surroundings on a steep flight of steps. But for the moment it remains a beautiful but ruined and lifeless square in which even the charming fountain and flower garden mentioned by Macaulay have been replaced by a dusty clay-coloured void. On the highest part of the square, some forgotten poet has been commemorated by a plaque that has today a special poignancy, the house it marks being a ruin overlooking larger ruins. 'In this house,' it reads, 'loving life and poetry, there was born, lived and died Eliodoro Puche, poet, 1885–1963.'

The old town developed a more ochre, devastated and impoverished look the higher we walked from the cathedral in the direction of the crowning Moorish castle. A style of popular decoration highly characteristic of this part of Spain, whereby broken pots, jugs and tiles are attached higgledy-piggledy to the walls of a house, supplied the main note of colour and fantasy. However, there was little to induce a smile at the very top of the town, where the gypsies lived, and where there reigned a poverty of a kind I had never seen before in Spain. I peered behind the ogee-arched portal of a ruined sixteenth-century church, and found that a family of gypsies had set up home in the narthex, the children all asleep on an old sofa with the stuffing falling out.

Between the last of Lorca's houses and the sad masonry of the neglected Moorish castle stretches a rugged wasteland. In its higher reaches we were offered our first view of the landscape to the north, and stood for several minutes miserably observing a distant strip of green in the middle of a monotonous ochre expanse over which was settling a greyish-white film caused by smoke from an enormous concrete works. Only then did laughter take hold of us. In the caked earth of the foreground, surrounded by thistles, weeds, tins, and yellowing strands of dead grass, was a sign suggesting that the Lorcan ecologists had not been altogether idle. It exhorted the visitor to 'respect the plants'.

The experience of Lorca finally persuaded my travelling companions to return to Granada. They left me on a late-afternoon bus to Cartagena. The bus was packed with young men on military service going home for the weekend. They shouted, ignored the 'No Smoking' signs, and nearly rebelled when it became clear that the bus driver was not going to put on a video.

Dramatic storm clouds gathered in the late August sky, and the bus was waved to a halt a few yards from a wrecked, overturned car, from which bodies covered in blood were being pulled out. Two of the trainee soldiers pretended that the human carnage was a traditional pig slaughter, and collapsed into a fit of giggles after one of them had squealed, 'They're making black pudding, they're making black pudding!'

The Murcians are said to have a special sense of humour.

14

Journey to Nowhere

JUAN JOSÉ MILLÁS, a contemporary Spanish writer, spent part of his youth as an agent for a pharmaceutical company, selling to taxidermists and natural history museums a special substance that destroyed the entrails of animals without having to extract them. In one of these museums he befriended a madman who had spent many years devising an atlas of imaginary places. To the future writer's surprise, these places included the whole region of Murcia. Murcia, the man explained, did not exist. It featured in maps purely to fulfil some mysterious 'geo-political balance', the region's imaginary status being of course a closely guarded government secret. And the thousands of people who holidayed each year by the Mar Menor? These people were almost certainly suffering from summertime hallucinations induced by injection with a special drug. In reality they probably spent their summer vacations asleep in warehouses under the glare of infra-red lamps.

Shortly before Cartagena the bus from Lorca stopped at Mazarrón, a popular coastal resort which had been the setting of a 1960s film by the prolific and ubiquitous Fernando Fernán-Gómez. The film had been released under the title *Crime at Mazarrón*, the original title having been rejected by Franco's censors on the grounds that it might be prejudicial to the region's burgeoning tourism. The director had wanted to call the film *Journey to Nowhere*.

'Cartagena exists!' was the reaction of a Madrilenian acquaintance of mine on first setting eyes on this port from the train window. She had been invited to take part in a history conference there, but convinced herself of the reality of the conference only when she finally arrived at the railway station and was presented with indisputable evidence that Cartagena, like the rest of Murcia, did indeed exist.

If the region in which it is situated is a mystery to most

Spaniards, Cartagena itself is its mysterious heart, thanks both to its name and venerable antiquity. The name derives from Carthage, the ancient city mythically founded by Dido. Cartagena's origins are so remote as to be similarly shrouded in myth, its foundation being sometimes attributed to the legendary King Testa, who was active around the middle of the fifteenth century BC. Possibly the oldest city in Spain, it owes its importance largely to its magnificent natural harbour, which is formed by a gilded ring of rounded, barren mountains. In ancient times, Cartagena was second only to Carthage itself as the Mediterranean's liveliest port, and drew additional wealth from the nearby and celebrated 'Wells of Hadrian', where lead, copper, zinc, sulphur, tin and even silver were all mined.

Cartagena was briefly the capital of Spain under the Visigoths, but was less well treated by the Moors, who developed instead the inland town of Murcia. Cartagena lived on as one of Spain's leading naval bases, and in the late nineteenth century saw the beginning of an economic boom inspired by the revival of the local mining industries. In 1873 it attracted the attention of the world when a group of revolutionary insurgents turned the town into an independent canton within Republican Spain. This uprising prompted a lengthy pamphlet from Karl Marx, and also provided the setting for one of the funniest novels ever written about an Englishman resident in Spain, Ramón Sender's *Mister Witt in the Canton* (1936).

At the turn of the century, Cartagena was almost entirely rebuilt in the latest eclectic and art-nouveau styles, and was considered by at least one traveller to be an even livelier place than Seville. This period would prove to be the town's Indian summer. The local industries collapsed after the Civil War, and though some of them later recovered, the town's economic decline would be halted only at the expense of further contamination of an atmosphere said to be one of the most polluted in Spain.

The travel literature on the town gives either no impression of what Cartagena is like today, or else an extremely unfavourable one. Rose Macaulay, usually the most enthusiastic of travellers, found the town 'too large, too noisy, too modernized and industrialized', but praised the beauty of its harbour, and wrote prolifically about the town's Classical past, of which hardly a trace survives. Modern Cartagena is apparently too rough even for the authors of *The Rough Guide to Spain*, who warn the reader of the dangers of the port, and urge those brave enough to spend the night there to write in with any favourable impressions.

I had wanted for many years to visit Cartagena. My closest friends in Madrid were 'Carthaginians', and had captivated me with their numerous tales about the town and the life they had led there. They and most of their childhood circle were children of prominent members of the Spanish Navy, but all of them had reacted to their Francoist upbringing by becoming socialists with strongly critical views on issues such as the 1992 celebrations and the naval presence in Cartagena. Prominent in the stories that I had heard about them all were the brothers Antonio and Perico Garrido, who worked respectively as a union representative and a university professor of economics. Antonio was famous for his passionate and scholarly love of food, while Perico, the shyer of the two, had the distinction of having been a candidate for the Communist Cantonal Party of Cartagena, a party fired in its ideals by the example of the town's 1873 insurgents.

Antonio and Perico headed the small and unexpected reception committee waiting for me at the bus station. They knew me only as a friend of friends, but they welcomed me immediately into their group, and had even set aside a few days to show me around their home region.

The old town of Cartagena is much smaller than Rose Macaulay suggested, and was easily seen in the course of my first evening there. The walk on which I was taken began in grand style on the Paseo Marítimo, a palm-lined promenade running between the beautiful harbour and the sturdy, defensive walls erected by Charles III. Beyond the lugubrious hulk of Isaac Peral's pioneering submarine of 1888 we came to the splendidly domed neo-Renaissance town hall, where we turned into the narrow Calle Mayor and headed into the heart of the old town. Entering this pedestrian, café-lined street, I succumbed fully to the charms of Cartagena, which was revealed to me not so much as an ugly town but as an extraordinary survival from the turn of the

century, with tightly packed rows of glazed balconies, cur-
vaceously expressive ironwork and wood-panelling, and an art-
nouveau casino, outside which sat groups of old men dressed in
ties and faded, shabby suits.

I was not the only English traveller to have been so taken by
Cartagena. When we reached the former Gran Hotel at the end of
the Calle Mayor, Antonio told me of an Englishman known as
'Don Jaime', who spent the last twenty years of his life in this
hotel, dying there only shortly before the building was converted
into the headquarters of a bank. Antonio vividly remembered
Don Jaime's habitual bow-tie and white linen jacket, in which
attire he was to be seen wandering to every corner of the town,
making friends as easily among the high society of Cartagena as
among the sailors and fishermen around the port. Whether under
the gilded arabesques of the casino, or in the slimy green taverns
of the fishermen's quarter of Santa Lucía, he could invariably be
heard asking in a precious voice for his beloved whisky and
almonds, a combination he always referred to in the diminutive
as 'un whiskito y almendritas'. No one knew why he had settled in
Cartagena, for, unlike the inherently serious Mister Witt, he had
not come here in any Consular capacity, and indeed gave the
impression of never having worked in his life.

The Gran Hotel, where Don Jaime had his suite, is a building
whose wedding-cake ornamentation and sweeping entrance
canopy in ironwork and frosted glass could easily be mistaken for
a building belonging to the French Riviera. Other buildings in the
town reflect instead the impact of Gaudí and Catalan art nouveau,
Cartagena being one of the furthest important outposts of this
style in southern Spain, and a place where the cosmopolitan
architectural tastes of the Levante meet up with the Andalusian
obsession with the neo-Moorish. Especially remarkable is the
extent to which turn-of-the-century Cartagena has been preserved
down to the humblest of shopfronts, and to elaborately wrought
street-lamps and kiosks that elsewhere in Spain would have fallen
victim to progress.

But the further we walked away from the Calle Mayor the
tackier and dirtier the whole city became, so that in the end I
could not help thinking that Cartagena was the closest European

equivalent to the decayed Amazonian rubber town of Manaus. At dusk I was taken behind the modest 1950s frontage of a department store and into a covered shopping arcade almost as grand as Milan's Galleria, but it was entirely neglected and had a skylight so thick with dirt and bird droppings that virtually no light could penetrate it. That the remnants of an older Cartagena had fared little better became apparent after we turned into the short side street that climbs up to the old cathedral. The cathedral was little more than a dilapidated Gothic portal rising above litter and dereliction. The surrounding district was the domain of drug addicts and prostitutes, but at night it was animated by a number of fashionable bars located in the half-abandoned buildings.

The night of my arrival marked the end of Cartagena's annual *fiesta*, which climaxed in a procession that fleshed out the Pope's vision of a 'neo-pagan' Spain. The theme was Cartagena's Classical past, but the presentation involved an exceptionally high number of slave girls, who paraded the streets of the old town in a state of near nudity, their nipples barely covered by tassels more appropriate to a sleazy revue bar than to an enactment of history and legend. The prime mover behind the whole event was the town's *concejal de cultura*, a man whose brain had been addled by alcohol. In the procession he played the part to which he and so many of Spain's *concejales de cultura* were ideally suited. With his ample, naked belly, bloodshot eyes and evident relish at being attended by so many lascivious slave girls, Cartagena's *concejal de cultura* made the perfect Bacchus.

Our night ended with my first taste of an *asiático*, a drink that in future years will probably have the same effect on me as Proust's lime tea and madeleines. The drink encapsulates the whole spirit of Cartagena.

The basis of an *asiático* is condensed milk, a milk substitute once used throughout Spain out of necessity but for which a special and inexplicable taste developed in the region of Murcia, where it is still preferred to real milk. In the making of an *asiático*, the condensed milk is combined with coffee, two types of locally produced cognac, and a sprinkling of cinnamon, the whole then being served up in a special conically shaped glass made only in Cartagena.

The origins of this concoction's curious name are said to lie in the use of the drink as a popular remedy during a serious outburst of yellow, or Asiatic, fever in the 1920s. The exotic nature of both its name and its rich, sensual texture belies a drink that can be made – so I was assured – only from the cheapest and most basic of ingredients. Antonio claimed that he had once tried to make an *asiático* from the best Italian coffee and an excellent French cognac. But it had not worked, the over-sophisticated and sickly result being 'something you might expect from Valencia'.

THE ELEMENTS of the kitsch and the exotic that make up the pungent cocktail that is Cartagena were revealed again the following morning, when I was taken to two places on appropriately opposite sides of the town. The first of these, straddling an arid, rocky inlet, was an outlying hamlet where the poorer Murcian families traditionally went for their holidays. It was officially known as La Algameca Chica, but everyone called it 'Shanghai'. A notice on its outskirts warning the visitor to 'look after your children' provided a menacing and faintly ridiculous introduction to what turned out to be a deserted, claustrophobic shanty community of coloured wooden shacks, roofed with corrugated iron, and resting on stilts in the oil-discoloured sea.

'Have you seen anything like this in Europe?' Antonio asked me in a tone close to local pride. 'But the best is still to come,' he added, as we got into his car to drive to the eastern side of town. 'We're off to see the ugliest building in the world.'

Not only did Cartagena exist, but so did 'Murcian taste': here was its apogee – the Regional Assembly Building of Murcia.

'We all call it', Antonio said, 'the work of Gaudí's demented son.' Sure enough, the undulating, mosaic-encrusted exterior was a grotesque parody of Gaudí, with parabolically shaped buttressing in diseased concrete supported by sturdy half-columns inspired by those in the peristyle of Barcelona's Parc Güell. But the interior had a different character and was even worse. The Delfos at Mojácar could not compete with the stylistic chaos with which I was now confronted. Art-deco lighting, neo-Plateresque ornamentation, abstract Expressionist murals, Symbolist mosaics, a wealth of blue plastic dolphins in an Andalusian-style courtyard all jostled for attention, but were of minor interest when compared to the incomplete assembly hall, where, in a heavily marbled setting inspired by the Royal Pantheon at the Escorial, the architect himself was still at work painting a ceiling decoration based on that of the Sistine Chapel.

The building had become a local joke, but it was a joke laced with a story of political corruption. 'All the marble you saw,' Antonio explained once we were outside, 'comes from the Almerian quarry at Micael, the owner of which happens to be the architect. He's a notorious entrepreneur, and the owner of a large property empire.' But how on earth did he get the commission to design such an important building? 'A public competition was held, of course,' said Antonio. 'But he was the only contestant able to bribe the president beforehand with a holiday villa in the Mar Menor.'

The Mar Menor, a half-hour's drive away to the south-east of Cartagena, is a vast, inland sea separated from the ocean by a narrow strip of land which Antonio and Périco remembered from their childhood in the 1960s as part of a large hunting estate looked after by a solitary gamekeeper. Today the place has grown into a Murcian Benidorm or Torremolinos, the appearance of which, with its imported lawns and castellated tower blocks, makes a stunning contrast to the rocky landscape a few kilometres away. This landscape is no less of an ecological scar than the Mar Menor, but it has the same compelling pungency and perverse fascination as Cartagena itself.

This landscape, with its dominant coastal range, is entered immediately beyond the southern outskirts of Cartagena. The devastation caused here by drought and erosion has been exacerbated by the mining industry, which has finally succeeded in turning the whole area into a large Surrealist painting. A giant slag-heap, as changing in its colouring as Australia's Ayers Rock, rises above La Unión, a town born of the brief but spectacular mining boom of the late nineteenth century, but now reduced to a dirt-encrusted sprawl of single-storey houses, from which stand out a market building reputedly designed by Eiffel and a pompous office block uncannily resembling a decayed structure from pre-revolutionary Russia.

The main surviving mining company in the area is the French-owned Peñarroya S.A., which, from the 1940s onwards, briefly revived La Unión's economy through tin mining. It also caused, at the nearby village of Portmán, one of Spain's greatest ecological disasters.

Portmán is a coastal village lying within the municipality of La Unión, in a magnificent bay enclosed by mountains whose slopes form an oasis of green in this otherwise arid stretch of country. It was a port of ancient origins whose English-sounding name is due not to some English duke but to the important Roman settlement of Portus Magnus. In the late nineteenth century, Portmán emerged as a popular summer resort for Murcians and Carthaginians, and remained such until the 1950s, when Peñarroya S.A. was given permission to use the bay to dispose of mineral and toxic waste.

Antonio and Perico drove me out to what was once Portmán's harbour, but only the distant strip of ocean could be seen. The jetty no longer jutted out into the sea but into a birdless swamp of an estimated 60 million tonnes of waste, covering over 8 square kilometres of the seabed.

The ministerial decree that gave the Peñarroya company the go-ahead to embark on this campaign of destruction stated that all work should cease the moment the bay showed signs of silting up. However, this clause was rescinded in 1969, at a time when the company began doubling its waste disposal to a rate of 10,000 tonnes a day. Only in the spring of 1990, when the damage was virtually irreversible, did Peñarroya cease its activities at Portmán. Guiltily acknowledging its responsibility for having ruined the bay, the company financed the construction of a new harbour at Cabo de Palos, 10 kilometres to the north. There was even talk of 'cleaning up' Portmán, a ruinously expensive scheme proposed less for altruistic reasons than for further profits to be derived from the construction of a new 'holiday city' to accommodate up to 100,000 people. 'For once,' a Murcian ecologist, Pedro Baños Paez, demanded optimistically, 'and if only for once, let social and environmental interests in Portmán take precedence over private gain.'

But human and ecological issues continued to be disregarded, as was revealed when we reached the mining village of Beal del Llano. Mining activity here has dwindled almost to nothing, and the company who owned the land would probably have moved on elsewhere had they not discovered, a few years back, new seams directly underneath the village. The company assumed that the inhabitants of this singularly ugly and impoverished village would be only too pleased to be relocated and given more work. However, the inhabitants showed themselves to be both stubbornly attached to their community and bitterly opposed to any further damage to their environment. Perico, who lived in a nearby farmhouse, was himself taking part in a round-the-clock vigil set up to ensure that the company did not secretly move in at night and begin excavation. The villagers' protest caught the imagination of the national press, who were now portraying the scandal in terms of David's fight with Goliath.

The vigil, now in its third year, had as its headquarters the local Casa de Cultura, the walls of which were covered on the outside with murals reproducing Goya's *Second of May* and Delacroix's *Liberty Leading the People*. But we did not stop to look inside, for Antonio was insisting on taking me to a building a few yards further down the street, where he promised a surprise that had nothing to do with either ecology or local politics.

The building was a typical miner's shack, that looked from the outside as if it was held together largely by tape and wooden crutches.

'You'll never eat a better rice dish than here,' Antonio told me, furnishing me with further evidence that the greatest Spanish meals can often be had in the most unpromising of restaurants.

The tiny dining-room was taken up by an enormous Westinghouse fridge with a broken door through which a family of mangy cats was struggling to push their heads. Antonio was surprised to find that the place had recently been given a 'face-lift', and disappeared behind a blackened curtain to congratulate the owner on the 'new décor'.

The owner, a local celebrity, came to sit with us after our

delicious meal of rice cooked with a rabbit he claimed had been caught by one of his cats. A sprightly man in his sixties, with incessant repartee, he was known to everyone as 'El Chupa del Llano', the word *Chupar* being the slang for eating and drinking to excess. The tales about Chupa were legion. He feared, first of all, that EC sanitary regulations would lead to the closure of his restaurant. Then, for my benefit, he repeated the tale of his visit to England, where he had been invited by two of the obviously eccentric foreigners who patronized his establishment. They lost him at the airport, and he consequently experienced one of the proudest moments of his life when the ridiculous nickname of 'El Chupa del Llano', was broadcast over Heathrow's loudspeakers.

When we got up to leave, Chupa presented me with a most impressive visiting card. On one side was an uncharacteristically serious photograph of him, placed above the words 'Casa El Chupa'. The other side featured two elaborate crests flanking large lettering reading 'Gastronomía Nacional'.

For my last night in Cartagena a farewell dinner was organized at a place called the Denver.

The Denver is situated at the very heart of the old town, and has occupied since its foundation in the 1950s a central position in the social and cultural history of Cartagena. Its name – suggestive of some seedy American cafeteria yet somehow exotic in its Carthaginian context – was coined as a gesture of friendship towards some American officers once stationed at the local naval base.

Pink plastic lettering spelling the words 'Restaurante Denver' hangs over the façade. The entry is through what might be described as a secular narthex, featuring the red-striped awning of a stand where waffles used to be sold. Beyond is the large, unprepossessing bar – Formica with pale lime-green walls shiny with grease. The actual restaurant is a small, windowless section at the back, where the smoke from the clients' cigarettes mingles with the fumes from the kitchen.

Despite its appearance the Denver has always been a centre of poetry and *tertulias*. In its literary heyday in the 1950s and 1960s, the *genius locii* of the Denver was the little-known Augustín Mesaguer, a poet of Sevillian tendencies whose life began inauspiciously in 1914 with what he would later refer to as his 'baptism of anís'. A poet of another kind is Denver's present cook and proprietor, Alfonso Ortega, a man who has concentrated his poetic gifts exclusively on the creation of food that has echoes of places as far apart as Murcia, Galicia, Italy, France and the Orient, but that forms altogether a strange distillation that can be described only as a *capriccio* of Alfonso. The *cognoscenti* of the Denver never ask for a menu, but put their faith implicitly in him, their sole contribution being to name the price they wish to pay.

On the night of my farewell dinner, we volunteered a larger price than usual, and waited expectantly for what was a theatrical spectacle, beginning with a curtain-raiser of marinated chicken livers draped on cherries, and proceeding to such wholly poetic combinations as a salad of cod's roe and diced pig's testicles served on a phallic leaf of chicory. As always, Alfonso served dish after tiny dish, improvising as he went along recipes that would probably never again be re-created, and giving up only when inspiration failed him. Egged on by our large and appreciative gathering he went on that night to produce over eighteen courses, the climax being reserved for a flambéd concoction that had the effect of a grand fireworks display. We clapped loudly and ordered a round of *asiáticos*.

The participants at this special dinner included a real poet, a tall and boyish-looking man called Fernando Blanco Inglés. A descendant of an aristocratic Carthaginian family who had owned an outstanding Gaudí-inspired palace on the Plaza de San Francisco, Fernando was one of those Spaniards I thought existed only in literature: a courteous *hidalgo* who had fallen on hard times. Accident-prone and thoroughly disorganized, he was working as a porter, and living alone in an untidy flat filled with volumes of Spanish verse, and what was probably the largest collection in private hands of stolen *asiático* glasses. The night of my farewell at the Denver, he was in unusually flamboyant form, though without losing in his drunkenness the dignity appropriate to a *hidalgo*. He dedicated to 'Mister Mikel in the Canton' one of his privately printed books of poems, and provided me with a final memorable image of Cartagena.

The conversation turned to Valencia, to where I was going the next day. None of the group had a good word to say about the city, least of all Fernando, who had married a Valencian woman who had subsequently returned there, taking with her their only child. Everyone agreed that the Valencians were basically unfriendly and overly sentimental, and that I would be better off staying on in Cartagena, where I could carry on the tradition of Mister Witt and Don Jaime. I argued for the cultural riches of Valencia, its great artistic and literary traditions, but these were all dismissed by Fernando as being 'cloyingly sweet'. I then mentioned the Valencia-born designer Mariscal, who had been responsible for devising the mascot of the 1992 Barcelona Olympics. I used Mariscal's name as part of my excuse for having to leave Cartagena, for I had arranged an interview with him in Barcelona the following week. As if to prove that I was not lying, I produced Mariscal's visiting card. The card was immediately seized by Fernando.

'This is worth nothing,' he said indignantly . He placed the card in his mouth, where it disappeared from sight. We all expected him to retrieve it, but he began chewing in earnest. Then he took hold of his *asiático*, and within seconds the last traces of the fashionable name of Mariscal were being flushed by a rich, soothing liquid down the gullet of a poet.

15

The Wart on the Lip

TWO IMAGES came to mind as I approached Valencia.
One of these had already been appropriated by the Valencian tourist board and was featured on posters and brochures promoting the city. It was of a limpid sunlit beach along which strolled two barefooted young women with straw hats, parasols and long, diaphanous white dresses. The image was derived from the canvases of the once internationally celebrated turn-of-the-century Valencian painter, Joaquín Sorolla, an artist whose sentimental but exhilaratingly fresh works bring to life an elegant, bygone world.

The other image was not of Spain at all but of an abandoned garden on the outskirts of Menton. Sorolla's friend, Blasco Ibáñez, then the most successful Western writer after H. G. Wells, came to Menton to spend the last years of his life, as an exile from his native Valencia. On settling there he emulated the example of so many other expatriates on the Côte d'Azur, and set about re-creating the distant world of his youth. Whereas others had built for themselves Scottish baronial hills, half-timbered English cottages or even Indian fantasies inspired by the Taj Mahal, Blasco Ibáñez transformed a characterless group of buildings into a cheerful, colourfully tiled Valencian villa and named it the Fontana Rosa. The villa, divided up into flats in later years, is now empty, and its garden – known as the 'Jardín de los Novelistas' – has been left as a jungle of weeds, ivy and cracked Valencian tiles. Neighbours will tell you vaguely that a 'Spanish writer' once lived here.

In coming to Valencia, I wanted above all to see what was left of the world Sorolla had painted and Blasco Ibáñez had yearned for. Others, instead, once came to Valencia hoping to find traces of the 'city of the Cid'.

*

THE CID took Valencia from the Moors in 1094 and died there five years later, having made numerous devastating incursions into the surrounding, Moorish-held *huerta*. The same medieval chronicles that later transformed this ruthless self-serving soldier into the hero portrayed by Charlton Heston gave also, and with greater justification, a glowing picture of Valencia and of the fertile landscape around it.

Throughout the Middle Ages, Valencia was one of the most prosperous and important cities in Spain. It was also a major centre of Catalan culture, with a flourishing literary life that culminated – so ironically for a city perennially associated with a historical figure distorted by chivalric gloss – in the publication in 1490 of Joan Martorell's *Tirant lo Blanc*, a chivalric epic whose hero takes part in exploits that rarely stray far from the plausible. This great work of Catalan literature, though praised by Cervantes for its realism, was greatly neglected in later years, victim not so much of changing literary tastes, as of the Castilian suppression of Catalan culture. Valencia itself suffered greatly from the dictates imposed from Madrid, and went into severe economic decline at the beginning of the seventeenth century. The region's agricultural economy had been heavily dependent on the Moriscos, whose expulsion from Spain had been strongly opposed by the Valencian nobility. This issue proved a prelude to more widespread antagonism between the two cities, a low point in Valencia's history being reached after 1715 when the place – together with Barcelona – was seriously punished for having opposed the Bourbon succession to the Spanish throne.

Economic recovery in the nineteenth century changed the face of Valencia. Romantic travellers came here expecting a city of picturesque medieval appearance, and were encouraged in this hope not only by the medieval chronicles, but also by Hugo's *Les Orientales*, which refers to Valencia as 'the city of three hundred towers'. They were disappointed by the reality. 'Valencia', in the words of Théophile Gautier, 'scarcely corresponds to the idea one forms of it from romances and chronicles. It's a large town, flat, sprawling, and confusing in its layout.' The city's medieval monuments had been either badly neglected or demolished, and were soon engulfed by a burgeoning modern metropolis that would become the third largest in Spain. Richard Ford found the whole place to have an atmosphere of menace and intrigue, and was enthusiastic only about the walk around the city's ramparts, a walk that, in his opinion, gave a good idea of this 'very Moorish and closely packed city'. But by the time of Augustus Hare's visit in 1871 these ramparts had been taken down, leading Hare to comment that nothing remained of the city of the Cid. 'No breath from those heroic days now blows upon Valencia, which is the very concentration of dullness, stagnation and ugliness.'

Not until the 1950s, when Valencia's old town was rapidly becoming overshadowed by towering office and apartment blocks, did travellers begin looking at the city in a more serious and open-minded way. Sacheverell Sitwell, one of the first English amateurs to take an interest in the Spanish Baroque, was entranced by Valencia's many seventeenth- and eighteenth-century palaces, and compared the city to that jewel of the southern Italian Baroque, Lecce. His visit to the city, however, coincided with the last days of the Fallas, a festival that appears to have offended the sensibilities of this irrepressible aesthete. While the Valencians were enjoying themselves with all their shouting, music-making and pyromania, Sacheverell Sitwell was trying to concentrate on the Valencian Baroque, and battling in the process with dense clouds of smoke, bustling crowds, and an intense distaste for the effigies that were being burned: he seems to have made no connection between the baroque monuments he so admired and the exuberantly festive spirit that went into the making of these sublimely gaudy figures.

Sitwell, for all his limitations, was singled out by Rose Macaulay as one of the few people to have shown any liking for Valencia in modern times. Macaulay herself, while highly critical of many of its aspects, undertook a thorough reappraisal of Valencia, a place that revealed exceptional charms once she had made her way through the modern development and stumbled across the city's unspoilt old parts. She was taken by the same palaces that had so impressed Sitwell, and was prompted by them to summarize the appeal of the city in terms of an 'eighteenth-century gentleman, unpretentious, a little down at heel, happy and at ease, though brooding a little wistfully over his past'.

At almost the same time that Sitwell and Macaulay were praising the charms of Valencia, the city was being discovered and enjoyed in an entirely different way by the drama critic Kenneth Tynan. Tynan's appreciation of this city – a place his widow Kathleen would describe as 'Ken's Mecca' – was greater and more perceptive than that of any other traveller in the past, but it was not one that was likely to have earned him an instant contract from the Valencian tourist board.

It developed, conventionally enough, out of his love for spectacle and bullfighting. Believing that no other Spaniards were as 'rapturous, exasperated and pitiless' in their devotion to bullfighting as the Valencians, Tynan regularly attended Valencia's summer Feria, where his pleasure in the fighting was complemented by his characteristically erotic absorption in the city's spectacular fireworks displays, which he saw as a 'prolonged spasm of organized fire' followed by trails of 'spermatazoa squirming for survival'. The gaudiness that so repelled Sitwell in the Fallas was precisely what Tynan admired in Valencia. He also enjoyed shocking his compatriots by developing a taste for all that was camp, ugly and 'obsessively unsmart' in the city. He was praising rather than damning Valencia when he described it as 'the wart on the Mediterranean lip', and he used the city and its 'horrors' as an initiation test for his young second wife, Kathleen. 'If a relationship can survive Valencia,' he commented, 'it can survive anything.' Elaborating on this theory, he wrote that Valencia was a place where you could 'loaf not so much solitary as truly alone'. 'Some people', he continued, 'go on vacation in order to meet strangers. Others go to meet themselves. For this group, Valencia, world hub of anti-tourism, is the predestined haven and hiding-place.' In Valencia, Tynan had found what Brenan had discovered in the Alpujarra, a place where – in the words of Kathleen Tynan – you could 'live in your own emotional climate' and 'create your own private myths'.

I WAS ALONE in Valencia, experiencing a vision of an empty cityscape dripping with icing and treacle, to which a dense layer of dirt and flies had attached itself. Induced by a Saturday afternoon stroll through the old town, the vision had coagulated into its final form after discovering that the closest Valencian equivalent to an *asiático* was known as a *bonbon*.

The new town of Valencia has shaken off the 'obsessive unsmartness' of Tynan's day, but the sleek designer look that has replaced it draws greater attention than ever to the decay of the old town. The faded gentility Macaulay admired is no longer applicable to today's 'historic centre', which has gone the way of so many other such districts in Spain, and lost its artisan nucleus to a growing marginal population injecting itself with heroin.

I immediately found myself in the thick of this seedy world through my unwise choice of a place to stay. I had little money and an exhausted credit card; I wanted to be in an old building in the city centre; and, being on my own, I preferred staying in a small, family-run establishment than in some impersonal hotel.

The Hostal San Martín did not seduce me with its charms, but I let myself be persuaded by its cheapness and by its central location, just around the corner from the unmarked house at 4 Calle Mantas, where the future painter of cheerful beach scenes, Joaquín Sorolla, was brought up. I tried to overlook the *hostal*'s dingier aspects, and was not even put off by the long climb up a filthy and echoing nineteenth-century stairwell. The rooms of the five-storey *hostal* had dark padlocked doors arranged, prison-like, around a gloomy hall with missing wall- and floor-tiles. A couple of itinerant African street vendors were standing talking with a friendly young teenager who was feeding her baby. The teenager showed me into a cell-like room and insisted on keeping the key. I was inspecting the unwashed sheets when another young woman entered without knocking.

'They're treating you well,' she said with a big smile. 'They've given you the best room.'

The full horror of the Hostal San Martín did not become apparent until nightfall. In the meantime I continued touring the city, my impressions of an encroaching seediness balanced by the sweetness, preciousness and camp evoked by the word *bombón*. Even the magnificent eighteenth-century palaces began to be perceived by me more as *bonbons* than Bourbon, their style, strictly speaking, being not baroque at all but a fully fledged rococo, which was both antipathetic to the tastes of the Spanish Bourbons and rare in other Spanish regions. A fondness for stucco ornament, 'another peculiarity of this insubstantial city', reached here its rococo climax in the Palacio de Dos Aguas, a building I had once known only from photographs that had concentrated on the struggling atlantes of its portal without showing any of the imitation, pastel-coloured marbling, *rocaille* window surrounds, and other flippant rococo features of the rest of the façade.

Against all odds, a considerable amount of Ford's 'insubstantial city' has survived, together with a handful of exuberantly decorative art-nouveau masterpieces that were mysteriously neglected by baroque enthusiasts such as Sitwell and Macaulay. At the same time, however, Valencia has changed so radically over the last hundred years that little remains of the city known to Sorolla and Blasco Ibáñez. In searching for traces of their city, I began to experience some of the frustration earlier travellers must have felt on coming to Valencia in search of memories of the Cid. Eventually I went into the main tourist office to see at least if there was some museum or monument to them I had overlooked.

The unusually helpful woman who worked in the office telephoned a colleague and brought me unexpected good news. The seaside villa where Sorolla had painted his famous Valencian beach scenes was still standing. I would find it, she said, in the coastal suburb of Malvarrosa, a former village that had become enveloped in the urban sprawl of Valencia. She could not give me an exact address, but she believed it to be one of the seafront houses near to 'Blasco Ibáñez's'. She mentioned the latter house as if it were one of Valencia's better-known sites, even though none of the books and leaflets I had with me suggested that such a place still existed.

'It's still in private ownership,' she added, noting my look of disbelief, 'but there's a caretaker who's happy to show people around. It hasn't changed much since the writer's day.' I thanked her for her help and turned to go, but she stopped me as I walked towards the door. 'I hope you're not going there today,' she warned. 'The situation could still be dangerous. The riots have been going on since the morning, and the police have cordoned off the area. Just a few hours ago a desperate tourist rang me up to say that he was stuck in Malvarrosa, and wondered if I had any suggestions as to how he could get out of there.'

The inhabitants of Malvarrosa had apparently taken the law into their own hands and set out in a large mob to attack all the drug addicts and gypsies who had moved into the neighbourhood. The number of injured was said to be very high.

'Everyone's gone crazy,' the woman continued. 'The police are lashing out at anyone who seems to be a protester, while the protesters are attacking anyone with longish hair and strange looks.'

Violent riots, police cordons, and drug addicts did not exactly correspond with my idyllic vision of Sorolla's land of parasols, serene sands, and nonchalant women. None the less they could well have been scenes from the life and work of Blasco Ibáñez.

Sorolla and Blasco Ibáñez have much more in common than would outwardly appear, but their lives could hardly have been more different. Sorolla's was by far the most straightforward of the two, being essentially the story of a happily married man who began precociously at the Valencia Academy of Arts, and went on effortlessly to achieve international fame as a virtuoso landscapist and figure painter in an impressionist vein. Whereas Sorolla's life offers little material for the sensationalist biographer, Blasco Ibáñez's life is so full of melodrama as to be scarcely believable. A lifelong political radical and trouble-maker, he was imprisoned at least thirty times, fought street battles with his political opponents, had notorious love affairs, took part in three duels, and was almost lynched after founding a disastrous agricultural colony in Tierra del Fuego. Fortune and a more settled life devoted solely to literature would come only in his later years, following his vast international successes, *Blood and Sand* and *The Four Horses of the Apocalypse*. But his finest literary achievements would always remain those dating from his youth in Valencia, when he was still, in his own words, 'a man of action who writes in his moments of leisure'.

Social injustice provided the constant and unsurprising theme of Blasco Ibáñez's novels, but in those of his so-called 'Valencian period', the theme was not treated in an overly political way.

Instead, it was implicit in his realistic, unsentimental and very believable accounts of the impoverished lives of the local peasantry and fisherfolk. Subject-matter of this kind was also a feature of the early works of Sorolla, an artist who would later concentrate on capturing the effects of brilliant sunshine and share with Blasco Ibáñez only the latter's fast and 'impressionistic' working methods.

Blasco Ibáñez has often been compared to Zola, but he lacked Zola's meticulous striving for realism, and was content to sacrifice factual accuracy and close attention to detail to overall mood. Critics have rightly commented on his 'painter's eye', and he himself disclosed his painterly approach to novel-writing by once confessing to Unamuno that all he needed were 'first impressions'. In the eyes of Gerald Brenan, Blasco Ibáñez's whole approach to writing was that of a pure *levantino*, the defining qualities being a vigorous, coloured prose, a complete absence of humour and irony, and a 'pagan feeling for nature'.

To SEE the Valencian world Sorolla had painted I would have to visit Malvarrosa; to see the settings of Blasco Ibáñez's greatest Valencian novels I would have to go outside the city and into the *huerta*. I postponed Malvarrosa to the following morning, and tried to decide which of the novelist's favourite rural scenes I would visit in what remained of my first day in Valencia.

The most intriguing was perhaps the freshwater lagoon of the Albufera, where Blasco Ibáñez set *Mud and Reeds* (1902), the story of a handsome wastrel whose illicit love affair with his childhood sweetheart ends in suicide. The Albufera is only 10 kilometres to the south of the city, but is described in Blasco Ibáñez's novel as belonging to an isolated, cut-off world, where everyone speaks in a Catalan dialect, and where city-dwellers come either to eat a traditional *paella* of rice, vegetables and eel, or else to hunt in the mysterious forest that covers the Dehesa – the strip of land between the lake and the sea.

The fate of this area is suggested in Blasco Ibáñez's novel, one of the principal characters of which is an old hunter and fisherman who views as a sorry indication of changing times his son's decision to abandon the insecure but free existence of his ancestors in favour of the subservient life of one of the many new rice-growers who were radically transforming the lake's western shores. Since Blasco Ibáñez's death, a great deal more of the lake has been drained for rice-growing, and even the island featured in his novel – an island epitomizing the former self-sufficient and proudly independent world of the Albufera's inhabitants – has been joined to the newly reclaimed land. The insecticides used by today's farmers, combined with the dumping of industrial waste on the lake's southern side, has greatly reduced the number of birds who come here and has killed off many of the fish.

I had a brief glimpse of Albufera when I woke up on the overnight bus from Cartagena. My view was of a lake surrounded by a ring of main roads and motorways, with a distant coastal development marking the former forest of the Dehesa.

I preferred to keep the Albufera a fictional memory, and decided instead to go to the north of Valencia, and visit the part of the *huerta* that inspired Blasco Ibáñez's *La Barraca* (1898), a tale of a traditional farming community which ostracizes and destroys a hard-working Aragonese labourer who has moved into its midst. The *huerta* is this novel's real protagonist, and makes its prsence felt throughout. Described in the opening pages as an idyllic, fertile expanse touched by the early morning rays of the spring sun, it becomes at the book's close a cruelly impassive force triumphant on a sad winter's dawn over a man who contemplates the last of his property disappearing in flames.

The bright-green fields and market gardens of today's *huerta* come right up to the edge of Valencia's growing urban sprawl, as if trying to hold their own against the advance of the modern developer. I took a late-afternoon commuter train to the suburb of Alboraia, which is said to be the rural district on which *La Barraca* is based. In its centre I stopped to have a *horchata*, a sweet and milky Valencian speciality made from orgeat. The young woman who served it to me was talkative and inquisitive, and was soon asking what I was doing in Alboraia. I mentioned something about Blasco Ibáñez and *La Barraca*.

'We have to study it in school,' she said excitedly. 'The story happens here, in Alboraia. Well, it's really set in the *huerta*, but we in Alboraia like to think that this is the actual place. We're just like the people in the book. Well, we're not quite as bad.'

I wanted to ask her why the inhabitants of Alboraia were so keen to be identified with Blasco Ibáñez's *huertanos*. But time was short, and I went on instead to the local town hall, where I found an informative employee with a great interest in literature. We talked about Blasco Ibáñez, and he told me that I could not possibly leave Valencia without visiting the writer's home at Malvarrosa. I wondered if there was any place specifically associated with the writer's life near Alboraia itself, and he mentioned a former inn between Alboraia and the neighbouring community of Sant Llorenc. This building, he warned me, had been totally modernized, but I would pass right next to it if I were to take his advice and walk part of the way back to Valencia along the old Valencian road. As in Blasco Ibáñez's time, this road went right across the *huerta*, where, he said, I would even be able to see one or two of the district's surviving *barracas*.

A *barraca* is the Spanish word for a hut, but it refers in Valencia to the thatched, steeply roofed mud dwellings that are the traditional home of the poorer *huertanos*. Sacheverell Sitwell, who came here when the region was dotted with them, wrote about their 'magic name' which 'recalls or evokes Valencia'. 'As a poetical or pictorial symbol,' he added, 'we would give it the importance of the cubical, whitewashed box of Pulcinella under the tall vines of Aversa, in the plain of Naples.'

My short walk across the *huerta* was carried out in conditions recalling the end rather than the beginning of Blasco Ibáñez's novel. The first cold wind of the incipient autumn was building up, blowing dark clouds across a sky that would eventually turn black, save for a lurid red strip dramatically silhouetting the distant apartment blocks of Valencia. In the middle of this landscape I came across the Bonsai Garden Centre, and a number of fields where crops were being grown under the fashionable plastic sheets. The narrow, empty road tortuously made its way around a scattering of modern farms and an isolated football stadium. I failed at first to see the promised *barracas*, but caught a glimpse of one towards the end of the walk: approaching, I noticed that its original thatch had been replaced by corrugated iron. Further on, within sight of a tiny railway station, was the inn I had been told about. I intended to ask its present occupants if they knew anything about Blasco Ibáñez's supposed stay there, but the place was empty and locked. The ticket collector at the station was unaware of the inn's history, but informed me that the place was occasionally used today by a strange old man who crafted some of the images for the Fallas.

With the onset of night, I made my way back to the Hostal San Martín, trying all the time to reassure myself that the place could not possibly be as bad as I remembered it from earlier in the day.

It was worse. Junkies with withered limbs hung around on the street outside, kicking rubbish, and eyeing me suspiciously. Someone had been sick on the staircase, possibly the young woman who was rushing up and down the steps, screaming hysterically and banging hard on all the doors. No one wanted to let her in – or me for that matter, for I had to wait an interminable ten minutes before the *hostal* door was finally opened, by one of the now inebriated African vendors. The prostitute 'receptionist' had collapsed with a needle in her arm, directly beside her screaming baby. I took my luggage, and got out, fast.

The modern hotel to which I moved was manned by a young student who made light of what I had seen at the Hostal San Martín. In the middle of Brazil, he told me, he had stayed in a hotel where he had caught the male receptionist 'servicing a maid from behind'.

The student was a jovial person who was anxious that I should form a more favourable impression of his city. Valencia, according to him, had a livelier night life than anywhere else in Spain. People were now coming from all over the country just to spend the weekend there. I should be out joining them, having fun, he insisted. He said he recognized in me someone 'with a love for the curious', and knew exactly the sort of bar that would interest me. It was called the Johann Sebastian Bach, and was owned by the person who had previously created the Murcian bar of La Granja, the flamboyant and eccentric establishment I had first heard about in the Delfos at Mojácar.

'But there's no comparison,' the student said. 'This is a far stranger and more ambitious place than La Granja.'

The Johann Sebastian Bach brought my day to an end with a flourish of rococo *cursi*. The bar occupied the whole of an enormous eighteenth-century palace, conceivably a film set created by Peter Greenaway. Its elegant clientèle, many in evening dress and dinner-jackets, sat at gilded wooden tables in a covered patio dominated by a grand marble staircase that swept downwards like a great flow of honey. There were altarpieces and religious statuary; there were also the urns, potted palms, draperies, and other Classical paraphernalia of the Delfos. But so obsessive was the concern for style that all sense of humour, taste, and human proportion had been drained away, leaving kitsch of the worst kind – serious kitsch with the soporific after-effect of rich food.

The soft strains of baroque background music closed my eyes, and I was unsure at first whether or not I dreamed the angelic, diaphanously veiled choir that was descending the staircase, led by a young black page in eighteenth-century costume. I rubbed my eyes and looked again. I had not been dreaming.

THE SUNDAY MORNING had the sunniness and clarity of a Sorolla painting. I rose early to visit Malvarrosa, hoping that the neighbourhood disturbances of the day before had cleared away like the clouds. The driver of the bus I caught assured me that the last stop was directly outside the 'Chalet Blasco Ibáñez'. The bus journey to the coastal suburb from the city centre takes up to half an hour, the sea having receded a good 2 miles since the time of the Cid. As the bus cruised through the empty streets of the modern city, I looked at the local newspaper, which had a full report of the Malvarrosa troubles.

The cover photograph was of the crumpled body of a drug addict and AIDS sufferer who had been set on by an angry mob. One of the leading protesters had been his father. In the hospital afterwards, the victim said that the locals were quite right to make their own stand against drugs, but that they should not have picked on a defenceless addict such as himself but on the notorious dealers, or *camellos*.

The bus came to its final stop between a long, sandy beach

and a row of cheerfully tiled villas. I asked the driver which of these was Blasco Ibáñez's, but he appeared to point to a vacant site before suddenly setting off back again to the city centre. The area was virtually deserted, but I found a solitary passer-by who told me that the villa had been pulled down at least four years before, and that the vacant site was all that was left of it. I refused to believe him, and waited around for someone else to ask. An old man turned up some ten minutes later and confirmed that it had been demolished, 'about ten years ago'. He said that there had been much talk about turning it into a foundation for students and admirers of the writer, but somehow plans for this had been abandoned.

'And Sorolla's villa?' I asked.

'Oh, that,' he replied, throwing up his arms. 'That went so long ago that I can't even remember.'

The day was so clear that the coastline could be seen for miles. Looking north I could make out the holiday flats and towering hotels that had replaced the fishing village where Blasco Ibáñez had situated *Flor de Mayo*. I walked slowly in the opposite direction, towards Valencia's port. Some of the villas I passed had been turned into restaurants and discotheques; others had been abandoned and taken over by gypsies; in the background hovered the tattered, pink blocks where the *camellos* reputedly lived. Turning my back on them, and strolling out on to the beach, I directed my glance solely to the sea and the sand, which, in the beauty of the morning light, brought back memories of Sorolla's paintings – of naked children playing in the waves, and smiling young women changing behind bamboo screens into flowing bathing robes. Now there was no one around, except for a distant jogger and a fat, middle-aged woman taking a dog for a walk. I went to look more closely at the wooden signs that had been placed at regular intervals along the beach. They had been put there by the Generalitat de Valencia and recommended the visitor 'not to swim in the polluted sea'.

By Sunday evening I was in Barcelona, and stepping out of the railway station into the Plaça dels Països Catalans. The square is one of the many recent urban spaces conceived as part of wildly ambitious plans for the 'new Barcelona'. It is a large bleak rectangle, with an incoherent scattering of metal poles, canopies and other abstract forms supposedly suggestive of railways; it has been enthusiastically described by the design historian Guy Julier as a 'lyrical minimalist essay which ensured its revival as a viable aesthetic beyond post-modernism'. The subtleties of the square are lost on most visitors, and were certainly not appreciated by the large and sinister crowd of skinheads that was forming here at the time of my arrival in Barcelona.

I made my way to the house of two journalist friends with whom I was going to stay. I got there only to find an apologetic message saying that they had been unexpectedly called out and would not be back until that night. They returned shortly before midnight. They had come directly from the hospital, where one of their colleagues from the *Observador* had been taken following a vicious attack.

The skinheads I had seen gathering at the Plaça dels Països Catalans had gone on a rampage through the streets of Barcelona, hitting with crowbars anyone who got in their way. The colleague of my friends was felled in the very centre of the Gothic quarter, in the beautiful square overlooked by the town hall and the Palace of the Generalitat. He might have been killed had his attackers not been momentarily distracted, allowing him time to hide in the arcades of the town hall. The police stood by apparently doing nothing, just as they had done during the right-wing protests that had taken place in the uncertain weeks after Franco's death.

The skinhead rampage was the subject of outrage in the next day's papers. Then, it was soon forgotten, brushed aside by the officially induced euphoria and triumphalism that heralded Barcelona's forthcoming year as Olympic Capital.

PART FIVE

OLYMPIAN HEIGHTS

16

The Greek Labyrinth

HIDDEN among trees on the upper slopes of Barcelona is a park known as the Laberint d'Horta after the maze that lies at its centre. Once a private domain where spectacular festivities were held in honour of Spain's royalty, the Laberint d'Horta is run today by Barcelona's municipality, and is one of the quieter corners of a now over-exposed city.

Laid out on a steep slope, the park forms a cool and mysterious complex crisscrossed by water channels and cypress avenues, and dotted with fountains, ponds, Classical statuary and enigmatic inscriptions. Its creator was the late-eighteenth-century Marquis of Llupià i Alfarràs, a typically learned figure of the Enlightenment who appears to have devised the place as a playful philosophical puzzle. This puzzle, obscure in much of its detail, is broadly concerned with the different forms of love, beginning, at the lower level, with Classical reliefs apparently denoting love's origins. Further up, statues representing the rapes of Amphitrite and Europa bring the visitor to the level of divine if not especially elevated love. The third level is occupied by the famous maze, which gives visitors the opportunity to participate more actively in the game of love, a challenge that is taken too literally by some of today's more eager couples, who use the hedges as convenient screens to hide activities associated with love's more physical forms.

The maze, with its central statue of Eros, is intended to suggest the 'realization of love', and has an inscription outside encouraging the visitor to penetrate it. 'Enter,' it reads. 'You will emerge without difficulty. The labyrinth is simple. You will have no need of the thread that Ariadne gave to Theseus.' Unfortunately, love is not always so easy to realize, and many visitors have had to force the process by resorting to crawling through hedges. But, however love is achieved, the outcome is not necessarily happy, for on leaving the maze one is confronted by a grotto alluding to the tragic myth of Echo and Narcissus: 'In a burning frenzy,' an inscription reminds you, 'Echo and Narcissus fell wildly in love, she with him, and he with himself.'

On the whole, one would be better off climbing the adjoining steps up to the level of 'sublimated love', where an impassive Venus observes those who struggle in the maze below. The game is still not over, however, and one has to solve more Classical riddles before finally reaching, at the end of a long, shaded, rectangular pool, a languidly posed nymph signifying the peace at the end of love's journey.

The Laberint d'Horta is a corner of the greater labyrinth comprising Barcelona. Emerging from the park, the post-modernist visitor of today will be looking for signs to help make sense of this other labyrinth. Above a multi-laned ring road lie the upper outskirts of Horta, one of the former townships now incorporated into Barcelona's outer sprawl without being adequately connected to each other by public transport. Horta, a place heavily populated by Navarrese immigrants, and with its own Navarrese social centre, has retained a pleasant, small-town character but is interesting largely for the monuments on its periphery. These include a seventeenth-century seigneurial farmhouse, or *masia*, which has been converted into an elegant restaurant whose prices substantiate the claim that Barcelona has become a more expensive place to eat in than New York. In incongruous proximity to this relic of Horta's rural past is a reconstruction of the pioneering modernist pavilion built by Josep Lluis Sert as Republican Spain's contribution to the 1936 Paris World Fair, and for which Picasso painted the controversial *Guernica*. The seriousness of the pavilion's associations are deflected somewhat by the proximity of a monument by the American artist Claes Oldenburg that has enjoyed a popularity far greater than any other of Barcelona's numerous civic embellishments of the last few years: it consists of a gigantic group of coloured matchsticks strewn over the pavement as if in a giant game of pick-up-sticks.

Higher up the hill, in between the ring road and the Laberint d'Horta, there is a further revealing group of monuments for the visitor to examine. The largest of these is the Velodrome, a stadium which was erected for the now forgotten World Cyclng Championships of 1984, awarded an architectural prize in 1985, and then virtually abandoned, only to be resuscitated for the 1992 Olympics. On the grassy slopes beside it, and resembling from a distance what could either be some scanty traces of a Roman villa or else the emptied contents of a builder's lorry, are the scattered concrete shapes of a 'visual poem' by the Catalan artist Joan Brossa. The shapes are of letters, broken letters, and – appropriately enough – question marks. Finally, menacingly thrust high in the air above the stadium, are two enormous shapes covered in graffiti inspired by a combination of Joan Miró and Antoni Tàpies. These are gasometers, and are colloquially known as 'Los huevos de Porcioles', a reference to the testicles of the notorious Francoist mayor, Josep Maria de Porcioles, whose long period of civic leadership saw some of the city's most brazen developments of the post-war years.

Porcioles's Balls provide a suitable vantage point from which to study Horta's relationshp to the rest of Barcelona's labyrinth. As one observes the vast cityscape falling away towards the sea, the mess Porcioles made of his city will be apparent, but the panorama also reveals the attempts made over the centuries to apply a rational, underlying order to the city. Barcelona might be an amalgam rather than a single unity (the local writer Vázquez Montalbán gave the title *Barcelonas* to his book on the city), but it has none of the amorphousness that seems to characterize Madrid. As with a maze, Barcelona becomes comprehensible when seen from a plan or from a great height, its constituent parts fitting together with a satisfying and almost geometrical precision.

The kernel from which Barcelona grew – the Eros at the centre of the maze – is formed by the Roman settlement of Barcino, whose oval shape can still clearly be made out through extensive surviving sections of the original defensive walls. With the city's rapid growth in the thirteenth century, the oval became encased by a rhomboid which was bordered to the west by a seasonal torrent, or *rambla*. In the fourteenth century the city was further extended by attaching to the other side of the *rambla* a walled, lozenge-shaped area called the Raval. After 1704 the walls that still separated the Raval from the rest of the city were gradually demolished, leading to the former *rambla* being metamorphosed into the plural Ramblas, one of the world's great promenades.

The creation of this new artery supplied only a temporary solution to a city that was soon festering and suffocating within its medieval grid. In 1857 the engineer Ildefons Cerdà devised a solution that got rid of the remaining outer walls while turning the otherwise intact old town into a heart enclosed within a grid of a regularity and scale unparalleled in Europe. The realization of Cerdà's plan coincided with the industrial and cultural renaissance that fostered such luminaries of turn-of-the-century architecture as Domenèch i Montaner, Puig i Cadafalch, and Antoni Gaudí. Barelona was transformed into the 'city of marvels', and at the centre of this was a grid so lined with magnificent Art Nouveau façades that it came to be known as the 'Golden Quadrangle'.

The clear, rational way in which Barcelona has expanded reflects the proverbial characteristics of the Catalans, who have invariably been portrayed by other Spaniards as being sensible, earnest, hard-working, efficient, and more interested in money than in matters of the spirit. The Catalan word generally used to summarize these qualities is *seny*, a word that means, literally, 'common sense', but also implies an ordered, methodical approach to life. *Seny* has its opposite, *rauxa*, a word denoting uncontrollable emotion or outburst, applicable to sprees of drinking, sex, violence and other forms of socially provocative behaviour. The Catalans are said to find relief from *seny* in *rauxa*, examples of which have been found in such diverse phenomena as the Catalan love of fire and fireworks, the region's violent anarchist tradition, and the local passion for obscene and scatological humour.

One Catalan writer, Victor Alva, believed *rauxa* to be the 'ultimate consequence of *seny*', an idea perhaps illustrated by the urban development of turn-of-the-century Barcelona. This same city, so keen to present an orderly, progressive image was also seething with the inevitable social and urban problems that resulted from Cerdà's inherently idealistic plan falling victim to the selfish interests of private speculators, who did away with the green and open spaces that had originally been envisaged, so as to fit as many offices and apartments as possible into each of the grid's blocks. The new city was certainly no ideal community to the thousands of labourers who had come in to build it, many of whom were forced into outlying shanty towns comparable to those that later developed on the outskirts of Brasilia.

In the meantime the old town went even more seriously to seed, with the Ramblas experiencing a complete reversal of its social make-up. The once smart and aristocratic lower half of this promenade became affected by the growing poverty and sordidness of surroundings that continue to this day to give the impression of a city continually flushing out its dregs and undesirables in the form of rubbish, faeces, hypodermic needles, junkies, prostitutes, drunken sailors, muggers and psychopaths. Unamuno, in a 1906 essay on Barcelona bringing together many of the Spanish-held prejudices against the Catalans, criticized the city in a way some might feel pertinent today. For him Barcelona was a place more interested in making cosmetic improvements than in dealing with fundamental problems. Coining the word *fachadismo* ('façade-obsessed') to define this mentality, he poked gentle fun at a city so concerned with its buildings' façades that there was even an annual, municipally sponsored competition to decide the most artistic. The façades, he admitted, were splendid and astonishing, but what was the point of them in a city where typhoid was spreading alarmingly through lack of a proper drainage system?

One of the most polemical of contemporary Spanish writers, Vázquez Montalbán, recently discussed with the radical lawyer Eduard Moreno the way in which the people of Barcelona have suffered from grand urban schemes that ultimately have benefited only those with money and power. Sadly, one can only speculate as to what would have happened to the most genuinely socialist of these schemes, the so-called Plan Macià. Drawn up in the early 1930s, under Catalonia's Republican government led by Francesc Macià, the plan was intended to meet the demands of a population grossly swollen by the first major wave of immigration. The plan was the creation of GATCPAC, a group of socialist architects heavily under the influence of Le Corbusier, who was keen that Barcelona should adapt what Communist Russia had rejected – his vision of the ideal workers' city of the future. Had the plan not been thwarted by the Civil War, and had it been carried out exactly as intended, the city would have been subjected to a geometrical layout far more tyrannical than that of Cerdà's grid: the whole of Barcelona would have been reduced to massive blocks parcelled up into zones that were divided according to different types of activity. Despite all its provisions for greenery, beaches and recreation zones, this 'cité radieuse' would probably have ended up as lacking in radiance as the grey concrete ruins of Marseilles's Unité d'Habitation.

In comparison to the cold Utopianism of the Plan Macià, there was at least something reassuringly human in the incompetence, shoddiness and lack of planning that characterized much of Barcelona's urban development in the years between the Civil War and the 1970s. Francoism, and in particular Porcioles – who served as mayor from 1957 to 1973 – are usually named as the principal culprits for having made Barcelona an even dirtier and more chaotic city. Yet, to be fair to both Franco and Porcioles, the urban policies they adopted were little different from those that were taken up in most other Western cities after the Second World War: the depressing banks and office blocks that made the Plaça de Catalunya such a visual disaster were certainly no worse, say, than the modern development that engulfed London's St Paul's Cathedral. As with Europe generally in the 1950s and 1960s, private speculators were given free rein, and little concern was shown in preserving the past, especially not the nineteenth- and early twentieth-century past. While many of the wonderful old buildings in the Eixample were being razed, insensibly altered, or uncared for, ugly and cheaply built residential blocks were randomly sprouting up in the surrounding areas, in the midst of those shanty communities that inspired Francesc Candel's powerful novel, *Where the City Changes its Name*.

The makeshift, illegally constructed architecture of the city's poor and unemployed made, of course, an easy target for developers, whose bulldozing of these communities only exacerbated the city's worsening housing problems. Increasing hostility towards the developers culminated, near the end of the Franco period, in a successful mass protest against a private scheme to erect high-rise middle-class housing in the decayed, working-class area of Poble Nou, the site chosen being one earmarked earlier for future use as parkland. Among those who protested were members of the present socialist municipal government led by Pascual Maragall.

Maragall, the grandson of one of Catalonia's most famous poets, was elected to office in 1982, shortly after the city had been put forward as a candidate to host the 1992 Olympics. Mounting Olympic fever, combined with the growing mood of Catalanism, encouraged Maragall in his plans to undertake a major urban renewal to make good many of the mistakes of the Porcioles era. In his book, *Remaking Barcelona* (1986), he used as the underlying motto behind his plans Shakespeare's phrase, 'The City in the People', a phrase he attributed erroneously to some 'old professor from Boston'.

Maragall's promise to 'remake' Barcelona would not prove an empty one, for Barcelona has been changed so radically over the last ten years that one might be excused for thinking that it has become simply a toy for the amusement of a generation of architects, designers, planners and sculptors who have become drunk on too much freedom and money. In addition to the stadia and other facilities built specifically with the Olympics in mind, the city has seen a proliferation of museums, monumental statuary, squares and public parks. A great many old buildings have been brilliantly restored, and an equal number of the Porcioles era's ugly additions been removed; more startlingly, the city, notorious for having turned its back on the sea after the Middle Ages, has been given one of the finest seafronts of any Mediterranean city, complete with smart promenades and cheap beaches. And the process of transformation by no means ended with the Olympics, one of the many ambitious projects currently underway being the creation – at the intersection of the city's two largest thoroughfares – of a megalomaniacally sized post-modernist temple designed by Ricard Bofill to house the new National Theatre of Catalonia.

In an age when innovative modern architecture and planning are thwarted by committees or lack of funds, it is undoubtedly thrilling to witness what is happening to Barcelona. None the less it is understandable that many of the city's inhabitants – in particular the older generation – are disconcerted by the speed with which the changes have been introduced. The theatre director Albert Boadella, a native of Barcelona now living in the countryside, told me of the unease he feels every time he has to visit the city: seeing the much loved landmarks of his childhood and adolescence disappear from one moment to the next deprives him of a sense of security. And, as he and others of his generation might well ask, are these changes really fulfilling Maragall's pledge to serve the people of the city, or are they motivated instead by political propaganda and the familiar bugbear of the private speculator?

Vázquez Montalbán firmly answered this question by comparing aspects of Maragall's urban policies to Porcioles', quoting as an example the way that the illegally built street bars and restaurants that once gave so much character to the popular district of Barceloneta have all been pulled down to make way for an elegant but lifeless promenade. But the greatest irony of Maragall's Barcelona is that the site chosen for the thwarted Plan de Ribera has now been usurped by the luxury housing development of the Vila Olímpica. Supported by the same people who had opposed the Plan de Ribera, the Vila Olímpica, with its large marina and enormously tall hotel towers, is one of the city's most expensive districts, with high prices that must seem obscene to the older inhabitants of the still-decayed Poble Nou: it is a wealthy ghetto that might one day become an urban fortress in the middle of hostile surroundings.

So many of the changes made in Maragall's Barcelona are wholly in the spirit of the *fachadismo* noted by Unamuno nearly a century before. The idea of making purely cosmetic improvements to the city was even emphasized by the use of a cosmetics-inspired slogan to try to encourage the owners of buildings to restore their property: 'Barcelona, posa't guapa' ('Barcelona, make yourself beautiful') was the message beneath a picture of a woman applying make-up. Shortly afterwards a book was published entitled *Barcelona Guapa*, featuring beautiful women posing naked outside the city's famous old and modern sights.

Though naked women and women with heavy make-up are deemed essential to the image of 'Beautiful Barcelona', prostitutes apparently are not. The up-market prostitutes who accept credit cards were forcibly removed from their favourite stamping-ground near the Barça Football Stadium and placed – for at least the duration of Olympic year – in a distant and unprofitable suburb. Meanwhile, the traditional home of Barcelona's lower-priced prostitutes is being affected by the campaign to clear up Barcelona's old town. Whole streets of the notorious Barrio Chino are being rebuilt, thus lessening the unrelievedly sordid look of an area much admired by those who come here with a hankering for the Barcelona of Jean Genet. The underlying social problems, however, have only partially been dealt with, the nearby Plaça Reial, for instance, being now no less of a junkies' meeting-place than it was in the past, despite its recent facelift. A great deal of medieval Barcelona remains a muggers' paradise, but the tourist showpiece of the Gothic quarter gives little hint of this. It has been subjected to so much restoration that it has acquired the innocuous look of a large, outdoor museum.

The aspect of the 'new Barcelona' that best illustrates the mentality of *fachadismo* is the much publicized mania for 'design', 'design' being now the hallmark of Catalan cultural identity. Every type of establishment, from shops to petrol stations, seems to be competing for the awards annually presented by the Federación de Arquitectos y Diseños, whose acronym of FAD, in English, about sums it up. The strange phenomenon of the 'designer bar' originated in Barcelona and has a seriousness lacking even in fashionable Madrid. The tourist board has produced a detailed map entitled 'Drink and Design', and there are a number of recent guidebooks on the city that discuss bars purely in terms of their design rather than their atmosphere: this emphasis proves often to be the right one, for the most visually striking places are frequently antiseptic in character, an inevitable consequence perhaps of attracting a clientele heavily made up of design-obsessed drinkers of mineral water. At least Unamuno's complaint that the Catalans ignore their drains for the sake of their façades is not applicable to these bars, which attach so much importance to the design of their toilets and washrooms that these are often the features that can clinch an establishment's reputation.

As one shits in the designer cubicle, it is worth reflecting again on the polarity between *seny* and *rauxa*. It's a polarity that might come to mind when reading Eduardo Mendoza's hilarious *No News of Gurb* (1990), which is set in a Barcelona of the near future and tells the story of an extraterrestrial's search for the elusive and equally extraterrestrial Gurb. The search takes the protagonist through all the city's fashionable bars, and details are given of whether or not the place has received, or was a finalist for, the prestigious FAD award. Eventually, at 4.21 a.m., after visiting a succession of designer bars that includes the Poble Nou bar which won the 'FAD award for the renovation of urban spaces', the protagonist throws up in the Plaça Urquinaona, and then in the Plaça de Catalunya, and again on the pedestrian crossing at the corner of Muntaner and Aragón, and finally in the taxi taking him home after his nocturnal ordeal through a designer hell.

IN RECENT years Barcelona has become the epitome of the 'new Spain'. The unstuffy traveller, fascinated by modernity, tends to think of Barcelona as representing all that is exciting in Spain, just as earlier travellers, searching for romantic Spain, found Barcelona to be what Edmondo de Amicis described in 1880 as the 'least Spanish' of Spanish cities. Madrid may not have lived up to romantic expectations of Spain, but at least it had its *majos* and bullfighters, its austere and unmistakably Castilian surroundings, and its sense of remoteness from the rest of Europe. By contrast, the appeal of eighteenth- and early nineteenth-century Barcelona had nothing to do with the unfamiliar and the exotic, but lay instead almost exclusively in the town's balmy climate, and its lush and pleasant situation overlooking the Mediterranean. Comparisons with French towns were frequently made, its industries and its port reminding some travellers of Marseilles, its temperate and agreeable climate and situation reminding others of the then flourishing winter resort of Nice. Théophile Gautier, walking through the streets of Barcelona, almost felt that he was in France, a feeling that helped him to acclimatize to the transition from 'exotic Spain' to his more prosaic, if also more civilized, native country.

The excellently preserved Gothic architecture of Barcelona was not at first widely appreciated, not even by the middle of the nineteenth century, when medievalism was at its height. The Catalan Gothic is unusually austere, which is perhaps why so pronounced a medievalist as Augustus Hare could describe the streets of Barcelona's Gothic quarter as 'thoroughly dull and unpicturesque'. But the city's greatest failings, in the eyes of most nineteenth-century travellers, were to be found in its modern, industrial and cosmopolitan aspects, aspects that were totally at variance with romantic notions of Spain. These failings would become more apparent than ever by the end of the nineteenth century, when they seem to have induced in the English traveller Edward Hutton an almost clinical depression. 'Alone of all the cities of Spain,' he wrote in 1904,

> I found Barcelona hateful; and even now I cannot think of it without a sort of distress . . . It is a city of the North, full of restlessness, an unnatural energy, haunted by the desire for gain, absolutely modern in its expression, that has made one of the oldest cities in Spain a sort of Manchester, almost without smoke it is true, but full of mean streets and the immense tyranny of machines that for the most part Spain has escaped so fortunately.

The qualities Hutton found hateful about Barcelona were among those that contributed to the city's growing popularity from about the 1930s onwards. Writers of the Existentialist generation, such as Genet, went out of their way to search for the more squalid aspects of Barcelona, and found nirvana in the absinthe and easy sex of the Barrio Chino. More healthy minded travellers, such as Rose Macaulay, enjoyed the place for its cosmopolitanism and liveliness, qualities that were especially salient in the post-war years, when other Spanish cities such as Madrid bore more visibly than Barcelona the repressive marks of the Franco regime: 'After Barcelona,' Macaulay noted in 1949, 'Madrid seems almost a genteel and soundless city' – a comment that could hardly have been made in any other period. Whereas travellers failed generally to perceive the intense cultural life of post-war Madrid (largely because this life was a literary one, hidden away in the *tertulias*), they enthused about the cultural vitality of Barcelona, a city that had won much attention in the 1920s and 1930s for having nurtured such distinctive talents as Miró, Pau Casals, Josep Lluis Sert, and Picasso. In the 1950s, 1960s and early 1970s, the continuing presence here of outstanding younger artists such as Tàpies, the beginnings of a design boom initiated by Studio Per, and the avant-garde theatrical productions of Nuria Espert and Albert Boadella led the outside world almost to think of Barcelona as the cultural conscience of Spain.

But it was above all the renewal of interest in the buildings of Gaudí that gave momentum to Barcelona's rapidly rising fortunes as a tourist destination. In the 1920s and 1930s Gaudí's work, along with art-nouveau architecture in general, had reached its nadir of popularity, and there were many people, Catalans included, who would have wished, like Orwell, for an anarchist bomb to have destroyed the unfinished Sagrada Família. Evelyn Waugh, virtually alone among the English visitors of this period, bravely defended Gaudí, but argued that the completion of his culminating monument should be left to a millionaire who was not 'quite right in the head'. The Surrealists, headed by Salvador Dalí, emphasized the notion of Gaudí as the mad genius, and were instrumental in encouraging the growing fashion for his works in the 1940s and 1950s. Gaudí's architecture still remained improperly understood, however, and most visitors to the city during this period would probably have argued with Rose Macaulay's view that the buildings were highly entertaining while being little more than 'magnificent extravaganzas of bad taste'. The Gaudí craze, particularly among the young, took off in earnest with the advent of mass tourism to the Costa Brava, and the arrival in the 1960s of LSD and psychedelia. Largely unaware that their idol of unorthodoxy had been a man of notoriously bigoted and reactionary views, these new admirers liked Gaudí because he was 'really weird', and many of them placed posters of his architecture alongside paintings by Dalí, engravings by Escher, and the face of Che Guevara.

Gaudí survived all this misplaced adulation to become more

widely popular than ever, with people of every kind admitting him as their favourite architect. By the 1980s Gaudímania had spread with unprecedented frenzy to Japan, where his buildings seem to be loved for being diametrically opposed to that country's traditionally linear, serene and horizontally proportioned architecture. Gaudí's Casa BatLló, the most expensive town house ever to have featured on the world's property market, is currently up for sale for many millions. It is likely to be bought by a Japanese businessman.

The popularity of Barcelona has grown in tandem with that of Gaudí, with just a brief hiatus in the years immediately following Franco's death, when world attention was momentarily distracted by the rise of Madrid's *movida*. For so much of its history Barcelona has been under the domination of Madrid, and there is perhaps a certain poetic justice in the way in which it has now firmly succeeded in convincing the world that it is the livelier and more interesting of the two cities. With Olympic year in mind, nearly forty guides and other books were brought out in English, one of these being an exemplary 500-page monograph by the Australian art critic Robert Hughes.

Barcelona is one of Europe's best-loved cities, but its admirers can be divided into two main camps, one of which is represented by the fashion-obsessed journalist Robert Elms, who believes the city to be witnessing a new era as culturally exciting as that of the turn-of-the-century. The other camp is occupied mainly by middle-aged men – including Hughes himself – who fondly remember Barcelona in the 1960s, when they spent much of their time either eating seafood in the now defunct dives of Barceloneta, or else following in Genet's footsteps among the artists, writers, sailors and down-and-outs who hung out in the seedier bars of the Barrio Chino. They are highly critical of Barcelona's more recent developments, and feel that the city has become a colder, more superficial and anaemic place than before; they ridicule the current obsession with 'design', and are generally in sympathy with the Peruvian writer Mario Vargas Llosa's controversial view that the present mood of militant Catalanism – which allows no criticism of what is happening in Barcelona, and encourages Catalan-only labels to be appended to the works of art in the city's museums – has managed to turn Barcelona from a truly cosmopolitan centre into a mean-spirited provincial one.

The recently inaugurated Torres de Ávila Bar encapsulates the gulf between the two opposed camps. A piece of futuristic kitsch built by Mariscal and Alfredo Arribas within the mock medieval entrance gate of the city's Poble Espanyol, the bar is for Robert Elms 'a hedonist's wonderland' and the ultimate symbol of the 'new Spain'. For Robert Hughes it is 'the most seriously unenjoyable *boîte de nuit* in Spain, or maybe the world'. Hughes is a rather more persuasive critic than Elms, but, in attacking the likes of Mariscal, Bofill and other fashionable froth, he unwittingly reveals at one point in his book the way in which each generation will always find something to criticize in the succeeding one.

Nostalgic for the Barcelona of his youth, Hughes rejects the 'latest frippery of Catalo-Californian cuisine' in favour of the 'ancient, dark taste' of the meat and seafood stew known as a *mar i muntanya*. Unfortunately, Hughes does not realize that this 'ancient' dish was in fact a Barceloneta invention of the 1950s, and one moreover that had incurred at the time the strong disapproval of the leading Catalan writer and gastronome, Josep Pla. For Pla the *mar i muntanya* was just a tourist fashion reflecting the decadence of traditional Catalan cuisine.

OVERWEIGHT, balding, cynical and drily humorous, Pepe Carvalho is a middle-aged *bon viveur* and Communist who shares many of the views expressed on his native city by foreigners such as Vargas Llosa and Robert Hughes.

Pepe Carvalho is Spain's best-loved detective. The fictional creation of Vázquez Montalbán, he emerged from a shady political past shortly after the death of Franco, and has been commenting since then on all the changes that have befallen Barcelona, observing these with a mournful demeanour that recalls his Czech contemporary, Lieutenant Borůvka, the detective hero of Josef Škvorecký. He lives in the upper reaches of suburban Vallvidriera, which gives him a panoramic view of the city, as well as a quiet place of retreat after the urban onslaught below. Unmarried, he has been conducting over the years an on-and-off affair with the proverbial prostitute with the heart of gold, Charo, a woman who is becoming as much of an anachronism in the new Barcelona as Carvalho himself.

As with Britain's detective bachelor, Inspector Morse, temptations are continually crossing Carvalho's path in the form of glamorous women met in the course of his investigations. But just as Morse prefers in the end to listen to opera rather than to become entangled in relationships, so too does Carvalho reject emotional attachments in favour of bizarre pastimes such as burning books in irritation at much contemporary thought and literature. A more substantial pleasure is derived from his love of eating and cooking. Not only does this sublimate the sensuality of his nature, but also momentarily obliterates the problems of a world that for him is sinking rapidly into global mediocrity.

Carvalho once savoured Barcelona with the relish of Galdós for Madrid, but the democratic process for which he had fought for so long is making his city ever blander. With the approach of the Olympic year, he finds that his socialist companions of old have abandoned their ideals and are busy 'preparing showcases for prize athletes from the worlds of sport, business and industry'. It is less with pleasure than with masochistic curiosity that he continues to wander around this city, dismayed as much by the disappearance of the old and familiar as by the burgeoning of such silly ephemera as Mariscal's giant harbourfront prawn, a work described by Hughes as a *falla* that, unfortunately, is incombustible.

Carvalho's reflections on the changing Barcelona take up many of the pages of the latest Carvalho novel, which was published in English under the opportunistic title, *An Olympic Death*, but had originally appeared in Spanish as *The Greek Labyrinth*. As with many of Vázquez Montalbán's novels, the reader's attention is held above all by the wit and wisdom of its opinions, and by the stylistic flair with which they are expressed. These provide the bones to support a particularly thin and flimsy plot involving a French couple's search for a young, beautiful and bisexual Greek painter. In helping them find the boy Carvalho is dragged into terrain filled dangerously for him with 'Olympian painters, Olympic wheeler-dealers, dealers in Olympic culture'.

The search through this Olympic labyrinth nears its conclusion at a 1960s theme party at which a young American woman, writing a dissertation on life in post-Franco Spain, is taking notes as she watches a group of hippy look-alikes embark on a musical homage to the 'gathering of Canet', the Catalan Woodstock.

The night is far advanced when a clue is finally given as to the whereabouts of the young Greek. Carvalho offers there and then to accompany the French couple to the place where the man might be hiding. Once outside in the street, however, Carvalho baffles the couple by telling them the name of the place they are going to. They think for a moment that they are being spirited away to the land of Mount Olympus, but in fact they are being led no further than a district 3 kilometres north-east of Mariscal's prawn. They are going to Icaria – Icaria, Barcelona.

The original, Greek Icaria is a small Aegean island named after Daedalus' ill-fated son, whose body was thrown here by waves, and then buried by Hercules. An island associated with a figure whose wings had melted after flying too close to the sun would not seem the first place to spring to mind when devising an ideal society. But, in the 1830s, an eccentric French philosopher, Étienne Cabet, decided to give the name Icaria to one such Utopia which he had dreamed up after a period of intensive reading in the British Museum. The resulting book, *A Voyage to Icaria*, was published in 1834, nearly ten years before Cabet finally attempted to put his dream into practice by sailing off with sixty-nine of his disciples to start an experimental colony near New Orleans. Three of these disciples were Catalans who had belonged to a Barcelona Icarian group founded by, among others, a future leading light in the Catalan musical revival, Josep Anselm Clavé, and a socialist editor and inventor called Narciso Monturiol i Estarriol.

The colony, as might be imagined, proved as disastrous as Icarus' flight, a special drawback being the swampy, mosquito-ridden land on which the would-be Utopia had been established. In the meantime Monturiol waited patiently in Barcelona for news of what was happening, and was encouraged by a false report from one of the Catalans saying that Icaria had so far been an enormous success and would one day be the 'centre of all knowledge and understanding'.

The settlement was already breaking up, with its founder on the point of dying, when Monturiol wrote to Cabet to ask if he could join it. His letter went unanswered. Monturiol later directed his imagination into pioneering the Catalan submarine, in which capacity he would possibly serve as the model for Captain Nemo in Jules Verne's *Twenty Thousand Leagues under the Sea*. As for the vision of Icaria, this continued for a while to raise men's hopes, but only in Catalonia, where the name of the failed Utopia was later bequeathed to the working-class district that grew up in the 1950s just to the east of the Ciutadella Park. While the workers dreamed of Icaria, their bosses preferred to think of Manchester, a place that symbolized for them their dreams of a prosperous industrial future.

By the turn of the century, the 'Catalan Manchester' had disintegrated into an enormous slum, and the city fathers, worried by the socialist memories attached to the name Icaria, had given the place the less controversial and more prosaic name of Poble Nou, or New Town. But Icaria had not vanished without trace, for its memory was preserved in Poble Nou's long avenue, known to this day as the Avinguda d'Icaria, which in turn has provided the Vila Olímpica with its official name of Nova Icaria, the New Icaria.

On their nocturnal journey to Icaria, Carvalho's group skirts the edge of the future Olympic village, which, in its half-built state, appears to Carvalho as a cross between Dresden and Brasília. It is a devastated, bulldozed landscape lying 'between the bare, ugly sea and the terrorized left-overs of what remained of Poble Nou'. As they continue towards their final destination they would have passed the old cemetery of Barcelona, which blocks the eastern end of the Avinguda d'Icaria, and had been built in 1818 in what was then open countryside. This neo-classical, symmetrically arranged complex, with its obelisks, pyramid-shaped mausoleums and pedimented chapel inspired by Hansen's revolutionary cathedral at Copenhagen, had been in its day a model of modernity, a reflection of the Enlightenment ideals of the city's planners in the early nineteenth century. Converted later into a civic cemetery, then badly neglected, it is today one of Barcelona's more haunting ruins, overgrown, crumbling, deserted and with a large sign prohibiting the morbidly minded visitor from taking photographs. It is a *memento mori* preparing the visitor for the decayed industrial landscape beyond, where Carvalho's group find themselves entering a labyrinth of empty avenues, abandoned factory buildings, dangling cables, discarded car bodies, broken office furniture, rusting rail lines, and piles of cardboard boxes that have been moulded by the weather into white mountains.

But, in the midst of this apparently deserted world of factories and warehouses, Carvalho's clients discover to their surprise a hive of nocturnal activity. A group of photographic models disappears into one of the buildings, while from another come the distant sounds of a ballet corps gyrating to rock music. Then, in a dark, hall-like space, they come across an artist working on what seems, to Carvalho's horror, to be a gigantic artichoke. The face of the artist is recognized by Carvalho as being that of someone 'fairly well known around town', but for the moment he cannot place the name. 'Marcial, or Marisco . . . something like that.'

Only a short time later does it dawn on Carvalho that the man in front of him is 'the creator of the strange shellfish erected at the Moll de la Fusta, the smiling prawn that towered over the little bars like a monster out of some Japanese film where the monsters are all conscious of being *papier mâché*'.

MARISCAL DOES indeed have his studio in Poble Nou, in an industrial complex largely given over to designers. By the early 1990s writers on modern Spain had begun to drop in there to pay their respects to the great Mariscal, just as nineteenth-century travellers to Italy had rarely passed Venice without visiting the studio of the neo-classical sculptor Canova. Dutifully, one sunny, late-September morning, I took my place in the long line of Mariscal interviewers.

I had prepared myself carefully for the occasion, and was

determined not to ask the sort of question that is put to him with such wearying regularity that one could hardly expect anything but the pattest replies – questions that probe for his views on Barcelona's obsession with design, or on the cultural changes in post-Franco Spain, or on the expenditure of so much talent on the creation of bars and nightclubs. I wanted to try a slightly different line of questioning, and was interested, for instance, in discussing the *cursi*, and whether or not he saw his witty and irreverent creations as a comment on Spanish bad taste.

I would also have liked to have found out if he agreed with any of the criticisms of the new Barcelona voiced by the likes of Vázquez Montalbán. On this subject, however, I knew that he would almost certainly be very guarded, for he was now heavily dependent on the patronage of his friend Maragall. In earlier days this former radical had been quite outspoken, but he had learned his lesson after a newspaper had quoted him as saying that Catalonia was ruled by a dwarf (a reference to the president Jordi Pujol), and that the 'problem with Catalonia is the Catalans'.

The former engineering works used by Mariscal and other designers looked from the outside little different from the other examples of grimy, redbrick, industrial architecture that filled the austere, rubbish-filled grid of wide, empty streets extending to the metro station of Poble Nou. The first hint that I might be reaching somewhere special was the modest corner bar, which at one time must have been an ordinary, squalid dive, but now had a menu outside brandishing the Olympic 'Cobi' mascot and listing designer salads and various brands of mineral water.

Once across the factory threshold, I had the sensation of being either in a museum of industrial archaeology, or else in one of those recent Barcelona squares or parks where the ruins of old factory chimneys have been tastefully incorporated into the over-all design. A labyrinth of designers' studios had tunnelled its way behind every wall, just like the complex of craft shops that have been crammed into London's Camden Lock. Mariscal's was the most outwardly discreet, its entrance marked by a pale-green metal door and a tiny label inscribed not with a name but with a characteristically Mariscal squiggle.

I pushed the bell at the appointed hour of twelve o'clock. I was now in punctual Catalonia, and, contrary to my normal Spanish practice, had fixed my meeting several weeks before. The metal door gently opened like a safe, the treasure inside being a long and open-plan shuttered space with atmospheric lighting and rich blue walls. Mariscal has claimed that he enjoys the confusion caused by having to work with many people, and that a certain amount of chaos is essential to him. But the studio exuded an atmosphere of calm and efficiency far greater than I had noticed in most offices. The mood was reflected in the young publicity manager who came to meet me, wearing a red uniform, and projecting the amicable blandness of an air hostess. She had a quieter but otherwise almost identical assistant who joined us as we sat in a small conference room ringed with Cobi dolls.

I waited for Mariscal to appear, but it became obvious after a few minutes that I was going to have to endure a preliminary session with the two hostesses. The room I was in had the same function as a decompression chamber, helping normal people such as myself to adjust to the rarified atmosphere. The women saw that I was not only nervous, but also the sort of person whose friends eat Mariscal's visiting cards.

They tried to calm and indoctrinate me, but, as with the Muzak meant to relax anxious passengers before a flight, their droning, monotonous voices succeeded only in gradually working me up into a frenzy. A large blue catalogue of Mariscal's work had been placed on the desk in front of me, and its pages were turned one by one with a reverence and carefulness normally reserved for the handling of valuable incunabula. Slowly, the over-familiar story of Mariscal's career was related to me in a commentary that was little more than a reading of the catalogue's captions.

'. . . Mariscal now moves from Valencia to Barcelona . . . Mariscal continues to work with underground comics . . . Mariscal shares a flat in the Plaça Reial with the abstract painter Miquel Barceló . . . Mariscal designs his first bar . . . Mariscal is taken up by the Vinçon store . . . Mariscal breaks out into furniture, ceramics, textiles, jewellery . . . Mariscal designs Cobi, the Olympic mascot . . .'

I've always enjoyed Mariscal's works. The colours and vitality of his childish graphics cheer me up, as do his comic creatures, called *Garriris*, his Scooter-shaped office chair, his 'Tio Pepe Seat', his *Garriri* Seat, his diagonally poised glass trolley, his air fans that cut slices through columns, his plate marked 'By Appointment to the *Garriris*', and even his giant prawn. But it was not until I had been subjected to over an hour's session with his assistants that I had realized the extent to which such whimsy was meant to be taken seriously. The fun was now over.

The session, however, was not. The much-awaited closing of the last page of the catalogue was followed only by a display of Cobiana stretching back to the original prototype conceived over three years before. Cobi plates, Cobi statuettes, Cobi ashtrays, Cobi glasses and Cobi T-shirts began to cover the table. I was increasingly obvious that I was not going to meet their creator, who appeared to be using the two women to fob off the most recent crop of journalists. I was angered by his tactics, but began to feel as indifferent to the probability of not seeing him as I was by the discovery of what kind of creature Cobi actually is. Cobi is not a cat, as Robert Elms thinks; nor is he a bear or a malformed *Garriri*. Cobi is in fact a dog, 'of a type much loved in Catalunya'.

There was a moment of dramatic tension when we got up from our chairs, walked into the main studio, and headed towards a darkened corner where a man who was unquestionably Mariscal was sitting. The moment passed, however, when we changed course and sat down in front of a video screen to watch *Cobi Discovers the Lost Planet*. A technical fault happily prevented the film from being shown, and for the first and only time in our meeting the two women showed some sort of emotion, and apologized profusely for the failure of the video. They were so sorry that they decided to show me slides of every single one of the illustrations that had gone into the video's making. They began explaining, flatly, everything Cobi was doing on the screen, anxious that I should not miss out on a single detail of his exciting adventures.

'. . . Here you see Cobi at home, relaxing with his friends the *Garriris* . . . In this picture Cobi is getting into a space rocket . . . His woman friend comes with him . . . Now Cobi has left the space craft and is floating in space . . .'

My glance wandered over to Mariscal's distant desk, where the designer himself could be seen at work.

'. . . As Cobi travels back from the lost planet he becomes happy when he sets eyes once more on Barcelona . . .'

The desk was made of glass and glowed in the surrounding darkness. Mariscal rose from his seat, opened the shutters slightly, and returned to make a few quick gestures with his brush. A shaft of sunlight sharply illuminated his shock of black hair and turned him briefly into a Rembrandt alchemist.

As Cobi's adventures continued in our corner of the studio, I tried to look more closely at Mariscal's large head, but it moved continually, and eventually vanished out of sight, whisked off by a Japanese businessman in a dark suit. I had not even shaken the great man's hand.

SUCCESSFULLY accomplishing his quest for the young Greek in Poble Nou, Pepe Carvalho returns home to Vallvidriera. I decided to follow him there, to shake off memories of my thwarted voyage to Icaria, and to climb up to a quiet and old-fashioned suburb where I would be able to look down on Barcelona from a great height, and reduce to a distant smudge the dregs of its industry and design. I also looked forward to meeting Carvalho himself, who would surely treat me better than Mariscal had done and have no hesitation about speaking his mind.

The initial signs were promising, beginning with the immediate appointment I was able to fix up with him simply through a quick phone call from Poble Nou: no question of booking a time several weeks beforehand. Then, on the turn-of-the-century funicular that climbs up to Vallvidriera, I met up by chance with his young Andalusian cleaner, whom I overheard telling a friend how 'kind and gentle' her new employer was. I struck up a conversation with her, and we continued talking as we walked together towards his house, following an uphill road fragrant with pines and dotted with villas that stared out over an immense urban panorama. 'He is basically a very straightforward, unpretentious person,' she said, 'very different from the intellectual who appears on television.'

Pepe Carvalho is of course the fictional *alter ego* of Vázquez Montalbán, who also happens to live in Vallvidriera, be a long-standing member of the Communist Party and have an obsessive passion for gastronomy. Through his fictional creation, Vázquez Montalbán is not only able to live out middle-aged, Existentialist fantasies about being free, unmarried, and faced with daily dangers, but he can also express in entertaining and accessible fashion his deeply felt and controversial views on food, politics and the new Spain. No one else has spoken or written so prolifically as he has on the failings of Maragall's Barcelona and the Spain of 1992.

With the Olympics nearing, his enemies multiplied, and he was repeatedly branded in the press as a party-pooper; at the same time, any journalist who wanted an articulate alternative view on 1992 invariably went to see him. I failed to understand how he could always find time to talk to people, for his productivity is far greater than Mariscal's – and puts to shame that of most other writers.

Having begun his career essentially as a political journalist and food writer, he then wrote the first of the Pepe Carvalho books before trying his hand at serious fiction; later he branched out into the theatre, and had a recent success with a musical about a Barcelona cabaret artist, *Flor de Nit*. He has also done the screenplay for the film version of *The Greek Labyrinth*; the director of which was amazed at the way the writer produced the script while completing his political novel, *Galíndez*, and compiling a guidebook to Moscow. Vázquez Montalbán is certainly one of Spain's greatest living writers, but his work has a characteristic common to much Spanish literature and one that lessens its chances of being widely appreciated outside Spain. His enormous *œuvre* is memorable not for specific books but as an entity that cannot be separated from his life and personality.

The modern villa where he lives lies almost under the shadow of Norman Foster's newly completed Communications Tower, a bold, soaring structure with a modular framework and an under-lying philosophy of achieving the maximum of effect with the minimum of structural means.

'We're just about getting used to it,' commented the woman

who had accompanied me up the hill. Entering the house, she showed me into a spacious sitting-room reminiscent of that of some successful socialist intellectual living in London's Hampstead or New York's Greenwich Village. Lined with books, and beautifully decorated with African sculptures, restful ceramics and other works of art recalling the modernist tastes of the 1950s and 1960s, the room featured also a small safe marked 'CIGARS'.

The writer came downstairs to invite me up into his study, where a newspaper photographer was completing a session with him. While waiting for this to end I looked carefully at my surroundings, noting a small bust of Lenin and a number of humorous sketches and photos, including a photographic mock-up of Prince Charles embracing a naked Lady Di. Above his desk he kept books apparently relating to his current projects, one of which I knew to be a fictionalized life of Franco, a subject he was researching with the aid of an impressive array of historical and socio-political works. On the other side of the study – and an immutable feature of the room, so I was later told – was a specialist library on food and drink rivalling the one the late Elizabeth David presented to London University.

After the photographer had gone, Vázquez Montalbán slumped back into his chair and called his maid to bring up some cognac and a bottle of malt whisky. Even without the help of the whisky, I felt myself relaxing in the writer's company, and had the immediate impression of being with somebody whom I already intimately knew. Inevitably Pepe Carvalho came to mind, and from that moment onwards I have never been able to distinguish between Vázquez Montalbán and his fictional creation.

Bespectacled, flabby, with a drooping moustache and a thin covering of black hair attached to a shiny ball of a head, Vázquez Montalbán spoke in a deep, soft voice, his features breaking out into an occasional hesitant smile before sinking back into an expression of weary pensiveness. His whole manner denoted an endearing mixture of affability, shyness and healthy scepticism. The words with which he opened our conversation corresponded exactly to my feelings on emerging from Mariscal's studio. 'Culturally, you know, Barcelona today is a disaster.'

My own viewpoint on the new Barcelona lay, like my age,

somewhere in between his and Robert Elms's. I timidly suggested that the city had at least produced in recent years some stunning architecture, not least the Foster Tower behind his home. But he did not concede even on this point.

'Architects today', he said, 'seem to have forgotten that architecture has a function. Buildings shouldn't be thought of just as beautiful objects.'

The conversation moved on from the cultural disaster of Maragall's Barcelona to the provincialism of Pujol's Catalonia, then to the sad decline of recent Spanish literature. He singled out for solitary praise the young novelist Antonio Muñoz Molina, whose enormous new work, *The Polish Rider*, evoked for him the 'collective consciousness of the Franco era' in a way remarkable for somebody 'too young really to have experienced this era'. Otherwise Spanish writers were condemned for their lack of content, and for being 'too literary and precious'. Travel-writers were not exempt, and he felt that no good travel books had been written on Spain since the 1950s, when the *tremendista* generation had addressed the shocking social problems of areas such as Las Hurdes and Extremadura. As the conversation continued, and growing numbers of recent writers and current cultural fads fell victim to his censures, I appreciated more how his detective hero has little hesitation in consigning books 'to the everlasting bonfire'.

Though Vázquez Montalbán had himself come increasingly under attack in recent months, his own highly critical views on the various subjects we touched on did not seem to reflect any bitterness on his part, but revealed instead a taste for polemics and controversy, as well as a nostalgia for an earlier, more repressive era when issues were passionately debated and hope was placed in some future democratic society. I could easily understand how he had thrived as a political dissident under Franco, and how he could recently have claimed – jokingly – that people were better off in opposition to Franco than they were now, under democracy.

When eventually we got round to talking about food, I thought that at last we had reached an uncontroversial subject. I was proved wrong when he pulled out from one of his shelves a recent book he had written, *Against Gourmets*. Criticism about food snobbery, the vacuous chic of many Spanish restaurants and other related topics were none the less skimmed over when the two of us launched with gusto into an exchange of recent gastronomic experiences. I mentioned the Denver in Cartagena, and he was anxious to discover if the combination of pig's testicles and cod's roe was a happy one. He enthused over the rabbit and rice dishes of that region, before mentioning in an aside that he himself had Murcian blood, and that his grandfather's family had been among those numerous and much abused Murcian immigrants to Barcelona in the post-war years.

I refrained from asking if this Murcian connection had any bearing on his attitude towards Barcelona today, but I could not help saying how happy I had been to find in Cartagena a city that seemed so distant from all the hype of 1992. The conversation was brought full circle, and we were back once more to *that* subject. Vázquez Montalbán referred to the current mood of 'triumphalism', which he said reminded him of the Franco period.

'No one', he stressed, 'is allowed any longer to criticize anything. No one can speak out against what is happening in Spain today, no one can suggest that all is not right with the country. And what is true of Spain is becoming progressively true of the rest of Europe. One nation, one currency, one idea.'

BETWEEN MY visit to Vázquez Montalbán in the autumn of 1991 and the closure of the Olympics in the following year, the writer found himself increasingly on a limb in Catalonia, where the 'spirit of triumphalism' would continue unchecked. Significantly, on the day the Olympic torch arrived in triumph at the Catalan coast, a lone official was heckled and booed for giving a speech in Spanish rather than Catalan; but of these jeers not a mention would be made in the next day's papers, which referred only to the unmitigated success of the whole occasion.

But miracles also happen. Who would have predicted that in the 'magic year' of 1992, the Barça football team would win first the Catalan Cup, then the Spanish League, and finally the European Cup? Even their captain became so convinced of the miraculous that he felt obliged to go with his team to offer their thanks to the Black Virgin at Montserrat, a place he and his companions had not visited since childhood.

And the greatest miracle of all: the Olympics themselves. Few could have hoped for an Olympic month so unclouded by trouble and terrorism; and not even the greatest optimist could have imagined that Spain would have gained quite so many medals. Was it not a triumph, and not an illusion of triumph, when Fermín Cacho touched the finishing post in the 1500 metres, or when Luis Peñalver – 'El Superman Murciano' – became, at the end of the decathlon, the greatest all-round sportsman in the history of Spain?

Spain had finally come of age as a sporting nation. The achievements and culture of the Catalan nation were now recognized by the whole world. Wild promises had been kept, and a vision fulfilled. The purveyors of triumphalism had emerged from the labyrinth and could enjoy, for a brief moment, a satisfying sense of order and rational progression.

17

A Vision of the Future

FACING away from the sea, on the northern slopes of Vallvidriera, is an eighteenth-century villa rising above extensive parkland carpeted with Mediterranean pines. The beauty of the wooded parkland was celebrated early this century in the verse of Joan Maragall, while the villa itself was the final residence of Maragall's great poetic predecessor, Jacint Verdaguer.

Wasted away by fasting and poverty, prematurely wrinkled, and with eyes that were exhausted from too much reading, the fifty-seven-year-old Verdaguer arrived at the Villa Joana on 17 May 1902, hoping that the clear air and peaceful surroundings would help him to recover his ailing health. The villa, owned by a wealthy admirer of his, had an upper terrace, where the poet would lie on a sedan dining-chair, enjoying on clear days the distant sight of the strange rock formations of Montserrat.

A man of peasant origins who had risen in the world through the priesthood, Verdaguer had acquired by this later stage of his life an ambivalent look characterized by an Italian journalist as that of a simple and benign country priest who was 'afflicted by some inner pain'. Formerly the great hope of Catalan nationalists, Verdaguer had by now lost many of his supporters among the Catalan clergy and industrialists, but was gaining instead the growing admiration of the intellectual Left, who saw in him a misunderstood victim of the Establishment. Verdaguer's immense popular appeal had fortunately survived all this, and when he eventually died – only three and a half weeks after his arrival at the Villa Joana – unprecedented crowds gathered in Barcelona for the funeral. On its way to the cemetery of Montjuich, the cortège traversed the whole length of the Ramblas, passing on one side the palace where Verdaguer had lived during his years of glory as chaplain to the Marquis of Comillas, and on the other the church of the Betlem, where, towards the end of his life, the disgraced and impoverished poet–priest had been allowed once again to say Mass. With the death of Verdaguer, the Catalan renaissance had lost both its greatest writer and a poet whose early achievement had signified to many that the Catalan language as an instrument of national self-definition had come into its own.

Whereas the socialist followers of Étienne Cabet had placed their hopes in an island named after Icarus, the conservatives associated with nineteenth-century Catalanism had found their vision of the future in an epic poem inspired by Atlantis. The genesis of this work dates from Verdaguer's student days at the seminary at Vic, where he undertook a number of long, ambitious poems, including an unfinished epic on Columbus. Several of these early works were well received at the poetry competitions known as the Jocs Florals, which were held in Barcelona and represented the most important outlet for those who were re-newing Catalan as a literary language. The competitions were a revival of a medieval tradition initiated by the troubadours, whose example was also followed by the Félibres of Provence, a literary group headed by Verdaguer's future friend, Frédéric Mistral.

The Félibres, whose ideals were closely similar to those of the Catalan Renaissance, used to hold open-air meetings outside a château near Avignon. Inspired by reports of these gatherings, Verdaguer and a group of fellow seminarians at Vic founded a literary circle called Esbart in 1867. The members used to recite their poems around the fountain of a farmyard on the outskirts of Verdaguer's native village of Folgueroles. Alone of his generation, Verdaguer went beyond the mere level of sentimental medieval pastiche and – in a way common to the finest verse of the Félibriges – forged a persuasive nationalist mythology through a potent mixture of Christian imagery, and Classical and Celtic legends.

The destruction of Atlantis, and the consequent restoration by Columbus of the 'cosmic balance', would form the basis of the long-planned *Atlántida* (1878). In this mythical reworking of history, Verdaguer provided the Catalan people with the first literary epic dealing with their origins. For his next epic, named after the Pyrenean peak of Canigó, he indulged to the full in the nationalist activity of *excursionisme*, and undertook numerous trips into the Catalan Pyrenees to research the various legends surrounding the medieval foundation of Catalonia.

In 1896, one year after the work's publication, Verdaguer was crowned 'National Poet of Catalonia' in a ceremony officiated by the Bishop of Vic in the ancient Pyrenean abbey at Ripoll. But, after attaining such a position of eminence, Verdaguer immediately suffered from a mental and physical crisis which led him to fall foul of the Church authorities, who sent him on a rest cure to a sanctuary near Vic, banned him from preaching in Barcelona, and finally suspended him from the priesthood. By the time he was pardoned, his verse had already begun to go out of fashion in Catalan literary circles, to whom the heroic ideals of the Catalan renaissance had come to seem excessively quaint.

Verdaguer would always be remembered for his role in the renewal of the Catalan language, and, in the aftermath of the Civil War, when the language was repressed, he was turned into a symbol of the Catalan nation by the exiled Catalan intelligentsia. But are his works much read today, particularly among the new post-Franco generation of Catalans? I put this question to the director of the Verdaguer museum in the Villa Joana. Naturally, she was very defensive about his reputation, and said that a new critical interest was being shown in his works, and that a group of young scholars was currently preparing the first comprehensive edition of his *œuvre*. She predicted a forthcoming surge in popularity in Verdaguer, and, as if to stress his universality as a poet, mentioned the influence of his work on the verse of the Italian writer and film director Pasolini.

The complete absence of visitors at the time of my visit to the museum semed to belie the argument that a Verdaguer revival was imminent. Attendance figures were at present disappointingly low, the director admitted as she led me round a building that had a gloomy atmosphere appropriate for the circumstances in which the poet had stayed there. The original eighteenth-century furnishings were stripped in the last century, but the place continued to exude a strong turn-of-the-century character, which evoked for me an old sanatorium for sufferers of tuberculosis. The museum's director was a smart, distinguished-looking woman in her fifties who spoke about Verdaguer as if he had been a member of her family, and qualified her proud enthusiasm for him with occasional lapses into sadness as she recalled the poet's tragic moments. The sparse furnishings and objects of the museum included a pair of amateurish, three-dimensional models of two key places in Verdaguer's life, one of these being the farmhouse where the young seminarian had gathered with his literary friends to read out poetry.

'Those were happy days,' the director said, before leading me on to the model of the Sanctuary of La Gleva, to where he had been sent by his bishop in 1893. 'How sad he was then,' she sighed, trying perhaps to put me in the right frame of mind before coming to the highpoint of our tour – the actual room where the poet had died.

The room had white floorboards, panelling in pale olive green, cream-coloured walls, and a painted dado of sickly flowers. A crucifix and a portrait of Christ hung above a simple bed on which there was a dying floral tribute, placed there the previous week as part of some commemorative occasion. A number of books and other items of the poet's were displayed behind a vitrine, but the furnishings themselves, including the bed, were apparently not the original ones, but merely 'in the style of the period'.

The actual deathbed of Verdaguer may no longer survive, but I was told that the cradle in which he was born could be seen in the Municipal Museum of Vic. I already had plans to visit Vic and the surrounding *comarca* of Osona, an area that has often been described as the heartland of Catalan culture.

Verdaguer made his name with an epic poem about the sea, and was buried in a cemetery that looks out over the Mediterranean. But to understand the roots of his art, one has to turn away from coastal Catalonia and head north into the mountainous interior.

CATALONIA was divided by Unamuno into 'urban or Mediterranean Catalonia', and 'rural or Pyrenean Catalonia'. The former was characterized progressive, open-minded and imperialist; the latter, conservative, reserved and suspicious. Unamuno was reminded of the polarity in Argentina between the civilized world of Buenos Aires and the 'barbarism' roaming in the land of the gauchos.

Rural Catalonia has always been symbolized by Vic, an episcopal centre as well as a traditional stronghold of the reactionary Carlist faction. When I told my two journalist friends from Barcelona that I was going to Vic and Osona for a few days, their immediate reaction was that I would be visiting 'la Catalonia profunda'. They insisted that I should read beforehand *Laura in the City of the Saints* (1931), a novel by the Barcelona-born author Miquel Llor, a writer much influenced by Joyce, Svevo and Gide. Set in a provincial town, clearly Vic itself, the novel angered many in rural Catalonia by dealing with a sensitive and refined young woman from Barcelona who confronts the cruel, gossiping and hypocritical world of the provinces. The book ends with a distraught Laura back again in Barcelona, having just written a letter to a man she has left behind in the 'city of the saints'. While she searches for consolation in the seductive expanse of the Mediterranean, the man puts down her letter to contemplate surroundings that seem perpetually hidden in a dense fog.

The ancient episcopal town of Vic lies at the heart of a wide, fertile valley set between a coastal range to the south and the Pyrenees to the north. Predominantly grey in the colouring of its architecture, and with a look more northern than southern, Vic is ringed today by modern development, at the edge of which are the modest blocks of the town's recently founded university. The old town, separated from the new one by a turn-of-the-century promenade, has been restored with a thoroughness typical of modern Catalonia. Clean, pedestrian streets lined with stone residences converge on to an irregular, arcaded main square. A light autumnal drizzle was falling the day I was there, forcing the friend I was with to hurry me along under his umbrella to the Municipal Museum.

The friend who acted as my guide in Vic was also my host in Osona. Manel was a farmer in his late thirties who had married into an English family whom I had known for many years. His father-in-law, a retired director of a local textile factory, settled in the 1970s in the nearby town of Manlleu, where his two daughters, Debbie and Belinda, both met their husbands. Quiet, sensitive and well travelled, Manel preferred to speak to me in English rather than Spanish, a preference I would find among many of the others I got to know in this area, several of whom had as hesitant a command of Spanish as Verdaguer's had supposedly been.

The Municipal Museum of Vic is a stuffy, old-fashioned institution with one of the best collections of medieval art in Spain. Founded in 1891, it was the first Spanish museum to draw the public's attention to the expressive beauties of the Catalan Romanesque, and pioneered the collecting of Romanesque frescos from the remote and ruinous mountain churches of the region. In my guided tour, Manel duly concentrated on the medieval period, and dismissed a group of darkly lit upstairs rooms as having miscellanea 'of purely local interest'. I insisted none the less on having a quick look at these rooms, and was soon confronted by the cradle I had heard about in the Museu Verdaguer.

Manel told me that it had belonged to a nineteenth-century poet, and was somewhat surprised when I revealed an interest in the man. 'My grandparents' generation had to read Verdaguer's work in school,' he said. 'But today's children have been spared this.'

The rain had momentarily stopped outside, and, as we walked slowly towards the cathedral, Manel talked to me about the Vic Verdaguer knew, and about how important the city was at that time as an ecclesiastical centre. The seminary where Verdaguer studied was no ordinary one, but had a reputation for learning unrivalled at the time in Catalonia. An enormous influence on the seminary in the early nineteenth century was the locally born priest and philosopher Jaume Balmes i Urpia, who, while never advocating Catalan separatism, argued against a Spanish centralist government and denounced as pure myth the idea of a unified Spain. Elsewhere Balmes wrote nostalgically about the characteristically Catalan love of the homestead and need for a rural patriarchy. This sentiment, known as *pairalisme*, would be expressed more strongly at the end of the century by the future Bishop of Vic, Josep Torras i Bagès. An out-an-out separatist, Torras i Bagès found the concept of the homestead preferable to that of the 'nation'. Believing in the family as the 'substance and base of social organization', he discovered the family spirit to be strongest in those parts of Spain in which the regional spirit was also the strongest.

Monuments to Balmes and Torras i Bagès can be seen in the cathedral, a great, dark mass of a building expressive of the disunity the two men had criticized in the Spanish nation. The bell-tower, and the lower level of the cloisters, are pure Romanesque, but the rest of the building is largely the result of neoclassical bowdlerization and twentieth-century redecoration. The clerestory has been turned into a 'Museum of Sacred Art', where Manel showed me a number of fine medieval treasures taken from deconsecrated churches in the diocese.

Once again I surprised Manel, by being less interested in these than in the extraordinary modern fresco cycle that goes round the entire cathedral. The frescos – incomplete at the time of the artist's death in 1945 – occupied much of the life of José Maria Sert, the last great practitioner of the large-scale decorative tradition of Michelangelo and Tiepolo. Melodramatic, daringly composed, and theatrical in their use of drapery, chiaroscuro, and illusionistic trickery, Sert's works at Vic struck me as among the most powerful religious decorations of the twentieth century. But if Verdaguer had gone out of fashion, Sert had been almost consigned to oblivion, a victim not only of changing tastes but also of present-day Catalanism.

Though a Catalan himself, Sert sullied his future reputation by working after the Civil War for Franco; moreover his works are wholly idiosyncratic, and do not fall into the categories of *modernisme* and *noucentisme* in which the new generation of Catalan art historians like to place all their region's artists. For these very reasons Sert has now been excluded from Barcelona's Museum of Modern Art, an exclusion that smacks of the petty provincialism to which Vargas Llosa has referred. *Pairalisme* might be an admirable concept, but regionalism can hardly be admired if it does not admit pluralism.

We drove back to Manlleu, where Manel and Debbie had their own *casa pairal*, or homestead. Manlleu is a smaller, uglier version of Vic, with an old quarter that has retained only a poorly preserved handful of its medieval palaces.

Manel's family had worked for generations as farmers on the outskirts of Manlleu, the original farm building being one of those massive stone blocks that are found throughout north-west Spain and perfectly convey the notion of a rural patriarchy. Manel's aged parents still lived in the old home, but Manel himself had recently moved with Debbie and their two children to a modern building at the back. I stayed with them there for several days, adjusting to a change of life-style that made me think at times I had left Spain and was back in northern Europe. Meal times were early, water only was drunk, and cows had to be milked at a time in the morning when I might previously have been pondering which would be my next bar.

Everything about Manlleu was different from what I had become used to over the preceding months. On my second day, I went to see the town's mayor, and found a man resembling an amiable bank manager working in a town hall that seemed like the headquarters of some international company. The building was old but had recently been given a 'designer' face-lift, exaggerating the contrast with many of the provincial town halls I had visited elsewhere in Spain. The mayor was very proud of the town hall's new look, and gave me a thorough tour including not only the toilets but also the lockers where the local police kept their guns. Though tourism had yet to arrive at Manlleu, visitors such as myself were provided at the town hall with informative and beautifully produced booklets dealing with every aspect of the town, from its economic and political history to its musical life. From these I discovered that earlier this century homely, health-conscious Manlleu had nurtured a composer who had made his name with a work entitled *Cocaine Tango*. I also learned more about the local textile industry, which was apparently the main source of Manlleu's economy and resulted in the place having one of the largest immigrant populations of any Catalan town.

Manlleu's immigrants were mainly Moroccans and Andalusians, who were completely integrated into the town's life, according to the mayor. Investigating on my own, I found that the Andalusians formed a close-knit community living in one of the ugliest parts of town. The original Andalusian immigrants were from the same small village in Jaén, and all spoke Spanish among themselves in the bars. They had a *Peña flamenca* and every year held a mini-*romería* in imitation of that of the Rocío. Two young girls who came into one of the bars in search of their grandfather were persuaded to improvise some *sevillanas* for my benefit. As I stood watching them, the grandfather told me that he no longer enjoyed his return visits to Andalusia, and could scarcely recognize his native village. In Andalusia, he said, the Andalusian immigrants are disparagingly referred to as 'the Catalans'.

In Catalonia, the immigrants are frequently criticized for not speaking Catalan. Pere, a young Catalan chemist and English student, was one of these critics, as well as someone who thought that the Moroccans were contaminating his home town of Man-lleu. He was otherwise a bright and amiable person who formed part of a friendly group of young Catalans with whom I went out one Friday night to an isolated rustic restaurant about 20 kilo-metres from Manlleu.

As it was the end of the week and a celebratory occasion, I was surprised that everyone was still drinking water, and that no one was helping themselves to the wine in a small pitcher in the centre of our long table: such abstinence could hardly be imagined in any other part of Spain. I felt like a pariah when, eventually, I timidly poured out a small glass of wine for myself. This seemed to set a bad example, for we all found ourselves later that night in Manlleu's most fashionable bar, naughtily drinking fruit juices. The spirit of carefree abandon that had taken hold of us led Pere, at two in the morning, to show me something he said he had shown few other people. He took me into his father's house, and amazed me by unlocking a large room with timber-panelled walls lined with nearly a thousand eighteenth-century pistols. Pere explained that the nearby town of Ripoll had once been one of the main centres of gun-manufacturing in Europe. My image of Ripoll as essentially a spiritual centre was shattered, but Pere told me that there are few people today who know anything about the town's former reputation for guns. 'Not even the townspeople,' he added.

On the way back from the restaurant to Manlleu we had taken a winding country route and passed through a small village which seemed to be covered with stone plaques engraved with lines of poetry. Inadvertently, I had stumbled across Verdaguer's native village of Folgueroles, and I went back the next day to have a look round. A statue to *L'Atlántida* in the form of an egg, supposedly suggestive of cosmic fermentation, stood at the entrance to what turned out to be a charming stone village of a type liable to induce nostalgia for rural life. The newly formed Friends of Verdaguer Society had certainly been active, and had liberally applied snatches of the poet's verse to every building remotely associated with him.

There is some confusion as to where exactly Verdaguer was born, the birthplace chosen by the society being a different one from that marked by a commemorative plaque earlier in the century: the former building has been turned into a small and characterless Verdaguer museum, the principal attraction of which is a video show about the life of the poet. The activities of the society have spread well beyond the actual village, and enthusiasts of the poet can now follow a numbered 'Ruta Verdagueriana', which leads one to every Verdaguerian landscape within a radius of about 15 kilometres.

I only got as far as Number Ten – a tiny hilltop hermitage on the outskirts of the village. According to a guidebook I had purchased in the museum, this hermitage was both the spiritual heart of Verdaguer's world and a place where the visitor could contemplate all the local sites that had been dear to the poet. The old tree-lined avenue that approached it had been abandoned in favour of a wide and well-graded modern road, which appeared indicative of the large amount of money the municipality now had at its disposal. In front of the hermitage, I sat down next to a fountain, and, following the advice of my guidebook, began reading a poem of Verdaguer's inspired by a childhood memory of overhearing the music of an itinerant harpist in this very spot.

The combination of these Celtic strains and the beauty of the surroundings had stirred in the young Verdaguer a vision of a landscape paradise in which the Muse of Catalonia had appeared in the sky. I turned from the poem to a landscape of woods, rolling fields and distant snow-capped peaks. Still in a poetic frame of mind I walked round to the back of the hermitage, where the Friends of Verdaguer Society have thoughtfully planted a small 'Verdaguerian Garden'. A metal, free-standing letterbox has a notice attached to it encouraging the visitor to turn the key and borrow from inside the box a book containing all the poems that Verdaguer had ever dedicated to flowers. All these flowers can be found in the garden beyond, arranged, as in the book, in alphabetical order. This could only be Catalonia.

Excursionisme is as popular and emotive an activity in Catalonia today as it was in Verdaguer's time. Every town and village in Osona organizes regular group outings to local beauty spots that are often teeming at weekends with professional-looking hikers. I participated in this weekend *excursionisme* and visited a number of sites Verdaguer himself probably would have appreciated. Among these were the rocks of Savassona, where Celtic human sacrifices had reputedly been practised; another site was the ruined and supposedly haunted Romanesque monastery of Sant Pere Casseres, which stands on a promontory above the wild shores of the Sau reservoir.

My main excursion was a Sunday outing to the mountainous landscape around the village of Rupit, where Manel's English parents-in-law had retired to. It was a perfect autumnal day, and my arrival at Rupit was a near idyllic moment, the culmination of an uphill journey along a road offering ever more extensive views of the Pyrenees before disappearing into a hidden valley where the air was crisp, the forests dense, and the fields as bright as a photograph on a calendar. The proverbial bubbling stream was there, rushing directly in front of the village of Rupit, which was lifted above it on a wave-like outcrop of rock, its houses forming a cluster of stone walls and flower-filled balconies, and its castle clinging in ruins to the wave's crest.

Someone had clearly been well versed in the rules of the picturesque and had been thoughtful enough to provide a perilous-looking suspension bridge with some of its slats missing.

Nothing seemed out of place, or jarringly modern, and yet the longer I stared at Rupit from a distance the more suspiciously clean and tidy the whole village appeared. It took me only a few minutes on the other side of the bridge to realize that the rustic idyll was in fact a carefully disguised group of restaurants, craft shops and weekend homes. Villagers whose forefathers had eked out a living gathering faggots in the forest had grown rich by selling tastefully packed local specialities, including an abundance of sausages and salami. By lunchtime the car-park was congested with cars and coaches bearing *excursionistes* from as far afield as Barcelona.

I had lunch with Manel's sister-in-law, Belinda, who had recently moved with her husband and children to an isolated house near to her parents. Her husband's family, who lunched with us, were wealthy citizens of Manlleu who had made their money from bathroom installations. The husband sat next to me at table, and began telling me about the strict building regulations now in force in the Rupit area. His father interrupted him, indignant that his son was speaking in Spanish, and was only partially appeased by being told that I had not as yet spent enough time in Catalonia to have picked up Catalan. The conversation was resumed, with the son unwittingly explaining why Rupit had seemed to me so perfectly medieval when I had first seen it: all house owners, he pointed out, were now obliged to hide their television aerials underground. After lunch we drove out to their new house, which belonged officially to the scattered community of Pruit, and stood at the top of a narrow wooded valley. From afar this house looked like a traditional stone dwelling, but close inspection revealed a modern villa entirely clad in stone. Anything modern, I was told, had to be hidden under traditional stone walls, even the swimming-pool.

Lower down the valley, and a welcome intrusion in this excessively quaint and tasteful landscape, was a green metallic dome that looked as if it had landed from Mars. This geodesic structure arrived at the end of the 1960s and would certainly not have been granted planning permission today. A loud battery of kettle-drums shook the sides of the dome as I approached it for my appointment. I was there to see the man who has used the space as a rehearsal studio for his theatre troupe, Els Joglars, for the last twenty-five years.

I took an instant liking to Albert Boadella. A youthful, white-haired man with an expressive manner, his attitude towards the new Spain is similar to that of Vázquez Montalbán, but he expresses himself in a more cheerful, extrovert and matter-of-fact way. He is an anarchist of a peculiarly Catalan type – an anarchist with such a good head for business that since 1962 he has managed to run a self-supporting theatre troupe dedicated to making fun of everything Spain holds sacred.

'Sacred' is the operative word, for, like most of the great Spanish satirists, the object of his most vicious satire has usually been the Church. He has been a devout atheist since his childhood in Barcelona, when he once publicly made known his views on the clergy by stuffing his mouth full of holy wafers and then pointing out to his shocked companions that he had not been felled by a bolt of lightning; afterwards he encouraged them all to urinate in the holy wine, an action that led the priest to taste an unexpected flavour while celebrating communion.

Most of Boadella's theatrical productions have been in the same provocative spirit, and there have been inevitable outcries, such as the time he mocked the Virgin of Montserrat. The production in question, *Te Deum*, was his most blasphemous to date, and was banned by the bishops in a number of Spanish towns. In several of the places where it was staged, members of the local clergy processed outside the hall, carrying crosses, reciting rosaries, and generally creating a spectacle that Boadella obviously enjoyed. But how, I asked, did he get away with his satires during the Franco period?

'I didn't always get away with them,' he laughed, reminding me that he had been put away in prison for a play satirizing the Guardia Civil. 'But', he continued, 'that was at the very end of Franco's life, when I felt more confident about taking liberties. Before that we had, of course, to be quite careful, and much more subtle.'

Boadella spoke with fluent enthusiasm – anecdotes about himself and his troupe were effortlessly succeeded by abstract reflections on the theatre, a medium he saw as ideally suited to the expression of irony and cynicism. Audiences, according to him, believe that what is said in the theatre corresponds more to reality than what is said in the cinema. Despite its stylization, the theatre conveys in his view 'an illusion of reality', and is therefore able to influence people more deeply and more subtly than the cinema.

A great uproar – loud moans, grunts, banging on tins, and swinging on ropes – distracted me briefly from what Boadella was saying. I regained my concentration to ask him more specifically about his working methods, and found that each of his productions develops from a rough written draft which is then improvised by actors over a period of many weeks. The actors are subjected to a strenuous physical regime, and their days always begin by jogging to the green dome from a country mansion about 5 kilometres away. As I watched nervously a group of men hanging in the air by their ankles, Boadella stressed how important it was for actors to be in top physical condition. 'Once an actor loses his energy,' he said, 'he loses something important as an actor.'

Boadella talked to me about the production he was currently rehearsing. It was called *Yo tengo un tío en América* ('I've Got an Uncle in America'), and was set in an imaginary mental hospital at Pruit. The patients are being treated with 'psychodrama therapy', and are enacting the life of an American tribe before the arrival of Columbus. Influenced by the most visionary among them, their imagination slowly gets out of hand, with an ensuing confusion between the present and the past, history and fantasy, illusion and reality. The ropes of the hospital gym, in which the play is set, alternate as bars and trees; the doctors become flamenco-dancing conquistadors intimidating the patients with giant syringes, and a visiting health inspector is transformed into Queen Isabel la Católica masquerading as the present Spanish Queen, Sofia. With a sweeping gesture of his arms Boadella indicated how the production would climax with eighty-odd ropes suddenly collapsing as a group of prospectors chase away the Indians with machine-guns and a chainsaw.

For the first time in the history of Els Joglars, the production that they were working on had been commissioned and funded by the State. This powerful, imaginative, if not always subtle attack on the 1992 celebrations would be appearing by courtesy of Spain's Fifth Centenary Committee. Boadella did not seem to be unduly concerned about this, and told me that one of his conditions for receiving the patronage of the Committee was that he would be allowed to do whatever he liked. In any case, he stressed, most members of the Committee were on his side, and it was only its President, Luis Yáñez, who would be likely to cause any trouble.

As Boadella predicted, Yáñez did refuse to see the play when it was eventually premièred early in 1992. The play was not allowed to be performed within the grounds of the EXPO, but Boadella got his own back by incorporating a joke about Yañez in the text, and by performing to packed houses in Seville's Teatro Lope de Vega. I would catch up with the production at that year's Edinburgh Festival, by which time a controversy of a different nature had arisen.

Spaniards were complaining that Spanish drama should be represented at the Festival only by a Catalan group, and misguided British critics were strengthening the Spanish case by claiming that the oppressed people in the play were not just the Indians but the Catalans themselves. I went backstage after the Edinburgh performance, and had a talk with Boadella's wife.

'It's the first time that Albert's been to England,' she told me. Gently reminding her that we were in fact in Scotland, I said, half jokingly, that I had always thought that the Catalans prided themselves on their affinities with the Scots. 'Oh, what nonsense!' she joked back.

Boadella's critical views on Catalan nationalism were made quite clear to me at Pruit, where he had said that he was in complete sympathy with Vargas Llosa's comments on the provincialism of presentday Catalonia. Barcelona was taking itself too seriously; the current nationalist fever was a dangerous symptom of paranoia, and the absurd slogan 'Freedom for Catalonia' was an insult to Spain. What should really be celebrated in 1992, he suggested, was the Fifth Centenary of the Spanish Union, a controversial suggestion he considered revolutionary rather than reactionary.

Before leaving Boadella at Pruit, I wanted to find out what his feelings were about this part of Catalonia, where he had lived for so many years. Was it not curious that a man of such strong anti-clerical and anti-nationalist views should have settled in the heartland of Catalan clericalism and nationalism? He was quick to reply that he no longer lived here, that he had recently moved to the lower Ampurdán, and that he now stayed at Pruit only during rehearsals. Then he confessed that he might have been wrong ever to have moved to Pruit, and that he had failed to make any close local friends in all the time that he had been there. The district capital of Vic appalled him even more than presentday Barcelona, and he ridiculed the place for having thirty-five churches for only 35,000 inhabitants, and for having a seminary whose only seminarist today was a man called García (the Spanish equivalent of Smith). He had been attracted to the district by its beauty and tranquillity, but even these had palled after a time. He had ended up hating to have to live in a 'picture-postcard village', and had recently gone out of his way in search of the ugliest place possible in which to set up a new home. He and his wife had now found their ideal home in what he described as one of the least attractive villages of the lower Ampurdan, a village where there were thankfully no tourists taking photographs, buying up houses, or exclaiming continually how beautiful the whole place was.

I was fully in sympathy with Boadella, but I soon went back to being one of the tourists he had scorned, ending my day as I had begun it – overwhelmed by the spectacular beauty of the scenery. At dusk I was walking to the house of Belinda's parents, being pulled along an overgrown forest path by her eight-year-old daughter. Roles were reversed and, as we made our way through the dark forest, the young girl teased and frightened me with tales of wolves and bears. The path turned out to be a Roman road crossing an ancient bridge and passing alongside the abandoned, arcaded shell of a large Renaissance mansion. Night was fast falling, and the girl rushed me along, dragging me out of the forest just in time to see a dark pink glow light up the white crests of a horizon that seemed the creation of some visionary landscape painter. An old farmhouse, commanding an uninterrupted view of this celestial backcloth, stood isolated among fields that fell steeply down into a wild valley at the foot of distant mountains. I was later told that the house was the birthplace and family home of a man who might one day be thought of as the saviour of Catalonia. To many of his growing number of followers, this man is known by the suitably angelic name of 'Six Wings'.

'Six Wings' is the nickname of Angel Colom i Colom (*colom* is the Catalan word for 'dove'). In his teens, wanting perhaps to fulfil the angelic potential of his name, he envisaged a career as a priest, and later joined the likes of García in the seminary at Vic. His studies for the priesthood were soon abandoned, and he became an intrepid traveller, journeying extensively through Iraq and India.

In the late 1970s and early 1980s he finally acquired his future taste for politics while working in the student organization known as COM, which was dedicated to a militant promotion of the Catalan language. At this stage in his career he was still a follower of the right-wing Catalan President Jordi Pujol, but he would later turn strongly against Pujol, especially when the latter insisted on Catalonia remaining within the Spanish Union. Angel Colom joined in the mid-1980s what had already become by far the most important of the Catalan separatist parties, the Esquerra Republican de Catalunya; by 1989, still in his thirties, he was elected its leader.

Since then he has had significant electoral success, and has greatly broadened support for the party, ridding it of some of its crackpot student image and making it more acceptable to members of the banking and business fraternity.

I went with Manel to see him at the party's headquarters in Barcelona. The tiny letters ERC marked the doorbell of a small and cheerful office papered with posters promoting 'Freedom for Catalonia' or showing a star symbolizing Catalonia being inserted into the round galaxy of the European Community,

Angel Colom does not have the obvious look of a charismatic politician, and resembles rather a very studious and retiring teacher. He is a gentle, soft-spoken man, with gold-rimmed spectacles shielding blue eyes, a large head covered with light brown hair, and an insubstantial beard. Courteous and friendly, he did not mind talking to me in Spanish, even though in public he feigns hardly to know the language. On hearing that we had come to see him from Manlleu, he invited us to the party conference to be held in Vic the following week. He also talked about the recent closure of two of Manlleu's textile factories, a closure he did not blame on a general recession but on the disastrous consequences of Catalonia's economic fortunes being tied to those of the rest of Spain.

I made the mistake at first of referring to his party as 'separatista', and I was immediately put right.

'We are not separatistas,' he said, 'but independistas. There's a great difference, you know. It's you, the English, who are the separatistas, with your great desire to separate yourself from the rest of Europe.'

After I had strongly dissociated myself from the Thatcheristas, I sat back and tried for a moment to be seduced by Colom's romantic vision of an independent Catalonia within a federal Europe.

'It's only a question of time,' he said, 'and though it might not happen in my lifetime, I feel strongly that the next generation will live to see it.'

Weakly, I referred to the nationalist problems of Yugoslavia and Eastern Europe, and though he agreed that the situation there was complex, he insisted that Spain and Western Europe were an altogether far simpler story. I stopped myself from mentioning Northern Ireland, Belgium, the Italian Tyrol and other such places, and let him air his views on the nationalist problems within Spain itself.

'Take, for instance, the Basque country,' he said. 'The only problem there is Navarre.'

But where, I asked, would this whole process of breaking Spain down into different countries end? With an independent Cartagena? And what about the huge immigrant population within both Catalonia and the Basque country?

Colom calmly attempted to assuage my sensationalist fears, and insisted that the immigrants did not constitute a serious problem, as most of them eventually became completely assimilated within their new environment. Nor did he see Spain being turned once again into a bloodbath, and especially not Catalonia, where a tradition of pacifism had been established since the Civil War. In contrast to the main independence party of the Basque country, Herri Batasuna, the ERC was completely opposed to seeking solutions by violence. He told me how his experiences in India had made him a dedicated follower of Gandhi.

While I listened to Angel Colom, I could not help thinking back to the idyllic landscape surroundings in which he had grown up. I was not alone in doing so, for a recent article had appeared in *El País* stating a connection between these surroundings and Colom's political views.

Hesitantly, I asked Colom if he was conscious of any influence of his Pyrenean upbringing on his way of looking at Catalonia today. He replied by saying that the landscape he had known as a child had of course left an indelible impression. Manel fortunately interceded at this point by telling Colom that my fascination with Osona and its landscape stemmed partly from my love of Verdaguer. Colom seemed both pleased and slightly amused.

'In the nineteenth century,' he began with a faint smile, 'an interest in the literature and culture of the Catalan people formed the basis for the renewal of the Catalan nation . . .' I hoped against hope that the conversation would be lifted into the higher realms of Verdaguer's world, where nationalism becomes a distillation of history, myth and poetry. 'However,' he concluded, firmly, 'we have now to be more practical. We have to think of money and finance.'

PART SIX

TO THE END
OF THE WORLD

18

The Cult of Relics

SPANIARDS on their honeymoon have traditionally paid a pilgrimage to the Aragonese town of Teruel, to visit the mausoleum where the relics of Spain's most famous pair of lovers can be found.

The tragic conclusion to the lovers' story is portrayed above the main entrance, in a pre-Raphaelite frieze showing a woman, Isabel de Segura, collapsed on top of the coffin of her childhood sweetheart, Juan Diego de Martínez de Marcilla. Five years before, Diego had pleaded for the hand of Isabel in marriage, but had been told by her parents that this would not be considered until he had become a wealthy man. After the five years allotted to him to achieve this aim, he returned triumphantly to Teruel only to find that Isabel had been forcibly betrothed to someone else. The frieze depicts the moment Isabel falls into a mortal swoon on kissing the dead Diego. He has died of grief after having stolen secretly into her house and been refused a kiss in order to seal their love.

Inside the small and dark mausoleum, the visitor is confronted by the tombs made for the two lovers in 1902, nearly 700 years after their deaths. The recumbent effigies, by an uninspired sculptor called Juan de Avalos, are shown with their hands reaching out to meet across the gap between the tombs. By kneeling or lying down on the floor, the more sentimental or morbidly inclined can peer between lattice stonework to catch a glimpse of what the poet Ted Walker has described as 'enormous chrysalides, shudderingly awful and . . . enough to guarantee at least a fortnight's impotence for even the lustiest of grooms'.

The story of the lovers, according to a leaflet handed out at the mausoleum, 'is based upon an old and well-documented tradition'. The documentation is in fact dubious, and the 'old' tradition goes back no further than the mid-sixteenth century, the story being entirely and suspiciously absent from all the medieval chronicles and romances of Aragón. The love affair between Diego and Isabel was first popularized in a poem, published *circa* 1555, the year when two mummified bodies were exhumed and transferred to a different chapel within the Teruel Church of San Pedro. Several literary versions of the story soon appeared, including, in 1616, a 'tragic epic' by a local notary called Juan Yagüe de Salas. Juan Yagüe, in his legal capacity, turned up three years later as a signatory testifying to the authenticity of two documents that were brought to light following the rediscovery of the mummies in the course of excavation work in San Pedro's. One document, said to come from the box in which one of the mummies was found, was a piece of paper marked simply, 'This is Don Juan Martínez de Marcilla who died of love.' The other document was reputedly a copy of a thirteenth-century original in which the full details of the lovers' story were outlined. This later manuscript gave no indication of where the original might be, and was written in a pseudo-medieval style that clearly belonged to the early seventeenth century, some of its lines of poetry being curiously identical to verse by Juan Yagüe.

An Aragonese historian of this period, Vincencio Blasco de Lanuza, remained rightfully unconvinced by this 'evidence', but most people unquestioningly accepted both the identity of the mummies and the story attached to them. Turned in 1635 into a successful play by Tirso de Molina, the story continued to grow in popularity, thus ensuring that the poor mummies would never be allowed to rest again peacefully under the earth. No one quite knew what to do with them, and from 1708 right up to the middle of the ninetenth century they suffered the undignified fate of being kept upright in a closet in the cloister, their identity recorded by an inscription euphemistically referring to the closet as a 'pantheon' in which "lie the celebrated lovers of Teruel'.

Interest in the lovers reached a peak in the early nineteenth century, when Juan Eugenio Hartzenbusch retold their story in the play that turned him overnight into one of the key figures of Spanish Romantic literature. In contrast to his Romantic contemporary Mérimée, who invented a bogus documentary framework to enhance the power of his historical fiction, Hartzenbusch followed up his fiction with an article expressing his genuine belief in the existence of the lovers. By now the whole issue of their existence had become a matter of national and Aragonese pride, and people such as Hartzenbusch simply refused to believe that the tale of the lovers was little more than a quaint courtly romance. Archivists, for all their searching, had failed to uncover a single new document about the lovers, and had merely dismissed once and for all the ones signed by Yagüe; furthermore, literary scholars had proved almost conclusively that the Teruel tale was based on one from Boccaccio's *Decameron*. But even so Hartzenbusch and later writers still held firmly to their convictions, and dared even to suggest that Boccaccio's tale, far from being the source of the Teruel one, was actually inspired by it, the story of the Teruel lovers having been popularized in Italy by the numerous Aragonese merchants then resident in the country.

'All those whose hearts have been touched by the tender flame should visit the cloisters, in which are preserved the "lovers of Teruel".' These words, uttered in 1845, are not those of a romantic Spaniard but of Richard Ford, one of the more cynical and down-to-earth commentators on Spain, and a man ever quick to dismiss anything smacking of the phoney or the ridiculous. His Protestant views, like those of other English travellers, led him naturally to make fun of the relics of Catholic saints, but he should perhaps have perceived that the cult of Diego and Isabel was directly comparable to the cult of saints, a cult that in the Middle Ages led Christians to undertake long pilgrimages to shrines that had grown up around mortal remains as dubiously authentic as Teruel's mummies.

The subject of saintly relics takes on a particular relevance in Aragón, where the traveller who heads north will eventually enter the orbit of one of the most famous of all pilgrimage routes – that of Santiago de Compostela. The reasons why Christians from all over Europe undertook the hazardous journey to Santiago were many and varied, and included such profane ones as getting away from the wife, escaping taxes, and profiteering from the sale of plenary indulgences. But the principal one was connected with the belief that the relics of saints had some of the qualities of the saints in life, and as such were able to assuage the very real fear of evil that existed in the Middle Ages.

The cult of relics developed around the fourth century, the original relics being largely those of the early Christian martyrs. From the start there were those who likened the cult to pagan idolatry, but opposition of this sort was rare right up to the Reformation, and was condemned by the Church as heretical. The Church's stance was an understandable one in view of the amount of money and propaganda that could be made from the pilgrimages, but was also increasingly untenable as more and more relics were discredited, as others were turning up embarrassingly in more than one location, and as many more still were being stolen, often to meet the insatiable demands of wealthy collectors, who amassed relics with the same fervour that later collectors would reserve for works of art.

Among the relics the Church was keenest to uphold were those of St James, whose corpse had mysteriously made its way from the Holy Land to a remote corner of north-west Spain, and had then resurfaced in the ninth century at a time when most of the rest of the country was in the hands of the 'infidels'. In order to sustain the cult of St James, and the profitable pilgrimage in his honour, the Church adopted such measures as exploiting the confusion beteween James the Apostle and James the Lesser, and by incorporating into Jacobean legend the mythical deeds of Roland, thereby endowing the former with an appealing chivalric gloss. More drastically, the Church was forced to invent the bloodthirsty figure of St James the Moor-Slayer, whose posthumous intervention on behalf of the Christians during the imaginary battle of Clavijo would result in Spaniards having to pay an annual tax offering to the saint's shrine in Santiago right up to the early nineteenth century. From the time of the Reformation, when the Santiago pilgrimage came under serious attack, this unpopular tax provided a powerful motive to those critics of the

Church who were anxious to disprove the authenticity of the St James relics. The Church retaliated in 1588 by uncovering the so-called 'leads of Sacromonte' in Granada. These were a number of supposedly ancient leaden plaques with multilingual inscriptions proving, among other things, that the saint had indeed come to Spain. The plaques aroused a number of initial suspicions, but it was not until late in the seventeenth century that they were finally exposed as one of the more spectacular forgeries in history. By the mid-nineteenth century, the Santiago pilgrimage had almost died out, and the Church was obliged to play its final card. The Church authorized excavations to be carried out in Santiago Cathedral, and these succeeded in 1879 in locating the apostle's skull, which, by some miracle, had a missing section corresponding exactly to a fragment of his skull kept in the Italian town of Pistoia.

The forefathers of today's numerous pilgrims to Santiago were responsible for what has often been described as the beginnings of mass tourism. For the benefit of these early pilgrims, the main religious orders established along the route a series of efficiently run hostelries comparable to modern hotel chains such as Trusthouse Forte; and a French priest called Aymeric Picaud wrote in the early twelfth century what was probably the first guidebook in history. Diversions were clearly necessary on the journey, and these were partially supplied by visits to a well-scattered group of lesser reliquaries, places that were uplifting not only because of what they contained but also on account of their often notoriously sumptuous settings. Picaud's guide listed the essential reliquaries no pilgrim should fail to miss, in the same way that the Michelin Green Guides give three stars to those obligatory sights 'worth the journey'.

Close parallels can be found between the medieval cult of relics and present-day sightseeing, both phenomena involving duty as well as pleasure, a belief in the life-enhancing properties of objects, and an almost ritualistic desire to 'tick off' a given series of places. Sightseeing is at its closest to relic-hunting when the sights in question are connected with particular people, usually famous writers, artists, or political or spiritual leaders. The sentimental traveller can justify journeys in search of associations and mortal remains by quoting St Thomas Aquinas: 'He who loves someone', the saint wrote, 'reveres the things that they leave behind them.'

A sense of being on a pilgrimage intensified as soon as I entered Aragón, and not only because I was nearing the pilgrim's road to Santiago. My initial destination on leaving Catalonia was to the home town of a childhood hero of mine who had overthrown idols, ridiculed relics, and brilliantly parodied the Santiago pilgrimage in a film – *The Milky Way* – that had shown two elderly medieval pilgrims hitchhiking by a motorway. The place I was heading for was Calanda in the north-eastern corner of Teruel province. The idol was Luis Buñuel, one of the best-known sons of a Spanish region with a particularly brutal image.

THE REGION of Aragón presents such a strong contrast to verdant Catalonia that one might easily forget that for over three centuries the two kingdoms were joined together in an alliance that brought the Catalan nation to the height of its political and economic power. Aragón, with its dual historical loyalty to Castile and Catalonia, should be thought of as a link between these two opposing regions, and yet has frequently been characterized by Castilians as more Castilian than Castile, and as such a bastion of anti-Catalanism.

The very landscape of the region, as Unamuno noted, is even 'drier than that of Castile', 'more robust', 'more desolate', and with a 'darker-coloured earth'. Then there are the Aragonese themselves, who have been viewed as a distillation of all the worst qualities of the Castilians, stereotyped as the obstinate, sullen and uncouth peasant known as the *baturro* – as much of a Spanish cliché as the *majo*.

Richard Ford was not voicing purely personal prejudices when he summarized Aragón as a 'disagreeable region' filled with 'disagreeable people'. For the tourist it is a region of scattered attractions, the greatest concentration of which are in the northern half of Huesca province, where there is spectacular Pyrenean scenery, and an extensive series of Romanesque monuments dating from the heyday of the Santiago pilgrimage; at the opposite end of the region, in southern Teruel, is a barren, mountainous district enclosing the walled showpiece town of Albarracín, one of the best preserved old towns in Spain. Between these two extremes, and covering most of the region, extend what Unamuno called the 'tragic lands of the Aragonese plateau'. Enormous flat expanses, with cultivated fields alternating with crumpled areas of erosion, make up a landscape that travellers glance at indifferently on their way between Madrid and Barcelona. Unamuno spoke for many when he said that he had crossed the plateau numerous times without having had the slightest wish to stop.

The scenery may be uninviting, but its dry monotony makes an undeniable impression, just as its many unprettified towns leave in the consciousness a scarred ochre residue, with traces of tall *mudéjar* towers, broken roof tiles and higgledy-piggledy walls in exposed brick. Having only recently left the 'picture-postcard' village of Rupit, I enjoyed stepping out into my first Aragonese town of Alcañiz, and finding a place of strong personality with a sloping square supporting an arcade of squat bars, a weathered, reddish mass of a church, a sturdy grand hotel well past its prime, and a Renaissance town hall displaying official lettering dating almost from the days of Buñuel's youth.

I was approaching Calanda in the same way that Buñuel had always done, alighting at Alcañiz to cover the remaining 20 kilometres by local transport. I held out little hope for Calanda itself, which Buñuel called the sole eyesore in a region of attractive towns and villages. The only writer to show Calanda in a truly flattering light was Antonio Ponz, who, writing in the late eighteenth century, had been so impressed by its hard-working inhabitants and by the fertile, well-maintained surrounding fields that he had predicted that the place would soon grow into a large and flourishing market and industrial centre. Nothing of the sort happened, and by the time Buñuel was a young man there the place was an impoverished, backward-looking community with 'fewer than 5000 inhabitants and nothing to offer the tourist'. When Buñuel returned to Calanda in his later years, its earlier poverty had been eradicated, but its ugliness had increased, cancelling any qualms the film director might have had in using the word 'horrible' to describe his beloved childhood home.

There are two main sources for Buñuel's life. One is by his fellow Mexican exile, Max Aub (an experimental novelist associated with the 'Generation of '27'), and comprises a massive transcript of conversations between him, Buñuel and the latter's family, friends, colleagues, and childhood companions. The other source is Buñuel's witty and profound *My Last Breath* (1982), perhaps the greatest autobiography ever written by someone connected with the cinema. Aub, reflecting on his own attempts to save Buñuel's life for posterity, refers to history as semi-fiction based on distorted and unreliable memories and on the accounts of scholars whom he likens to 'rubbish collectors and scrap merchants who exhibit their finds in showcases'. Buñuel himself, opening his autobiography by recalling his mother's total loss of memory in old age, asserts that 'memory is what makes our lives', but that, 'Our imagination, and our dreams, are forever invading our memories; and since we are all apt to believe in the reality of fantasies, we end up transforming our lies into truths.'

In Buñuel's memory, Calanda was a town where the Middle Ages had lasted until the First World War. Wholly feudal in its make-up, and dominated by the clergy and a handful of wealthy landowners, the Calanda of Buñuel's childhood was a place where traditional costume was still worn, where the poor begged for food on Fridays outside the church, where motor cars were unknown, and where one woman could create a scandal by bringing a bidet into her home. 'Life', in Buñuel's words, 'unfolded in a linear fashion, the major moments marked by the daily bells of the Church of Pilar.' Religion permeated every aspect of the villagers' lives, and, as in the Middle Ages, death too was an omnipresent force, regularly announcing itself through the loud wails of the professional mourners who accompanied the funeral cortèges from the church to the cemetery.

The son of a wealthy citizen who had made his money in Cuba, Buñuel lived a privileged life in Calanda, staying there only during the holidays. The rest of the year was spent in Zaragoza, where his father worked. Money and a family home in Zaragoza, however, did not make the influence of Calanda any less powerful. This influence would be reflected in the strong medieval atmosphere of his films, in their grotesque anti-clericalism, and in the blackness of their humour; his fund of future images would also be heavily indebted to early experiences in Calanda, such as the time when he came across the swollen body of a dead donkey being devoured by vultures and dogs. Those who knew Buñuel as a child in Calanda remembered him for his toy theatre, his showing of films in his parents' house, his near fatal exploration of a cave, and his provocative, proto-Surrealist behaviour which would lead once to his feigning to be the dead Christ by lying naked with a fake wound and a false beard.

The sun was always shining relentlessly in Buñuel's Calanda, and whole years would pass without a single cloud being sighted. It was entirely overcast on the morning I travelled by bus from Alcañiz to Calanda, a journey the young Buñuel had always made by horse-drawn carriage. Under a grey sky the approach to Calanda could not have been bleaker or more colourless, the overall impression being of flat, interminable olive fields, and a predominance of mournful ochre. Arid rocky outcrops spiked the horizon, and formed a backcloth to the handful of factory chimneys.

'Horrible' is the only word to describe the appearance of Calanda itself, a small town with hardly any vestiges of the past or any colour, but composed instead of forbiddingly shuttered houses in brick or concrete. There are no monuments or plaques to Buñuel, the only reference to him apparently being in the name of a recently formed cinema club. To try to find out more about Calanda, I went to the town hall, where I had the feeling that strangers were as much of a novelty in the town today as they had been in Buñuel's time. The welcoming mayor insisted that one of the local policemen should give up the rest of his morning to accompany me on a tour of Calanda. We would begin with the Church of the Pilar.

One of the people whom Aub had interviewed at Calanda had said that his town, though outwardly less attractive than Alcañiz, was the superior of the two places for having given birth to three men 'of universal significance'. Buñuel was of course one of these;

the seventeenth-century guitarist Gaspar Sanz was another, and the third was Miguel Juan Pellicer, a man whom most people in the town still regarded as the most important of the three.

Pellicer would be a completely forgotten person today had he not suffered the misfortune in 1637 of having his leg crushed under the wheel of a cart. The leg was later amputated and buried, and Pellicer was forced to make a living by going to Zaragoza to beg outside the shrine to the Virgin of Pilar – the Virgin St James had seen on a pillar during the Roman occupation of the town. While asleep back in Calanda in 1640, Pellicer had a vision similar to that of St James, and woke up the next morning with a new leg. This unusual transplant operation was verified by doctors, and officially confirmed a miracle by the Zaragozan archbishopric; Pellicer was received shortly afterwards by Philip IV in Madrid. Buñuel believed implicitly in the miracle up to the age of fourteen, though he wrote a garbled account of it in his autobiography. My police escort gave me his own version, as we stood in Pellicer's actual bedroom, which has been incorporated into one of the chapels of the neo-classical church commemorating the miracle. The policeman did not seem a great believer, but he was adamant that this miracle was the only authenticated one in the history of Catholicism.

Having dealt with Calanda's principal claim to fame the policeman took me on to the Buñuel family home, a large mansion whose size and central location, almost in front of the town hall, indicated the high position the family had held in this town. The turn-of-the-century brick exterior emulated *mudéjar* architecture, but the interior was said to be in an Art Nouveau style which at the time of the house's construction was a source of much wonder to the poor of the town, who stood open-mouthed at the door, gazing inside. The house was closed for the season, but Buñuel's family still owned it, one of the film director's sisters still continuing to divide her time between Calanda and Zaragoza.

As we started walking away from the house, I expressed my surprise that the only public statue I had so far been able to find in the town had not been of Buñuel but of the Aragonese painter Goya, who, as far as I was aware, had no association whatsoever with the town. The policeman told me of plans to build a roadside monument to Buñuel on the outskirts of Calanda, but said that the idea of commemorating a former Republican and Communist sympathizer had always been opposed in this traditionally right-wing town. If I was really interested in Buñuel, he continued, the person I should go and see was Tomás Gascon, who was one of the film director's few surviving old friends here. He was also the town's drum-maker and master drummer.

A whole chapter in Buñuel's autobiography is devoted to 'The Drums of Calanda'. The town is one of several in this part of Aragón that belong to what the local tourist board calls 'La Ruta del Tambor', a reference to the custom of beating drums on Good Friday. This custom, honouring the darkness, thunder and earth-quakes that befell the earth on Christ's death, was said by Buñuel to date back to the late eighteenth century, though the first documented mention is as late as 1856.

ᵗ The custom died out towards the end of the last century, but was revived almost immediately by a local priest, and supposedly made an impression on Buñuel when he was still in the cradle. Buñuel began participating in the event as a child, and almost experienced his earliest trauma when his father threatened one year not to allow him out of Zaragoza on Good Friday. He would take part in the ceremony right up to old age, and was even rumoured once to have interrupted filming in Hollywood to return to Calanda for the occasion. The sound of loud, incessant drumming obsessed him, and was an important element in the soundtracks of many of his films, in particular *L'Age d'Or* and *Nazarín*. It was a sound that aroused in this notorious atheist a powerful, mystical sensation.

The policeman opened the door of Tomás Gascón's house, and shouted up the stairs for him. A young man with dyed, cropped hair and a huge belly rolling under a stained T-shirt emerged to tell us that his father was out. He slouched back grumpily to a room where loud rock music was playing on a radio. Before he disappeared from sight, the policeman managed to persuade him to invite me upstairs to see 'the room of the photographs'.

I went on my own up the poky staircase of a house entirely

covered with patterned wallpaper the colour of dark mould. The music was turned off, and the son led me into a sombre front room given over entirely to a display of drums and photographs of drummers, among whom could be seen Buñuel, Chaplin and the actor Fernando Rey. The son became gradually more hospitable, and when I had told him of my interest in Buñuel, he opened a cupboard and put into my hands what was to me almost a sacred relic. I turned it round slowly, hoping perhaps that some mystical force would rub off on me. I was holding Buñuel's drum.

Tomás Gascón was due back shortly, and the son suggested that I should wait for him in the sad little kitchen crammed between a corridor and a chaotic workshop packed high with drums, skeins and wires. On one side of the room a cat was sitting on a large pile of washing, while on the other was a large television set with a collection of videos scattered over the floor. The son was searching through the videos when his old and meekly smiling mother came into the room to apologize for all the mess and to offer me some food and beer. She confirmed that her husband had been a drinking companion of Buñuel's for over forty years, and showed me a copy of Buñuel's autobiography inscribed 'To my friend Tomás Gascón, master drummer, your friend Luis Buñuel'. The son grunted as he found the video he had been looking for. The lights were switched off, a can of beer was put in my hand, and within seconds the house was shaking to the drums of Calanda.

I had expected a film about the town's Easter activities, but the architecture was clearly Parisian. In 1985, the son explained, a year before Buñuel's death, a homage to the great film-maker was organized there. He and his father, together with fifty drummers from Calanda, were invited to take part in a procession from the Mexican Embassy to the Pompidou Centre. Fernando Rey, Jeanne Moreau, the screenwriter Jean-Claude Carrière and other celebrities all attended, but Buñuel himself was too ill to come, and in his stead an effigy of him from the Waxwork Museum in Barcelona was sent.

Tomás Gascón headed the procession, and could be seen in the video as a lithe, distinguished man with a bushy moustache and a grave demeanour. Behind the drummers, and carried by hooded men, came the effigy of Buñuel, seated on a director's chair on top of a holy processional float that would usually have been reserved for Christ or the Virgin. 'Thank God I'm an atheist' is the line invariably quoted to illustrate Buñuel's ambiguous relationship to the Catholic Church, but the dichotomy of this sentiment was yet more blatant in the strange spectacle of an atheist being paraded around Paris in a parody of a Spanish Semana Santa. Some of the participants were crying, and the sound of the drums, combined with the pathos of the occasion, and the pathos of the room in which I was sitting, brought a few tears to my eyes as well.

The video show was ending when Tomás Gascón entered the kitchen and sat down next to me. He muttered some words about drums being made today not with wood but with metal. Then he told me the story of Buñuel's last visit to Calanda.

It was the morning of Good Friday, and the square was already seething with a crowd waiting for noon so that they could strike the drums. Buñuel's son, Leonardo, approached Tomás with a message from his father saying that he wanted to meet him there and then in the square. The meeting took place, with the two men warmly embracing each other in front of an applauding crowd. Buñuel whispered into his friend's ear. 'Tomás,' he said, 'I'm in a bad way . . . I'm worn out. I know that this'll be the last year that I'll be able to make it to Calanda, I don't think I'll last much longer.' Overcome with emotion, Tomás insisted that the film-maker take up his drum one more time. Buñuel accepted, and, as the drums broke out at noon into their apocalyptic roar, he stood amidst the massed ranks of his townspeople, beating with what little strength he had left his final drumrolls.

FROM CALANDA I moved on to Zaragoza, where I returned to the scene of Buñuel's youth, and entered Goya's.

The Baron of Menglana, a schoolboy friend of Buñuel's from the Jesuit College at Zaragoza, spoke to Max Aub of Buñuel's sadness on coming back to Zaragoza in the 1950s, over twenty years after his last visit. Buñuel had fond memories of the old

Zaragoza and was almost tearful at seeing how it had been engulfed by a high-rise development that was turning it into 'a city like any other of its size in the world'. Yet Zaragoza seems never to have had an immediately obvious appeal, and rarely won the hearts of travellers, most of whom had agreed with Ford's assessment of the place as 'dull, gloomy and old-fashioned'.

After several hours of walking in the rain in search of somewhere to stay, I almost felt that I should have followed Unamuno's example and gone no further than the railway station. Zaragoza may not be a major tourist destination, but it was full on the night of my arrival with both pilgrims and travellers passing through. The Virgin of Pilar finally took pity on me and found me a place among elderly pilgrims in an establishment angelically named the 'Inn of Souls'. Nominated when it was built as 'The Finest Hotel in Aragón', the Inn of Souls now stood on the edge of the town's prostitute district, and had kept from its heyday in the 1920s only its ceramic-tiled vestibule, and its grand exterior, in a traditional Aragonese style. Massive, and with elaborately carved and widely projecting eaves, it was a building that imitated one of those typical Zaragozan palaces that had seemed to Ford more like castles than houses. Palaces such as these, in Ford's opinion, would have given the city a dignified aspect had it not been for all the 'rude rustics' who had taken them over from the absentee nobility, and who 'talk about bullocks in stately saloons, and convert noble patios into farm-yards and dung-heaps'.

Zaragoza still has a centre that is old-fashioned in character and lacking in elegance. That evening I walked up and down the two main streets of the old town, looking at department stores unchanged from the 1950s, as well as at religious shops selling the obligatory souvenir for all those making the pilgrimage to Zaragoza – a block of inedible, rectangular-shaped candy wrapped in a picture of Our Lady of Pilar. The old and predominantly *mudéjar* monuments I saw at dusk behind these streets lost some of their appeal by being surrounded by a poorly planned post-war development which had also managed to isolate one of Spain's greatest Moorish palaces – the Aljafería – in between a railway line and a spaghetti junction.

At nightfall, so I discovered, many of the pilgrims who had purged themselves of vice by day ended up in a narrow, claustrophobic street leading off, bathetically, from the pompous Plaza de España. Known locally as the 'Tubo', it was like a tunnel blocked with ageing bars, restaurants, porn shops, nightclubs, newspaper kiosks, and shoe-cleaning stands, the whole forming a museum to the seamier side of Franco's Spain. I was lucky enough to visit the Tubo in time to attend the poignant and last ever show at La Plata, a music-hall where women of a certain age sang risqué songs in a tarnished setting of plush red velvet and mirror tiles. With the closure of La Plata, Spain lost one of the last of this country's *cafés cantantes*, institutions that had played a major role in Spanish popular life since the middle of the last century. An old man, who had been present at the final show, sighed as he left the building, but then smiled as he pointed out to me a nearby old shop which was not likely to be closing down in the near future. Its window was like that of a traditional confectioner's, but its glass shelving, instead of displaying pastries, had a delicate arrangement of condoms and dildos. 'They always sold them there,' he said. 'I remember the shop as a boy, hasn't changed a bit. Even priests would go in then, in plain clothes, you understand. No, hasn't changed a bit.' The shop had a delightful name: it was called the French Orthopaedic Shop.

The Tubo is the hidden side of a city that presents an image of the Church Triumphant to the outside world. The antithesis of the Tubo is the Square of Our Lady of Pilar, which I appreciated at its best on my first morning in Zaragoza, when brilliant sunshine highlighted the sparkling detail and vast scale of a space that could almost have been built to bolster the ego of a Hitler or a Ceauşescu. Roman walls and a cathedral built over a mosque form the two ends of a square whose principal side is taken up by an archbishopric, a Renaissance stock exchange, a town hall, and the massively domed and turreted eighteenth-century bulk of the shrine itself, where pilgrims queue up within a marbled, gilded, frescoed gloom to pay their respects to the Virgin of Pilar, patroness of the Guardia Civil. The square, I was told, once had a more homely character than it has today, and was split into two levels, one of which functioned as a chaotic car-park. But by the autumn of 1991, it had just emerged from a cripplingly costly remodelling which had left it more totalitarian-looking than ever. Cars had been banished to below ground, and lay entombed underneath massive marble paving slabs, above which rose a long row of soaring, stadium-style lights of a sort Albert Speer might have devised for Nuremberg. Modern statuary of ambiguous significance provided the odd visual hazard, while real dangers were supplied in the form of large, unguarded pools into which the unwary visitor, contemplating the Pilar, could easily fall. A thought had at least been spared for dogs, who were now encouraged to relieve themselves above zinc-plated holes with rushing water.

In the new refurbishment of the Pilar Square, special prominence had been given to Goya, who had been turned into a secular idol to balance the sacred one contained within the shrine. A bronze, full-length statue of him stood on a huge plinth projecting above a pool flanked by recumbent bronzes of a *majo* and *maja*. Near by, and resembling an elegant pillarbox, was the funerary urn where his ashes had lain in Bordeaux, while enclosing the whole commemorative complex was a wall inscribed with the famous line, 'Fantasy abandoned by reason produces monsters, but, united with it, is the mother of all the arts.'

Goya is Aragón's most famous painter, but he is also an artist who has come to epitomize the Spanish genius, much more so than Velázquez, whose work is more limited in its subject-matter, and was largely conceived within the enclosed world of Madrid's Royal Palace. A combination of Spanish nationalism and romantic legend has transformed Goya into a painter of the people, an upholder of liberty, a fervent patriot, an embodiment of macho-ism, and a tormented genius. This is an image that has no place for the Goya who adored pigeon-shooting, regularly attended his shareholders' meetings, and had a long homosexual affair which has recently come to light following the little publicized discovery of a series of love letters. More seriously, it ignores the fact that Goya seems to have painted for anyone who would pay him, and actually executed a portrait of Napoleon which had to be changed quickly into an allegory of the Second of May. The art, it will be argued, is what matters, but the art in Goya's case is more uneven than that of any other painter of his stature. Whereas Velázquez's paintings unfailingly convey a magical and effortless naturalism, Goya's frequently reveal the hand of a hack who makes little attempt to cover up either his clumsiness or his boredom.

The works of Goya on show in Aragón are mainly religious decorations of Italian baroque inspiration, and certainly do not live up to the image of immortal genius projected in the Pilar Square. It was more out of interest in the idol than in the real person that I set off once again on the trail of relics and went to visit the artist's birthplace at Fuendetodos, about 40 kilometres south of Zaragoza. The only bus of the day that went there from the city left in the late afternoon, from a bus station of such darkened and sordid appearance that it brought to mind Goya's 'Black Paintings'. Twenty kilometres outside the city, the bus left the main road and the fertile Ebro valley to climb slowly into an empty landscape of olive trees and arid slopes. The light was quickly fading and only the faint profile of a municipal rubbish heap could be seen before we plunged into a near total darkness, just as we arrived at Fuendetodos.

I was the only person to get out of the bus, and I had optimistically brought my luggage with me in the hope of a place to stay. The darkness was such, however, that for a brief, frightening moment I thought that I had been dumped in the middle of the countryside. Not a single light was visible, and it was only after standing around for a few minutes, and disturbing a number of dogs, that I was able to make out a few distant signs of life. The village was tiny and apparently half deserted. Its sole bar was open only during the tourist season. The mayor was away on business, and the *concejal de cultura* had not yet returned from the farm where he worked during the day.

I found a teenage girl to open up Goya's supposed birthplace for me. It is a sturdy and unadorned stone structure, not quite the peasant's cottage of romantic legend, but then possibly nothing to do with Goya at all. The man responsible for commemorating Goya at Fuendetodos was the Basque painter Ignacio Zuloaga, a supporter of Franco, a lover and practitioner of bullfighting, and a devoted follower of Goya. In 1920 Zuloaga erected a monument at his own expense with the inscription 'To Goya, so that the spirit of the immortal artist, whose fame has spread throughout the world, lives on in the village where he was born.' In the same year Zuloaga purchased the house traditionally associated with Goya's birth, the only house of note or antiquity in the village. Goya's links with Fuendetodos are slight and entirely connected with his mother's family, the Lucientes, minor aristocrats whose name is still borne by some of the inhabitants here. The mother came back to Fuendetodos only for her son's birth, and returned soon afterwards to Zaragoza, where her husband worked as a master gilder, and where Goya would spend most of his childhood and adolescence. The 'birthplace' at Fuendetodos, a ruin when Zuloaga had bought it, now has a sparsely furnished, whitewashed interior, presumably intended to foster the myth of the 'people's artist' having been brought up in an environment of stern, rustic simplicity.

The girl with the key to the house said that none of the furnishings had anything to do with Goya, but were just 'bits and pieces' that Zuloaga had collected. I inquired about an organ loft Goya had painted in the local church, but she said that the original had been destroyed during the Civil War, and that the present organ was a modern copy. Bringing up a matter of more immediate importance, I asked if there was any chance of my finding a place to stay the night in Fuendetodos. She shook her head, but allowed me to use the phone in her parents' house.

A miracle happened. For the first time ever, I managed to get through to the car phone of my *bon viveur* friend, Javier Landa, whom I had last seen waving me off at the bus stop at Lorca. He was driving in the vicinity of Zaragoza, and offered to come immediately to pick me up. An hour later the darkness of Fuendetodos was illuminated by the beam of a smart red Audi.

'Michael,' he said, opening the car door, 'why do you always end up in the most Godforsaken places?'

ARAGONESE TASTE, according to Javier Landa, is of a similar degree of awfulness to Murcian taste, but it has its own distinctive qualities. It lacks the entertaining pretentiousness of the latter, and is just downright awful, without style, lightness, or any sense of design or quality.

'Take this tourist brochure,' Javier said, picking up a leaflet with a dark orange border and large, heavy lettering. 'It's a disaster.' He took a glass of local red wine and shook his head. 'They can't even make good wine here . . . And as for the food . . .'

The place we were in was not the best in which to contest his theories. We were having a late lunch in an empty self-service cafeteria, done up in the style of an American log cabin. Javier had done his best to improve the conditions of our lunch, and had successfully exercised his charm and forcefulness of character to make substantial changes to the set dishes on offer, and to try out before paying a selection of the small bottles of cheap wine near the cash till; he had even made up for 'the inexcusable lack of a tablecloth' by covering our bare wooden table with a number of paper napkins. But, in the end, Javier decided that there was nothing for it but to eat as quickly as possible and then go out and enjoy the beauty of the landscape, before continuing northwards.

We were in the most romantic corner of Zaragoza province, in the grounds of the Monasterio de Piedra, a former Cistercian abbey which in the nineteenth century had been turned into what was now a lugubrious hotel, with rooms arranged along dark and echoing Gothic corridors, decorated in 'typical Aragonese taste' with imitation-leather furnishings. The grounds themselves, an oasis of green hanging high above a landscape of distant ochre peaks, were laid out in an English romantic style, and had an exhilarating complex of waterfalls that flushed from my lungs the accumulated Aragonese dust of the previous days.

I had embarked with Javier on a tour of north-east Spain, and we were heading slowly towards a part of Aragón where Javier had been based for many years, an exile from the neighbouring region of Navarre. Javier, as a proud native of Navarre, found that Aragón greatly improved the closer you approached the Navarrese border, and though he loved the beautiful Monasterio de Piedra, he was especially keen to reach the northern province of Huesca, a province that had formed the original nucleus of the former kingdom of Aragón and had been briefly allied to Navarre in the Middle Ages.

We left the monastery and then the province of Zaragoza, and went to stay for several days with friends of Javier in Huesca itself, a town with a loftily situated medieval centre with views over a landscape reminiscent of those southern parts of Navarre where intense lushness is offset by dramatic areas of erosion. Having failed to find the truly 'unspoilt' Spanish village in the Almerian interior, Javier promised me that we would find such a place in the now seriously depopulated Pyrenean foothills to the east of Huesca. But even here we would arrive too late, discovering in this case that a vanguard of French canoists had begun to popularize the area.

Inevitably, with Javier as a guide, food became a major priority of our tour; and fortunately the food of this part of Aragón had benefited from proximity to Navarre. When we left Huesca to drive towards the north, we stopped only 15 kilometres outside the town to have lunch at a restaurant considered to be one of the best in all Aragón. The Venta del Sotón is a roadside inn with a history highly indicative of the social changes in Spain since Franco's day.

The place started up over twenty years ago as a sideline to the adjoining petrol station, and was originally a modest *asador* specializing mainly in roast meats for passing lorry drivers. The oven was a traditional clay one, the quality of the meat excellent, and many of the clients were drivers carrying produce from the great gastronomic centres of northern Spain. Deals were done, and soon the restaurant was receiving daily consignments of Navarrese vegetables ('the best in Spain'), Asturian *charcuterie*, and Basque and Galician seafood. The prices soared, the lorry drivers went elsewhere, but in their place came regular crowds of businessmen making special journeys out from Huesca to lunch and dine there. The petrol station is now a minor adjunct to a luxuriously appointed restaurant, one of the owners of which fuelled us for our journey with a home-made liquor rather more toxic than petrol. Back in the car, and prompted by the excellent food of the *venta*, I was soon dreaming of the gastronomic rather than the spiritual delights that sustain those travelling across northern Spain.

Two years earlier, in 1989, Javier had sent me off to Santiago de Compostela in a decidedly unspiritual fashion. I was reminded of that journey an hour away from the Venta del Sotón, when we saw the first of the Council of Europe signs that now mark the whole length of the pilgrims' route.

I HAD BEGUN the so-called 'Milky Way' at the hotel Javier owned at Candanchu, a skiing resort on the French border, occupying the site of what had been one of the most important pilgrim's hostels of medieval Europe. Javier had insisted on a dawn start, but by the early afternoon we had got no further than the neighbouring town of Canfranc, where I was gripped in reverential awe not by some Romanesque sculpture but by a monumental, turn-of-the-century railway station which had been transposed to Tsarist Russia in the film version of *Doctor Zhivago* (why had none of the many guides to the Santiago pilgrimage ever mentioned this remarkable building?). Javier had offered to accompany me at least as far as Pamplona, and naturally we were going there in his red Audi rather than by any of the more officially recognized forms of pilgrim transport – foot, horse, or bicycle. However, at Jaca, the original capital of Aragón, Javier decided that I needed to obtain a more *bona fide* status as a pilgrim, and took me immediately to the bishopric. The bishop was not in, but, through a friend of Javier's who worked in the secretariat, we were able to get the necessary 'pilgrim's passport', which claimed that the bishop himself had blessed me in Jaca Cathedral at the start of my pilgrimage.

The ceremony had of course been performed by Bishop Javier Landa, and in rather less august surroundings than the cathedral; none the less this dubious document would allow me to stay in the pilgrims' hostels along the route, and also to receive, at the end of my journey, a Latin certificate that would confuse my less knowledgeable friends by placing the name Michaelem Jacobus alongside that of Sancti Jacobi. The passport also put me into a holier frame of mind, at least until we reached Pamplona, where unholy distractions were provided at a famous nightspot known as 'The Knowing You Is Loving You, Baby'. Javier stayed on with me a few more days, until we reached the wine-growing district of the Rioja, where our 'Milky Way' lost whatever traces it still had of milkiness.

A sense of heading towards some ultimate goal began to affect me only once Javier and his Audi had left. I had begun to walk up to 30 kilometres a day, carrying a rucksack weighed down with books and pamphlets, washing in freezing streams, and sleeping fully clothed under old blankets in village halls, churches, school rooms, or the houses of priests. The hardships and the slow pace made me enjoy more than ever before the natural beauty and variety of northern Spain: the rolling vineyards and distant mountains of the Rioja; the forested hills east of Burgos; the unrelieved flatness of the upper Castilian wheatfields; the snow-capped peaks of the Cordillera Cantábrica; the empty mountainous district of the Maragatos; the almond blossom of the Bierzo Valley; the granite greyness of Galicia. The modern world – motorways, industrial expanses, high-rise suburbs – intruded on large stretches of the pilgrims' route, but there were times when the experience of the pilgrimage seemed to have changed little since the Middle Ages, as when the villagers of remote communities came out of their houses to say, 'May you arrive in peace!' Or when an old hermit invited me once to have lunch in a kitchen where a Latin inscription reminded the visitor that 'God resides in the saucepans.'

Frequently I felt a complete fraud, a participant in an absurd medieval charade. I had little respect for the cult of St James, and was largely motivated as a 'pilgrim' by reasons unconnected with the spirit: principal among these were a love of walking and of new places, and, above all, a fascination with the different peoples, cultures, and gastronomic traditions of northern Spain. Furthermore I was beset for much of the journey by two nagging anxieties that lessened my chances of arriving anywhere in peace. One of these was an almost pathological fear of dogs, which increased with the *minifundios*, or smallholdings, of Galicia, where dogs rushed out to bark at me every hundred metres or so. The other fear was less rational: a fear of meeting the genuine pilgrim.

In contrast to those taking part in the Andalusian pilgrimage to the Rocío, the pilgrims to Santiago are an altogether more serious group of people. The southerners' pagan sense of religion, and their passion for dressing up and exuberant merry-making, are replaced on the Santiago route by orthodox Christianity, sensible hiking gear, a taste for sporting challenges, and a wholly sentimental nostalgia for the Middle Ages. Before going to Santiago I had joined the British Confraternity of St James, and had cringed at descriptions of pilgrim reunions where guitars had been taken out and 'Greensleeves' sung. I had experienced a similar embarrassment along the route while looking through some of the hostels' visitors' books, which were usually filled with lyrical descriptions of birds and babbling brooks, together with photographs showing people dressed in medieval pilgrim's garb, complete with tricorn, scallop shell and gourd. To judge from the dates on many of the entries, it would be only a matter of time before our paths would cross. Further mounting unease resulted from talking to some of the villagers, who warned me of certain strange pilgrims on the route ahead, and told me repeatedly to be on my guard against one particular drug addict who was prone to violent attacks.

By travelling to Santiago off-season, the likelihood of meeting many pilgrims is actually slight, and in the whole of my four weeks on the route I was to meet only seven. The first was a young and lonely Dutch woman whose slow, heavy manner and perpetually sad expression spread melancholy wherever she went. The second, in contrast, was an irritatingly jaunty Belgian of clear paedophile tendencies. He was going to Santiago to collect a consignment of juvenile offenders who had been forced to undertake the pilgrimage. Then came a German who had walked all the way from Frankfurt, barefoot and with a rucksack of over 30 kilos: he said he was punishing himself for having been an errant husband.

The moment I had most dreaded came at the beautiful Galician monastery of Samos, when one of the kind monks showed me into a small dormitory with a most overpowering smell. I had caught up at last with a Messianic-looking trio from Paris, who had not washed for three months in the expectation of a literal and symbolic cleansing on the outskirts of Santiago. To make matters worse, they had taken under their wing – in the hope either of exorcizing the devil or redeeming a soul – the drug addict of whom I had heard such fearful stories. Their idea of night-time entertainment was to lie on top of their beds, taking it in turns to read out the Bible, while doing their best to ignore the occasional scream and evil laugh of their addict protégé. A brief distraction from this religious nightmare was provided by the worldly monks, who asked me for help in translating into Spanish part of an Amstrad computer manual. This task completed, however, I was subjected to an intensive French interrogation. Why was I going to Santiago? Was I looking for the truth? Surely I was not following the route just because I'd been commissioned to write an architectural guide? Could I not see how this poor drug addict had begun to see the light under the guidance of St James?

EVERY JOURNEY away from one's home is a pilgrimage, according to Dante. But there is something special about the Santiago pilgrimage that has nothing to do with relics, religion, self-discovery, cultural sights, or any of the numerous ephemeral pleasures along the route. In walking relentlessly every day in the direction of the setting sun, there are moments when one can almost convince oneself of the existence of some magnetic, mystical force that has drawn worshippers, long before Christianity, to what was once the end of the world.

19

Basque Routes

THE LANDS of the pilgrims' way, from Navarre to Galicia, are united by what the Basque philosopher Fernando Savater referred to as 'not only a pastime but also a way of life'. Known in the strange language of the Basques as a *txikiteo* (the *tx* is pronounced *tsch*), this pastime is a type of bar crawl special to the north of Spain; it is not really a crawl at all.

First-time participants in a *txikiteo*, accustomed perhaps to the leisurely bar life of a southern city such as Seville, will still be sipping their first drink when they are suddenly rushed off by their group of friends to another bar, then another, and another, until sometimes up to twenty bars are visited, the speed of the process being made possible both by the exceptionally high concentration of bars to be found in specially prescribed streets and districts of northern towns, and by the smallness of the measures available there. Wine comes either in tiny straight glasses, or – in Galicia – in shallow cups of white porcelain; spirits can be ordered in half measures; cider covers only the first few centimetres of a wide tumbler; and beer is frequently drunk in thimble-like quarter-measures.

Standing up is essential to maintain the pace of a *txikiteo*, and *tapas* are needed to prolong the whole experience, the particular gastronomic specialities of the various bars being important indicators as to whether or not these places are to be included in the drinkers' itinerary. The often manic speed of the *txikiteo* precludes too much time spent either in choosing the food, or waiting for it to be prepared. Many of the bars assist the hurried drinker by specializing, say, only in cheese or octopus, or else by arranging a large selection of canapés on the counters, the quantities consumed being estimated afterwards by the person in the group who is paying for the round. Despite the smallness of the individual quantities of food and drink, the accumulated effect of several hours of this leaves one with the impression of having taken part in a vast speeded-up banquet with scarcely a pause between courses, a moving rather than a movable feast, and something better evoked by a Futurist painter than by a Hemingway.

The *txikiteo* is more than just a feature of the life of northern Spain. It suggests a journey across a part of the country where much of the population is concentrated in intense clusters, often separated from each other by poor communications, and by rigid historical and geographical frontiers, yet forming altogether a bewilderingly diverse succession of cultural riches of which the traveller can have only a brief taste before moving on.

I like also to think of the *txikiteo* in more general terms: as a metaphor for a journey in its later stages, a journey that began with a relaxed sense of time stretching ahead, but which has now reached a point where the limitations of time have become only too apparent, forcing one into a near-hysterical rush to see as much as possible in what little time remains.

SHORTLY BEFORE noon, on the day of St Fermín, crowds of people dressed in white can be seen running along the high-rise avenues of modern Pamplona, carrying glasses and champagne bottles, and heading towards the Plaza del Castillo, the large arcaded square at the entrance to this town's small and congested historic centre. When the town's bells strike twelve, the bottles are opened, the champagne is poured, red neck-ties and berets are donned, and everyone starts kissing and embracing each other, and exchanging best wishes for the ensuing week-long festivities of the Sanfermines.

The scene from the centrally positioned balcony of the town's casino, where the privileged families of Pamplona are ensconced, is one of Bacchanalian chaos, a turbulent sea of white and red, speckled with hundreds of drunk and bedraggled young foreigners who have been sleeping rough, and sporting their ties and berets long before noon, in blissful ignorance of the local superstition that this is a harbinger of bad luck.

Saber beber (the drinking equivalent of *savoir vivre*) is a quality Spaniards consider lacking in most foreigners, but the distinction between those who have it and those who don't becomes an increasingly tenuous one as the Sanfermines wear on, and foreigners end up indistinguishable in their drunkenness from the more loutish of the *sanfermineros*: this is the most democratic of festivals, and, as such, an antithesis to the élitist Seville Feria, where the many foreign tourists fade into the background, and where extreme drunkenness is unacceptable unless accompanied by style or wit.

The Sanfermines reminded H. V. Morton of a Scottish Hogmanay, but the Sanfermines last over seven times as long and produce after only a few hours scenes of mass inebriation rarely encountered elsewhere in Europe. By nightfall not a single white shirt remains unstained by wine or beer, and the cheerful throwing around of drink and bottles will continue until dawn, when the route to the famous *encierros* or bull-running is strewn with broken glass and bodies. At seven o'clock one morning, a few minutes before the start of the *encierros*, I once came across a foreign woman so tired and drunk that she took off her belt, fastened herself to one of the columns of the main square, and fell asleep. Other foreigners, in a state scarcely more alert than hers, have been goaded by friends into running in front of the bulls. They are likely to provide the main casualties of this tumultuous event.

A feature of the Sanfermines no less striking than the festival's drunken confusion is the efficiency of the local ambulances and rubbish vans, the former arriving within minutes on the scene of an accident, the latter battling all day and night to maintain a modicum of tidiness such as one would never expect on the pilgrimage to the Rocío. But foreign observers of what Kenneth Tynan described as Pamplona's 'annual orgy, or ordeal by noise and wine' prefer to ignore these signs of Navarrese organizational excellence, and think of the festival either as a display of 'southern passion' or else as an endorsement of Aymeric Picaud's view of the Navarrese as drunken, pugnacious semi-savages who dress worse than the Scots, and make sounds while eating comparable to those of 'dogs or pigs gulping gluttonously'.

The Sanfermines clearly upset such an effete northerner as H. V. Morton, who detected in them 'the only touch of what looked like urban vulgarity in Spain', a viewpoint that would have been heavily contested by Hemingway, Pamplona's most famous apologist. Those who have done their best to try and avoid traces of Hemingway in Madrid will find his presence inescapable in Pamplona, where a monumental bronze bust of his head is set, appropriately enough, outside the Spanish ring where the subtleties of bullfighting are the least understood. The publication in 1927 of Hemingway's *The Sun Also Rises* turned Pamplona into what Tynan described as a 'magnet for American Left-Bankers', many of whom congregated at Hemingway's beloved Café Choco, where Tynan spotted several of them wearing 'the black smocks of Basque peasants'.

To the disciples of Hemingway, Pamplona and its Sanfermines express the passionate, *macho* essence of Spain itself, an attitude that seems to corroborate Victor Hugo's view that the city was 'well and truly the real Spain'. Yet, in terms of its history, culture and geographical position, Pamplona should really be seen as a city between two worlds, between a Spain that is unmistakably Spanish and a Spain that some would not consider Spanish at all. Below the city extends lower Navarre, where cereals, vines and olives are cultivated in a rolling landscape of yellow, grey and reddish tones; fertile, irrigated areas flank the banks of rivers, and provide, in the vicinity of Tudela, a verdant contrast to a neighbouring expanse of badlands reminiscent of the Almerian desert. In contrast, immediately to the north of Pamplona is a land where Basque is widely spoken and which is characterized throughout by a scenery that travellers have often compared to that of Switzerland, a scenery composed of pine forests, mountains, fields of Alpine lushness, and timber-roofed farms that have the toy-like neatness of Swiss chalets.

IN THE AUTUMN of 1991, driving north from Aragón with Javier Landa, we remained on the pilgrims' way only as far as Pamplona, where we broke our journey for a couple of nights before continuing towards the coastal town of San Sebastián. The main road between Pamplona and the coast has now been converted for much of its length into a motorway, the completion of which has been endlessly delayed by a combination of ETA bombs and ecologists' protests, the advocates of conservation being some-times confused with the agents of destruction.

The alternative route to San Sebastián, longer and more politically correct, takes the traveller through some of the most beautiful mountain valleys of upper Navarre and a countryside especially rich in associations with Basque folk culture. We chose this slower route, and set off from Pamplona in the late morning, emulating the example of Pope John Paul II by stopping off shortly afterwards at the Venta de Ulzama, a restaurant so famous for its *cuajada*, or curd dessert, that the very bowl out of which the Pope had eaten his has been hung on the wall, together with a reverential inscription.

Sanctified by the eating of a *cuajada*, we resumed our climb into the mountains, but soon lost sight of the landscape in dense fog and blinding rain. The rain was still falling, and dusk was nearly on us, when we deviated from our route at the small town of Santesteban, at the base of a steeply ascending valley featuring a near-perfectly preserved series of tiny villages and what are called in Basque *baserrik*, the farming homesteads that form the traditional backbone of rural Basque society.

In the first of these villages, Ituren, we stayed in a cheap, spotlessly clean *pensión* of a tasteful simplicity very much in keeping with the surroundings. The building itself, as with so many others in this part of Navarre, was of enormous size and sturdiness, with whitewashed walls, huge stone quoins, flower-adorned wooden balconies, and a Swiss-style pointed roof. Characteristic too of this region was the narrow gap separating the building from its neighbours, a gap representing in Javier's eyes the proud individualism of the Navarrese people, and their abhorrence of living in a connected row of houses, as in most other Spanish villages.

The only other occupant of our *pensión* was an eccentric painter friend of Javier from Pamplona, Joaquín Echevarría, who spent several weeks in the valley every autumn, recording the landscape in expressively bold canvases. Prevented by continual rain from doing any painting in the preceding days, he was in a depressed, complaining mood when we arrived.

'Can you imagine!' he said, referring to the charming family who ran the *pensión*. 'They actually gave me *frozen* fish last night! I've been coming here for twenty years, and then they treat me like that!'

An elegant and mannered bachelor from one of Pamplona's wealthiest families, Joaquín was bossy and snobbish, and made a point of cultivating aristocrats whose names he would continually drop. He had lived for a while under the patronage of some marquis in the Italian town of Asolo, and was such an Italophile that he larded his conversation with innumerable Italian expressions. He was also a man of great contradictions that seemed to reflect the political and cultural complexities of this part of Spain.

Typically, for a man of romantic, aristocratic leanings, Joaquín grew up espousing Carlism, a monarchist cause fought in the last century with particular ferocity in the Basque country and Navarre, where it gained its main Spanish stronghold, thanks to the traditionally reactionary, wealthy and ultra-Catholic rural classes of these regions. Carlism later disappeared almost completely from the Spanish political scene, the most recent pretender to the throne, Carlos Hugo, having confused his few remaining followers in 1976 by forming a political party advocating left-wing socialism and workers' control.

As for Joaquín Echevarría, he had gone on to adapt an ambiguous, ever-changing political stance that had nothing to do with real politics. Unable to speak Basque, and hostile at first to its culture and political aims, he became for a while an extreme Spanish nationalist, favouring the Guardia Civil and the right-wing Partido Popular; later, under the influence of his sojourns in the valley of Santesteban, he came to take the side of the Basque countryfolk, 'simple, warm-hearted people' whom he forgave for such frequent acts of vulgarity as serving frozen fish. He was converted to the cause of Basque separatism, and believed, like the most radical of the separatists, in a Basque state that would include the whole of Navarre, a region he regarded as the heartland of the Basque nation. I could only assume that Joaquín's feelings were allied to the right-wing PNV (Partido Nacional Vasco), but so irrational and confused were his views that I would not have been surprised had he emerged as a supporter of ETA, the left-wing terrorist group, which has many of its hideouts in the valleys of upper Navarre, and is widely tolerated there out of a sense of Basque brotherhood.

Joaquín Echevarría was a mad and maddening person, but the unpredictability of his moods and opinions, and his arrogant presence, made him compelling company, if only in short doses. At nightfall I happily joined him and Javier in a mini-*txikiteo* beginning in Santesteban itself and gradually making its way up the valley, stopping off at rustic bars that openly displayed ETA collection boxes. At carnival time the small winding road up the valley forms the route of a celebrated folkloric procession headed by men in bear-costumes known as *ioaldunak*. The first Saturday of November could not provide us with such spectacular anthropological entertainment, but near the top of the valley we did stumble across a local festival of pronounced Basque character.

The setting, to which I would return by day, was a scattered idyllic community of about twenty farmsteads, with a mountainous backcloth, an isolated wooden church crowning a hill, and a small *pelota* court adjoining one of the hamlet's two bars. The festival was centred around the *pelota* court, where, on the Saturday night, young girls in local costume were dancing *jotas* to the accompaniment of an accordionist. Women and children were the main onlookers, most of the men preferring to stay drinking outside, some of them exchanging hearty jokes in Basque with the sturdy champion of an earlier display of log-sawing (a characteristic sport of the Basque lands).

People were constantly arriving and leaving, and, after an hour or so, we decided to follow one of the departing cars, which eventually drew up on the outskirts of Santesteban, outside one of the largest discotheques I have ever seen – a hyper-discotheque intended to serve the entire valley, with a huge neon sign drawing attention to the place for miles around. On the night of our visit to the valley, carloads of increasingly drunk people were restlessly alternating between the discotheque and the festival, between modern rock culture and Basque folk culture. Joaquín insisted that we return to the latter, but by the time we arrived back in the hamlet, at around two in the morning, the traditional festival had lost all semblance of rural dignity. The bloated red faces of middle-aged men seemed to be laughing at us, particularly at Joaquín, who was making disparaging comments about them in high-pitched Italian. An unglamorous-looking local band, mingling *jotas* with Michael Jackson songs, was occupying the now crowded *pelota* court, wresting from a disgusted Joaquín a sigh of 'Che schifo!'

A smiling old man pulled us away from the court, and started making theatrical gestures, his eyes half closed. The background noise and his drunken state made him almost inaudible, but the gutturals I could catch were clearly Basque. The voice grew louder and succeeded, in the interval between the band's sets, in attracting the attention of some of those around us. The man was reciting, as he apparently always did, at every bar, at every gathering. He was a Basque archetype: the village storyteller.

The telling of stories has been the life-blood of Basque culture, a culture based on an obscure language, isolated both from Spain and from the rest of the world, and condemned at one time to extinction. Until recently, a mere hundred or so books had been written in the Basque language, and it was only with Bernardo Atxaga's *Obabakoak* (1980), a novel arranged as a series of stories, partially recited, that Basque literature achieved both national and international recognition.

In an afterword to this book, Atxaga says Basque writers of today might lack antecedents – books from which to learn how to write in Basque – but they did not lack tradition, for all writers of the late twentieth century have at their disposal 'the whole of the literary past'. 'The world', as Atxaga put it, 'is everywhere and Euskal Herria [the Basque country] is no longer just Euskal Herria but . . . "the place where the world takes the name of Euskal Herria".' The stories of *Obabakoak* (the title means, roughly, 'Stories from Obaba') begin with childhood scenes from the imaginary mountain village of Obaba, go on to include the narrator's experiences of living in an isolated Castilian community, and end up by covering a vast range of countries and periods, the narrative thrust being provided by what the narrator defines as his 'search for the last word', a search that ultimately takes over the narrator's life to become a parable of the passionate quest for Basque identity.

The Basque nation did not need a Verdaguer to create its own mythology. Its origins are so distant and mysterious that innumerable legends have grown up to explain them, the most popular of which bear out Atxaga's belief that the greatest of stories have the quality of poetry and transcend the anecdotal and particular to achieve a universal significance. Long before Verdaguer wrote *L'Atlántida*, Basque storytellers were relating how these people were originally the inhabitants of the lost island of Atlantis. Etymologists have rationalized this by saying that Plato's name for the island's capital, Basileia, was derived from *Batzileya*, the Basque word for the island of the dead. Another story has it that the first Basques were among the earliest families of mankind and that they came to Europe from the Orient in search of the sun. Yet another story, still surviving in the folk traditions of the Guernica district, claims that Noah's Ark ran aground in the Basque country, and that one of Noah's grandsons, Tubal, left the boat here to found a new nation with his wife and children.

Scientific investigation into the origins of the Basque people has on the whole been scarcely more convincing than the folk tales. Unamuno, in his 1883 doctoral dissertation on the subject of Basque origins, concluded by saying that 'we know almost nothing about the prehistoric culture of the Basques'. Subsequent researchers would discover that the Basques have a higher percentage of rhesus negative blood type than any other people in the world, and that some of the stereotypical features of present-day Basques, such as high foreheads and long, straight noses, are comparable to those of Cro-Magnon man. None the less, Julio Caro Baroja, the distinguished author of *The Peoples of Spain*, remains convinced that the very concept of a 'Basque race' is a problematical one, given the inability of scholars to come up with any scientifically rigorous explanation of the origins of such a race.

Caro Baroja, one of the most respected survivors from an encyclopaedic age of Spanish scholarship, is an authority on Basque matters rivalled until recently only by Father José Barandarián.

Barandarián, who died in January 1992 at the age of a hundred and one, achieved in later life an almost bardic stature among the Basques, many of whom considered him to be a scholar much closer to their hearts and interests than Caro Baroja. He approached his work in a spirit of idealistic fervour and with the conviction in the existence of a Basque race dating back 50,000 years. Believing in the decadence of urban and technological culture, he concentrated his academic interests on primitive and rural societies, whose culture he thought essential both for an understanding of the present and for a judgement of the future: he was a mystic driven by a powerful eschatalogical sense. In contrast, Caro Baroja is the supreme empiricist, a man whose only god is scholarship, and whose writings are dry, clear-headed, and lacking in abstract speculation. He has none of the pure Basque credentials of Barandarián, nor any of the latter's romantic qualities; yet he has – in the upper Navarrese village of Vera de Bidasoa – a house that is in itself a legend.

ON A SUNNY day washed clear by the heavy weekend rains, we left the valley of Santesteban and continued slowly north by way of Vera de Bidasoa. The mountain fields had a *Sound of Music* greenness, and exaggerated the make-believe appearance of the countless old farmsteads and villages we passed. The district we were in, so redolent of wholesome, unchanging rural life, was also one that fascinated both Barandarián and Caro Baroja for its associations with witchcraft. A wooded mountain range is all that separates Vere de Bidasoa from the notorious caves of Zugorra-mudi, the former location of what is known in Basque by the one word this language has given to the world at large – an *akelarre*, or witches' coven.

Vera de Bidasoa lies among extensive pastures at the upper end of the Bidasoa valley, within walking distance of the French frontier. Caro Baroja's house, known as 'Itzea', is on the outskirts of the village, and to reach it one has to show one's passport at the Spanish border post. Itzea seems to belong to a neutral land between countries, which is perhaps appropriate for a house that is its own cultural entity enclosed within the greater enclave of the Basque country.

A traditional stone farmstead of characteristically large size, Itzea was purchased as a ruin by Caro Baroja's celebrated uncle, Pío Baroja. The leading novelist of the Generation of '98, Pío Baroja was someone with an ambivalent relationship with both Spain and his native Basque country. A critic of mindless patriotism (he thought it ridiculous that something should be praised simply because it was 'very Spanish'), he saw himself as an arch-European, and was proud of having Italian blood through a grandmother from Como, which conferred on him roots that stretched from the two great mountain barriers of Europe, the Alps and the Pyrenees. His novels, hastily written, in short paragraphs, and filled with action, often had Basque settings; his trilogy, *Basque Land* (1900–1909), incorporated tales he had heard from his father about the Second Carlist War.

The popular Spanish press caricatured Pío Baroja as a ferocious, beret-wearing Basque brandishing a sheet of paper; to Gerald Brenan, he was at heart a 'Basque mountaineer and *aldeano*', whose professed belief that 'art, music and books . . . are of no importance' was typical of a people 'noted for their lack of aesthetic feeling'. Yet Pío Baroja himself was loath to reach any straightforward conclusions about the Basque character, and wrote about his region not as an ideologue, but as an often critical observer. Strongly anti-clerical and profoundly nihilist, Pío Baroja delighted in his reputation as an *enfant terrible*, and was almost flattered, shortly after purchasing Itzea, that the local children knew him as the 'Bad Man of Bidasoa'. Such a nickname gave glamour to an inherently shy bachelor whose adventures were limited almost exclusively to his novels.

Caro Baroja, another lifelong bachelor, has also emulated his uncle in dividing his life between a flat in Madrid and his home at Vera. Itzea is almost an open house to scholars, who drop by to consult the celebrated library founded here by Pío Baroja and continued by his nephew. Javier and I were met at the massive oak door to the house by Caro Baroja's old housekeeper, who, by coincidence, turned out to be from Javier's native Navarrese village of Dicastillo. Discovering that her master was at home, Javier asked her to tell him that 'Javier Landa from Dicastillo' was passing by and had brought with him 'a scholar from England'. She went upstairs to see if he was in a position to receive visitors, and returned with a smile to direct us into an ante-room, where she said that he would shortly be joining us. This old-fashioned way of welcoming unexpected visitors seemed to belong to the same distant era in which the house itself had obstinately remained. We were not so much in a private home as in a museum to the Generation of '98, dark, musty, with creaking floorboards, a smell of polish, and decor apparently untouched since Pío Baroja's day. Breaking the silence of the ante-room, Javier confessed that he had personally never met Caro Baroja, but that he had a sister who had spent much time here while researching a thesis on witchcraft.

Caro Baroja finally made his entry, having apparently donned a jacket and bow-tie in order to greet us in the proper style. Nearing his eightieth year (a mere youngster in comparison to Barandarián), he had retained a nimble step and a near-perfect memory. He was able to recall every detail of Javier's sister's stay, down to the actual day when she first arrived at Itzea. With his neatly trimmed moustache, small, delicate features, serious, quietly affable manner, and disinclination to wander in his conversation, he evoked in person the main qualities of his writings – lucidity and economy of prose, a vast intellectual range, and a more limited emotional one.

He gave us the salient facts about Itzea and his family, and then guided us through rooms that were pale and faded in their coloured wallpaper, but heavy in their furnishings and memories. The simple writing desk, the small brass bed and other mementoes of the quiet, solitary life of Pío Baroja dominated living quarters that were hung with the dark Whistlerian portraits and landscapes by Pío's versatile brother Ricardo, a painter, film director and essayist. The library, the largest private one that I had ever seen, seemed to weigh the whole house down, covering as it did the entire upper floor, and extending into a barn-like attic of massive wooden beams. Rambling in appearance, with wooden shelving that had spread like an ancient oak into every darkened recess, the library was divided into sections corresponding to the many areas on which Caro Baroja has wrtten, from Spanish Judaism to Golden Age literature, from prehistoric archaeology to twentieth-century ethnography. One section, made up almost entirely of vellum bindings and sixteenth- and seventeenth-century manuscripts, featured the most important collection in Spain of primary material relating to witchcraft, and to its persecution by the Inquisition.

For my benefit Caro Baroja took me into the part of the library dedicated to foreigners' travel-writing on Spain. He told me that he greatly admired Gerald Brenan, whom he had known personally, but that he believed that foreign writings on Spain had in general become progressively less interesting from the late nineteenth century onwards, and were full of inaccuracies and distortions while having little of the freshness of the writings of the Romantic period. The subject of 'inaccuracies and distortions' was afterwards revealed to me as one that itself was of interest to him. At the time of our arrival, he had apparently been sitting in the one heated corner of the bitterly cold library, proof-reading a book entitled *The Falsifications of History*.

THE ENGLISH neo-Gothic architect, George Edmund Street, entering Spain through the Basque country in 1865, wrote that 'so little has it been the fashion hitherto to explore the north of Spain in search of artistic treasures, that it was with somewhat more than usual of the feeling that I was engaged in an adventure that I left Bayonne on my first journey west of the Pyrenees'. Scarcely aware of the pilgrimage that had once made the north of Spain one of the great thoroughfares of Europe, the nineteenth-century traveller tended to head immediately in the direction of Andalusia, where, in the words of Street, 'most English ideas of Spain and the Spaniards are formed'. Of the romantic travellers to Spain, it was principally the French who seem to have taken more than just a passing interest in the Basque country. Prosper Mérimée's *Carmen* may have been the book that immortalized the hackneyed vision of southern Spain, but one should not forget that its unfortunate male protagonist is a Basque who, in his first conversation with the gypsy with whom he becomes obsessed, mentions to her that he is from the upper Navarrese village of Eliozondo: 'If you're from Eliozondo, then I'm from Echalar,' she cheekily retorts, referring to a village near Vera de Bidasoa which no Andalusian gypsy woman of the nineteenth century could possibly have heard of.

The Bidasoa river, which Javier and I followed after leaving Itzea, marks in its last stages the French frontier and passes alongside 'the island of pheasants', a site that unfailingly provoked the curiosity and amused scorn of French travellers. The curiosity was due to the island having been the scene of the celebrated marital exchange negotiated in 1659 by Louis XIV and Philip IV; the mirth and disappointment resulted from the discovery that the island associated with this glamorous event was just a sad strip of green in which the pheasants had been replaced – by Victor Hugo's day – by 'one cow and three ducks'.

The site today is more desolate still, for it lies within earshot of the motorway between Bordeaux and Bilbao, and only a few hundred metres from the industries of Irún. Javier was quick to remind me that we had left Navarre a few kilometres back, and were now in what was officially known as the Basque country. The rural architecture is identical to that of upper Navarre, though in Javier's opinion the villages and farmsteads are less well maintained, and more sullied by modern additions, as if the predominantly rural interior has been contaminated by the sprawling industrial conglomeration of the valleys behind the coast.

The coastal town of Irún is not an immediately appealing sight, but it is one that has often excited travellers coming from France. It marks the arrival in Spain, and the crossing of a frontier that had once seemed as much of a frontier in time as a political and geographical one. The sudden shock of Spanishness made a particularly acute impression on Théophile Gautier, who succeeded in convincing himself that on entering Spain at Irún he had entered the Middle Ages. For him the place was 'unlike a French town in every possible respect', the town having 'whitewashed walls in the Oriental manner' and quaint local costumes that seemed to him to be medieval.

Victor Hugo entered Spain at Irún in 1843, three years after
Gautier, and thirty-two years after he himself had last been there
– as a child of eight in the company of his father. The crossing of
the Bidasoa brought back memories as romantic as those of the
adult Gautier, but Irún itself bore little relation either to the place
he remembered from childhood or to the one Gautier had
described. He now found Irún to be 'more Empire and precious
than Paris', and summed it up as a Spanish Batignolles. 'Where',
he asked, 'has its history gone? Where is its past? Where is its
poetry?' Fortunately this disillusion with Spain was momentary,
and he was soon entranced by the Basque country.

As a Hispanophile, Hugo is usually thought of as a devotee of
medieval Castile (the setting of his play *Hernani*) and Moorish
Andalusia (mythologized by him in his epic poem *Les Orientales*);
but his sole travel book on Spain was the one to come out of his
journey to the Basque country and Navarre in 1843. In this
delightful short book, *Les Pyrénées*, Hugo describes how he
originally intended to spend a long period in San Sebastián but
moved on after a few days to the nearby fishing village of Pasajes,
where he had been lured by the harpy-like women who ran the
ferry service between the two places. Hugo had no idea what sort
of place he was being taken to until his boat passed a headland
and there suddenly came into view, 'as if by magic', a 'ravishing
spectacle' composed of green mountains rising above a sparkling
inlet and a long group of narrow, balconied houses in white,
green and saffron. Hugo described this 'resplendent Eden' as one
of the most beautiful villages that he had ever seen, and claimed
that it 'would be admired if it were in Switzerland and famous if
it were in Italy'; but, of course, had it been anywhere other than
in the Basque province of Guipúzcoa, he would not have been
able to relish the sense of superiority in being in a place 'which no
tourist visits'. He also clearly enjoyed the shock he caused on
returning to his hotel in San Sebastián and announcing to the
receptionist that he would be transferring to Pasajes the next day.
'What are you going to do there, sir?' the man asked. 'But it's a
hole. A desert. A land of savages. But you won't even find a
hotel!'

Hugo found lodgings in a picturesque old house overlooking

the sea, and continued to be enchanted by the village he had 'discovered'. A mood of *dolce far niente* is not normally associated with Basque fishing villages, but this is precisely what Hugo encountered in Pasajes, a village where 'Some people work, many dance, everyone sings.' By the end of his stay in Pasajes the author of *Les Orientales* had not 'died of hunger or been devoured by savages', as the people of San Sebastián had feared, but had begun to succumb to those oriental delusions that usually took hold of romantic travellers south of Despeñaperros. Walking down Pasajes's main and only street, he now imagined himself further away from Guipúzcoa than ever. He had come to perceive the street as 'unmistakably Arab' and almost had the sensation of 'being in Tetuan'.

On our drive from Irún to San Sebastián, I persuaded Javier to make a brief detour to Pasajes, so that I could see for myself whether there was anything left of Tetuan in a place that from the outskirts resembled Swansea or Cardiff.

Industries and tall, grey blocks of flats, heavily populated by Galician immigrants, had mushroomed to the south of the town centre and along the whole of the western side of the estuary, where they joined up with the working-class suburbs of San Sebastián. But once we had left our car and entered the central, pedestrian district of Pasajes, we came to an unexpectedly well-preserved fishing village. Crammed in between the sea and the dark green slopes behind, this old quarter was tied together by a long street which narrowed at times into the darkest of alleys, and passed through the occasional arch that might have deluded Hugo into thinking that he was in a Moroccan *souk*. That the sturdy stone buildings could only have been Basque, however, was reinforced by the black graffiti proclaiming freedom for the Basque country and victory for ETA, a list of whose prisoners was featured on a long banner draped from the town hall: the 'resplendent Eden' of Victor Hugo had become one of the main strongholds of ETA's political wing, Herri Batasuna, which apparently had the vote of 35 per cent of the town's electorate. Even at the northern end of the town, where the street turned into a footpath hugging a wild headland, politics were not forgotten, the slogans being now appended to the massive granite boulders that fell into the sea.

We reached the end of the town and then turned back, to look once again for what we had so far failed to find – some form of commemoration to the stay in Pasajes of the towering genius of nineteenth-century French literature. The old quarter of Pasajes was so intact that the seafront house where Hugo stayed was certain to have survived; but in the absence of plaques marking it, we were forced in the end to call in and see a friend of Javier's who owned one of the many restaurants in Pasajes that cater for Sunday excursionists. She confirmed that there was indeed a 'Hugo house', and pointed out to us a picturesque building projecting into the sea.

'Right up to a year ago,' she said, 'the house had hardly changed since Hugo's day. But then a bank bought it, and the whole interior was stripped to make a cultural centre.'

She had a surprise for us, however. We followed her upstairs into her family's living quarters, where we were confronted, in the corridor, by a large lithographic portrait of Victor Hugo, signed by the man himself and dedicated to her great-grandfather. This work, she explained, had once hung in the restaurant's dining-room, next to old photographs of her family. However, her stern Basque mother had protested strongly about this, and indignantly asked her what 'this Frenchman' was doing next to the family portraits.

Victor Hugo's memory had been consigned to the upstairs corridor, but seemed to have scored some subliminal victory over the woman with whom we were talking. She had married a man called Victor, and they had named their son Victor.

'THE FIRST glimpse is magnificent,' wrote Victor Hugo of San Sebastián. 'The second is merely amusing.' The beauty of San Sebastián's shell-shaped bay, with its twin emerald-coloured peaks guarding its entrance, has never been doubted, but the town itself has often been improperly appreciated by foreign travellers for the same old reasons: it's too modern, and corresponds too little to notions of what a Spanish or even Basque town should look like.

The English romantic traveller had virtually nothing to say about San Sebastián, which is perhaps just as well, for it was the English, led by the Duke of Wellington, who razed it in 1813 with a Dresden-like thoroughness, thus ridding the place of most old monuments of potential appeal to conventional romantic sensibilities. The English justified their action on the grounds of ousting the French, whom they claimed had started the fires; motives of commercial jealousy were suspected by the Spaniards, who never fully forgave the English, even after they had tried to assuage their consciences by building the present neo-classical market for the townspeople.

The new San Sebastián, described by Hugo in 1843 as being 'as regular and grid-like as a draughts board', became subject later in the century to a rigid, hierarchical extension that consigned the wealthiest citizens to the centre, and the working-class people to the southern suburbs out of view of the bay. By the 1880s, the Irún–Madrid railway line, and the interest shown in San Sebastián by Spanish and European royalty, had helped to turn the town into an obligatory summer residence for Spain's aristocracy and rich middle classes. The superb neo-baroque and neo-Renaissance monuments imitated the architecture of the smart French resorts, the influence of which was further stressed by the existence of a Paseo de los Franceses, an Anglophobic response to Nice's Promenade des Anglais.

Pío Baroja was a native of San Sebastián, and hated the town. Its great potential beauty, in his opinion, had been destroyed by a shallow, pretentious architecture and by a 'lamentable spirit' whereby 'no one ever read', or had 'any interest in science, in art, in literature, in history, in politics, or in anything other than the King, the Queen Regent, yachts, bullfighting and the cut of trousers'. Pío Baroja's views on San Sabastián, and his wish to have been born instead 'in a mountain hamlet or coastal village', mirrored the concern of the Generation of '98 with what they saw as the spiritual void at the heart of modern Spain. But in the more unashamedly hedonistic and materialistic Spain of recent years – a Spain of which one of the principal apologists is the San Sebastián philosopher Fernando Savater, a witty neo-pagan – the qualities in San Sebastián once thought of as spiritual failings have now emerged as exemplary virtues. Presentday San Sebastián, minus the strong presence of ETA, represents an ideal to which much of modern middle-class Spanish society aspires: elegant yet relaxed, clothes-conscious yet informal, cosmopolitan yet intimate. The town has also a reputation for Spain's finest cuisine, with traditional delicacies such as *kokotxas* (or fish cheeks) of such delicacy and dainty sophistication as to confound all preconceptions about the heartiness of Spanish food in general. San Sebastián is in many ways the sybarite's paradise, which made me understand why Javier Landa referred to the town as his 'spiritual home'.

It was fitting that we should have stayed in San Sebastián with a couple who ran a hairdresser's and beauty parlour. The wife, Inma, was for Javier a model of feminine beauty, with her exquisitely wrought, doll-like features, and her crisp black curls of hair that seemed never to fall out of place. Her manner and way of dressing, according to Javier, were unmistakably those of a Donostiarra (a woman of San Sebastián), a type immediately distinguishable from other Spanish women and characterized by what was for him a natural elegance and sophistication.

But as well as being a beautiful Donostiarra, Inma had a family connection many a Basque would have envied: her mother had been brought up by the young widow of Sabino de Arana Goiri, the founder in 1895 of the Basque Nationalist Party. Arana, a nationalist of a most extreme and reactionary kind, made his name in the field of philology by trying to strip the Basque language of the many Castilian-derived words that had crept into it, and by replacing them with suitably ancient-sounding and difficult Basque ones; it was he who coined the term *Euskadi* ('a community of Basques') to define the vision of a united Basque nation covering all the French and Spanish areas populated by Basques. Guided by a dream of a pure, immigrant-free Basque nation of pre-industrial innocence, Arana advocated racial as well as linguistic purity, and put his beliefs into practice by turning down the love of a sophisticated Castilian woman in favour of a Basque sixteen-year-old of humble origins, who happened to be the great-aunt of Inma. After Arana's death, the widow betrayed her late husband's principles by marrying a Castilian Guardia Civil, thus initiating a Francoist trend in Inma's family.

Inma herself, raised in this Francoist environment, had never learned Basque, but she was now picking up the odd word or two from her children, who had compulsory Basque classes at school. Though opposed to ETA and Herri Batasuna, she was sympathetic to the idea of an independent Basque country, and thought that such a place would function more efficiently as a result of not being controlled by a government in Madrid. She was also a Basque in a way that would have pleased the ethnologically-minded: she believed implicitly in witches, even if the ones she spoke to me about were not the bedraggled, long-haired old women of popular imagination but essentially benign people who had a power to foresee the future, and regularly visited her salon to have their hair done.

WITCHES, Sabino de Arana, Donostiarras, ETA, a fizzy white wine called Txacoli: all were bubbling away in my imagination without cohering into a unified mass I could unhesitatingly call 'Basque'. Inma and her husband were talking, and Javier was driving; we were travelling west of San Sebastián, aiming for a Basque site of renowned symbolic importance, and hoping to take in on the way three places associated with famous Basques.

The main riches of the Basque country, Unamuno once claimed, were not its natural resources but its people; however, he said this in a speech – given in Bilbao in 1901 – that shocked Basque nationalists by urging the Basques not to be too insular and parochial in their outlook, but to extend their ambitions away from the *patria chica* ('small homeland') and on to 'the greatest and only *patria*, the *patria humana*'. The greatest Basques, in his opinion, were people of truly international significance, one of whom was Ignacio de Loyola, the founder of the Jesuits, 'a school of cosmopolitanism'.

Loyola's birthplace, a phonily restored medieval palace, is encased in an enormous Baroque sanctuary, Italianate in character and based on designs by the Roman architect Carlo Fontana. A nationalist Basque historian has recently discussed the sanctuary as an example of 'Basque Baroque', a term he defends on the grounds that, 'All works are Basque that have existed on Basque soil and have inspired emotions in Basque men and women.'

Inma and her husband had been to the sanctuary only as schoolchildren, when the main emotion it had inspired in them had been one of boredom. They were far keener to show me the nearby fishing village of Getaria, with its delightful old centre of traditional Basque houses arranged one on top of the other on a steep slope leading down to the sea. Getaria was the birthplace of another of Unamuno's Basque heroes, Juan Sebastián Elcano, who expressed his cosmopolitanism by being the sole captain to survive Magellan's global journey of 1519–22. A tough and resilient adventurer such as Elcano was perhaps the inevitable product of a village that had produced generations of whalers and cod-fishermen. But the same cannot be said of another of Getaria's celebrated sons, Balenciaga, a pioneering designer who conquered the world's fashion houses, and lies buried in his native village under a playful art-deco tombstone.

Between such opposed manifestations of the Basque spirit as Elcano and Balenciaga can perhaps be placed Ignacio Zuloaga, whose summer villa is situated just along the coast from Getaria, at the entrance to the wide, green bay of Zumaia. Zuloaga was someone who moved in the same sophisticated circles as Balenciaga, but had a bluntness of personality and obsession with physical prowess that might well have made him a brash adventurer in some earlier incarnation. Unamuno, a friend of his, saw him as the supreme Spanish artist of his day, a man who epitomized 'the noble tragedy of our nation, its austere and fundamental gravity, the inward-looking side to its soul'. But Zuloaga can also be linked to a specifically Basque tradition of painting which includes contemporaries of his such as Gustavo de Maeztu and Ramón de Zubiaurre – artists whose works seem to reflect the forcefulness of the Basque spirit in their use of sombre, flat areas of colour, and by their black and vigorous outlining of forms.

The Basque and Spanish sides of Zuloaga's personality are united at Zumaia in a stylistic hotchpotch. The villa itself is in the inappropriate style of a traditional Basque *baserri* (a type of building more suited to the mountainous interior than to the temperate coast), while the chapel next to it has elements of northern and Castilian inspiration integrated within a structure of predominantly Andalusian character. The brilliant sunshine illuminating the quiet November day on which we visited the villa's empty grounds induced in front of the chapel a nostalgic vision of a festive *romería*.

West of Zumaia, our historical pilgrimage was briefly distracted by a succession of beautiful bays indenting a hilly, wooded coastline which in the sunshine had a sparkling greenness of a kind that has always coloured my most vivid impressions of the far north of Spain. But the small rollercoaster of a road we were on slowed us down considerably, and there were storm clouds in the far distance, threatening to bring to an end the days of Indian summer Javier and I had enjoyed ever since entering the Basque country.

We left the coast to drive by motorway along the industrial valleys of the interior. The rain and dusk fell shortly after crossing from Guipúzcoa into the province of Vizcaya and lent a particularly sombre aspect to the largely rebuilt town of Guernica. Under these bleak conditions, we visited the town's famous oak, symbol of Basque liberty. I felt slightly let down on being told that the massive oak dominating the garden of the neo-classical assembly hall was not the actual tree at which the Basque people's liberties, or *fueros*, had been sworn in 1371. Even the charred specimen near by, encased in a Classical tempietto, was scarcely more 'ancient', being no more than three centuries old. But the rain soon forced us indoors, into the building where the Basque parliament held its meetings until the abolition of the *fueros* in 1876. The marble, elliptical interior, seen in the half-light of dusk, had the sad solemnity of the Sanctuary of Loyola.

From Guernica, Javier and his friends set off back towards the more cheerful world of San Sebastián, leaving me to continue by train into the grey smokiness and perpetual rains of a Basque city unloved since those distant days when an eighteenth-century Irish geographer, William Bowes, called it 'one of the neatest towns in Europe'.

★

ON THE evening commuter train between Guernica and Bilbao I took out a newspaper and caught a glimpse on the front page of a smiling, slender-legged teenage girl, dressed in a miniskirt for her school dance. The accompanying story involved another terrorist atrocity, justified as part of the armed struggle for the liberation of the Basque people, and doomed ultimately to be a forgotten incident in the long history of blame and counter-blame that trails away into the mists shrouding the ancient oak of Guernica.

If blame has to be apportioned, one has to go back at least to 1876, when the outrage caused by the abolition of the Basque liberties supplied a rallying cry to nascent Basque nationalism. The passionate desire for an autonomous *Euskadi* soon became the dominant political conviction in the region, with the result that the inherently conservative Basques of Guipúzcoa and Vizcaya would side during the Civil War not with Franco, as they would otherwise have done, but with the Republicans, who had offered them in 1932 the choice of future autonomy, and had kept to this promise by giving them at the outbreak of the war a provisional statute of home rule. Basque allegiance to the Republicans led to Franco's notorious bombing raid on Guernica so famously depicted by Picasso. The extent of the devastation caused was probably exaggerated by the Basques, but the viciousness of Franco's retaliatory measures against them could hardly have been greater.

ETA (an acronym for Homeland and Freedom, as well as the Basque word for 'and') was founded towards the end of the 1950s, but did not become an active terrorist group until a decade later. Thereafter it began gaining considerable popular support throughout Spain, particularly after 1973, when it brought off its most spectacular coup by assassinating Franco's prime minister and probable successor, Admiral Carrero Blanco, whose blown-up car is still one of the attractions of Madrid's Army Museum. With democracy, however, and the granting of semi-autonomous status to the Spanish regions in the late 1970s, ETA lost more and more of its followers within the Basque country, and those that remained became divided into splinter groups, which in turn were shattered into further splinters; acronyms flourished (LAIA, EIA, KAS, HASI, HB, etc), as did qualified acronyms such as ETA-

militar and KAS-*alternativa*. The principal divisions revolved around the issues of violence and non-violence, support or rejection of Spain's democratic progress, and the extension or not of the Basque conflict into other struggles, such as international class conflict and battles against drug-running and pollution. 'Mr Herri Batasuna', as a *Times* correspondent once mistakenly personified this party, is now the only Spanish party not to have denounced ETA, but it has none the less suffered over the last few years from growing internal rifts, some of its many factions being as appalled as the wider Spanish public by ETA's more recent terrorist tactics.

Politicians, the army, and above all the Guardia Civil may be 'legitimate targets' for ETA, but in attacking them, innocent members of the public have suffered, especially children. In November 1990 a sixteen-year-old girl was killed by a bomb intended for her father, a member of the intelligence services; in May 1991 four children aged between seven and fourteen were among those killed by a car bomb directed against Guardia Civil families resident in Vic. Later in 1991, there were Spaniards I knew personally who were calling for the death of 'all Basques' following a bomb attack perpetrated in the Madrid suburb of Carabanchel and shown afterwards on television in such graphic detail that many of those watching the report felt ill.

A collapsed middle-aged woman, wondering what had happened to her daughter, was seen struggling to try and stand up, unaware at first that she had lost her arms. The daughter lay a few feet away, alive, but without legs.

The legs were those of the teenage girl featured on the paper I was reading on the Bilbao train. 'She loved dancing,' read the caption.

I ALIGHTED from the train at the edge of the old town, at a dark, little-used station which hung over the Nervión river. The river, continuing its journey towards the sea, disappeared below the twin arches of a stone bridge before emerging next to an art-deco market which cast, like some ghostly ferry boat, a faint yellow glow over waters made Stygian by the rain and the night. The view reminded me of Glasgow, but the Baroque profile of a foreground bell tower also had overtones of Central Europe, and reinforced a sensation that I was arriving in some Hungarian, Polish or Bohemian town during the Communist period, when travellers could indulge in the fantasy of participating in a *film noir*.

Walking away from the river, I thought again of Central Europe after discovering that the pollution, grey blocks and industries of Bilbao encased an enchanting old core composed of a grimy but intact grid of narrow eighteenth- and early nine-teenth-century streets. The proliferation of tiny bars was some-thing that one could have found only in the land of the *txikiteo*, but the young men who huddled together within them had the conspiratorial look of students under a repressive regime.

I arrived at the arcaded and elegantly neo-classical Plaza Nueva bearing an address that could almost have been Hungarian. It read 'Santimaminek Kobak, 2' and was scrawled in pencil on a crumpled piece of paper I had miraculously unearthed from a trouser pocket filled with a decomposing accumulation of notes, tissues and used tickets. The address referred to a travel bookshop in an alley off the Plaza Nueva, and had been given to me several months before by a Basque friend in Madrid. The shop had just closed for the night, but the person I had been told to go and see there, Javi Pascual, was standing outside it, as if he had actually been waiting for me, waiting perhaps to clarify my confused ideas on the Basque country, to give some ideological direction to my search for the Basque spirit.

'Before we go any further,' he said after I had introduced myself as someone who was travelling around Spain, 'I must give you a word of advice. You should try not to talk about the Basque country as if it were Spanish. Of course, you're a foreigner, and no one would really mind, but it makes a better impression if you always distinguish between Spain and *Euskadi*.'

He told me this as if he was exchanging a confidence between close friends, which we would almost become after repairing to one of the bars in the Plaza Nueva. Tall and blue-eyed, with a mop of light-brown hair, a severe green donkey jacket, and a capacious old pullover, Javi had something about him of the student leader and social worker, and also reminded me in his looks, informality and directness of manner, of certain dissidents whom I had got to know in Hungary in the early 1980s. As with those Hungarians, he was soon arranging a 'programme' for my visit to his city and insisting that I shouldn't waste any money by staying at a hotel.

Javi's home was no longer in his native Bilbao, but in the outlying village of Larrabetzu, which we reached in a ramshackle van piled high with posters. He lived with his partner, his partner's sister, and his partner's sister's partner, in a cramped, scruffy block at the centre of a village he had described beforehand as 'traditionally Basque'. The village, with its untidy mixture of the old and the new, was not picturesque, but it was friendly and warm. For Javi it was a terrestrial haven.

'I love travelling,' said Javi, 'but I feel homesick whenever I'm away for more than four weeks. I miss my people too much.'

I envied him this sense of belonging, and felt a growing desire to immerse myself in Basque culture as we stood talking in a small bar.

'It's quiet in here tonight,' he said. 'Everyone must be at the meeting.'

'The meeting?'

'Yes, we usually meet up every Thursday night in the village school.'

I found out only then that we were standing in the local social club of Herri Batasuna.

'You've heard of them, haven't you?' Javi asked, noting the strange look on my face.

We went to the meeting to pick up Javi's partner, whose straight black hair emphasized an American Indian look said to be characteristic of many Basque women. Javi introduced her to me as 'Marifeli', and then placed his hand on her heavily pregnant belly.

'And this,' he added, 'is the new member of our family.'

The rain stopped, and a full moon emerged briefly to light up the fields and pine trees we passed on our van drive up the hill behind the village. An owl was hooting (at least it was in my imagination) outside the solitary restuarant where we went to have supper, which was served by a large, laughing man who treated us as if we were his family, heaping huge helpings of charcoal-grilled meats on to our plates. In the course of our supper, I learned that Marifeli had been born and brought up in Larrabetzu, and that she worked for Kukubiltxo, a children's theatre company based there. She had spoken Basque since childhood, unlike Javi, who learned it only in his twenties, 'with great difficulty'. Javi was now publishing books in Basque, the company that ran the travel bookshop off the Plaza Nueva having also a small imprint specializing in mountaineering. The company, known as Sua, functioned as a cooperative, with everyone receiving exactly the same salary.

'By and large,' Javi said, 'we're a happy group.' Marifeli smiled, and told me that Sua and Kukubiltxo had recently got together on a book project based on one of the latter's productions. Javi took out of his duffle-bag a book containing a politicized, comic-strip version in Basque of *The Song of Roland*.

I slept that night on a sofa below a crowded bookcase, in a time-warp. I had regressed to a world of innocence and idealism. The books were those that might have been found in a student flat of long ago: Marx, Engels, Walter Benjamin, Rosa Luxemburg, Lenin, Che Guevara, Régis Debray, Marshall McLuhan, Mao Tse-tung, Simone de Beauvoir . . .

I woke up to a typically Bilbaine day, with the landscape softened and greyed by a *chirimiri*, or Scotch mist. The accompanying drizzle became heavier as Javi drove me in heavy traffic to the centre of Bilbao, from where I began a journey by foot and local train through the urban sprawl that follows the Nervión all the way down to the sea.

Known sometimes as the 'Daughter of Iron and Water', Bilbao rose to prominence not only because of its protected position at the foot of the Nervión estuary, but also because of its iron industries, which were developed in earnest in the second half of the last century. In the first stage of Bilbao's dramatic expansion after 1870 the city came to incorporate the former township of Abando, which stands on the other side of the Nervión, and features today the American-style towers of the city's commercial centre. From the town's art gallery, on the northern edge of Abando, I looked north towards what was once a string of fishing villages, but which is now a uniform grey mass. From it protrude smoking chimneys, shipbuilding works, and cranes that loom in the mist like giant, futuristic birds. I reached the sea at Portugalete, an old working-class township staring across the Nervión to a coastal suburb of wealthy villas and apartments. These two extremes of Bilbaine society are joined together by the 'moving bridge', a spectacular piece of turn-of-the-century industrial architecture that transport cars and pedestrians in an open ironwork box suspended between two massive towers. Rain and wind seemed to shake the whole structure when I used it, making me perceive the sea beyond only as a Turneresque blur.

The life of Bilbao's most famous son, Miguel de Unamuno, coincided with the years of intense industrial development that led the city to spread like a grey dragon down towards Portugalete and the sea. Searching for traces of Unamuno in present day Bilbao, I went back to Abando to have a drink at the Café Iruña, a surviving testament to Bilbaine literary life *circa* 1900, with a neo-Moorish interior of green ceramic tiles and *artesonado* ceilings. But to enter the world of Unamuno's childhood I had to return to the beautiful grid of dark streets that radiate from the Plaza Nueva. Much of his life up to 1896 was spent at 7 Calle de la Cruz, a house at the centre of the crowded small district where he was born, went to school, and met his future wife. Unamuno recalled his family home as having an enclosed balcony 'from which I first looked out on to the outside world', one of the early incidents he observed from here being the Carlist bomb that fell on the house next door in 1874. Something else seemed recently to have hit No. 7 itself; for when I went in search of it, I found it to be the one gap in an otherwise intact pedestrian street.

In 1901 Unamuno returned to what he called his 'maternal Bilbao' to give the speech that would transform a potentially triumphant homecoming into a catcalling fiasco. Before embarking on his attack on Basque parochialism, he did at least stress that he owed his 'spiritual roots' to Bilbao, and that the city had provided the seed from which grew the tree that later bore fruit in Salamanca. But the early infuence on him of Bilbao itself was a largely negative one, the gloomy mists and industrial smog that seemed always to hang over this claustrophobic city inspiring in the youth a yearning for open countryside, blue skies and mountain tops.

> The fine mist of sadness rains in my
> soul like that of your sky, and like you
> I dream my dream of restlessness among
> the iron-cored mountains.

His mother's family, the Jugos, came from the mountains behind Bilbao, and had an old homestead in Galdacano, a place he loved to visit as a child, and which stirred in him some of his earliest poetic visions.

> Here, in the austerity of the mountains,
> with the wind of leaves that purifies itself
> among the oaks, my forefathers held high
> their noble breasts . . .

A love of the countryside, nurtured during the constant excursions he undertook to wild places often little more than a half-hour's journey from Bilbao, made the future writer and philosopher turn to Sénancourt's meditative novel, *Obermann*, the work that had done so much to instil in European Romantics a sense of the spiritual consolation of nature. Obermann's reflections in the Alps particularly interested the young Unamuno, whose overriding obsession at this time was with mountains, above all with the peak of Arnotegui, which had first impressed itself on his youthful imagination as a distant, majestic form rising symbolically above the dark streets and human anthill of Bilbao. 'When', he had asked himself, 'would I be able to scale its peak up there, where at times the clouds would rest to bathe themselves in God's air and sunshine?'

As a teenager he went with his schoolmates on regular Sunday outings to the top of Arnotegui, and climbed the mountain repeatedly in later life, making a detour to its summit as part of the mammoth walks he sometimes took when visiting his fiancée in Guernica. The panoramic views from Arnotegui engendered profound reflections that were included in his first and longest novel, *Peace in War* (1897), and helped him to evolve the basic philosophy which informed his greatest work, *The Tragic Sense of Life*. The sight far below of the sea crashing against the rocks came to symbolize for him the constant struggle between peoples and races, 'the clash that produces life'.

The spiritual emotions and philosophical reflections that mountains engendered in the young Unamuno have developed into nationalistic sentiments among those many Basques who love mountaineering. Thus Joaquín Gorostidi Artola, a convicted terrorist, claimed at his trial in 1981 that his political ideals had been influenced by membership of the 'Club Alpino Usturre' and that 95 per cent of the climbers whom he had known were in sympathy with ETA.

The fact that Javi's publishing co-operative produced books on mountaineering did not immediately strike me as being of great political significance. The penny dropped, however, on my second night in Bilbao, when a group of us gathered outside Javi's shop to embark on a *txikiteo* through the historic heart of the city. The group included not only members of the co-operative, but also two of the best-known mountaineers in the Basque country.

One of these was Juanjo Sansebastián, a short, excitable man with a ruddy complexion, and a perpetual shy grin that reduced his eyes to slits; he gave frequent talks on mountaineering, and had been on numerous expeditions in Asia and Latin America, some with the British climber Doug Scott. Juanjo had the clean, wholesome look of an enthusiastic young priest.

Kike de Pablo, the other mountaineer, was impish, unshaven and long-haired, a youthful thirty-nine-year-old who could have been mistaken for a student backpacker. Kike had travelled as extensively as Juanjo, and had taken part in the Basque-led Everest expedition of 1980, the first organized by the 'Spanish State' to succeed in reaching the summit. A Basque flag had been placed there.

The subject of politics rather than mountaineering took over the conversation within minutes of our arrival at the first bar; it was still going strong about fifteen minutes later. Javi tried to involve me in the discussion, but much of what was being talked about related purely to local issues, and my attention was distracted by having to drink quickly, and by wondering how I could be fast enough to pay for a round. The one thing blatantly apparent as we moved with barely a pause from one bar to the next was that the discussion was becoming progressively more heated, and that everyone was gradually turning against Juanjo, whose complexion was getting ruddier by the minute.

'But they're maiming children!' he cried at one point. 'They're maiming children!'

The mounting toll of innocent victims in recent years had convinced Juanjo that terrorist tactics could never be justified. None of the others in the group wanted to play down the tragic consequences of ETA's latest attacks, but they did not renounce terrorism as Juanjo had done.

'A sixteen-year-old girl loses her legs,' said Javi. 'I don't even want to think about it. But do the same people who protest so strongly about this say anything about the thousands of children who were maimed and killed by Bush during the Gulf War?'

We moved on to what Javi referred to jokingly as 'Juanjo's bar', which was apparently favoured by members of Euskadiko Ezkerra, the party Juanjo had joined after leaving Herri Batasuna. EE is a moderate nationalist party of the left, with a stand on the Basque situation somewhere between Herri Batasuna's and the PNV's, and with liberal political sympathies broadly allied to the Eurocommunist parties.

'Juanjo is a wishy-washy liberal,' Javi told me with a smile before putting an arm on the mountaineer's shoulder. 'We can joke about these things today,' Javi continued, 'but in the past we'd be pulling out pistols.'

The mood turned more jovial with the alcohol, and I found myself talking with Kike de Pablo about something other than politics. Kike was vividly describing to me his treks through Nepal, and for a moment I was transported away from the continual rains and dark, smoky bars of Bilbao. I was walking along a narrow track thousands of feet high, ascending, breathless, to a sunlit heaven of monumental, snow-capped peaks.

*

It was a lower and less spectacular mountain range that was evoked for me on my final morning in Bilbao. Marifeli was talking to me about the Pyrenean pass of Valcarlos, where, according to an eleventh-century romance by the poet Turpin, Charlemagne's heroic knight Roland was tragically killed in a skirmish with the Moors. This skirmish, Marifeli explained, was in fact an ambush carried out by the Basques in retaliation for Charlemagne's unwarranted sacking of their city of Pamplona.

The less flattering Basque version of events was the subject of *Orreaga*, a play put on by Kukubiltxo in 1991. Marifeli tried to conjure up the spirit of this production as she led me on a tour of a dark, cold basement with off-white walls and a smell of rotting cod.

The basement, situated in a modern block, was the headquarters of Kukubiltxo, and was lent to them by the town council of Larrabetzu. Some of the younger members of the company were at work creating masks, puppets, and giant mannequins, modelling plastic into grotesque shapes, attaching wires inside figures of Tolkien-like inspiration, and using a machine that turned a chemical into spewing foam rubber. Mangled, rejected pieces of foam, plastic skins, felt sheets with footprints, and screwed-up pieces of coloured paper filled the chaotic rooms to overflowing, and joined company with placards and posters promoting Herri Batasuna.

'We all have the same political convictions,' said Marifeli. 'It makes life easier.' Intensely serious and committed, yet also patient and understanding, Marifeli was obviously a wonderful communicator with children. She was both an actress and a puppeteer, though her pregnant condition was forcing her to work temporarily in the company's administration. Roles in Kukubiltxo were completely interchangeable, and the company successfully projected the aura of a happy, close-knit family.

In the rehearsal room a rotund, cheerful-faced French Basque was giving a voice-and-movement class to three savage-looking youths, who were learning to jump and shout as he swung a huge stick under their feet. Marifeli took me backstage and showed me some of the props for *Orreaga*. Theatrical moans and the odd genuine cry of pain could be heard in the background, as

Marifeli donned the sinister, bird-like mask that had been used for Charlemagne. Cut-outs from Picasso's *Guernica* had accompanied the destruction of Pamplona, while the Republican song 'Ay, Carmela' had been sung during the emperor's subsequent defeat.

We went back into the office, where I met the company's director, who had the quiet, dignified authority of some Central European intellectual. We all huddled together near the two bars of a crude electric heater to look at photographs of past productions. Marifeli pointed out to me a young man with long, greasy black hair and a pointed beard.

'He was our Roland,' she said. 'But he's in prison now. They took him away in July, we were all shocked, we lived in fear for several weeks. Perhaps they'd close our company, perhaps they'd arrest someone else. I was interviewed three times by the police, we all were. They treated us brutally, they made us feel that we all were guilty. But no one had any idea that he was in ETA, we couldn't believe it. Membership is secret, not even partners tell each other. I could be a member of ETA, so could Javi, but neither of us would let on.'

'How was he caught?' I asked.

'Red-handed. On a mission with someone from France who was wanted by the police. He's still awaiting sentence, but I'll be surprised if he gets less than ten years.'

Marifeli lowered her eyes, then changed the subject by pulling out a folder containing sketches for their next production, *The Curse of Malinche*, which was intended for 1992. It would be their most ambitious work yet, and they were still raising money for it. The action would take place inside and in front of an enormous tent constructed like an Aztec pyramid. The 'Indians' would be playing wooden xylophones and hollow wooden tubs whose mellow echoings would contrast with the strident and metallic sounds introducing the cruel conquistadors.

The play, needless to say, would be an anti-1992 statement in which the plight of the Basques would be paralleled with that of the native Americans. The complexities of history and the Basque country had been reduced to a childlike legend which was strangely appealing and exciting in the context of the terrorized basement where we were sitting – a basement that seemed to embody Unamuno's notion of 'the clash that produces life'.

I was handed a copy of the play's title song – an old Indian song, so I was told.

> Curse of Malinche
> Illness of the present day
> When will you set my people free?

20

The Cradle of Humanity

AFTER several months of travelling on Spanish buses and trains, I must have seen every film Sylvester Stallone has ever appeared in. The choice of what is shown on the video screens is depressingly familiar, though there are occasional surprises. One was a charming Spanish film of the 1950s about the miraculous apparition of the Virgin of Fatima. The passengers, normally alert to every flexing of Stallone's muscles, had been sent to sleep by the Fatima film, just as they had been by the film being screened on the late-afternoon bus from Bilbao to Santander. This film, unusually for Spain, was subtitled, and the language being spoken sounded like my attempts at pronouncing Basque. The language was in fact imaginary, invented by Anthony Burgess for *Quest for Fire*, a film about man's earliest days on earth. Outside the bus, darkness had fallen, and rain was hammering against the windows.

Celluloid man had just discovered the delights of the missionary position, shortly after the Cantabrian town of Laredo, when a red-cheeked woman with an umbrella and a straw hat entered the bus and made her way to the no-smoking section. In trying to reach a window seat, she woke up an old woman in black, who politely greeted her with the words, 'Buenas tardes'. 'I'm sorry,' she replied in English, smiling falsely. 'I'm English and I don't speak Spanish.'

The arrival on the bus of the Englishwoman brought home a prosaic aspect of presentday Cantabria. She was one of the new breed of British colonizers of a once wild and dangerous part of Spain which medieval pilgrims to Santiago had preferred to avoid. Cut off from the rest of Spain by a daunting barrier of mountains to the south, Cantabria began to be more accessible to outsiders only after 1850, with the construction of the railway line from Madrid to the port of Santander. Santander was soon turned into a summer resort rivalling San Sebastián, and in the late 1920s an

English visitor to the town, E. Allison Peers, predicted that, 'In years to come, once Channel tunnels and faster trains have brought England nearer to Spain . . . the seaside resorts of northern Spain will hear as much of the English language in summer as the French Riviera does in winter today.'

The British who now flock to Cantabria on the Santander ferry to buy up or rent houses in the region are of a different kind from their counterparts in southern Spain: generally more discreet, more middle class, more interested in sightseeing. They love the mild climate, the quiet, sandy beaches, and the wealth of old churches and pretty villages to be seen on rainy days; and they are delighted by the traditional houses that they can hire from Casas Cantábricas, a British organization that has introduced into northern Spain such British customs as Suggestions Books for Visitors. Perhaps they enjoy as well the Britishness of much of the scenery: the green, rolling landscape of northern Cantabria has echoes of the wilder parts of England, while the dark, forested mountains to the south have reminded many people, such as H. V. Morton, of a Wales planted with maize. But – if a recent theory about Cantabrian origins should be proved correct – perhaps they are being lured by an altogether different and deeper force, and are responding unwittingly to a mysterious urge implanted in them by their distant ancestors who once searched for fire.

From the Middle Ages right up to the creation of the Spanish autonomies in the late 1970s, Cantabria was not a region at all, but a remote coastal province of Old Castile. Many centuries earlier, long before the so-called 'Reconquest' and the appropriation of the area by the Austrian kings, Cantabria was inhabited by a reputedly savage and proudly independent tribe whose distant ancestors might well have been the creators of the extraordinary cave paintings at Altamira, or, to go even further back in time, those people whose recently discovered bones in the Sierra de Atapuerca are thought to be the oldest human remains in the world. The prehistoric importance of Cantabria is unquestionable, but there is at least one scholar who believes that this land was once at the centre of the universe.

Whereas Asturias has been known merely as the 'cradle of the

Spains', Cantabria has been called the 'cradle of humanity'. The imaginative scholar who has designated Cantabria in this way is the toponomy-crazed Jorge María Rivero, who has scoured atlases of the world searching for correspondences with Cantabrian place names, and has concluded from these investigations that a name such as 'St Andrew's' is an obvious derivative of Santander. The fruits of his researches are gathered in a lavish, two-volume work entitled *Cantabria, Cradle of Humanity* (1985), which comes both with a dedicatory reference to the work's 'transcendental import-ance', and with a three-page autobiographical note listing Rivero's multifarious achievements, which include being the author of twenty-seven books, and the founder of Spain's first 'poetry co-operative', first heritage preservation society, and 'first stable and professional chamber ensemble since the Civil War'.

Rivero's theory of the origins of humanity is not so much a theory as an example of divine inspiration. It is backed up by not a single footnote or bibliographical reference, and continually accompanies its wild speculations with expressions of certitude such as 'it goes without saying' or 'there can be no doubt that'. Beginning with the premiss that the very name Iberia gave rise to the word 'universe' (which should really be known as the *uni-berso*), he goes on to concentrate his attention first on Cantabria, then on the Cantabrian mountain range of the Sierra Sagra, which he believes not only to be the subject of the famous Mappa Mundi in the eleventh-century Burgo de Osma Codex, but also the Paradise from which humanity was 'expelled', to spread first to other parts of Iberia, and then all over the world, bringing with it names that are still used today to mark the range's hamlets and natural landmarks.

From this point onwards Rivero's ingenuity knows few bounds. He manages to locate within the Sierra Sagra the whole Book of Genesis, and every possible Classical and ancient myth up to the Trojan Wars. No aspect of Cantabria is free from Rivero's fantastic theory, not even the humble *hórreo*, that quin-tessential feature of northern Spanish farms. To prosaic minds this roofed, rectangular structure in wood or stone is simply a place for storing maize, and is always raised on stilts in order to prevent rats from getting inside. To Rivero, however, the *hórreo* is none other than a copy of Noah's Ark, and was originally conceived both to keep alive the memory of the Flood and to serve as an emergency boat in case of a further deluge, the structure being one which would have floated away once the waters had reached the top of the stilts.

Santander did not remind me in any way of St Andrew's, but I did think of Rivero when I visited the private library of the most renowned Spanish scholar of the nineteenth century, Marcelino Menéndez y Pelayo.

Menéndez y Pelayo was a prodigy who began collecting and cataloguing books at the age of eleven, was fluent in ten languages at twenty-one, and died at fifty-five having amassed 50,000 volumes, all of which he had consigned to his prodigious memory: on his tomb are inscribed the words, 'How sad to have to die when I've still so much to read.' Whereas Rivero has applied his own enormous knowledge to an all-embracing theory of questionable value, Menéndez y Pelayo used his scholarship to chronicle the evolution of religion in Spain, to bring a much needed respectability to Spanish literary history, and give a methodological basis to Spanish academic studies in general. And yet, visiting his library in Santander, I also had the feeling of someone no less deluded than Rivero, of a person who had finally lost all sense of reality in his world of learning, and who ended up pursuing knowledge with the urgency of someone who had convinced himself that it had finite scope.

His library at Santander was for him a sanctuary, a place where he could continue his quest undisturbed by all the interruptions that continually upset him in Madrid. The present building, a marbled, neo-classical structure built after his death in 1912, was shown to me by a librarian who still considered the place as inviolable as a sanctuary, and was shocked by my suggestion that its collections, unaltered since 1912, would be more useful to the public if incorporated into the municipal library next door. The building was empty when I visited it, and so was the post of director; the most recent applicants had all failed to show the necessary proficiency in six languages.

An insight into Menéndez y Pelayo's private life was provided when the librarian took me in the pouring rain across a courtyard and into the scholar's neo-Gothic home, which had a peeling white façade covered in graffiti. This modest house, poorly maintained today through lack of funds, had always been simply furnished, even though Alfonso XIII had come to dine here with Menéndez y Pelayo at least thirty times.

'He had little interest', the librarian said, 'in material possessions or personal appearance. All his money went into the library.'

I was shown the bed in which he died, next to which was a framed letter Pope Leon XIII had written to him in the hope of getting to know him one day in person. A yet more telling memento, displayed on a small table, was a fan that apparently had belonged to one of his fiancées. 'As a young man,' the librarian explained, 'he was engaged six times, but he always remained a bachelor.' To the librarian, Menéndez y Pelayo's lifelong celibacy was an indication of the priestlike personal sacrifices that had to be made by those who dedicated their lives to 'higher matters'; others might instead have wondered what emotional disappointments and frustrations lay encased behind the tooled leather volumes of his library.

'He shared his life with his brother Enrique,' I was told as we entered the study where Enrique had worked as a doctor and minor author. On leaving the house I purchased a recent reissue of Enrique's posthumously published memoirs, which describe his life with Marcelino. They are entitled *Memoirs of a Man to Whom Nothing Happened*.

The house and library of Menéndez y Pelayo are among the few cultural attractions in the noisy and largely reconstructed centre of Santander. The town was devastated by an offshore explosion of dynamite in 1893 and again by fire in 1941. Its beauty lies in its situation on a narrow peninsula, and its elegant, palm-lined promenade, which in the summer months is enhanced by open-air bars and cafés, and by a continual flow of strollers. However, the bracing conditions of the November day on which I walked along the promenade did not show the town to advantage, and gave an especially sad look to the enormous seafront monument to Menéndez y Pelayo's novelist friend and fellow Cantabrian, José Maria de Pereda.

The heavily cloaked figure of Pereda, with his pointed beard and glasses, sits on top of an artificial, ivy-covered outcrop of rock, the sides of which are decorated with reliefs portraying characters from his novels. Santander schoolchildren, asked recently to comment on these reliefs, revealed a complete ignorance about Cantabria's most famous novelist, an ignorance that turned out later to be not much greater than that of their parents. Ironically, when the monument was inaugurated in 1911, children from every school in the city formed a long procession to place bunches of flowers at its foot. This crowded and glamorous occasion was presided over by Menéndez y Pelayo, who gave a speech praising his friend for having given literary identity and international fame to what had previously been 'little more than an obscure and placid corner of the Peninsula which many people had scarcely been able to distinguish from the neighbouring provinces'.

It was in fact Menéndez y Pelayo who first encouraged Pereda to turn his fictional talents to his native region, and thus to write what are always regarded as his two finest works. *Sotileza* (1884), a tale set in a poor and now vanished fishing quarter of Santander, was followed in 1894 by his great novel of the Cantabrian countryside, *The Peaks Above* (1894), which must be the only novel ever written to have its text interrupted two-thirds of the way through by a red cross. The cross, accompanied by the date, 2 September 1893, marks the point in the narrative when Pereda was distracted from his writing by the sound of his son shooting himself in a next-door room.

The novel itself offers nothing as dramatic as this real-life incident. Dealing with the visit of an idle Madrilenian to a small village in the Cantabrian mountains, it highlights Pereda's habitual reactionary theme of the morally improving nature of the countryside. It has endless descriptions of the mountain scenery, many incorporated into a lengthy account of the journey between the Cantabrian villages of Tudanca and Reinosa. Anyone wishing to retrace this journey, however, should bear in mind that Pereda himself never made the trip, and that the Cantabria portrayed in his works is an idealized and largely imaginary one. The topography of Cantabria, as the critic José María de Cossío noted in

1934, has been jumbled around by Pereda and transformed by his 'novelist's intuition' into an alternative reality.

Traces of the actual Santander known to Pereda and Menéndez y Pelayo became more extensive as I continued walking along the seafront towards the fashionable beaches of the Sardinero and the Magdalena. The views over Santander's beautiful bay widen, the town peters out into luxury villas, and the terrain narrows into a tongue flanked by two beaches and tipped by a wooded park enclosing the former summer palace of Alfonso XIII.

I turned off the coastal road into a long residential avenue named after the third of the great nineteenth-century authors associated with Santander – Pérez Galdós.

Galdós regularly spent the summers in Santander after 1871, and became intimate friends with both Menéndez y Pelayo and Pereda, even joining the latter on a Cantabrian tour he was later to describe in his short book, *Forty Leagues through Cantabria*. The friendship between Galdós and the two Cantabrians was perhaps surprising in view of their radically opposed political positions. Pereda was an ardent Carlist who publicly attacked the 1868 liberal revolution that had brought so much hope to the young Galdós. As for Menéndez y Pelayo, he was an orthodox Catholic who had established his theological credentials by denouncing 'Krausismo', the nineteenth-century German philosophy taken up by Spanish liberals as an excuse to retain a belief in a divinity while continuing to hold progressive, liberal ideas. But as befits friendships forged in the 'cradle of humanity', the intellectual differences between the three men were made insignificant by a mutual recognition of their worth as writers and individuals.

The Villa San Quentín, at 14 Avenida Pérez Galdós, has a modern gate and an entryphone. I pressed the bell, and posed a question that seemed to take the woman who replied to it off her guard.

'Galdós?' the distorted voice replied. 'But that was years ago! When did he die? Nineteen twenty, wasn't it . . .?'

The rain was getting heavier, and I was hoping to be invited inside. But I remained on the pavement, listening to an intermittent voice eventually made incomprehensible by the crackling sounds of the entryphone's speaker.

'The house, I think, was sold by the Galdós family in the 1930s . . . My father bought it in 1955 . . . No, it's all been changed inside . . . My husband's got modern tastes . . . too gloomy before . . . No, nothing left . . . nothing left . . .'

I LEFT Santander to go to a town I knew better from fiction than from reality. For me, Oviedo was 'Pilares', the name Ramón Pérez de Ayala gave to his native town in his whimsical, philosophical novels, *Belarmino and Apolonio* (1921) and *Tigre Juan* (1926). Above all, I knew Oviedo as 'Vetusta', the name under which the town is cloaked in *La Regenta* (1885–6), the remarkable novel written by Ayala's law teacher in Oviedo, Leopoldo Alas.

In Santander, I had embarked on a literary route embracing most of the great 'realist' novelists of the Spanish nineteenth century, beginning with Pereda and ending in Galicia with Emilia Pardo Bazán. A vital link in this literary chain was Leopoldo Alas, who, under the pseudonym of 'Clarín', had established by the age of thirty-four a reputation as Spain's wittiest and most mordant critic. In that same year, between his critical writings and his onerous teaching duties at Oviedo University, he managed, in the space of only a few months, to write a novel almost as long as Cervantes' *Don Quixote*.

La Regenta, the story of the adulterous wife of a judge, has a simple, melodramatic plot that parodies one of the Calderonian tragedies the cuckolded judge so loves. The beautiful heroine, Ana, tries for much of the novel to sublimate her sexual and emotional frustrations by absorbing herself in mystical and devotional readings under the guidance of the ambitious young canon, Fermín de Pas. When she realizes that de Pas has fallen in love with her she avoids him, but then succumbs in her despair to the advances of Vetusta's Don Juan, Don Álvaro Mesía, a prominent liberal member of the local gentleman's club. De Pas, in revenge, reveals the affair to the judge, who challenges Don Alvaro to a duel, and is killed. Don Álvaro flees Vetusta.

Alas might himself have felt inclined to flee Oviedo after publishing the novel. It created an immediate scandal, stirred up by Oviedo's bishop, Ramón Martínez Virgil, who wrote an open letter to his parishioners denouncing the work as a pernicious, perverted example of 'liberalism, Krausism and naturalism'. As a portrait of a stagnant provincial town beset by boredom, gossip, hypocrisy, jealousy, selfishness and sexual fantasy, *La Regenta* was hardly the sort of book to have gone down well in the town on which it was quite obviously based. But, given the many enemies that Alas had made for himself through his work as a critic, the novel's reception in Spain was unlikely to have been a fair one.

Alas relied heavily on his friends, among whom was Galdós, who wrote to tell him that, 'The characters and events of your novel follow me wherever I go'. When asked, however, to give an honest critical assessment, Galdós qualified his praise with numerous 'buts'. Menéndez y Pelayo was more hostile. He told Alas that he liked the book's style and the vividly sketched minor characters, but was antipathetic to the subject-matter, and to the exaggerated complexity of the protagonists. The book was soon forgotten, awaiting the day, like Alfau's *Locos*, when it would be discovered by a generation more understanding of its aims. The wait would be a long one. Azorín criticized Alas for his pompous, verbose style, and Brenan accused him of being an author who 'lacks the secret of making his scenes come alive and is extraordinarily long-winded'.

The book Brenan pronounced in 1951 as being 'dead' was finally resuscitated in the early 1970s. Since then it has come to be considered as a work of nineteenth-century Spanish fiction second only to Galdós's *Fortunata and Jacinta*. The complexity of its narrative structure, and its continual changes of viewpoint (even within a single paragraph) give the book something in common with Galdós, but it lacks the latter's narrative momentum, the development of the plot being endlessly interrupted by lengthy passages of brilliantly ironic social observation. The originality of the novel and the reason why the book took so long fully to be appreciated lie in its approach to psychology, which closely mirrors modern preoccupations.

Ana's numerous inner monologues recapture the rapid stream-of-consciousness illogicalities that characterize the way in which the mind actually works. Neurosis and hysteria are uncovered, and sex is revealed both as their underlying cause and the dominant motivating factor behind all human behaviour: one of the sexual climaxes of the book comes when Ana, in an act of penitential exhibitionism, 'prostitutes herself' in front of the whole town by walking barefoot in a Holy Week procession. The importance of role models and childhood traumas is suggested, dreams are analysed, and the workings of memory deconstructed. Thus Ana, caressing her cheek against the sheet when she goes to bed, reflects on her past, confusing memories with dreams, and ultimately questioning whether memories of certain incidents and people are not just memories of memories, or even memories of memories of memories . . .

I ARRIVED at Oviedo at about the same time of day that *La Regenta* opens, when the inhabitants of the town were still sleeping off a heavy lunch of Asturian stew or *fabada*. The weather was typically Vetustan; between October and May, Alas maintained, the town is subject to near continual rains.

It had been raining without a break since Santander, and dense, low-lying clouds obscured much of the green and hilly coastal scenery, as well as all the potentially extensive views of the rugged Picos de Europa. Clouds intensified the ugliness of the coal-mining valley between Gijón and Oviedo, and had shrouded, on the outskirts of Oviedo itself, the famous mountain of Naranco, where the Asturian kings had made their residence. But by the time my bus had reached the station, a strong wind had blown up, and would shortly clear the sky. The sun came out as I walked towards the centre of the town; Alas would have described it as a typical mid-November sun, 'a different sun, hurrying about in farewell visits with the preparations for its winter journey weighing on its mind'.

I went straight to the medieval cathedral. It is the pivot both of Vetusta and of Alas's book, which begins high up in its tower, and ends on the floor of its nave. The novel's opening scene brings together two opposed extremes of Vetustan society. One is the grotesque figure of a child orphan and bellringer, who enjoys the heights of the tower for reducing the pedestrians below to the insignificance of scurrying mice, on whom he can heap his scorn by throwing pebbles and scraps of rotting baked potatoes. The other extreme is the canon theologian, Fermín de Pas, who has first experienced the sense of divine superiority to be gained from observing the world from a lofty eminence in the course of a childhood in an Asturian mountain village. From the top of the cathedral tower, he concentrates his gaze entirely on the city, which he observes with the aid of a telescope, exploring 'its anatomy not like the physiologist whose only concern is to study, but like the gastronome who searches out the tastiest morsels'. One of these morsels is of course Ana.

The west façade of Oviedo Cathedral, with its solemn, deeply recessed Gothic portals, is entirely overshadowed by its sixteenth-century tower, a structure that climaxes in a flamboyantly crocketed openwork spire. George Borrow, normally the least effusive of writers when it comes to architecture, described the tower as 'one of the purest specimens of Gothic architecture at present in existence'. I paused briefly to look up at this Gothic hyperbole, before entering through a side chapel into what Borrow referred to as the 'simple and unadorned' interior. Once I had reached the dark, squatly proportioned nave, I walked towards a solitary old man who was rearranging the pews for the early evening Mass.

In the closing moments of La Regenta, Ana wanders into the empty cathedral and nervously shuffles towards the confessional, from which suddenly emerges the black figure of Canon de Pas, shaking with rage, and barely restraining himself from attacking her. He retreats into the sacristy, leaving Ana to fall in terror face downwards on to the black and white marble floor. The bellringer of the opening scene, arriving to lock up the chapels, discovers her unconscious body and decides to carry out a physiological experiment. Pressing his 'vile face' against hers, he kisses her on the mouth. She comes back to life with an overwhelming sense of nausea. 'For she thought that she had felt on her lips the cold and slimy belly of a toad.'

As I approached the sacristan he disappeared into the shadows, vanishing as if by some hidden door. The sacristy was deserted. A surly woman, cleaning the floor with a mop and bucket, had no idea where the man had gone to, nor could she help me out herself by showing me the way into the tower. I tried a flight of steps off the south aisle, but found myself instead in the Cámara Santa, a ninth-century chapel Alas fictionalized as the 'Chapel of the Holy Relics'.

Had I come here with the likes of Vetusta's self-appointed tour guide and local historian, Don Saturnino Bermúdez, I would probably not have been allowed out of this over-restored chapel for at least an hour. An anarchist bomb in 1934 and a deranged man in 1977 did away with many of the fabled relics Alas described, including a portion of the bread used at the Last Supper, and some of the Virgin's milk (presumably in powdered form); but much remained to merit lengthy explanations from a latterday Don Saturnino. However, I could not stay long, as I was anxious to see before nightfall the view Fermín de Pas had scoured with his telescope. The person who had sold me my ticket into the Cámara Santa seemed surprised when I came out of the chapel just a few minutes later, having managed to assimilate in that short space of time objects of such weighty stature as Alfonso II's gold-plated, jewel-encrusted 'Cross of Victory', St Andrew's wallet, five thorns from Christ's crown, one of St Peter's sandals, and a version of the Holy Shroud that had not been subjected to carbon-dating. I told the ticket-seller that my particular interest was in the cathedral's tower. She said that it was closed to the public, and that its steps were dark and dangerous.

I finally caught up with the sacristan, who just shook his head and kept on insisting that I needed the permission of the cathedral's canons. He mentioned two specific names, but then said that they would not be coming back to the cathedral that day, and would be leaving early in the morning for a Holy Year Conference in Santiago de Compostela. Could I speak to them at their homes? I could, he replied, but he did not want to tell me where they lived. 'That would be betraying a friendship of over thirty years.'

My search for the canons proved futile, but in wandering restlessly around the small squares surrounding the cathedral, losing my sense of direction amid all the convents and churches, and going repeatedly from one ecclesiastical office to another, I gained at least some first-hand experience of the claustrophobic,

Church-dominated world Alas evoked. I also encountered a venerable relic from Alas's Oviedo after knocking at one of the doors in the Casa Sacerdotal.

The door was answered by a priest of such remarkable age that his chin drooped as if a weight was attached to it, elongating his nose and ears, and pulling his skin into a chasm of folds and wrinkles. I could barely conceive the physiological effort it must have taken to hoist these features into the smile he gave me. Before he could say anything, however, a housekeeper took him to one side and told me that I had come to the wrong door. The following year I would see the old man's face again, in a newspaper article recording the death in Oviedo of the 'oldest priest in the world'. The priest was called Don Luciano López García-Jove, and had been born on 17 January 1885, two months after the publication of the first volume of La Regenta.

Unable to climb up to the cathedral tower, I had to content myself with a ground-level comparison between Alas's Vetusta and present-day Oviedo. I went, at the hour of the early-evening paseo, to the Alameda, which is described by Alas as an outlying site threatened by the encroaching suburban villas of modern Vetusta, or 'La Colonia'. Today the alley of poplars has been absorbed into a large park, which is boxed in by busy streets and a Madrid-style development of high-rise offices and apartments. The new town of Oviedo corresponds at least in its essentials to La Colonia, a place Fermín de Pas describes as 'mapped out in straight lines, dazzling with vivid colours and steely reflections'. De Pas is dismayed by La Colonia – a symbol of new wealth and middle-class vulgarity – and actively hostile towards the then small and inaptly named industrial district of 'El Campo del Sol', a hot-bed of anarchism populated by coal and iron workers.

The action of La Regenta is centred almost entirely on the historic heart of Vetusta, a district known as 'La Encinada' and considered by de Pas as his 'natural empire'. In contrast to the brash modernity of La Colonia, La Encinada conveys a sense of dignity and continuity, its buildings being emblazoned with aristocratic crests, and blackened and mildewed by centuries of damp. Walking through the dark, oppressive heart of Oviedo's old town, I could in certain moments have imagined myself in La

Encinada, a delusion furthered by a number of street names identical to those in the fictional district. Quite apart from the cathedral, there were also specific sites I could visit such as the Plaza Mayor, which is identifiable as Alas's Plaza Nueva, a square 'forever sunk in gloom'; then there is the sturdy eighteenth-century block of the Palacio Valdecasana (now the law courts), which once housed the town club frequented by Alas and was almost certainly used by him as the model for the gentleman's club of Vetusta. But as Juan Cueto Alas (one of the novelist's descendants) has recently emphasized, scholars, journalists and other readers of La Regenta have spent so much time trying to find similarities between Oviedo and Vetusta that the fictional town has ended up looking like the real one: as with the 'six characters' in Pirandello's play, Vetusta has freed itself from its author and has come to seem more real than the reality. The actual similarities between the two places are not in fact as great as one is sometimes led to believe, for Alas, like Pereda in Cantabria, used recognizable topographical references only as a point of departure, and then mixed them together in the creation of a wholly fictional world, one that in his case served as a microcosm of provincial life in general.

By night-time, the old town lost for me any remaining resemblance to the district de Pas admired for being populated by a mixture of old aristocratic families and the town's poor. The quiet, dying streets of heroic Vetusta had been replaced by the noisy routes of nocturnal bar crawls. I forgot literature completely and joined the Friday-night revellers in a bar that I discovered only later, removing a beer mat from my pocket, was called 'La Regenta'.

JUST OUTSIDE the old town of Oviedo, on a hill leading down to the railway station, is a group of ugly modern bars, where I spent the greater part of a Friday night absorbed in the characteristically Asturian spectacle of drinkers making their way through large plates of sea urchins while pouring out cider from a great height. The inevitable spillages oozed along the floor, and swept up the dirt, urchin shells, and cigarette stubs to form a slushy liquid lapping at the soles of my feet. A miasma of cider and smoke would still be hanging in the air a few hours later when I returned to the street, at six o'clock on a drizzling, deserted morning, to catch the only train of the day to the Galician port of El Ferrol.

It is possible to travel by train the whole length of Spain's northern coast, but the railway is single-track, the stops are continual, and the trains local and uncomfortable, without cafeterias, and sometimes without toilets. I travelled on the line only between Oviedo and El Ferrol, but that journey alone took me ten hours, and I was forced to use the gaps between the carriages to rid my body of the remaining dregs of my night's intake of beer and cider. Fortunately, there was little chance of my being discovered in this embarrassing and precarious activity, for there was no one else on the train for most of the journey. Not surprisingly, there are plans to cut the service.

Renewed gusts of wind cleared the rains and mists shortly after Oviedo, enabling me to benefit fully from the experience of being possibly one of the last passengers to travel on what is the most beautiful of Spanish train routes. The train, travelling towards a land where railways had preceded roads, closely hugged the green and wooded coast, passing next to villages and small towns reduced to silence by the end of the summer season. Crossing a narrow, shallow-sided estuary at Ribadeo, the train entered Galicia, where the grander and more dramatic estuaries of the Rías Bravas soon came into view, the line of the Spanish coast becoming wildly indented at its western extremity, as if shattered by the full force of the Atlantic. Manoeuvring through woods and over hills, the train emerged continually at the head of bays and estuaries that I had visited once before, with Galician friends who had introduced me to the lobsters, goose barnacles, spider crabs, and other delicacies of a coast so renowned for its seafood that Japanese biologists have recently been investigating the mysterious qualities of the waters that breed it.

Promontories, known for their wild horses, protruded far into the sea, their distant rocky headlands lit up by fleeting patches of sunlight. Hidden on the other side of one of these estuaries, but vividly clear in my memory, was the crude cliffside sanctuary and hamlet of San Andrés de Teixedo, where the inhabitants use a bread-based substance to fashion fantastical and luridly painted crosses, ex-votos, and lucky charms that recall uncannily the popular art of Mexico.

'Quel pays barbare,' said George Borrow's travelling companion, Antonio. 'The further we go, my master, the wilder everything looks. I am afraid to venture into Galicia.' Borrow, one of the few romantic travellers to have come to this region, entered it not at Ribadeo, but through the barren, mountainous district to the south, which still features some of the wildest parts of Spain. Hamlets, virtually unvisited until recent times, contain a handful of families who continue to live with their livestock in round stone huts that suggest even to the most prosaic imagination the dwellings of prehistoric man. This district, the Galician province of Lugo, is crossed in its southern half by one of the most haunting stretches of the pilgrims' way to Santiago, a stretch that genuinely conveys a sense of regression in time, and takes the traveller across a landscape of heather, granite, and rough pastures, where fields are terraced and divided by upright stone slabs resembling menhirs.

Galicia is a land that encourages myths, though myths of a different kind from those found in other regions of Spain. Galician nationalists, no less than sentimental travellers, think of Galicia essentially as a Celtic land, even though the Celtic presence in this region is not significantly greater than in parts of Spain one does not think of as Celtic at all – Almería, for instance. The physical resemblances between Galicia and such Celtic extremities of Europe as Ireland and Brittany cannot be denied; and there are local traditions such as bagpipe music that are associated with the same regions. But the term 'Celtic', when applied to the people and character of Galicia today, is so vague and contradictory as to become almost meaningless.

Annette Meakin, the author in 1909 of one of the first general books in English on this region (bizarrely entitled *Galicia: The Switzerland of Spain*) wrote that the Galicians have a 'Celtic predilection for spontaneous wit'. John Hooper, in *The Spaniards*, summarizes the 'Celtic' characteristics of the Galicians as 'a genius for poetry, a love of music, a fascination with death and a tendency towards melancholy'. Ted Walker, categorically referring to the Galicians as Celts, explains that they differ from other Spaniards in being 'a squat, thick-set, lumpish, physically unattractive race' (a very different opinion from that of Camilo José Cela, who has always insisted that the women in Galicia are the most beautiful in Spain). More offensive still, and yet more ludicrous, is the notion that the Galician tendency to emigrate has largely been in response to the 'migratory urge' of Celtic peoples. The Galicians have left their homeland for the same reasons that the Irish have done so – to escape terrible poverty.

Celtic mists have clouded the minds of those who have visited Galicia, but they have also contributed to the region's mysterious, exotic allure. This allure has been compounded by the extremity of Galicia's position, at the end of Europe's greatest pilgrimage route. The exciting sense of finality felt by generations of pilgrims on reaching Galicia is an emotion the more romantically inclined can share when confronted by the primeval expanses of the interior, or by the gaunt promontories of the Galician *rías*. Galicia fascinates and attracts in what is sometimes a morbid way, the place's associations with a journey's end having also their mortal connotations. It is a dying region, with a population that in the interior has been reduced to half of what it was in the 1950s. The ghostly character of much of the interior cannot just be blamed on Celtic rites and superstitions, but is also due to the thousands of abandoned old houses that are unlikely ever to be done up as holiday homes for the wealthy. Though abandoned, they are generally still in the possession of their emigrant owners, who, suffering overseas from that proverbial Galician malaise of *morriña*, or homesickness, maintain their properties in Galicia in the habitually vain hope of returning one day for good, not to work, but to die.

IF GALICIA can be called the cradle of anything, it should be called the 'cradle of dictators'. Fidel Castro is of Galician descent, and recently came to Galicia to visit the mean, stone huts in the Lugo village of Lancara where his father was born over a century ago. The right-wing president of the Galician 'Xunta', Manuel Fraga, himself the son of Galician emigrants, accompanied Castro on this visit and is said to have offered him a Galician refuge in the case of the Cuban's fall from power.

But the most notorious Galician was Francisco Franco Bahamonde, who was born at El Ferrol in 1892, and whose granite-like obstinacy and phlegmatic disposition have been seen as unmistakable attributes of the people of this region.

My train from Oviedo finally drew up at El Ferrol around four o'clock in the afternoon, on what was, coincidentally, the day of Franco's death, 20 November. An international Fascist rally was taking place that day in Madrid, but El Ferrol remained outwardly its quiet provincial self. Friends from the nearby town of Betanzos collected me from the station, and took me to eat in a small restaurant whose owner mysteriously recognized in us Francoist sympathies, and furtively produced for our benefit a bottle of 'Vino Nacional': on the label were emblazoned Franco's portrait, the illegal Falange crest, and the words '¡Arriba Espana!'

Driving out of the town we encircled the main square, which continues to be dominated by a monumental bronze of Franco seated on a notoriously well-endowed horse. Repeated bombing has led to reconstruction of nearly all the surrounding buildings, and succeeded in giving the plinth the craggy, pitted look of the Galician coastline. But the Generalísimo has lived up to his phlegmatic image, completely unscathed by all these explosions, as if miraculously preserved by some Celtic sorcery.

21

Chasing Phantoms

THE MAIN square of the ancient Galician town of Betanzos has a statue featuring perhaps the earliest sculptural representation of a telephone. Dating back to the early years of the century, the statue is of the brothers Juan María and Jesús García Naveira. The two men are shown standing, their generous handlebar moustaches bristling with a Victorian pride in technology and commerce. The telephone is held to the ear of the elder brother, Juan María, whose free arm embraces Jesús as if to transmit by touch the message he is receiving. Jesús responds by pointing with his left arm enigmatically into the distance.

The protagonists of this strange construction were local heroes and benefactors who made their fortune through commercial activities in Argentina. They began their lives as the semi-literate sons of a poor agricultural worker and were brought up in a Betanzos that had scarcely emerged from the Middle Ages. Remnants of the Betanzos they knew then can be seen behind the square's Art Nouveau bandstand, within a complex of dark streets that lead steeply down to the estuary between El Ferrol and La Coruña. Among the discordant and eclectic twentieth-century buildings are squat, balconied houses trimmed in a mossy granite, and medieval-looking taverns with nothing outside to indicate their function other than dying vine branches attached to the lintels. At the heart of the old town, standing on its own on the rough-hewn floor of a Romanesque church of cellar-like gloom and simplicity, is the late-medieval tomb of Fernán Pérez de Andrade, whose effigy is stretched out on a coffin decorated with playful hunting scenes and supported by marble boars. A symbol of wealth and power, as well as a wonderful display of fantasy, this famous work might well have been an early inspiration to the García Naveiras, who, on their return to their native town from Argentina in the early 1890s, assumed a status comparable to the feudal lords of old.

Returning emigrants from Latin America are known in Spain as *indianos*. Throughout Spain, but especially in the northern half, the *indianos* have left their mark in their native towns and villages by constructing pretentious villas differing in every possible respect from the simple, traditional dwellings in which most of them were raised. The architectural tastes of the Naveiras were no different from those of other *indianos*, but their munificence towards their home town was greater than most, as was their imagination.

At the time of the construction of the railway line from El Ferrol to Betanzos, the brothers assisted the path of progress through the financing of such projects as a municipal wash-house, a sanatorium, a hostel for 'abnormal girls', a cultural centre, a poor people's home, and – next to the church of Andrade's tomb – a local school in neo-Byzantine style. But the attention of the brothers, and of Juan María in particular, was concentrated above all on the outlying gardens of the Pasatiempo. Juan María began work on this in 1893, and devoted much of the next forty years of his life to creating what was to become one of the most unusual landscape gardens in Europe.

The range of influences on the Pasatiempo was quite extraordinary, and reflected the extent of Juan María's travels and interest in other countries. Argentina of course held a special place in the whole conception: blind arcading along one of the garden's main avenues was adorned with shields of all the Argentinian provinces, while elsewhere there was a Chinese *mirador* inspired by one in Buenos Aires, a city featured at the very centre of a large relief of clocks that gave the time in all the world's main capitals.

Other follies and statues resulted from a trip the two brothers undertook at the very end of the century to Italy. Two sleeping lions in Carrara marble, copied from those guarding the entrance to the tomb of Clement XIII in the Vatican, were placed outside the park's main entrance, while further marble copies of Italian works were used to create a long avenue of Roman emperors. The 'Sacred Wood' or 'Monster Park' at Bomarzo made an understandable impression on the brothers, but so did the Roman catacombs, which inspired the shape of some of the Pasatiempo's many grottoes. The influence of Classical and Renaissance art was later supplemented by Juan María's discovery of such masters of contemporary fantasy as Gaudí and the visionary French postman Ferdinand Cheval. Gaudí's Parc Güell led Juan María to create a different style of grotto, while Cheval's extraordinary structures at Hauterives encouraged him to broaden the scale and scope of his fantasies by executing them in cheaper materials such as concrete, broken glass and seashells.

Concrete hastened the Pasatiempo's decline into downright ugliness, and it was used in such diverse and unfortunate contexts as a reproduction of Canova's *Eros and Psyche*, and a complete series of papal busts from St Peter up to Pius X, all made from the same mould with minor variations. But concrete also allowed Juan María to carry garden art into new territory, the world of modern technology: thus the very first biplane to be seen in Galicia was the one reproduced here in concrete on an enormous wall relief recording Juan María's visit to Egypt in 1910. Kitsch of such magnitude is perhaps unique in the history of landscape gardening, and extended even into the topiary of the Pasatiempo. Who else but Jose María would have tried to re-create in topiary the heavy, ugly forms of contemporary dining-room and bed-room furniture?

Scholars have inevitably uncovered a labyrinth of hidden symbols within the park, and have established a relationship between the place and the world of Freemasonry. But the Pasatiempo was essentially a public park, and one intended not only to entertain but also, and more importantly, to educate. The García Naveiras reacted against their own lack of education as children with such a fervent didacticism in later life that they not only gave free classes to those who helped to build the park, but also conceived the whole place as a series of lessons in subjects ranging from geography to business administration. One Betan-zos teacher even claimed that children 'learned more about agriculture and natural history in a single visit here than they did in a whole year of theoretical studies and explanations given in the classroom'. A zoo formed an important part of the educational programme, but the major role was played by the childlike and often ghoulish concrete reliefs portraying such themes and scenes as Early Christians in the Colosseum, St Isabel Curing the Sick, the Execution of General Torrijos, Divers in their Diving Gear, the Investment of Capital, the Panama Canal, and the Sacrifice of Tupac-Amaru.

A small entrance fee was charged for all this entertainment and knowledge, but all the money earned from the ticket office and the sale of postcards went into financing the Betanzos poor people's home, a charity of special importance to the García Naveiras, and one that partly explains the enigma of Jesús's pointing arm in the monument to the brothers in the town square.

The monument was made originally for the Pasatiempo, where it stood within sight of a sculptural group representing Charity. The latter work, based on an engraving by an eighteenth-century Bolognese artist, depicted what is known as 'Roman Charity', a subject especially popular during the baroque period and one expressed in the somewhat questionable image of an imprisoned old man being suckled at the breast of a daughter overcome by compassion and, in some instances, by a more physical sensation. The bare-breasted woman in the Pasatiempo, however, appears coldly oblivious to the man at her nipple, for her attentions are otherwise engaged: she is speaking into a telephone.

Baroque art is full of what art historians refer to as 'correspondences', whereby – to give one example – an annunciatory angel appearing in the squinch of a chapel is directing her glance towards an altarpiece of the Virgin. In the Charity group at the Pasatiempo, this baroque theatrical device has been appropriated, but in an updated technological version. The woman is using the phone to contact Juan María, who, learning that charity is needed, relays the message to Jesús, who responds by pointing in the direction of the poor people's home.

The original appearance of the Pasatiempo can scarcely be gleaned from what survives of the place today. In 1991, Nacho Cabaño, the scholarly son of Galician emigrants to Uruguay, co-wrote the first full-scale study of the Pasatiempo, and accompanied me there to guide me around its present maze of concrete-mixers, barbed wire, Nissen huts, undergrowth, and hidden ditches and potholes.

The destruction of the place, Nacho explained, began only

three years after Juan María's death in 1933. At the onset of the
Civil War the gardens were taken over by soldiers for target
practice, the hundreds of busts of emperors and popes being of
course ideal for this purpose. When in ruins, the Pasatiempo was
stripped of the lead piping that fed its pools, and became a place
of ill-repute, a scene of copulation, prostitution and mugging.
This reputation did not stop couples from having their wedding
photographs taken there, but such was the state of the gardens by
the 1960s that only those with the gloomiest marital prospects
would have considered doing so.

Nacho, who began his researches into the gardens' history
before the current restoration programme, admitted that the place
had had a greater poetic appeal when it was overgrown and
ruined. None the less he had been pleased to hear of the plans to
restore the park, and had only been dismayed on learning that
there was no intention whatsoever of staying true to the place's
original spirit. The Pasatiempo, instead of being scientifically
restored to its original state, was simply being cleared of all its
debris and character, and was going to become a municipal park,
just like any other.

I asked Nacho, an Italophile, if he had seen what had happened
recently to Bomarzo. He shook his head; he had never been there.
I told him that I remembered Bomarzo from the time when a
solitary old woman under a parasol guarded the entrance to a
place so overgrown and unvisited that it had seemed like an
enchanted forest, inhabited only by demons and spirits. But all
that had changed now. A large car-park and souvenir shop had
been built; the grass had been cut, the trees clipped, and the
monsters fenced in and numbered, as in a nature trail.

'So they've defiled the Sacred Wood,' Nacho said with his
ironic, melancholy smile.

THE INHABITANTS of the Galician province of La Coruña are
proud of their woods. But the woods of Galicia are fast disappearing, victims today mainly of fires said to be caused not only by
careless campers but also by an ecological and nationalistic terrorism, prepared to destroy innocent trees in order to do away with

the dreaded eucalyptus, an Australian import believed to be eroding the true character of the region. But the sheer scale of the destruction, and the fact that the wettest region in Spain should also be the one with the highest number of fires, suggests at times that some evil, supernatural force is at work.

The fastest route between Betanzos and La Coruña passes next to the village of Cecebre, which was once enclosed in a haunted wood. Wenceslao Fernández Florez, a novelist and journalist from La Coruña, had a summer house here, and used the area in a novel of melancholy whimsy, *The Animated Wood* (1943), in which the principal protagonist is not a person but what the author refers to as the *fraga de Cecebre*. A *fraga*, in Galician dialect, is a wild wood crowded with a chaotic assortment of coniferous and deciduous trees, all of which, in Fernández Florez's novel, have a life of their own and talk together in the first chapter as if they were human beings. The remaining chapters deal with the actual humans who visit and inhabit the wood, and with their occasional encounters, real or imaginary, with such supernatural forces as the *Estadea*, a tall Galician phantom who prowls at night dressed in a white tunic. Among the humans are two middle-aged women who come there on holiday from La Coruña, and eventually flee back to the city, terrified by all the strange goings-on in the wood. Then there is the impoverished, wooden-legged and love-stricken Geraldo, who is rewarded at the end of the book by regaining his real leg and capturing the heart of the hitherto aloof Hermengilda.

Death, in the book's brief epilogue, arrives to wipe out 'all these beings and the stories of these beings'. Their spirits live on in the wood, but, as the narrator stresses, the wood is no longer as 'luxuriant or extensive as it was in the past'.

I searched for the wood as the bus sped past Cecebre on the motorway, but all that I could see was a handful of charred trunks in a rolling countryside of modern villas that lay within sight of the advancing grey and white apartment blocks of La Coruña.

I WAS GAINING a reputation as a harbinger of death. Galicia, like Andalusia, is a land of deep and widespread superstition, and it was unfortunate that my visits to La Coruña always seemed to presage a death in the family with whom I stayed. The Monteros, admittedly, were a large family, and my stays with them had coincided with more weddings than funerals; but it was the deaths that came to be associated with me, beginning with that of the father, who died on my first visit to the city, after many years of suffering from the effects of a stroke that had deluded him at times into thinking he was the King of Spain.

Before the father's working life was curtailed by his long illness, the Monteros lived in a grand, turn-of-the-century mansion in the centre of La Coruña, and spent their summers in an outlying villa surrounded by palm trees and magnolias. They had moved now to a modern block, but the world in which they had been brought up was evoked for me every time I visited their most elderly relative, Tía Antonia, a bird-like woman in black who had spent much of her ninety years in a house that conveyed the spirit of La Coruña's turn-of-the-century heyday.

The house formed part of one of Spain's most beautiful and unusual seafronts, a seafront of glazed balconies that rise several floors to create an enormous glass wall, which is divided up into rectangles by gleaming white frames and animated by the brilliant, swaying reflections of the town's yacht-filled marina. The interior of Tía Antonia's house had all the magic and mystery I imagined would lie behind the glass seafront. The daylight, passing through a rippling ocean of ancient Venetian blinds, was transformed into filtered, penumbral patterns that echoed, in their strangeness, the muffled sounds from the harbour front and the ticking of a multitude of old clocks. Art Nouveau designs and curious Symbolist watercolours by Tía Antonia's father, a well-known local architect, enhanced rooms that were crowded with ancestral portraits, Classical-style bronzes, Japanese folding screens, and armchairs and sofas shrouded in ghost-like white sheets. The presence of hidden spirits seemed to hang over the rooms, above all over the host of frail figurines that were displayed in cabinets like miniature Tía Antonias.

The small back windows of Tía Antonia's house looked obliquely over both the old town and a grand and eclectic civic square known as the Plaza de María Pita after a local sixteenth-century heroine who managed to outwit 'the pirate Drake'. The inhabitants of La Coruña claim the square is the only important one in the world named after a woman who was not a saint or the Virgin Mary – an indication of the high position held by women in Galician society. This is a region where even the landscape has been described as feminine, thanks not only to its rounded forms and the lack of a mountainous backbone of thrusting virile sharpness, but also to the predominance of women working in the fields, the menfolk being either at sea for much of the year or else trying to make money overseas. In a region such as this, where women have had to fend so much for themselves, it is perhaps more than just a coincidence that two of its greatest cultural figures should have been women. One of these was the mid-nineteenth-century poetess, Rosalía de Castro; the other was her younger and more socially advantaged contemporary, the novelist Emilia Pardo Bazán.

Pardo Bazán was brought up in La Coruña's old town, in what she would later recall as a 'forbiddingly silent old house, where I was never invited by any child of my own age to play and run about'. Married off to a lawyer at the age of sixteen, she was later separated from her husband after he had become increasingly disturbed by her growing notoriety as a writer. A liberal and a leading advocate of women's rights, she was also one of the protagonists of the 'realist' generation of Spanish writers that came to the fore in the early 1880s. She admired the *costumbrismo* of Pereda, but had a particular passion for Pérez Galdós, a passion that transcended the merely literary, as was revealed by the publication in 1972 of her intensely physical love letters to him.

Pardo Bazán's credentials as a realist were established by *La Tribuna* (1883), which told the tale of a noble and courageous *cigarrera*. This was one of the earliest novels in Spain to be centred on a provincial city and the first in modern Spanish literature to deal with urban working-class life. The city in question is obviously La Coruña, but it is disguised as 'Marineda' for reasons that are given in the book's preface. Though admitting that her novel was at heart 'a study of regional customs', Pardo Bazán confessed that the proximity in time of the events described, and her consequent unwillingness to be tied down too closely to factual exactitude, impelled her to create her own imaginary world and to 'situate the action in places that belong to that moral geography of which [Pereda] speaks, and which every novelist, great or small, has the indisputable right to bend to his or her particular needs'.

La Coruña, a city situated like Santander on a promontory, had, in Pardo Bazán's day, a shape reminiscent of an hour-glass, with the working class and the aristocracy living in the lower and upper extremities respectively. The city's bustling commercial and entertainment districts were situated in the tall, narrow neck of land in the middle. The central area of La Coruña is still a place for business and promenading, but the appearance and social make-up of the city have been drastically altered in recent times by demolition, reconstruction, massive expansion, and the inevitable pockets of decay. The narrow, picturesque streets of the gently sloping old town, formerly the haunt of the aristocracy, have gone somewhat to seed and have been taken over by a warren of student bars that have helped to consolidate the city's reputation as the liveliest in Galicia.

The tourist population of La Coruña is built up almost entirely of yachtsmen and summertime revellers. But the city's old town also continues to attract a trickle of mainly elderly British visitors, oblivious both of Pardo Bazán and of the more frivolous aspects of presentday La Coruña. They could almost be described as pilgrims, for they have come to La Coruña primarily to venerate at a tomb: the tomb of Sir John Moore.

Sir John Moore, retreating in 1809 from French forces led by Marshal Soult, was mortally wounded by a cannonball while undertaking a rearguard action that has variously been described as valiant or foolhardy. The death upset the marital plans of the eccentric Hester Stanhope, and became the subject of an impassioned debate in Parliament; but it would probably have passed into history merely as a footnote had it not been for the poem it inspired eight years later from the Reverend Charles Wolfe, an Irish curate who never set foot in Spain and would never write any other verse worth reading.

> Not a drum was heard, not a funeral note,
> As his corpse to the ramparts we hurried;
> Not a soldier discharged his farewell shot,
> O'er the grave where our hero was buried.
>
> We buried him darkly; at dead of night,
> The sods with our bayonets turning . . .
>
> Slowly and sadly we laid him down,
> From the field of his fame, fresh and gay;
> We carved not a line, we raised not a stone,
> But we left him – alone with his glory.

They buried the hero on a small battery of the old town, a spot George Borrow described in 1836 as 'sweet', with an extensive view of the ocean. By then a granite tomb had been erected with a 'simple and sublime' epitaph which Borrow favourably contrasted with the 'bombastic inscriptions which deform the walls of Westminster Abbey'. 'JOHN MOORE,' it read,

LEADER OF THE ENGLISH ARMIES
Slain in Battle
1809

Later in the century the tomb was embellished with urns and railings, and the surrounding area was turned into a small public garden with palm trees, cacti, and flowerbeds bordered by box hedges. The lines of Wolfe's poem, already one of the most quoted in the English language, were carved on one of the battery's walls, alongside a poem to Sir John written in 1875 by Galicia's most loved poet, Rosalía de Castro. Thanks to Wolfe's one-off work, based on a newspaper article, Moore won the affection of the Galician people, and, through Rosalía de Castro, entered Galician folklore. Rosalía's poem, written in Galician, is addressed to 'Poor John', and dwells not on the heroics of the death but on such characteristically Galician themes as absence, the sadness of the ocean, and separation from one's homeland.

A retired English diplomat and soldier I once encountered in front of Sir John's tomb was incensed by the 'disgraceful state' of the memorial and its surrounding garden, and was particularly upset by the disrespectful way in which the gardener had 'casually left his tools around'. He became so red in the face that for a moment I thought that he might soon be joining his hero. Fortunately he regained his composure and decided to write an immediate letter of protest to the British Ambassador in Madrid.

I only hope that he did not go on afterwards to the nearby British cemetery, which is an annexe to the municipal cemetery, and stands just outside the old town, in what is perhaps the dingiest and most dangerous district in modern La Coruña. The district occupies a magnificent coastal site, and could easily have been given over to parkland and attractive seaside residences and hotels. But, thanks to its cemeteries, it has become a dumping ground for gypsies, junkies, and everyone else the city's wealthier residents would like to forget about.

On a dark, late November day, the Monteros came to this part of the city for the funeral of an uncle, leaving me and a family friend to drive beyond the cemetery, beyond the grey council blocks and outlying shanty houses, and into an as yet unspoilt part of the headland, shaggy with wild grass and heather, and walled in by granite boulders that occasionally disappeared under the impact of the more ferocious waves. We got out of the car beside the Tower of Hercules, a severe sixteenth-century structure encasing the oldest lighthouse in the world; it was mentioned by Ptolemy and was founded, according to Irish legends, by the Celtic chief, Breogan. An inscription, recording its Roman architect, is protected under a nearby shelter, to which someone has added the now more pertinent message, 'No a la droga'.

Drugs, poverty and smuggling entered our conversation as we looked west along the rugged coast which leads eventually to Finisterre. The wild, rocky bays along this coast have always been the haunt of smugglers, who since Franco's day have traded largely in drugs, and have transformed Galicia into one of Spain's more drug-infested regions. The most notorious areas are not the deprived urban districts such as the one we had passed through on the way to the lighthouse, but the coastal villages we were now scanning. This is a coast where bleak winter conditions and long periods spent waiting around between fishing trips encourage boredom, loneliness and, occasionally, despair.

I had idyllic memories, from several years back, of the Galician coast in summer, but many of the acquaintances I had made then had warned me against returning in the winter. 'You might like it now,' they kept on saying. 'But come back in two or three months' time. It's so sad, so empty.' The idea of visiting the coast in what seemed set to be a relentlessly wet late November had not immediately appealed to me, but as I sat watching the waves, the rocks, and the imminent storm clouds, I came to welcome the prospect of desolation with an irrational excitement. I had half accepted an offer of a lift the next day to the southern, inland town of Ourense. But I was now gripped by an urge to head south on my own, preferably in winds and driving rain, along slow and indirect coastal roads that would lead me to the promontory at the end of the world.

'IT WOULD be difficult to assign any plausible reason for the ardent desire which I entertained to visit this place,' wrote George Borrow, describing his sudden decision to go to Finisterre in 1836. He tried subsequently to justify the trip as a way of thanking God for having saved him the year before, when he had almost been shipwrecked 'on the rocky sides of this extreme point of the Old World'. But ultimately it was Borrow's perversity that drove him to Finisterre, the same perversity that made him fall in love with Galicia at a time when few other foreigners went there out of choice. His account of his Galician journey, and in particular his trip to Finisterre, is perhaps the highpoint of *The Bible in Spain* (1840).

Borrow was one of those travellers who relish hardships and dangers, of which he seems certainly to have had his full share on his way to Finisterre, even if he probably exaggerated them afterwards in the telling. His journey to Finisterre began by being duped by the man who was originally going to take him there, after which he was entrusted to the guidance of a half-witted, retired sailor who soon revealed his complete ignorance of the route. By nightfall they were wandering lost on a moor, with the guide terrified that a mist would descend on them, bringing with it the much feared phantom, the *Estadea*.

The night was clear and a place to sleep was found, but they reached Finisterre the next day only to be put under arrest by the mayor, who threatened them with immediate execution. Such, according to Borrow, was the rarity of foreigners in this village, and such the gullibility of its people, that he and his guide were mistaken on arrival for the Pretender, Don Carlos, and his nephew, the Infante Don Sebastián. Borrow's rational attempts to show that they could not possibly be either of these two men were undermined by his failure to find any reasonable motives for having come to Finisterre.

'I endeavoured', he said, 'to convince the *alcalde* that I had come across the country for the purpose of making myself acquainted with the many remarkable objects which it contained, and of obtaining information respecting the character and conditions of the inhabitants.' However, the mayor was unconvinced by such motives, and was made especially suspicious by Borrow's assertion that he had climbed the mountain behind the village simply to enjoy the view.

'I have lived at Finisterre forty years,' the mayor protested, 'and have never ascended that mountain. I would not do it in a day like this for ten ounces of gold. You went to take altitudes and mark out a camp.' The lives of the two strangers were fortunately spared by the intervention of an old sailor, who had known other Englishmen and found Borrow's statements to be entirely consistent with what he knew of this race. '"The English", said he, "have more money than they know what to do with, and on that account they wander all over the world, paying dearly for what no other people care a groat for."'

Rural Galicia still has the feel of Spain's least developed region, but the lack of development works today in favour of the solitary traveller who has to resort to public transport. In trying to get on my own to an out-of-season Finisterre, I had half expected to further the English reputation for eccentricity and extravagance by having to take taxis; but I soon discovered that the wild and near-inaccessible areas of old are served today by one of Spain's most regular and extensive bus networks, a network necessitated by the relative lack of private cars and by the region's string of hamlets and *minifundios* ('small-holdings').

Almost disappointed to find how easy it was to get to Finisterre, I could none the less enjoy a sense of the remoteness of my destination, thanks to the lethargic progress of the direct bus from La Coruña. The weather changed repeatedly and dramatically on the journey, but a clear, late-autumn sun emerged during the afternoon, as the bus reached the coast and embarked on the final stretch of road, a narrow dead-end stretch threading its way around small, wooded bays, eventually reaching the exposed slopes rising above the small fishing village of Finisterre.

Covering the remaining three and a half kilometres between the village and the actual cape on foot, I climbed to the top of Borrow's mountain and shortly descended its ridge towards that famous point where 'the earth ends and the sea begins'. The first recorded journey to the cape was undertaken in around 150 BC by a Roman soldier called Decimus Junius Brutus, who, according to an account written by one Lucius Florus, 'did not want to turn around until he had seen the sun disappear into the sea, a spectacle that caused him remorse and a sense of having committed a sacrifice'.

A Celtic tribe apparently inhabited the peninsula, and placed at its cape an altar to the sun, at which sacrifices were said to be made. In Christian times a hermitage dedicated to St William was erected here, and in 1745 an itinerant priest, O. P. Sarmient, was told that a stone bed had been latterly kept inside it for the use of husbands and wives desperate for a child. Today there is just a lighthouse, and an abandoned weather centre which reminded me of the days when the BBC exotically mentioned Finisterre in its weather reports.

The weather was so clear that the Rías Bajas could be seen in their entirety, the promontories of the far distance fading into the ever paler blue gradations of a horizon in which the exhausted eye finally rested on the minuscule profile of the St Tecla mountain, on the border with Portugal. Nearer where I was standing were the sharply defined pines, rocks and cliffs of a froth-fringed, mountainous coast baptized by sailors 'the Coast of Death'.

A storm suddenly hit me in the back, making me turn round to face the north, where a distant fishing boat was rocking at the approach of dark, racing clouds carrying with them the diagonal streaks of torrential rain. The sight of the rain advancing at such speed was so exhilarating that I sought shelter only at the last possible moment, when the whole landscape I had been admiring was entirely obliterated. There was no sunset that evening.

On the outskirts of the village of Finisterre, a large crowd holding umbrellas stood in the twilight outside the much weathered Romanesque church of Santa María, where the exhausted medieval pilgrims to Santiago used to come to venerate the popular devotional images of the Virgin of the Boat and Christ Crossing the Waters. Two old men, clearly village idiots, mumbled something in Galician about a funeral, but the presence there of what seemed like most of the village argued for a funeral of particular importance.

'No,' another man explained to me. 'It's just an ordinary funeral. No one special.'

Afterwards the fishermen at the funeral went to play at the pinball machines in the bars around the harbour. The owner of the smartest of the bars told me in an American English that he had bought his establishment after spending over twenty years travelling around the world working as he went. Nothing, he insisted, would induce him to leave his village ever again, but he had enjoyed his years abroad, and always liked meeting foreigners, quite a number of whom now came there in the summer months.

'We always welcome strangers to our village,' he said, 'but especially those who show an interest in our culture and customs.' I said that a compatriot of mine, George Borrow, had not experienced this hospitality in the last century. 'Ah, but times have changed since then,' he replied. 'We've got an excellent mayor now. In fact he's a foreigner himself. He's a Peruvian, married to a local girl. He writes wonderful poetry.'

The next day I headed slowly south down the Coast of Death. I wanted to climb up into the frenetic outcrops of granite that crowned Mount Pindo, a mountain with a mystical and symbolical importance comparable to that of Croagh Patrick in the west of Ireland. In the village of Ezaro, I was told that the easiest ascent was from the village of Pindo; in the village of Pindo, they said that I'd be better off going back to Ezaro. I later met a person who had actually been to the summit, but he said that he had done so only as a child, and had heard that since then all the paths had become overgrown and difficult to follow. The persistently uncertain weather encouraged me to continue travelling south, past a wide, sandy bay guarded by 'the largest *hórreo* in the world', and into the estuary which separates the Coast of Death from a mountainous peninsula filled for me with memories of one Galician summer.

LONG AUGUST afternoons were spent with friends on the northern side of the Barbanza peninsula, on a sandy beach backed by pines and maize fields, and with a small, rocky promontory bearing the remains of a Celtic fort. Up to a dozen or so nudists, mainly intellectuals from Santiago University, shared the large beach with us, and provided a stark contrast to the heavily skirted Galician farm workers who came down periodically to the fields to collect the maize in ox-drawn carts with stone wheels. The worlds of traditional rural Galicia and urban liberal permissiveness would occasionally come into conflict, with irate locals descending on to the beach wielding large sticks, chasing away the nudists as if expelling Adam and Eve from paradise.

The southern side of the peninsula, where we had rented our house, presented a different and less immediately beautiful aspect of coastal Galicia. One of the Montero daughters had found the property for us, and had raised our hopes with descriptions of an isolated farm dwelling in a hamlet of three or four other houses. The contrast between what she had told us and what we actually found seemed to confirm that the Galicians were mad, deluded people with a fanciful perception of places.

From the town of Padrón, at the head of the Arousa estuary, all the way to our destination of Palmeira, we drove along a coast almost entirely built up, not with hotels but with bungalows and apartment blocks constructed over the previous thirty years in response both to the boom in the seafood industries, and to immigrants' demands for holiday and retirement homes. The coastal road was narrow and congested, and had a reputation as one of the most dangerous in Galicia, thanks to the many impatient drivers, especially those engaged in smuggling. When we arrived in Palmeira, we discovered that the 'hamlet' had a summer population of at least 2000 and was virtually a continuation of the neighbouring towns of Puebla del Caramiñal and Ribeiro, which itself was a modern conglomerate of several communities. The whole architecture of the coast was an excellent example of what many Spaniards refer to as 'Galician taste', which differs from Murcian taste or Aragónese taste in its apparently wilful defiance of Ruskinian ideals of simplicity, sturdiness and natural materials, and in its desire to substitute instead flimsiness, corrugated iron and ceramic cladding *preferably* in a bilious green.

Our own house in Palmeira had an orange-green porch in ceramic mosaics, and a neon-lit interior with such features as a plastic image of the Virgin inserted into an anchor made of imitation fur; our so-called 'orchard' was a tiny, tin-filled strip of wasteland adjoining a zoo-like concrete enclosure to which was chained a perpetually barking dog. On the day of our arrival, we stood depressed in the orchard under a light drizzle, looking towards an estuary completely obscured by fog. We might have been better off on a caravan holiday in Skegness.

Everything changed on the second day. The fog slowly lifted, revealing first tidy rows of 'mussel rafts' that gave to the ever widening prospect the sharply receding perspective of an Italian Renaissance painting. Rocks and tiny islands and a distant, mountainous strip constituting the southern shores of the Arousa estuary came successively into view to form an immense panorama in postcard blues and greens. In the early afternoon, the far-off sounds of explosions, bagpipes and dance music announced the first of the August festivals that would regularly transform the night sky above the estuary into a magical dome of fireworks.

Even Palmeira itself began to enchant me. Though I never went so far as to consider it a 'hamlet', I began to think of this sprawling and objectively unattractive place as a fishing village with the same endearing beauty as Dylan Thomas's Llareggub. The inhabitants of the village, like those of the Barbanza peninsula in general, flatly contradicted Ortega y Gasset's controversial assessment of the Galicians as 'submissive, suspicious souls, and with no trust even in themselves'. Though forming part of an intensely urbanized coast, Palmeira had retained the atmosphere of one of those friendly, uncorrupted old villages that exist more in the imagination than in reality: this was a place where doors were never locked, crime was non-existent, credit was given automatically in all shops and bars, and invitations were made immediately to drop into people's homes or to go on fishing trips.

I was the first Englishman ever to have holidayed in Palmeira, but I had never been before to a Spanish village where English was so widely spoken. Many of the men had picked up English on their long fishing trips, but the majority of the English-speakers were either emigrants on a home visit or else emigrants who had returned for good: the proportion of emigrants in this part of the coast is traditionally the highest in Galicia and once accounted for nearly two-thirds of the total population. Our fisherman neighbour fondly recalled a long stay in 'Great-yarmoof', while one of the small children who played in our street surprised me on my second day by saying 'Hi, Mike!' in a broad American accent. The *americanos*, who made up most of the emigrants, had settled mainly in New Jersey, where they tended to work in small businesses, garages or petrol stations. They sat for much of the day in the bars of the harbour, eating large plates of succulent mussels, and enjoying a reputation as sages on international affairs. The latest opinions and prognostications of the *americanos* on the issues of the day were constantly relayed to me, as I stood drinking a morning coffee at the oldest of the village bars, which itself was run by a former *americano*. At least one of them did indeed project a formidable image of authority, intelligence, and international glamour. He was said to have homes in California, Massachusetts and Palmeira, and though he claimed that he worked as a 'marine biologist', he had all the attributes of a Mafia godfather. On one occasion when he asked me to join him at table, where he always surrounded himself with female admirers, we got on to the subject of drugs in Galicia. Palmeira, according to him, had so far been spared the drug trade; but for the next two days a strange man would keep on approaching me as I sat reading on the village pier. He said that his life was in danger and that the drug barons were 'out to get him'.

Another, more representative of the *americanos*, invited me one clear and sunny morning to come with him by car to see what he described as the 'most beautiful view in the world'. We drove into the woods behind the village, and climbed into the Sierra de Barbanza, eventually rising above tree level and winding our way up a ridge from which we could see Finisterre to the north and the whole of the Arousa estuary to the south. We stopped two-thirds of the way up the mountain, at the viewpoint of La Curotiña, where a menhir-like monument was carved with a face featuring rounded glasses and a pointed beard of prophet-like length. The face stared across the estuary, and commemorated – according to the plaque below – a man who frequently walked up to this spot to 'contemplate and savour the landscapes of his ancestors and literary creations'. In coming to spend the summer on the Barbanza peninsula I had unwittingly entered the domain, half real, half imaginary, of Ramón del Valle-Inclán.

'The love of homeland is born and affirmed at the two opposite points of our lives. It is born in childhood, because the first marks that the world leaves on us are formed of impressions of one's native landscape and people; and it is affirmed in our last years when we turn away disillusioned from all the paths of life to immerse ourselves in the sentimental world of our childhood.' These words, by a minor novelist called Victoriano García Martí, served as part of the foreword to a lengthy history of Puebla del Caramiñal written by one of its emigrants in Cuba. García Martí was himself included in this book as one of the youthful participants of a *tertulia* held in a local pharmacy and presided over by Valle-Inclán, who spent much of his childhood in Puebla del Caramiñal and returned there in his fifties to write many of his greatest works.

In his poem 'The Traveller', Valle-Inclán expressed a wish for his memory to live on in a '. . . stoic house/walled in the stone of Barbanza'.

> I want to build a house
> Like the meaning of my life,

I want to leave my soul in stone
Erected.

Many years after his death the municipality of Puebla del Caramiñal claimed to have fulfilled this wish when they purchased a small Renaissance palace in the centre of his 'home village' and converted it into a museum to him. In the meantime, on the other, southern side of the Arousa estuary, the municipality of Villanueva de Arousa created another museum to Valle-Inclán, this one situated in the house where he was supposedly born. The fact that Valle-Inclán appears to have had two home villages might be confusing for those who are discovering this writer and are as yet unaware of his love of mystification and of playing games with reality. Valle-Inclán deliberately clouded his origins, and diplomatically contributed to the heated dispute as to where he was actually born by saying that his birth took place on a fishing boat halfway between Puebla del Caramiñal and Villanueva.

Valle-Inclán's birth certificate, in the name of Ramón Valle y Peña, is in fact held by the parish of Villanueva, though his childhood was indeed divided between there and Puebla, the northern side of the estuary being the ancestral land of his mother, the southern that of his father. An amalgam of places on both sides of the estuary would appropriately form the basis of 'Viana del Prior', the imaginary Galician village around which are centred those works inspired by his native land.

Though the professional life of this man of many masks was spent largely in Madrid, his period of greatest productivity coincided with his move in 1917 to a former priory outside Puebla, where he wrote the most important of his distorted tragicomedies or *esperpentos*. One of these was his Madrilenian drama, *Bohemian Lights*; the other was *Divine Words*, the tale of an adulterous sacristan's wife living in a vicious, gossip-ridden and impoverished Viana del Prior. *Divine Words*, with its grotesque array of characters, its clipped, exclamatory dialogue, and its poetic, impractical stage directions, is not just a precursor of the Theatre of the Absurd, but also a work in the spirit of a Galician folk tale, fantastical, morbid, and with a sense of lurking evil.

Suitably enough, the building where it was written – occupying an overgrown grass verge between the coastal road and some eucalyptus trees – is now a sinister, graffiti-covered shell, the place having been gutted by fire in 1989.

In 1921 Valle-Inclán rented a modest villa in the centre of Puebla, but the Galician period of his maturity ended four years later, when he returned on a more permanent basis to Madrid. By 1932, when Valle-Inclán was poor, ill and separated from his family, García Martí tried to raise money to realize Valle-Inclán's dream of having a Galician property in which his memory would be permanently encased in the stone. A subscription was taken up and then abandoned. But at least Valle-Inclán was to die in his native region, his withered body being transferred from Madrid to what he once described as the 'petrified city' of Santiago de Compostela. He died in a clinic there on 5 January 1936, and was buried the following day in a ceremony as gruesome as one of the scenes in his *esperpentos*. Just as the simple coffin was being lowered into the ground, on one of those proverbially rainy Santiago days, a young sculptor hurled himself at it to try and remove the wooden cross on its lid, placed there contrary to Valle-Inclán's insistence on an entirely civic funeral. The sculptor succeeded in carrying out the writer's wishes, but also managed to fall into the grave, break the coffin, and expose the corpse to the dark and muddy surroundings.

'HOW TERRIBLE it is to die among those greys!' Valle-Inclán remarked as he lay dying in a city whose melancholy beauty had enchanted him in his youth. 'Among vintage Spanish cities,' he once wrote, 'Santiago de Compostela is the only one that seems to be immobilized in a dream of granite, immutable and eternal . . . A mystical rose of stone, a rustic and romantic flower, it preserves the ingenuous grace of old, rhymed Latin as in the bygone days of its great pilgrimages . . . It has the solitude, sadness and strength of a mountain.'

Today's pilgrims to Santiago, arriving there after risking their lives and illusions on the ugly and congested approach roads to the city, will find, outside the tourist season and beyond the unprepossessing outer core, a place as eternal as the one evoked by Valle-Inclán. It is one of the few showpieces in Spain to give little hint of the fake, the artificial and the modern; instead, it overwhelms the visitor with an atmosphere both deeply affecting and difficult to define. To many people Santiago is a university town with the romance and mystery of Zuleika Dobson's Oxford, and indeed many Spaniards come here having read the Galician equivalent of Max Beerbohm's novel, Pérez Lugín's immensely popular *The House of Troy* (1915). To others, Santiago is a place more like Alas's Vetusta than Oviedo itself, a place under the icy grip of suspicion, rumour and the clergy. The atmosphere of Santiago is at its most powerful on autumn and winter evenings, when the claustrophobic, rain-washed streets and granite arcades are brought sporadically to life by groups of students, weaving in and out of lighted doors, crawling perhaps between the Paris and Dakhar bars, and avoiding the dark profiles of priests and canons who scurry forth from the variegated bulk of an omnipresent cathedral that is like a town in its own right. The apostle's shrine within this building was likened by Ford to a 'spider in the middle of its web, catching strange and foolish flies'; but I prefer to reserve this image for the cathedral archivist, Don José María Díaz, a canon of vast learning and intelligence, but moody, suspicious of foreigners, and with penetrating eyes that not only reduced me to stone when I once turned the pages of Picaud's twelfth-century pilgrim's guide, but which also preyed on gossip and controlled all the threads of a dark domain extending well beyond the archives.

Santiago de Compostela is timeless in the sense that when one comes here one cannot automatically ascribe it to a particular period. The common assumption is that it is a medieval town, but little of its architecture is outwardly medieval, and almost none of it is Gothic. No one would call Santiago a Renaissance town, and few people think of it as a baroque town, even though the majority of its great buildings have an idiosyncratic and imaginative baroque coating of florid and geometrical forms that might be called dreams in granite.

Even fewer visitors would consider Santiago a nineteenth-century town. However, when the Galician writer Torrente

Ballester was commissioned recently to write a book on Santiago concentrating on the most representative period in the city's history, he chose to write on neither the medieval nor baroque periods, but on the 'Santiago of Rosalía de Castro'.

Rosalía de Castro wrote little that referred directly to Santiago, but her work is thought to encapsulate the spirit of this town. There are monuments to her in the square where she was born, outside the church where her body was later brought, and in the middle of the beautifully situated Alameda Park, where people still come to have their photographs taken by an elderly man who frames his subjects in a heart.

Anyone struggling to define the essence not just of Santiago but of Galicia itself must at some time turn to Rosalía de Castro, whose life and work offer a summary of the proverbial 'Celtic melancholy' of the Galician people. The illegitimate offspring of a priest and a woman of high society, Rosalía married in 1860 the 'Galician Revivalist' and future director of the National Archives at Simancas, Martínez Murguía; he later contributed to Rosalía's burden of Galician sadness, or *saudade*, through his many infidelities and long absences from home. Socially ostracized on account of her birth, homesick while living away from Galicia, and exhausted through frequent illnesses and the strain of raising six children, Rosalía eventually died from cancer in 1885, at the age of forty-eight.

Rosalía did not have a wide following during her lifetime, partly through her belittlement as the wife of a famous intellectual, but largely because she wrote in Galician, a language little used and not wholly understood by the Galician middle class. In 1863 she published her first important book of poems in this language, *Galician Ballads*, which drew on and refined the then dying folk poetry of Galicia, a poetry Rosalía characterized as 'all music and vagueness, all complaints and sighs and gentle smiles'. Written with a Bécquer-like economy, and recalling in their lyrical tenderness the distinctive lilting manner in which so many Galician women speak, these subtle and movingly simple works form altogether a long poem to Galicia, its peoples, traditions, myths, and above all to its soft, green and misty landscapes. Rosalía preferred this countryside above all others that she had known in Spain, and clearly said so in a foreword in which even the 'famous *huerta*' of Murcia was described as being 'as tired and monotonous as the rest of that region'. Her next book, *Follas Novas* (1880), was written almost entirely in the Castilian village of Simancas, a village located in flat and dusty surroundings that made Rosalía wonder in one of the poems what God was thinking of when he created such an ugly place. Stuck in Simancas she found empathy with the Galician emigrant, whose plight, together with that of the oppressed Galician fisherman and labourer, provided the main theme of these new poems.

Rosalía's position in the forefront of the Galician Revival was consolidated by *Follas Novas*, but even among her Galician supporters she continued to be regarded as a folklorist rather than as a major poet. Was it out of a desire to be more seriously recognized and to reach a much wider public that she decided, in 1880, when already suffering from cancer, 'to write no longer in our native dialect, nor even to deal with themes of direct concern to our people'? Rosalía was a modest person, and she probably made this decision not out of any wish for self-advancement but out of a sense of the inability of literature to alleviate the problems of the Galician people. In any case it was a decision that lost her the favour of many Galician intellectuals without winning for her many new readers outside the region. Her next and last book, *By the Banks of the Sar* (1884), came out in a small edition that made little impact when it appeared; thirty years or so would pass before writers such as Azorín would consider it a work of similar importance to Bécquer's *Rimas*.

By the Banks of the Sar is not only one of the greatest books of modern Spanish verse. It is also the bleakest. The beauty of the Galician landscape, and in particular of the river valley behind Padrón, is evoked; but it is a beauty haunted always by sadness and death, as when she laments the destruction of oaks by disease and man, and her near-prophetic vision of a future barren land. The rain is always falling, death is relentless, 'phantoms' are everywhere, and the adjectives 'dark' and 'sad' are constantly repeated. Within the clouds of depression and confusion there stands out the image of a woman continually searching, but searching for she knows not what.

I do not know what I am eternally searching
on land, in air, and in the sky;
I do not know what I am searching, but it's something
Which I lost I know not when, and do not find.

THE BUS that drove me round the rocky shores of a deserted
Coast of Death continued inland to Santiago, from where I set off
again one morning to the sea, this time by train, following up to
Padrón a stretch of track laid out by the English grandfather of
Camilo José Cela. The grandfather had settled at Iria Flavia,
which had been a bishopric long before Santiago, but which was
later reduced to being a quiet, outlying suburb of Padrón. Cela
was born there, in a long mansion guarded today by an enormous
bronze bust of his head, and a yet more recent monument
incorporating the first train to run on his grandfather's railway.
The single track keeps its distance from Cela's birthplace, but
passes instead alongside the garden wall that protects the final
home of Rosalía de Castro, 'a modest little home full of memories,
with a small balcony covered in creepers', as Unamuno described
it, contemplating the place from his train window.

The house has since been turned into Rosalía's museum, with
a few items of furniture in cold, reconstructed settings, editions
of her books in several languages, and medals struck for her in
foreign lands; but her memories now seem to lie elsewhere, in the
gentle landscape outside, in the heavy morning mist trying to lift
itself above the River Sar, and in the names of nearby places that
sometimes appear in her works as in a litany, as if, in the words
of Unamuno, by their very mention images of tenderness would
be invoked.

> Padrón! Padrón! Santa María . . .
> Lestrove!. . . Farewell! Farewell!

Memories of Rosalía came and went as I caught glimpses of
names from a speeding train that continued south into the
sunshine, stopping briefly at Pontevedra, a place Pardo Bazán
remembered from childhood holidays as 'embraced by the blue
arms of a sea worthy of the Bay of Naples'. I changed train at

Vigo, a high-rise metropolis set in the lowest and most temperate of the Rías Bajas, an estuary that extended in front of me like a vast and glowing diorama in the crisp November sun. I had two hours to spare in which to walk down to the harbour front, thinking of Laurie Lee, V. S. Pritchett and other idealistic British travellers from the romantic days of the passenger ferry from London to Vigo. The harbour master assured me that the service had been suspended a good forty years earlier, and that not even cargo boats took passengers any more.

The small episcopal town of Tui, on the border with Portugal, sits with its squat, fortress-like cathedral above the Miño, its sad, cobbled alleys and cracked stone walls having given up the struggle to prevent the luxuriant vegetation of this mild and humid climate pushing itself relentlessly through the stone. In the empty Diocesan Museum, a man was taking down an exhibition on the theme of Death in Galicia. The words 'vida' and 'muerte' still hung on either side of the entrance door, while inside was a white panel asking the visitor a series of fundamental questions. How is death understood by our people? What exactly do we mean by it? And we ourselves? What do *we* think about death? The last remaining item was a theological treatise of 1581, written by a local author colloquially known as 'El Tudense' or 'The man from Tui'. His life's work, apparently, was a 'Discourse on the Brevity of Life'.

An elderly emigrant, returning to France, shared a compartment with me on a late afternoon train shuffling almost silently along the wooded, hilly banks of the Miño. He had gone off to France over thirty years earlier in search of work, 'as we all have to'; but he never got used to French life, and was hoping that his next stay would be his last. He grumbled about the length of the journey ahead of him, then fell into a deep sleep, leaving me to take out a book entitled *The Traveller in Galicia* (1989).

Álvaro Cunqueiro, the book's distinguished Galician author, describes the town I was heading for, at the confluence of the Miño and the Avia, a river which Cunqueiro regards as the etymological twin of 'Shakespeare's sweet Avon'. If Galicia had produced an Izaak Walton, Cunqueiro muses, then he would certainly have come to fish at the riverside town of Ribadavia, a town 'coloured like the autumn', and 'surely more beautiful than [Walton's] native Tornhill'.

Death and drink come together at Ribadavia in a very special way. The town is not only the capital of Galicia's most important wine-growing region, it is also the largest European manufacturer of coffins. In 1991, during the build-up to the Gulf War, the local coffin industry had been especially busy carrying out an enormous commission from the Americans; a vast surplus of coffins resulted, and by the time of my arrival here, a great many of the coffins were being sold off at cut-down prices.

I stayed in a half-abandoned house on the outskirts of the town, surrounded by hills and vineyards, and within sight of the warehouses of the 'coffin factory'. The house, enclosed by vines, belonged to the family of one of the Montero daughters-in-law, but had scarcely been used or dusted for many years. I had been invited to a small reunion of friends coinciding with Ribadavia's 'Third Festival of History'. The daughter-in-law, a native of Ribadavia, was keen on coming to the festival from La Coruña, and was with her husband, José Ignacio, who had chosen to risk stroke and heart attack by abandoning his recently adopted alcohol-free, low-cholesterol diet for this weekend. He could scarcely have done otherwise, given the presence in our group of his old drinking and eating companion, Jorge, a man of Rabelaisian size and tendencies, who had an entirely guilt-free approach to self-indulgence and was capable of ordering three large steaks in a restaurant one after the other. 'At least there's no shortage of coffins here,' Jorge joked, as we set off by night into the old town.

The granite-grey streets of an intact medieval quarter, rising above the leafy banks of Galicia's Avon, were hung with flags and coats-of-arms in preparation for the next day's festival. The night was clear but cold, and most of the inhabitants were indoors, the more elderly of the menfolk mainly in the dark, nameless bodegas installed in the medieval cellars. Walking down the steps that led into one of the largest, we interrupted a scene from another era. In a setting of yellowing posters from before the Civil War, old, unshaven men playing cards around a long wooden table were frozen in a raucous laugh at the very moment of our entry. The tavern's owner was seated with them, and reacted to our arrival simply with a drunken gesture of the hand, and a reminder that his establishment was 'self-service', and that we should help ourselves to whatever we could find. We entered a back room and poured out jugs of wine from giant oak barrels that became progressively dustier as they disappeared into the gloom of the high, vaulted ceiling.

The owner was a strange man. He charged whatever he felt like, and loved to tease new customers by keeping them standing for ages while pretending to work out some vast, imaginary bill. His old cronies giggled in the background, knowing too well that the sum asked for would almost certainly be a derisory one. He had genuinely no interest in money, and, while we were there, turned down a large sum offered to him by a television crew which had come to Ribadavia to film the festival, and, they hoped, his tavern. 'This is a place for drinking, not filming,' he said, to the accompaniment of laughs and approving cheers from his friends.

A similar line of argument, according to my companions, had made him previously reject the advances of a number of archaeologists who had wanted to dig underneath the tavern, where they were convinced that they would find one of the major relics from Ribadavia's past. In the Middle Ages, the town had an important Jewish community; its main synagogue, dating back at least to the eleventh century, was reputed to lie underneath the very room where Jorge was now expertly cutting slices from a large ham and where we were all sitting with our white ceramic cups, drinking a wine that Cunqueiro thought would have pleased such a 'peaceful, liberal and human man' as Izaak Walton.

On the morning of the festival, we went wine-tasting in the neighbouring valley of the Arnoia, where vines were succeeded in the steep and narrow upper reaches by dense woods in which old balconied houses, with caved-in roofs, waited patiently for the return of their emigrant owners. Pedro Verdejo was one of the few to have come back to his beautiful native valley, in his case to revolutionize traditional methods of wine production by introducing the latest in Japanese technology. He invited us to try his prize-winning wine in a hi-tech modern cellar with gleaming, stainless steel vats that clashed, futuristically, with the unspoilt valley setting, which, he claimed, held mystical enchantment for him.

The effects of the wine soon blurred the boundaries between the old and the modern worlds, and helped by lunchtime to ease the transition back to the Middle Ages in a Ribadavia that had become a medieval fair, with most of the town's population strolling between stalls of food and wine, dressed in improvised medieval costumes made from chains, cardboard and old curtains.

At night-time, a re-creation of the Inquisition was staged in the arcaded, quaintly irregular medieval square of the old town, which in itself resembled a large stage set. Before the evil tribunal of the Inquisition passed bloody judgment on Ribadavia's Jews, *conversos* and other heretics, the cast of hundreds began battling with the Galician television company, whose van and equipment were taking up much of the square and destroying the character of the event. The quarrel was only partially resolved as the reconstruction got under way, with the Inquisition marching in procession to the centre of the square to demand over loudspeakers the arrest of a long list of names. From upper balconies all round the square buxom women with low-cut dresses and lace-curtain veils were shouting, 'I am innocent! I am innocent!' But soldiers in comic fifteenth-century armour marched up to the doors of the houses and spoke gruffly into the modern entry-phones to insist on being let in. The screaming women emerged from their houses as straw dummies which the soldiers lustily threw into a massive fire warming the whole square and threatening for a few moments to engulf the television crew.

A MOST unusual and embarrassing death occurred in Ourense, the district capital. The young man was said to have been handsome and 'attractive to women', but, on the day of the accident, he forsook female company in favour of a hen. His bestial passion was consummated in a stone hut, where the earth moved, and so did the walls. A photograph appeared in the national magazine, *El Tiempo*, showing the trouserless man on top of the hen, and the walls on top of the man. The man's wife, according to the accompanying article, refused to pay for the funeral.

This sorry encounter was the sort of incident one might have expected from the most backward of Galicia's rural communities. In fact, it happened directly in front of the seven-arched medieval bridge leading into the centre of the ancient city where James Joyce's *Ulysses* – translated into Galician in the pages of the local literary magazine, *Nos* – was first introduced to the Spanish public.

All my preconceptions of a desperately provincial and inbred town were dispelled once and for all. My arrival in Ourense coincided with an animated Sunday evening *paseo* which merged imperceptibly at nine o'clock into a bar crawl that rocked the medieval streets around the cathedral. But the frivolous mood in which I had been put by my weekend at Ribadavia began to wear off when I reached the flat of José Ignacio's sister Matilde, a university lecturer who introduced me into the friendly but more sober and serious world of her colleagues.

'It seems completely stupid to drink too much alcohol,' said a young economics lecturer, as a group of us sat at night ordering coffee in one of the more traditional of Ourense's cafés. The conversation then switched to economics and to this teacher's theory that Galicia was on the point of experiencing the worst financial crisis of its history, now that the region's traditional local industries had been supplanted by huge national companies. The group nodded, and a classics lecturer brought a touch of poetry to the proceedings by turning to me and saying in a characteristically soft and sadly sweet Galician voice, 'This is a land forgotten by God.'

THE BODY had begun to tire after months of travel and abuse, and the spirit was in need of replenishment. With the onset of winter, I became sympathetic to the idea of spiritual retreat.

Galicia may be a land 'forgotten by God', but it is also a land of monasteries, a renowned group of which lies in the wild countryside north of Ourense. One bitterly cold afternoon, under a clear blue sky, I took a bus from Ourense to the village of Cea, from where I continued by taxi through a near empty valley to the remote, massive monastery of Oseira, 'the Galician Escorial'.

A Cistercian foundation of the twelfth century, the monastery stands isolated between hills, its medieval core hidden behind a heavy and severe eighteenth-century shell with crude rustication up to the level of the roof. An old monk eventually answered the large bell, and listened patiently, smiling as I told him something about myself and my interest in staying in the monastery. He replied in a slow, quiet voice that had obviously been acquired after years of contemplation and prayer.

'There was another English writer who used to come here a lot,' he said, his brow furrowing as he tried hard to remember the name. 'Greeyam . . .' he muttered. 'Greeyam . . . Greeyamgree?'

'Graham Greene?' I suggested.

'Yes,' he said. 'That's him! A good, kind man.'

The monk had forgotten what I had originally asked, and instead sold me a ticket for a guided tour of the monastery, led by himself. My hands became numb with cold as he slowly took me along dark, empty cloisters, up monumental stone staircases, and into a stark Gothic church. A small Cistercian community, numbering fewer than a dozen monks, had moved back into the monastery in 1929, and was still struggling with weeds, cracks, broken windowpanes and other damage caused by nearly a century of abandon.

I attempted to find out more about Greene's stays in the monastery, and learned that he had started coming there each year in old age, but always in the summer, and never for more than a night or two. My guide said that few of the monks had been able to have much conversation with him. The man who got to know the General never got to know Spanish. Greene had tried to communicate to the monks in broken Italian.

The monastery is described in detail in the closing pages of Greene's *Monsignor Quixote*. The eponymous hero, seriously wounded in a car crash after being chased by the Guardia Civil, comes here to die. In the course of his last night, he rises from his bed and wanders into the church, where, against the orders of his bishop, he says in his delirium a garbled Mass in which he places an imaginary communion wafer into the mouth of his kneeling atheist companion, the Mayor of El Toboso. Then his knees suddenly give way and he falls on the cold floor into 'the final silence'.

Witnessing this whole scene is an enlightened monk named Father Leopoldo, who is perhaps partially based on Father Leopoldo Durán, Greene's spiritual confessor in his last years. Durán, a former professor of English literature at Madrid's Complutense University, was the man who had first brought Greene to Oseira, and who always accompanied him on his visits here. At the end of my tour, I was introduced to the monastery's kind and formidably knowledgeable librarian, who told me that Durán was a native of Ourense now living in retirement in Vigo. The librarian gave me the man's telephone number, and said that he was sure that Father Durán would be delighted to talk to an Englishman about his friendship with Greene. As for my own wish to spend a week or so at the monastery, he recommended I come back in the summer when the guest room would be warmer. He asked me to pass on his best wishes to Father Durán, and looked forward to hearing about my meeting when I returned. The monk who had guided me gave me his blessing as I went off into the outside world.

'A small shop and a bar at the very entrance of the monastery grounds make up the whole village of Oseira,' wrote Graham Greene. I went into the bar. The owner remembered Greene as 'polite and stand-offish', but had warm memories of 'an English actor called Alec Guinness', who had come to Oseira to perform the title role in a television film based on Greene's novel.

'Señor Guinness', he said, 'had a way of making himself understood with just a few words of Spanish. He sometimes had us all in fits of laughter.'

While waiting for my taxi, I asked for a glass of the monks' homemade liqueur, which the bar owner reluctantly poured out for me.

'It's disgusting,' he warned. 'No one likes it around here. Señor Guinness was almost sick.'

When I made the appropriate coughing noises, he produced a liqueur he had distilled himself.

'I think you'll find this is much better. Señor Guinness got quite hooked on it.'

My young taxi-driver had only the faintest memories of Greene and Guinness, and thought Father Durán was a rock group.

'Duran Duran never came to Oseira,' he insisted, 'but Julio Iglesias did. I got to shake the singer's hand, he was really nice, he was. You know he's originally from Ourense? Just like Gorbachev, in fact.'

I knew about Julio Iglesias's Galician connection; the singer made much-publicized return visits to Galicia, mainly to gorge on seafood. The Galician ancestry of Gorbachev, however, was a new one.

'I'm not joking, you know, everyone here'll tell you that he's got Ourense blood. Comes from an old Galician family called the Gorbachos.'

Back at Cea, I used the phone at a petrol-station café to contact Father Durán in Vigo. I anticipated a calm and reassuring voice, and some future meeting in which my spiritual being would be enhanced, and I would be filled with that mysterious love the Mayor of Toboso comes in the end to feel for Monsignor Quixote. But I mentioned Graham Greene, and the voice that answered my call was sharp and tetchy.

'No! No! No! What happened between Graham Greene and myself was entirely between him and me.' I apologized for disturbing him, but then the man of the spirit revealed himself also to be a man of the world. 'In any case, I'm writing my own book about my friendship with Greene. It wouldn't be politic to discuss this with anyone else.'

Then he hung up.

I LEFT Galicia and returned to Castile, but to Old Castile, the land of deserts and mystics. The train from Ourense passed through a lonely and spectacular landscape, without roads or villages, but with soft and hazy mountain silhouettes receding to the south, and meadows, forests and snow-capped peaks sharply delineating the view to the north. The greens of the foreground gradually disappeared as the train slowly descended under the red glow of sunset into the rocky flat expanses that Rosalía de Castro had so dreaded.

A young couple who had quarrelled sat sullenly in my compartment, the woman barely repressing her tears. A mother stared vacantly at the floor, while her child pointed to a plane up in the sky.

'Mama,' he asked, 'why doesn't the train go there, up there?'

PART SEVEN

THE DESICCATED HEART

22

Journey into a Castilian Winter

THE STARS of a clear December night shone above the flat landscape. The train, which had left Ourense two hours late, had lost a further three hours in a succession of abandoned wayside stations, waiting for more important trains to pass. Night had thus caught me long before my destination, allowing me to look at the Castilian countryside under conditions that had traditionally encouraged thoughts of infinity.

Starlit skies over the vast expanses of Castile were a recurring theme in the writings of the Generation of '98, many of whose associates were rendered especially contemplative when travelling by train. Antonio Machado even wrote a poem claiming that he never slept on trains, but passed the time happily in daydreams, disturbed only by the thought of the journey ending.

At Toro, I stepped out into a cold and remote station so poorly lit that I was not entirely sure I had reached the right place. The stationmaster's whistle forced me quickly on to the platform, into a black and silent world where an isolated factory building obscured the stars with its smoke, and gave out an overpoweringly sickly smell like that of a brewery. I gathered my bearings in the darkness and walked uphill towards the as yet invisible town of Toro.

Toro, former residence of the Spanish kings, once epitomized for me the decayed grandeur and spiritual dignity of the Spain I had searched for as a teenager. One of the last of the country's steam trains, with gilded, velvet-lined carriages demoted from first to third class, had brought me from Zamora to Toro, a town I had perceived as a dying, empty place full of Romanesque churches with dusty altarpieces crumbling to the touch. I had stayed in an old *fonda* where a mad woman appeared in the dining-room at night balancing an omelette on her head, and I had found a quintessential Spanishness in a fifteenth-century devotional picture in which a large and miraculously painted fly had landed in the very middle of the Virgin's mantle. I had not been back since.

Had such a Toro ever existed, or was it the creation of a distorted memory? The Toro of 1991 bore no resemblance to the town I remembered from the late 1960s, having acquired in the intervening years a prosperous, well-maintained look, with families muffled in heavy, expensive coats wandering around the arcaded main square before suppertime.

I came across a barber's shop still open at ten o'clock at night, and went inside to have my hair trimmed by a lively and loquacious man who invited me afterwards to 'go gossiping' – the local term apparently for to 'go out drinking'.

'I can tell you're someone with similar views to mine,' he confided to me over a glass of beer. 'You see,' he continued, 'this town's a very reactionary one, gets more so every year. In fact I'm the only revolutionary left in Toro, the only one. People think I'm eccentric. I'm glad you've come, it's not often that I'm able to meet literate men of the world like yourself. Living in a small town has its advantages, and I've spent many years in Madrid and wouldn't go back there. But there are also many disadvantages, which my wife doesn't understand. I can't hold a single intelligent conversation with anyone here. I was brought up among simple countryfolk, and now I seem to be surrounded all the time by bankers and small businessmen. The town's been taken over by them, and that's why it's so expensive here. Do you know that the price of an apartment is almost as high as in Madrid? And just imagine, there are about 7000 of us living here, and we've thirteen banks. *Thirteen!* Who needs thirteen banks?'

The barber left me in the empty dining-room of one of the square's bars, and told the owner to treat me well. As I ate 'muzzle' in a tinned tomato sauce served by a grumpy waiter, I wondered if the Generation of '98 would find in the Castile of today images of noble suffering, spiritual fortitude, and historical continuity.

At least they would have found an unchanged Castile in the view from my hotel balcony, a view that I discovered the next day at sunrise. The hotel, 'a modern establishment in traditional Castilian style', shared with Toro's Romanesque cathedral a ledge perched high above the river Duero. The river, flowing through the arches of a medieval bridge, made a bold curve in a predominantly horizontal and treeless landscape of stubbled and desiccated fields stiff with early-morning frost: a landscape frozen in the past.

Unamuno once pined for the green and mountainous landscape of his native Basque country, in the same way that Rosalía de Castro pined for Galicia. The stark and endless Castilian plateau profoundly depressed him on his arrival at Salamanca from Bilbao in 1891. Soon, however, he came to see it as the most beautiful landscape in the world, and he surprised his colleagues at the university by walking after lunch not to the Plaza Mayor but to the Zamora Gate and out into the countryside.

Unamuno's love affair with Castile, and his consequent rejection of large cities in favour of small Castilian towns, were typical of the Generation of '98, whose leading members originated from Spain's periphery, and were later emotionally and mystically drawn to what they considered the Spanish heartland. Their obsession with the Castilian landscape, above all with its arid vastness, revealed a passionate interest in nature largely lacking among Spanish authors of the Romantic period, but which owed instead something to foreign travellers such as Gautier, who was praised by Azorín for having discovered the 'greatness' of Spain. In dwelling on Castile, and in their highly selective appreciation of this region, they developed their own mythology of Spain, a mythology given a special urgency by an underlying belief in national revival and spiritual regeneration.

The Generation of '98 were greatly influenced in their approach to the Spanish landscape by the determinism of the French writer and philosopher, Hippolyte Taine, who tried to give a sense of form and direction to the complexities of civilization by stressing that the character of a nation was mainly the result of geography and climate. Thus the harsh, arid and endless expanse of the Spanish heartland could be seen as an explanation both for Spain's strong mystical tradition and for its succession of ruthless and determined soldiers, such as El Cid and the conquistadors. The country's enormous regional variety was purposefully ignored by the Generation of '98, who in their search for an understanding of Spain sought out what they regarded as the essence of their country, or – to use Unamuno's phrase – the 'eternal features of the nation'. Angel Ganivet, in his famous work discussing the 'Spanishness' of Spain, *Idearium Español* (1897), ignored all regional differences and concentrated on the peninsula as a whole. Unamuno, in his essay *Del castizo* (1902) echoed many of Ganivet's views, but always referred to Spain as 'Castile' on the grounds that 'Castile, like it or not, placed itself at the head of the Spanish monarchy, and gave it its true character and spirit.' 'That which is Castilian', he concluded, 'is that which is truly Spanish.'

As well as grossly simplifying the complex cultural make-up of Spain, and neglecting the growing problems of regional separatism, the Generation of '98 showed remarkably little concern for the often desperate social conditions of the Castile they so admired. Castile was, for them, less a region than a metaphor and a state of mind, its current situation being evocative of a glorious past, of a slumbering present, and of the ashes out of which some future phoenix would one day rise: 'Does it hope, sleep or dream?' Antonio Machado asks of Castile in a celebrated poem encapsulating the dilemma both of Castile and of the poet himself – immersed continually in the passing of time, poised between 'hopes and memories', between 'something which is still to come', and 'everything which has already been'.

On a more ethereal level still, Castile was seen as a reflection of the soul, a reflection that epitomized the characteristically Unamuno-esque conflict between spiritual serenity and spiritual anguish. 'The infinity of the plains,' wrote Unamuno, 'fills us with the infinity of the spirit'; but, 'in the middle of all this aridity', one also glimpses the 'desiccated patches of the soul.'

*

374

FROM TORO I followed the river Duero, crossing by bus the whole length of Old Castile next to a river that is as much of a metaphor of this region as the Guadalquivir is of Andalusia. Both Unamuno and Antonio Machado dedicated poems to the river, the latter referring to the way in which the

> 'Duero crosses the heart of oak
> of Iberia and Castile.

I passed the isolated cone supporting the castle of Simancas, to the archives of which historians once travelled from Valladolid in a bus known as 'the bus of the researcher'. The surrounding countryside, flat and dreary, emphasized for me the plight of Rosalía de Castro, who would have found little to distract her in Valladolid itself, a city of immense historical importance, yet choked by industries and chaotic modern development. Near Peñafiel, a small town dominated by another of Castile's castles, I was confronted by the more cheerful sight of the wine-growing area of the Ribera del Duero, home of Vega Sicilia, a wine so exclusive that purchasers have to add their names to a long waiting list.

The owner of the Pesquera vineyards, the up-and-coming rival to Vega de Sicilia, gave me a sullen and intensely serious tour of his domain, and brightened up only after showing me a recent newspaper article mentioning that his wines had been judged by 'a panel of tasters . . . superior to those of Bordeaux'.

Roast squirrel, an illegal dish, was on offer that day at a well-known restaurant in the nearby market town of Aranda del Duero, a busy crossroads at the very heart of gastronomic Castile. I was in a land where the refined delicacy of the best Ribera wines contrasts with the earthy simplicity of a cuisine truly reflecting the harsh austerity of the Castilian landscape. Roast meats, usually lamb or pork, are the ubiquitous speciality, supplemented traditionally by the products of the annual *matanza*, or pig-slaughter, a day-long gastronomic ceremony practised throughout Spain but which is somehow emblematic of Castile, redolent as it is of violence, medievalism, and sacred ritual. Winter is the season of the *matanza*, and I could hear the deafening squeals of sacrificial pigs as I headed after lunch towards my night-time destination of El Burgo de Osma.

El Burgo de Osma has recently been dubbed the 'Vice-Royalty of the Pig-Slaughter'. An archetypal Castilian small town, with a half-forgotten and slightly sinister old centre cast up on the banks of a quiet tributary of the Duero, El Burgo de Osma was the home town of a seventeenth-century bishop who became Viceroy of Mexico. The name 'Virrey de Palafox' has recently been usurped by one of Castile's leading gastronomic dynasties, the founder of which was a baker from Aranda del Duero who settled in El Burgo de Osma after the Civil War and – as was the tradition in Castile – allowed his oven to be used by the towns-people to roast their meats. The subsequent history of his family takes the form of a typical Spanish progression from the simple to the *cursi*. The family's fortunes rose first with the acquisition of a modest *pensión*, then with the construction of a large and ugly roadside restaurant, and, finally, with the installation, within the very palace of the Palafoxes, of a luxury hotel of lavish pretentiousness.

The former baker, now in his seventies, hovered in the background with his beret and unshaved chin, as one of his grandchildren served me with salami made from a newly created breed of animal resulting from the crossing of a *cerdo* (pig) with a *jabalí* (wild boar). The animal had apparently been devised by a local farmer specifically with the restaurant in mind: it was known as a *cerdalí*.

At breakfast, under one of the sombre arcades of the quiet main square, a drunken, middle-aged man with a mop of white hair asked me courteously in a Latin American accent if I could give him some money. He had abandoned his girlfriend a few days ago, so he told me, and had been drinking until all his money had run out. Yes, he replied in fluent English to one of my questions, he was originally from Buenos Aires, 'the most Sur-realist city in the world, according to García Márquez'. He slumped, half conscious, into a nearby chair, leaving me to speculate as to what Surrealist impulse had driven this literate, romantic drunkard to such an out-of-the-way and moribund Castilian town as this. I walked to the cathedral, which, in its size, architectural splendour, and renowned treasures – such as the eleventh-century Mapa Mundi – seemed almost as incongruous in presentday Burgo de Osma as the Argentinian himself.

I found pathos at El Burgo de Osma, and medieval decay of a most haunting kind at Castañazor, a tiny hill village off the Soria road, entirely surrounded by the ruins of ramparts. I climbed up to the village though wheatfields and boulders, and was threatened on arrival by a mangy dog which had been playing with rubbish in front of a group of wood-framed houses on the point of collapsing above the remains of a cobbled alley.

Smoke from one of the conical chimneys peculiar to this district led me to a bar, where the surly-faced owner's family sat eating in silence behind the medieval counter, ignoring my presence. Was this the sort of Castilian village the Generation of '98 dreamed about? I continued my journey into the mountainous, wind-swept Castile of Antonio Machado.

'I have an enormous love for Spain, and a conception of Spain that is completely negative. Everything about Spain enchants and angers me at the same time,' wrote Machado in 1913, shortly after leaving Soria, the town that marked the turning-point of his poetic career, and where he experienced the two emotional extremes of his personal life.

Born in Seville in 1874, Machado moved to Madrid at the age of eight, and later lived in Paris, where he translated for a publishing company, and met Oscar Wilde, Verlaine and many of the city's Parnassian and Symbolist poets. By 1907 he was back in Madrid and in need of a job. He contemplated working as a bank clerk, but was encouraged to become a provincial school-teacher, a job for which he had no vocation, but which suited both his conventional if slightly shabby appearance and manner, and his serious, withdrawn personality. He was offered the choice of teaching French in either Ourense or Soria, and had he chosen the former some of the finest poems ever to have been written on Castile might never have appeared. Soria and its surroundings provided the immediate inspiration for his major work, *Campos de Castilla*, in which he perfected a sparse and resonant style to match the stark power of the Castilian landscape.

The productivity of Machado's Soria years was also influenced by the love affair and marriage of the by now thirty-four-year-old poet to the blonde and blue-eyed Leonor, the sixteen-year-old daughter of his landlady. Their marriage would later supply biographers of the poet with much-needed romantic material to enliven an otherwise singularly unglamorous life. In true romantic fashion, the marriage ended tragically after only three years, with Leonor falling fatally ill in Paris, where Machado had gone in 1912 to hear Bergson expound on a theory of time that corresponded closely to his own. After Leonor's death, Machado asked to be transferred to the northern Andalusian town of Baeza, where he composed the second part of *Campos de Castilla*. Writing and dreaming about Soria from his new Andalusian home helped to intensify his obsession with time, his tragic view of modern Spain, and his mythologizing of Castile.

Soria is famous for its roast lamb and freezing winds. On the colourless December day of my arrival the smells of smoke and meat hung in the air, and the winds were blowing so hard that some scaffolding collapsed in the town centre, killing two passers-by and creating pandemonium in this otherwise uneventful town. Old streets were blocked off, but none of them were inviting, for – unlike the beautifully preserved Baeza – Soria is a place that has lost most of its architectural charm through peculiarly bleak and insensitive development in recent years. The associations with Machado have been exploited to the full, with the poet's name constantly linked to that of Leonor, thus transforming their three years of marriage into an idealized poetic relationship, comparable to the love of Dante and Beatrice or Petrarch and Laura.

The modern *parador* on a hilltop above the town has been named the 'Parador Nacional Antonio Machado', and looks out towards another hill crowned by the Hotel Leonor. Between these two summits, of poetry and its muse, the town peters out as it falls down to the steep and wooded banks of the Duero, where Soria's true beauty is to be found. A path shaded by poplars closely hugs the northern banks and leads to the isolated, rock-hewn hermitage of Saint Saturius. This, Machado's favourite local walk, was recalled in one of the late poems of *Campos de Castilla*. I followed in the poet's footsteps, and made the depressing calculation that Machado was little older than myself when he wrote the lines that are now engraved in stone by the path's edge.

> I am walking alone,
> Sad, tired, thoughtful and old . . .

'SORIA, head of Extremadura', runs a local saying, referring to the town's position at the head of the seasonal trail used by shepherds guiding their flocks from Castile to Extremadura. At Soria I turned back, away from the Duero and towards Extremadura, following the trail in a south-westerly direction, into a plateau of giant boulders that seem to have been hurled from the massive sweep of granite peaks that mark the northern boundary of Old Castile.

Segovia, early on a sunny winter's morning, was looking its best. The Sierra de Guadarrama was capped with snow, and the streets of the old town were free as yet of the Sunday lunchtime crowds that would later descend from Madrid in a Rabelaisian scramble for suckling-pig. The view from the ramparts below the Alcázar remained as I had first known it, a view from a lithograph of Old Spain, with a donkey and cart meandering on the narrow road below, wheatfields and scrubland rising from the wooded banks of the quiet Eresma, and the rounded profile of the twelfth-century Templars' Church of the True Cross standing starkly on a bare, ochre ridge. Only later in the day would I discover that the present, unenlightened town council had plans to widen the road and allow developers to exploit this one area of Segovia where the old town still looked out directly on to an unchanged countryside.

In the two hours of silence remaining before the late-morning invasion of the town, I persuaded a young caretaker to let me into the former *pensión* where Antonio Machado spent his last tranquil year in Spain before fleeing to die an anonymous death in Collioure in 1939. In this house with its simple balconied rooms and tiny garden, I was offered further proof that the relics of Antonio Machado's life had, mysteriously, been better treated than those of most other Spanish writers. His former Segovian landlady, Doña Luisa, had kept every item associated with his stay in her establishment, and had later presented them with a long inventory to a local academy: everything down to the poet's stove, blankets, ashtray and chamberpot were itemized in this list, and have been brought together again in the Casa-Museo Antonio Machado.

I left the house-museum having got, I thought, as close to the domestic world of a great Spanish writer of the past as I was ever likely to. I would have continued to think so had I not lunched afterwards with a Segovian friend who succeeded in tarnishing even this illusion. He had spoken about the place to the aged Marquis de Lozoya, who had dismissed it as a 'complete fabrication'.

'The Marquis was adamant that the poet never lived there,' my friend told me, 'and that they chose that particular house simply because it was the prettiest on the street, and the only one that was free-standing. But the Marquis regularly visited Machado, and remembered clearly that Doña Luisa's *pensión* was in the building opposite.'

We lunched at José María's, the most successful and dynamic new restaurant in a town, christened 'The Culinary Archdiocese of Old Castile', where the battle for culinary excellence has come to dominate almost every other issue. José María spared us a few moments from his hectic Sunday cooking to tell us something about his career, his newly acquired vineyards at Peñafiel, his plans to have 'the best cellar in Europe', and his apprenticeship under Cándido, the high priest of the Segovian archdiocese, and the owner of the first Spanish restaurant to have achieved legendary international status. My friend and I were agreed about what a dreadful place Cándido's had now become, but José María remained diplomatically loyal to his former master. 'He was very great and important in his day,' he insisted.

Cándido began his career in 1931, taking over an inn of eighteenth-century origins situated under the arches of Segovia's Roman aqueduct. His genius as a publicist was evident from the start, for he soon revived an interest in traditional Segovian cuisine by surrounding it with medieval mystique. He promoted the now ubiquitous 'traditional Castilan interior', and turned his inn into a higgledy-piggledy series of intimate dining-rooms, with wooden-beam ceilings, pseudo-medieval lettering, stuffed animal heads, oak chests, leather-backed wooden chairs, and parchment scrolls. To match the essential simplicity of the fare on offer, and to reinforce the illusion of a medieval inn, the food was served on crude, poorly glazed earthenware plates and bowls that must have struck the illustrious international clients who came there as delightfully unpretentious.

Aided by a large bald pate which made him look like a Yul Brynner of the kitchen, Cándido was almost more of an actor than a cook, and loved to appear and be photographed dressed in a medieval-style waistcoat and sash, garlanded with his growing number of international awards. His most famed theatrical gesture, and one he performed in the course of countless publicity tours throughout the world, was his ceremonial slicing of a suckling-pig with the edge of a plate, a tradition reputedly of medieval origin, and one that involved an accompanying procession of chefs and bejewelled 'majoresses', and the recital of lines instigated at the time of Henry IV of Castile. In 1941 Cándido's restaurant was declared a 'national monument', thus giving his place the same order of protection as the aqueduct above it. But already Cándido himself, under the ridiculous title of 'Greatest Inn-Keeper of Castile', was a national monument, an international symbol of 'Spanishness', and a man so taken in by his own publicity that he had come to think of himself almost as the valiant upholder of Castile's noblest traditions.

By 1991 Cándido had long been in his dotage, his mind deranged by strokes and his portly body kept alive by a degree of medical intervention similar to that attendant on Franco in his last months. His less-gifted son, the 'Greatest Vice-Innkeeper of Castile', had taken over the running of the restaurant, and had counteracted the family tendency to baldness by the acquisition of a toupee. After lunch at José María's my Segovian friend took me to see the son's new establishment, which had just opened on the outskirts of the town on a site less suited for a restaurant than for a supermarket or petrol station. My initial reaction was shock, but I would later emerge from a tour of the interior laughing uncontrollably.

Even the noblest traditions of Spain are not free from the scourge of the *cursi*. The decline into kitsch, initiated by the mock-medievalism of Cándido senior, had reached a nadir of bad taste in the son's new restaurant, the 'Pórtico Real' ('The Royal Gate'). Built from scratch, with the help of an enormous grant from the local government of Castile and León, the so-called 'Palace-Restaurant' was supposedly imitative of a sixteenth-century palace, complete with a machiolated corner tower. The homely interior of the old restaurant had been replaced by chandeliered marbled rooms and halls, with knights in armour, eighteenth-century tapestries, and a wide variety of pretentious decorative styles – from Renaissance to rococo – intended as architectural mood music. The place was almost deserted when I went there, and was on the point of closure by the autumn of 1992, when the great Cándido himself finally died. Excess, deluded grandeur, farce, high camp and an unconscious Surrealism would be attendant on the funeral, with a huge cortège parading through the streets of Segovia, the corpse of Cándido carried by chefs to the grave like a suckling-pig to the table.

As EMBLEMATIC of Castile as Cándido and his suckling-pigs is the sturdy, unbroken line of walls surrounding the town of Ávila. The walls embody the military greatness of medieval Spain, but they have also come to symbolize the inward-looking world of the spirit, for they enclose the town of Spain's greatest mystic, St Teresa.

According to Unamuno, one has only to look at these walls, with their ring of towers, to realize how St Teresa came upon her metaphor of the 'Inner Castle' and its seven dwellings that led to union with God.

'This town of Ávila,' wrote Unamuno, 'so secretive, so silent, so withdrawn, seems a musical and sonorous town. In it sings our history, but our eternal history; in it sings our unquenchable thirst for eternity.' Ávila has become less of a town than a metaphor, but those who contemplate the quiet and lonely place of today make a great mistake in assuming that the Ávila in which St Teresa was brought up was a similarly suitable place for retreat and meditation. Sixteenth-century Ávila, far from being – as Azorín and many others have suggested – an ideal home for such an introverted man as Philip II, was in fact one of the liveliest and most prosperous of the Castilian towns, and also a place where St Teresa's reforming activities were by no means a unique and isolated phenomenon.

The change in Ávila's fortunes, and the beginning of its unswerving decline into the sad, stagnant community of later years, set in only after St Teresa's death, at the very end of the sixteenth century, when the town's importance was diminished by drought, disease, the collapse of the wool trade, and the removal of the élite members of its nobility to the court of Madrid. From a population of 13,000 in 1572, the town was reduced to a mere 5400 only sixty years later. The atmosphere of gloom, sickness and death that came to hang over Ávila has persisted up to recent times and was distilled, in 1948, into the powerful first novel of the Castilian writer Miguel Delibes, *The Shadow of the Cypress is Getting Longer.*

'I was born in Ávila,' muses the novel's orphan protagonist, 'the old city of the walls, and I believe that the silence and the near-mystical absorption of this city settled in my soul at the very moment of birth.'

A different sort of sadness has been induced in many by the sight of the numerous ugly buildings that now encircle the walls, seriously impairing the medieval fantasies that tourists and Hollywood alike have loved to indulge. Samuel Bronson, the Hollywood producer, bought one such building in the 1950s with the sole intention of pulling it down. Today he would find himself battling with whole estates.

The Convent of the Encarnación, where St Teresa spent most of her life, lies outside the walls, and is separated from them by one of the more recent of the housing estates, the comfortable brick residences of which did not strike me as particularly suitable abodes for potential mystics. The peaceful life of the convent was disrupted on the morning of my visit by an Austrian television crew, one of whose members explained to me that they were making a film trying to convey 'the essence of Spain'.

A young nun, stepping over cables, guided me round a modernized interior that included the saint's cell, together with the log she used as a pillow, and a water jug not unlike one I had seen the day before in the 'house of Antonio Machado'. From the saint's autobiography, written in a touchingly direct and economical style, we know almost every thought that passed through her head here – these thoughts being, of course, ones that attributed to divine, mystical love what others would have interpreted in a more straightforward, psychological way: the eighteenth-century traveller de Brosses, confronted with Bernini's statue of St Teresa's ecstasy, made the famous remark, 'If that's divine love, I know it.'

Teresa's possibly fetishistic fixation with arrows and other piercing objects was confirmed for me later in the tour when my guide told me that a grotesque statue of Christ impaled on seven daggers was a work that had 'greatly impressed the saint'. Even the saint's relationship with the convent's chaplin and confessor, St John of the Cross, did not seem entirely wholesome, as far as one could tell from the wording of an English-language inscription recording the 'parlour where, while talking to St John of the Cross, they were lifted in ecstasy'. But ecstasy of any sort was almost as difficult to envisage in the antiseptic setting of the presentday convent as some tale of mystical conversion in Welwyn Garden City.

I penetrated Ávila's metaphorical ring of walls in the hope of achieving a closer union with St Teresa. My principal destination was the Convent of St Teresa, built in the seventeenth century on the site of the minor nobleman's palace where Teresa spent a sickly childhood alleviated by the reading of books, beginning, as she herself confessed, with tales of knight-errantry. The tiny garden from the old palace has been kept, and is visible from a window of the convent church. I peered into it and found modern statues, like garden gnomes, of the child Teresa reading books with her brother, 'books about saints', of course. Unamuno found within this enclosed garden the source of St Teresa's metaphor of the garden of the spirit.

The empty granite streets of old Ávila were so cold and windswept that the most consoling image that came to mind was not an inner garden but the centrally heated cafeteria of the battlemented *parador*. A friend of mine from the Malasaña bars of

Madrid had a job in the *parador*, and was as greatly taken aback to see me there as I was by the sight of her regulation grey uniform and air-hostess hairstyle.

'You're lucky to catch me here,' she said. 'This is my last week in Ávila.' Any impression that she regretted her imminent departure was immediately corrected by her next words: 'Thank God!' Her pent-up emotions broke through the formal façade her job had imposed on her. 'I've been here three years,' she complained, 'and I haven't made a single friend. I've never known such a environment. I was in Soria before, and got to know the whole town within days. You're going to stay the night here? No, well, you're wise. Where's your next stop? I've got half a mind to pack it all in right now and come with you.'

When I said that I was going to Alba de Tormes, she decided to come with me only as far as the bus station.

'You'd have thought St Teresa was a confectioner,' she joked as she sat with me in the station, looking at a stall selling sweets and pastries. Sponge fingers named 'Bones of St Teresa' were on sale here, together with specialities such as *Caramelos Teresianos*, and the ubiquitous *Yemas de Ávila*, the sickly-sweet egg-yolk concoction St Teresa supposedly devised for the sustenance of the poor. 'I wouldn't buy those,' my friend said. 'They're probably what killed her.'

St Teresa arrived ill and exhausted at Alba de Tormes on 20 September 1582. 'How tired I feel,' she later told the nuns who had welcomed her. 'And I don't know how many years it's been since I've been to bed so early.' I reached the small riverside town after nightfall, the bus from Ávila depositing me alongside the incomplete shell of a neo-Gothic basilica begun at the end of the last century on a scale that seriously overestimated the number of future pilgrims to St Teresa's final resting place.

The upper part of the town lay in darkness under the glare of the floodlit gasometer constituting the remaining central core of the Castle of the Dukes of Alba. By ten o'clock at night the town seemed already asleep, with even the trend-setting Bar Manhattan on the point of closing its doors. 'We're a poor town,' the young owner told me. 'Everyone has to get up early for work.' The central heating was not functioning in my empty *pensión* and I spent a freezing night in a room overlooking the convent where St Teresa died fourteen days after her arrival there.

I entered the convent church shortly after daybreak, hoping to see her relics. A small, curtained opening off the left aisle looked into a modern reconstruction of the saint's last cell, featuring a wax model of the saint blissfully asleep under mauve silk sheets on a bed that looked distinctly more comfortable than the rusted, rickety structure where I had spent my own night in the town. But what I had really come to see lay locked and hidden behind wooden shutters flanking a high altar guarded by white marble angels. One of the relics was the saint's left arm, which had been kept by the deathbed of Franco, who deluded himself into believing that he had become the conscience of Spain and that the country's patron saint would come and give him succour in his last moments. The other relic was of metaphorical resonance; it was the saint's heart, a desiccated heart.

One of the Franciscan monks entrusted with the keeping of the relics told me that he was too busy that morning to open the shutters. I questioned him about the heart, and he spoke to me impatiently of the amazement this relic had caused over the centuries, and how doctors had never been able to explain why the heart had been fresh and bloody for so long after the saint's death.

'But what's it like now?' I asked, testing his patience further.

The reply was terse: 'Practically like wood.'

THE TORMES is a modest river without metaphorical pretensions; but beside its banks was born the infamous Lazarillo de Tormes, the literary rogue whose adventures – written up anonymously in 1554 – helped to initiate the picaresque novel.

Lazarillo de Tormes began his wanderings 20 kilometres upstream from Alba, beside the twenty-six arches of Salamanca's Roman bridge, where he was fooled by his first master, a blind man, into pressing his head against a stone bull so as to listen to 'a loud noise inside it'. The blind man then struck Lazarillo's head against the stone, teaching him to sharpen his wits.

A bronze monument to Lazarillo and his master marks the site today, a site that has remained as long as I have known it so remarkably grubby and uncared for that some modern tale of picaresque low life could easily be set here. The decrepit old houses behind it extend along the banks of the Tormes into Salamanca's prostitute district; across the river, on the outskirts of the town, makeshift gypsy dwellings huddle together in dried mud below the grounds of a weathered concrete and glass *parador* which might be mistaken for a factory or a housing project.

The guests at the *parador*, blocking from their vision the modern and decayed elements that have crept into the famous riverside view of Salamanca, will delight in the background towers and domes of the 'Plateresque' or 'Golden' city, where Renaissance sculptors and architects transformed into jewel-like surfaces a local sandstone that turns at sunset into a tawny gold.

Unamuno, according to a poet who knew him, was lucky enough to have lived for most of his working life in a city where it was possible to wander around undisturbed in dreams. But, as David Gilmour has pointed out in a recent book, *Cities of Spain* (1992), reality would impinge today too greatly on these dreams, the city having been subjected in the Franco years to rebuilding and demolition work on a scale unequalled in any other Spanish centre of such architectural and historical importance: a staggering 8000 of the 13,000 buildings built before 1936 were destroyed in the 1960s and 1970s, most of them to be replaced by tall modern structures that jar horribly with the remaining old monuments. The population of the small university town where Unamuno served for so many years as rector grew from 27,000 in 1900 to 167,000 in 1981, and inevitably lost much of the magic and quiet charm Unamuno found there.

However beautiful Salamanca must once have been, the town loved by Unamuno seems to have been as much of a creation of his own imagination as a real place. 'Whenever I'm speaking about myself,' Unamuno wrote in 1914, 'about my Spain, about anything, I'm always speaking to you about her [Salamanca].' Salamanca, Castile and Spain became in his mind synonymous concepts, while at the same time his self-identification with his country developed to such an extent that the man who had done so much to reduce Spain to metaphors ended up by becoming himself a metaphor. The tragic last day of his public life is documented in great detail, but seems to belong less to the real world than to the heroic, superhuman world of Classical myth and allegory.

The date was 12 October 1936. Unamuno, in his capacity as rector, had to preside over patriotic celebrations honouring the 'Day of the Spanish Race'. The Civil War had broken out four months previously.

The hall was filled with Fascists and Falangists, and above the dais there hung a large poster of Franco, who had hoped to convince the outside world that the great, internationally acclaimed philosopher was on his side. Speeches were made, including an aggressive, impromptu intervention by the one-armed, one-eyed General Millán Astray, who not only called half the population of Spain 'criminals' and guilty of 'high treason', but also referred to Catalonia and the Basque country as 'two cancers in the body of the nation'. The blue-shirt sympathizers of the General greeted his speech with shouts of the Foreign Legion slogan, 'Viva la Muerte', and incited the public to stand up and intone a shout of 'Franco, Franco, Franco!'

Unamuno alone remained seated, his face locked in a grimace of undisguised contempt which made the crowd uneasy and filled most of them with what one writer described as 'the voluptuous thrill of imminent tragedy'. The Bishop of Salamanca – a Catalan from Barcelona, as Unamuno would shortly remind him – tried to restrain him, but Unamuno, as the spokesman of the insulted Spanish race, could not be silenced: 'To be silent is at times to lie.'

'I can't stand any more,' he shouted. 'I won't stand any more.' The man who had thrived on shaping paradoxes expressed his utmost contempt for the words 'Viva la Muerte', which for him sounded depressingly close to 'Muera la Vida'. He could only assume, he said, that the slogan was a testimonial to General Millán Astray's being a 'symbol of death'. He used the General's appearance and condition to extend the man's metaphorical significance, characterizing him as a 'cripple . . . wont to seek ominous relief in seeing mutilation around him', a man who 'wants to see Spain crippled'.

The General unwittingly strengthened Unamuno's reasoning by shouting out 'Muera la inteligencia!', but was immediately corrected by the Falangist writer by his side, José María Pemán: 'No. Long live intelligence! Death to the intellectuals!' Unamuno, with his genius for metaphor, turned the whole occasion into a battle between reason and brutality.

'This is the temple of intellect,' he concluded, 'and I am its high priest. It is you who are profaning its sacred precincts. I have always, whatever the proverb may say, been a prophet in my own land . . . You will win, because you possess more than enough brute force, but you will not convince, because to convince means to persuade . . .'

Unamuno, narrowly avoiding being lynched, walked back alone to his house, the Plateresque decoration of which, with its tiny skulls, gave it the name 'the House of Death'. In the late afternoon, unable to bear the loneliness any longer, he went to the town club, and experienced one of the more telling consequences of his rejection from Spanish public life: he was turned away from his regular *tertulia* of friends.

His last months were spent under house arrest in the House of Death, his rectorship and honours stripped from him. He died in December of that year from what Ortega y Gasset referred to as 'sickness of Spain'. In the late 1960s, when I first visited Salamanca, the statue of Unamuno in front of his last house was repeatedly daubed red by students. 'Unamuno still bleeds for Spain,' was the accompanying slogan.

Unamuno was buried in Lot 340 of the municipal cemetery. But his spirit lies to the south, in the Sierra de Gredos, where he had asked to be laid in isolation on the range's summit, alone with his dreams, with the mountain as his mausoleum, his winding cloth bleached pure by the Gredos sun and woven from flax watered by the Duero. The banal and the ludicrous are ever attendant on the sublime: for several years the southern slopes of the Gredos range have been favoured as a holiday home by the British Prime Minister, John Major. Travel articles have already appeared referring to Unamuno's spiritual domain as 'Major Country'.

*

THE BUS from Salamanca led me across the Gredos range and into Extremadura, 'the land beyond the Duero'. Castilian in character in its northern half, Andalusian in its southern half, and with an admixture of Portuguese influence to the west, Extremadura is a cultural synthesis held together by a history of extreme poverty and remoteness. *Land Without Bread* is the title Buñuel gave to his third film, a savage documentary on the near-inaccessible mountain communities of the northern district of Las Hurdes. 'Crouching over a road as long and flat as a day without bread' is how Cela described the southern Extremaduran village in his Existentialist novel *Pascual Duarte*.

Tourism promotes Extremadura as 'the Land of the Conquistadors', a land whose desperate conditions in the past helped breed Pizarro, Cortés, Orellana, Balboa and many more hardened men who shaped Spain's 'Black Legend'. Art historians, instead, have found in the region's landscape a source for the near-abstract simplicity of the paintings of Francisco de Zurburán. Many others still talk of Extremadura as a 'Virgin Land' where the Spanish spirit has been preserved in its purest, most unsullied form.

Extremadura lay at the end of my journey, just as it had marked the final stage of the longer, metaphorical journey of Charles V. Ill with gout, and worn out after a lifetime of constant travel around Europe, the Holy Roman Emperor abdicated in 1556 and was carried in his sedan chair all the way from Santander to the Sierra de Gredos. He retired to the Hieronymite monastery of Yuste on the lush southern slopes of the range, overlooking a broad valley that inspired his words: 'Ver ibi perpetuum' ('Here is eternal spring').

While awaiting the completion of his quarters at Yuste, Charles V stayed at the Renaissance castle at Jarandilla de la Vera, a few kilometres up the valley. The castle, in ruins when Unamuno saw it, was turned in the 1960s into a *parador*. For me this hotel had always held the promise of satisfying imperial longings; but of course when I finally got there, I found that it had the disquieting sameness of all *paradors*, the same coats of arms, ceramic-tiled floors, heraldic flags, artificially blackened 'old-master paintings', and pseudo-antique leather and wood furniture. *Paradors* cocoon you from the world outside, in the same way as if you were to travel around Spain listening to a Walkman which only played medieval and Renaissance music. The pleasant illusion of old Spain which can be created within these hotels occasionally stays with you as you walk into the surrounding town or village. However, this was not the case at Jarandilla de la Vera, where I emerged at night from the neo-Renaissance blandness of the parador on to a main street of nondescript modern blocks that bore as the only trace of the Holy Emperor's memory a place named 'Charlie's Bar'.

A taxi took me early the next morning to Yuste. A slight fall of hail turned briefly into snow as we entered a wood and a deer rushed out across the road. The small palace–monastery would have been silent and undisturbed had not the Austrian television crew whom I had met in Ávila beaten me to it. The director and producer were standing around a large and stagnant fish-pond shouting in German, as cables and lighting were being taken into the palace, where the search for the 'essence of Spain' would soon be continued.

Richard Ford, visiting the place in 1832, had been able to achieve a certain illusion of closeness to Charles V by sleeping 'the slumber of a weary insignificant stranger' in the very room where the emperor had died. The sedan chair of the emperor's last journey, and the specially designed seat for his gouty legs, have been placed today, for authenticity's sake, in one of the palace's tiny rooms. But the now entirely reconstructed interior did not bring me back to the days of Charles V, but reminded me instead of the parador at Jarandilla, and supplied me with an epitaph with which to summarize attempts such as these to re-create the past: 'Here is eternal sham.'

The taxi-driver was cheerful and friendly, and encouraged me to continue my journey into Extremadura by a means of transport that I believe has never before been used by the long-distance literary traveller in Spain. Unamuno and Cela would not have approved, let alone the young Laurie Lee and V. S. Pritchett; but once I realized that I would lose at least two or three days by trying to reach my next and final destination by public transport, I decided to abandon all monetary restraint and puritanical objections, and go by taxi. The driver was unruffled by the possibility of the 200-kilometre journey, and said that he had taken someone only the other day all the way from Jarandilla to Valencia. The one problem with the driver was that he was so proud of his native valley that he would not allow me to leave it without showing me some of his favourite local sights. Thus, only a hundred metres or so from the monastery, we left the main road and continued along a side track.

'Where are we going?' I asked, wondering whether I would have been better off taking my chances with a bus.

'To the German cemetery,' came the unexpected reply. 'You're German, aren't you?' he added merrily. 'The Germans all love it here.'

The words 'Deutscher Soldatenfriedhof' were carved in Gothic script at the entrance to a small and tidy plot of land surrounded by trees, at the foot of the monastery's grounds. Above a light covering of snow stood regular rows of simple granite crosses, two of which had newly placed wreaths propped up against them. Who were these German soldiers, and what were they doing in such a peaceful spot as Yuste? The driver did not seem to know, but drew my attention to an inscription 'in your own language'. Those who were buried here, this revealed, were mainly submarine victims of the First and Second World Wars, supplemented by Germans who fought in the Civil War, either on the side of the Republicans or with the Nazi Condor division. They were brought to the cemetery from all over Spain as recently as 1983.

Charles V himself lay in Yuste for only seventeen years before being transferred to the Escorial. But the creators of the German cemetery had clearly felt that his spirit still lingered there, and that the sense of historical roots was a force so strong that Germans who died fighting for different causes five centuries later would derive comfort from being buried together under the shadow of their great emperor.

23

To the Extremaduran Siberia

'WE'VE GOT everything here,' said Carlos, the taxi-driver, as we drove south across the Valley of Eternal Spring. We had emerged from the woods around Yuste, and were now in the middle of cultivated fields planted with maize, tobacco, asparagus, and a host of other crops that Carlos named individually, his face beaming with pride.

'Don't expect anything like this in the place where we're going,' he added. 'It's another world over there.'

The horizon in front of us was broken by the savage, teeth-like profile of the Sierra de Guadalupe. On the other side was our final destination. Carlos, who had crossed the mountains only twice before, tried to describe to me the land that lay beyond. He evoked a vast emptiness, with an endless, flat expanse of olive trees at its centre, and an outer wall of pine forests visited only by the occasional hunter.

We were driving towards Siberia.

THE NAME of the dreaded Russian region of convicts and Arctic coldness is a derivative of Iberia, according to Jorge María Rivero. But Iberia has its own Siberia, extending along the Guadiana valley, at the remote, eastern end of the Extremaduran province of Badajoz.

I was travelling to a place largely on the basis of its exotic name, and had little idea of what the 'Extremaduran Siberia' had to offer. It was a land not only beyond romantic Spain but also beyond all the guidebooks and travel accounts that I had read; I could not even be sure that its name was anything other than a silly nickname until we passed, some 30 kilometres south of Guadalupe, a large, regional government sign proclaiming the official existence of a 'Comarca de la Siberia'.

There seemed nothing inherently Siberian about a landscape

of scrubland, olive trees and isolated rocky hills; but the sky had turned a dreary grey, giving the environment an appropriate bleakness. The empty road we were on became so narrow and poorly surfaced that Carlos thought for a moment that he had made a mistake, and was convinced otherwise only after seeing in the far distance the unmistakable outline of a nuclear power station.

'We're getting near,' he said, further heartened by the sight of lorries carrying materials to what appeared to be a motorway under construction. We crossed an enormous reservoir, and aimed towards a faraway hill where an isolated ruin, standing above fields of olive trees, guarded the approach to a large village of whitewashed houses. 'Herrera del Duque,' exclaimed Carlos, relieved that his journey into this inhospitable land was coming to an end.

We had reached the capital of the *comarca*, and entered the former fiefdom of the Dukes of Béjar, whose eighteenth-century descendant, the Ninth Duke of Osuna, was said to have been the man responsible for giving the whole area its name. He had been Spanish Ambassador to Russia, and had reputedly found the surroundings of his Herreran estate reminiscent of the Siberian steppes.

The town itself had a distinctively Andalusian appearance, and I looked forward to finding some old-fashioned *fonda* centred around a cheeful, ceramic-tiled patio. The main place to stay, however, turned out to be one of the incomplete, half-plastered cubes located in the outskirts of the town, where the urbanization petered out into rubbish and dust tracks. A large group of men in hunting gear stared at me as I pulled up in the taxi outside the Hostel del Duque, and walked with my luggage into the bar. 'A hunter,' said one of them.

The owner's wife took me upstairs to a room of *cursi* luxury, and mentioned a price far higher than at some of the more comfortable city hotels that I had stayed in. I was curious to know why I was being charged in mid-December a 'high-season' price. 'This *is* the high season,' she answered, surprised, before asking me if I was going to bring up my guns.

Downstairs in the bar, the owner and his clients were nodding their heads as Carlos, enjoying a brief drink before heading home, was telling them about his German passenger. This information, though helpful, did not convince them as to why anyone other than a hunter should want to come to Herrera in the middle of the hunting season. I joined in the discussion by saying that I was interested in seeing the former summer residence of the Duke of Osuna. But none of them knew of such a place, and were doubtful whether the Duke himself had ever come here.

Carlos became sidetracked in a conversation about the price of vegetables in Siberia, and could not contain his astonishment.

'Everything's twice as expensive here as in my *pueblo*,' he told me, before putting me in a similar state of shock after quoting the price of the taxi ride. I handed him most of what remained of my money, and he patted me on the shoulder and wished me a happy stay.

It was a Friday afternoon, and the next bus out of Herrera was not until the following Wednesday. A slight drizzle had set in, and the forecast was for worse weather over the coming days.

'WHY BOTHER to travel?' Azorín once asked. 'There comes a moment in life when we realize that the image of reality is better than reality itself.'

Unamuno, on a visit with a friend to the Castilian village of Brianzuelo de la Sierra, reached a similar conclusion. They had arrived at night, and Unamuno stayed late in bed the next day, happy simply to listen to the street sounds outside.

'Get up, you old lazy-bones,' his companion told him. 'Let's go and see the village.'

'See the village?' Unamuno said. 'Whatever for?'

'Whatever for? There's something up with you! . . . Why on earth have we come here?'

'To dream about it,' Unamuno replied, before proposing that they should spend the rest of the day in the room, imagining the village simply through its sounds and 'spiritual vapours', and continuing their journey only at nightfall.

There was nothing much to dream about in the Hostal del Duque. I preferred to go outside and confront my exotic imaginings of the Extremaduran Siberia with the reality of an unremarkable-looking town on a rainy December afternoon.

My reputation as a strange 'German' with no interest in hunting had preceded me. Mutterings of 'It's him' could be heard behind dark porches as I walked down the deserted main street, feeling like one of the villains in *High Noon*.

The bars off the pleasant main square, with its white arcades and palm-filled centre, went quiet as I entered them. Some of the drinkers anxiously awaited my ordering of coffee, so that they could test my accent. The curiosity of one young man got the better of him, and he came up to ask me where I was from, and what I was doing in Herrera. He said he was the village policeman, and invited me to come with him to the town hall.

In the town hall I was given a large, photocopied plan of Herrera's streets, and was introduced to the mayor, who assumed that the Osuna estate I was interested in seeing was the ruined castle on top of the hill. The castle, he said, was a good hour's walk from the village, and he advised me to put off my visit there until the morning. He was keen that I should make contact with the village's *concejal de cultura*, a man called Enrique. Enrique, unfortunately, was not at home, but the policeman volunteered to search for him, and to tell the man to contact me at the Hostal del Duque.

'Are you a friend of the Irish couple?' the mayor asked me just as I was about to go off on his recommendation to see the parish church. 'It doesn't matter,' he said after I revealed both my ignorance of the couple and a curiosity to find out more about them.

The policeman went with me as far as the parish church, and on the way pointed out a fifteenth-century convent, with a tree growing out of its roof, and a courtyard that had been turned into the village sports ground. The parish church, at the edge of the town, was a simple, late-Gothic structure with a large baroque altarpiece by a minor follower of Zurburán. I was left with the priest, a knowledgeable man who put me right about the castle, and said that the Duke of Osuna's estate was some 15 kilometres away, at a place called El Afuche. He also refuted the idea that the Duke was the man who had named the area 'Siberia'. He believed rather that the name had been coined initially as a pejorative reference to the unprofitability of the local soil, and to the terrible poverty that had once existed here.

'It's to our eternal shame,' he sighed, 'that we're still lumbered with this name.'

A small and apparently very bad booklet had been written on the history of Herrera, and I could buy it, if I really wanted to, in the local hardware shop. 'But I think you'll be wasting your money.'

The hardware shop had sold out of copies, but the owner said that I could probably obtain one from the author's widow.

'By the way,' she added, 'you're not staying with the Irish family?'

The widow of the local historian rented a room to a young priest, who was the first to tell her the good news that her late husband's reputation had already spread abroad, and that a foreigner had come to Herrera to buy his book. She was so pleased by the news that she refused to accept any money.

In the bar round the corner I read the book in under ten minutes, and particularly enjoyed the biographical notes about the famous locals after whom the village's streets had been named.

'May I be so bold as to suggest', the author commented after one entry, 'that Rodrigo Foronda and García de la Peña, Jewish ragmen, were not sufficiently worthy to merit the great honour of having streets dedicated to them?' Unreserved enthusiasm, on the other hand, was shown towards a certain Antonio Mogollón, whose two short verses eulogizing the Regentess Cristina had been considered by no less an authority than 'the chronicler Francisco Fernández Sorrano' to be justification alone for the poet's inclusion 'among the great Guadalupean writers of the nineteenth century'.

A class of young children giggled and rioted as I walked into the reading-room of the local library. The woman in charge had difficulties controlling them, and shouted at them for several minutes before eventually being able to attend to me. She smiled when I told her which book I'd just been reading, and then went off to a back room in search of more serious works on local history. I later found out that she was originally from Madrid, and had a sister there who she thought might be useful to me. The sister was a student of anthropology and had written a dissertation on 'Siberian Legends'.

I mentioned at this point Herrera's *concejal de cultura*, whom I said had also been recommended to me as an authority on local matters.

'Enrique, you mean?' she said, barely concealing her amusement. 'Well, if you're here for a few days you're bound to meet him.'

I said that the policeman was already trying to track him down for me.

'Yes,' she laughed. 'In the bars.'

A TALL MAN hovered in the dusk in front of the Hostal del Duque. When I got closer, I could see that he had blue eyes and blond hair, and was wearing a mauve tracksuit.

He shook my hand and introduced himself to me as 'Enrique Pires, *concejal de cultura*'.

The impression of sportiness was belied by a pot-belly and a shortness of breath that became more noticeable as we walked at great speed towards the town hall. He appeared driven by a mysterious urgency.

The building was locked for the night, but Enrique had his own key, and led me up the stairs to his office. No sooner had we sat down than a panting Enrique placed on the table a number of car stickers made from Herrera's coat of arms.

'They're for you,' he said. He appeared very knowledgeable about heraldry, and explained that the local coat of arms incorporated the crown of the Archbishopric of Toledo, the cross of the Order of Alcántara, the stripes of the County of Belalcázar, and the castle of the Dukes of Béjar.

'I designed it myself,' he announced. 'Two years ago the district council of Badajoz asked all the communities of the province to send in their coat of arms. The trouble was we didn't have one, or at least if there was one it had been lost years ago. Of course, I went immediately to do some historical research in the National Library in Madrid, where they've kept what remains of the Osuna archives. But most of the early material relating to the Dukes of Béjar has gone.'

I was becoming more confused about the history of Herrera and its rulers, and Enrique had to help me out by giving me a short summary.

Herrera, according to Enrique, was the site first of a Celtic settlement and then of an important hospital, and had a population in Roman times almost twice the size of its present one of 4500. In the early Middle Ages, after a period of decline under the Visigoths and Moors, Herrera and the surrounding district flourished through being favoured by Peter the Cruel, who frequently hunted here. But Herrera's medieval heyday came after 1421, when the fiefdom was presented by John II to Gutierre de Sotomayor, Master of the Order of Alcántara and father-in-law of the Duke of Béjar's daughter. The family's dominion came to embrace one of the largest of Spain's medieval counties, the county of Belalcázar, which stretched almost all the way from Badajoz to Córdoba and north to Toledo.

Enrique tried to keep a serious and sober manner, but as soon as he began evoking the greatness of the former county of Belalcázar his excitability increased, and he started to lose a sense of perspective on the importance of the whole district. His enthusiasm for Siberia, it soon turned out, was not that of a native but of a Madrilenian whose Andalusian-born father had got to know and like the area while hunting, and had settled there on his retirement.

Enrique had moved from Madrid with his parents, and though a resident of the village for only the past three years, he had already taken on the role of local historian. In contrast to other historians of his kind, however, Enrique seems to have had a vision of his new homeland that transcended both local pride and a pedantic concern with factual accuracy. Siberia, in his view, was no mere *comarca* but a microcosm of Spain, an important cross-roads on the pilgrimage route to Guadalupe, a former home of a large Jewish community, and a melting-pot of influences not only from the neighbouring regions of Andalusia and Old Castile, but from places further afield such as Galicia and Cantabria.

'Its complexity is evident even in its official status,' he

emphasized. 'We form part of the diocese of Toledo, while belonging civically to Badajoz and judicially to Cáceres.'

He then talked about ancient migrations from León and the wild Maragatos, about traditional local costumes originating from the Segovia area, and about the persistence to this day of 'squat, blue-eyed Celtic types' and of a local dance 'of undeniable Celtic inspiration'. And as he continued to pursue his theory of an Iberia within Siberia, the obscure Extremaduran district I was in began at last to assume for me the mythical identity most travellers unconsciously impose, sooner or later, on the places they visit.

From history, folklore and ethnography, Enrique turned to the subject of Siberian transport, and its great limitations until comparatively recent years. He himself remembered the days when the district was served by a single bus, the *Transiberiano*, made from the chasis of a British lorry, with its steering wheel on the right-hand side. Its roof piled high with luggage, this rickety bus experienced the most dangerous moments in its journey while crossing the Guadiana. The passengers all had to disembark and wait anxiously on the shore while the bus and their luggage swayed from side to side on a raft steered by a man called Tío Vito.

But in spite of his obsession with Siberia's past, and his evident fondness for the *Transiberiano*, Enrique was not just someone whose dreams were fed on nostalgia. His dreams also extended into the future of Siberia, a future he perceived in the most golden terms. The area, as he saw it, was on the point of radical change, and would no longer be a 'lost *comarca*'. The nearby nuclear power station, though currently incomplete due to ecological protests, was a source of great hope, as was the proposed factory for sparking-plugs in the hitherto unindustrial-ized Herrera. But the main changes would be brought about by the motorway between Madrid and Badajoz, which was due to be opened in 1992 and which would surely put Siberia into the economic and tourist mainstream of the new Spain.

'The tourist potential of this *comarca* is quite extraordinary,' enthused Enrique. 'We are surrounded by an almost virgin natural habitat full of rare birds and animals, even bears and imperial eagles.'

Then he lowered his voice, and addressed me in a way that implied I was on the point of being let in on a secret of universal significance.

'Only four of us know about this,' he said, furtively, pausing for a few moments. 'A family of black herons has recently been spotted down by the river.'

He told me to keep quiet about this, and then suggested that we should continue our conversation in a bar.

Before setting off, I asked him if I would have any difficulty in getting to see inside the Osuna estate at El Afuche. He furrowed his brow as if about to divulge another secret, then abruptly changed back to a more normal expression.

'You'll have to speak to the present owner, Miguel del Pozo. He lives at Puebla del Alcocer, a village about 30 kilometres to the west.'

The rain, as predicted, was heavier the next day, and clouds entirely hid Herrera's castle. By late morning everyone in the village not out hunting was taking refuge in the bars, including one of the guards from the nuclear power station. The guard pushed a beer in my direction, and invited me to join his friends, who soon began discussing how I would reach Puebla del Alcocer. 'Pedro!' one of them shouted across the bar to a ruddy-faced man. 'Get your car out, you're off to Puebla.'

Pedro, a modest man with a gentle smile, was a farmer who improvised occasionally as a taxi-driver. He apologized for the weather as the rain turned to hail, and clouds almost touched the ground of the flat expanse we were crossing. Puebla, a reputedly attractive hill village, appeared to us as a grey smudge, with only its lower, outlying district visible.

Miguel del Pozo, a plump man in his sixties, was waiting for us at a granary he owned at the edge of the village. He knew Pedro, and asked after his family before telling him to follow him by car to his home in the upper part of Puebla. 'I'll wait here until you've finished your business,' Pedro told me after we had climbed through the narrow streets and parked the car behind that of 'Señor del Pozo'. Pedro seemed slightly in awe of the man, and referred to him in a hushed voice as the *cacique* ('local boss').

Señor del Pozo lived in Madrid but spent the weekends at

Puebla in an eighteenth-century palace he shared with his two sisters, Encarnación and Conchita. The sisters were elderly and lively, and showed a great and inexplicable curiosity in me as I sat down on a sofa drinking a sherry brought to me by a maid.

'We've heard all about you and the Irish couple,' Encarnación said.

I started to explain that I did not know this Irish couple, and that I'd arrived in Herrera only the day before.

'But you're the German, aren't you?' Conchita protested.

Señor del Pozo, wishing to get down to business, interrupted his sisters before I had a chance to assert my true nationality.

'So you're interested in the Osuna estate?' he asked. 'I'm afraid that the house was demolished early this century, and all that remains is a modern porter's lodge, which we use as a store. You could, of course, visit the grounds. But on a day like this, I don't think you'll be able to see much . . .'

'You'll have to come back and visit us in the summer,' Encarnación interjected as her sister got up to retrieve a huge file from the bottom shelf of a bookcase. 'Conchita's compiling a scrapbook of local history,' I was told just as the volume was placed on the coffee table in front of me. Conchita opened it at the first page, and put her finger on a photograph showing a detail from one of the painted maps from the famous Sala delle Mappe in the Vatican. 'Look,' she said. 'There's Puebla del Alcocer, and there's Herrera.' The only other nearby places were Córdoba, Seville, Badajoz, Toledo, and what is now the small and decayed village of Belalcázar.

Señor del Pozo, trying ineffectually to keep some control over his sisters, returned to the subject of the Osuna estate, and began explaining how his family had acquired the place after the last of the Ninth Duke's direct descendants had died out. But, once again, Encarnación interrupted him.

'Both Conchita and I are fascinated by genealogy,' she exclaimed. 'I suppose you know all about the connection between the Sotomayors and the Osunas?'

I made the great mistake of saying no.

'Well, Gutierre Sotomayor, the hero of the Battle of Olmedo, had five sons . . .'

'I thought it was seven,' corrected Conchita.

'Well, let's say a number of children, the eldest of whom was Alonso de Sotomayor, who was made by Henry IV First Count of Belalcázar and First Viscount of Puebla del Alcocer. Alonso then married Doña María de Randona . . .'

'No, you've got it wrong. It was Gutierre, the father, who married Doña María. Alfonso's wife was Doña Elvira de Zúñiga.'

'Well, in any case, she was the daughter of Don Alvaro, First Duke of Béjar . . .'

'And their eldest child was Don Juan.'

'Exactly, who renounced his titles and became a monk.'

'Who was known as Fray Juan de la Puebla.'

'So Juan had to be succeeded by his younger brother, Don Gutierre, who went and married an admiral's daughter called Doña Teresa Enrique . . .'

Señor del Pozo, giving up all attempts to speak, slouched in his armchair, and was half asleep by the time the sisters had reached the eighteenth century. They had brought into their genealogical account almost every Spanish aristocratic family except the Osunas. I waited for the Osunas to make their appearance, and was encouraged by the news that Don Joaquín, the Twelfth Duke of Béjar, died heirless in 1777.

'The succession passed into the House of Benavente, beginning with Doña María Josefa Pimentel y Téllez Girón . . .'

'Who then became Sixteenth or Seventeenth Countess of Puebla del Alcocer . . .'

I wondered at first why the name of this woman seemed so familiar to me, until I realized that I knew her essentially as the Duchess of Osuna.

'Wasn't it she,' I asked, 'who created the Capricho outside Madrid?'

'Yes, that was her,' Conchita answered. 'She wanted something to do while her husband, the Ninth Duke of Osuna, was out in Russia.'

'Poor woman,' mused Encarnación. 'With such a husband as that, no wonder she got mixed up with all those French intellectuals. And to think how much time she wasted with that park of hers. There's nothing left of it, my brother tells me.'

The Ninth Duke of Osuna, it transpired, had many of the vices of the last of the Osunas, Don Mariano, whose high living would lead to the sale of the Capricho in 1882.

'The Ninth Duke would have been bankrupted himself had it not been for his wife's enormous fortune. They say that when he was in Russia he spent all his money gambling and buying expensive presents. He was a good friend of the Tsar, and lived beyond his means, trying to keep up appearances.'

I wanted to know if the duke had ever been to the Siberian steppes.

'Well, you know what these gamblers are like,' Encarnación replied, enigmatically.

Conchita spelled out the answer for me. 'They're fantasists,' she said.

I arrived back at the Hostal del Duque in the late afternoon to find that Enrique had been trying anxiously to contact me for the past few hours. Pedro and I had taken our time over the return journey, and had driven up to the ruined medieval castle above Puebla, where freezing fog and blinding rain had turned the Gothic arches and surrounding boulders into a scene from a Hammer horror film.

In the meantime, according to everyone at the *hostal*, Enrique had been pacing up and down the streets of Herrera in search of me. I was told to ring him immediately at his home.

'I hear you've been to Puebla,' said the rather hoarse voice at the other end of the line. 'Do you think that you could meet me in ten minutes outside the town hall?'

Enrique sat down with me again in his office. His face was grey, and his eyes watery and bloodshot. He gave the impression of having been drinking continually since I had last seen him.

He handed me a couple of photocopied articles on the history of the Extremaduran Siberia, and said I could have them. Though both of them had been published many years before, he had scrawled on their front pages the words 'To be used only for the purposes of personal research'. 'The author of the articles', he claimed, 'would not want this material to be widely disseminated without his permission.' Then he came straight to the point. 'I didn't want to spring this on you yesterday,' he began, 'because I needed to find out what sort of person you were. But now I know you a bit, I feel I can trust you.'

I expected some further news about Siberia's black herons; but he embarked instead on a subject of much weightier significance.

'When I lived in Madrid,' he said, 'I used to belong to this intellectual circle which held *tertulias* and talks in each other's homes. A classicist among us, a man of enormous learning, such as yourself, developed this remarkable theory which he explained one night to our group. He confessed that it was still in a very tentative stage, and that there were a number of details that he had yet to work out. But what he went on to tell us was so impressive and convincing that there was no room for doubt in our minds.' I had began moving in my chair, infected by Enrique's agitated manner. 'In a nutshell,' Enrique continued, 'my classicist friend believed that the Extremaduran Siberia was a fragment of the lost Atlantis.'

In the long pause that followed, I waited for some explanation as to how a fragment from an island could have ended up in the middle of Spain. Andalusia, Catalonia and the Basque country had all been linked to Atlantis; but they at least had the advantage of being by the sea.

'The evidence is in Aristotle,' Enrique finally revealed. 'When Aristotle describes the people who lived in Atlantis, he could almost have been talking about the inhabitants of today's Siberia. Haven't you noticed how so many of the locals here have that combination of dark hair and deep-blue eyes, and have that skin which is neither pale nor truly olive-coloured?' The conclusive evidence was still to come. 'After hearing my friend in Madrid, I knew I had to invite him down to Herrera to expound his theory on local radio. He protested that his theory was not ready yet for public consumption. But I persuaded him, and he gave an even better talk than before. He had polished some of the details, and had encountered some startling new evidence. The public response was extraordinary. Hundreds of listeners phoned in to say that they had been completely converted by his ideas.'

'And this new evidence?' I asked.

'I don't think I'd do it justice simply by summarizing it. You really have to listen to the talk yourself. We've got it on tape at the radio station. Let's go there and have a copy made.'

When we reached the station, Enrique left me in the main recording studio with a young woman who was presenting the early-evening programme. While Enrique was down in the basement searching for the tape, the woman was introducing records, and talking to me while they were being played.

'So you're with Enrique,' she said. 'I hope you don't believe a word he says.' She turned to put on another record, but before adopting her cheerful and bouncy radio manner, added a terse comment about my Herreran mentor: 'He's a liar and a cheat.'

Enrique emerged from the basement some twenty minutes later.

'I can't find the tape,' he said, sweat pouring from his brow. He assured me that he would look for it later, and would definitely get me a copy before I left Herrera. If the worst came to the worst, he stressed, he would send me the tape to wherever I wanted, 'by express post, of course'.

Successfully dissuading Enrique from getting his 'friend' the presenter to do an impromptu interview with me on the radio, I proposed that we should go instead and have a drink outside. Once we had left the building, however, Enrique said that he should really be going home to have a short rest. As it was a Saturday, he explained, a heavy night lay ahead, 'for the two of us'.

'Your visit to Herrera will be remembered for a long time to come,' he confided, as he turned to go back home. 'We had a negro spending the weekend here three years ago, and people are still talking about him.'

'And the Irish family?' I asked.

'Oh, they're a special case, a whole book could be written about them. They've got no passport, no papers, no money, and scarcely any Spanish. They just turned up here one day, and they're still here. The Guardia Civil could have them thrown out at any time, but the municipality is protecting them. I don't know for how much longer. I try to help them out by offering them work teaching English. But they're not interested, they say they've got enough money for their needs. Yet they live in squalor, without water or electricity. I don't understand them at all. They're a greater enigma than Atlantis.'

THE IRISH family lived at the end of the village, in a tiny converted stable between the parish church and the open fields. Outside was a sign with the words, 'Restoration of Antiques', together with a psychedelic crest, and an accompanying motto, 'Two Good Investments: Art and Education'.

I paid the family a visit while Enrique was resting, and found that they were not Irish at all.

'We say we're Irish,' Derek told me cheerily, 'because the Irish are better loved abroad than the British. And it was in Ireland that we started our journey.'

Derek was a bald Scot in his late forties, and was living with the blonde and much younger Josie, a woman from Hertfordshire. They radiated health, friendliness and a touchingly naive openness. And they were clearly adored by the community. In the three hours that I sat with them, elderly women in black from the surrounding houses kept on popping their heads round the door to ask after them, the conversation being largely conducted through smiles, gestures, and laughter. The particular object of local affection was Derek's and Josie's wild-looking two-year-old son, Dan, who apparently was constantly receiving gifts of food and toys. The neighbours were also very concerned about the present state of Josie, who was over eight months pregnant and preparing to give birth in the stable. She herself did not seem at all worried by this.

'Derek and I have a lot of experience with children,' she said with a big smile. 'Apart from Danny, we've already got twelve between us.'

They had had these other children with their previous partners, but had left them all behind in Ireland. They had not seen them for over two years, and were unlikely to see them ever again.

'Being parents of children doesn't mean you're their owners,' Derek said in a matter-of-fact voice, as if such an attitude was the most normal in the world.

Derek and Josie began what they referred to as their 'journey' almost immediately after they first met each other, in the spring of 1988. They toured the west of Ireland for three months in an old Volkswagen, but then took a boat to France and continued on foot. Josie was already four months pregnant with Dan, and the strain of walking with a rucksack was becoming ever greater. They rested in a forest to take stock of their situation, and devised a way of making money by selling pieces of carved and polished wood. With what they earned, they bought two secondhand bicycles, and continued heading south towards the country that had always been at the back of their minds without their knowing anything about it.

They were the true innocents abroad, travelling unburdened by preconceptions or metaphorical baggage. After the Pyrenees they had come to the Navarrese village of Echalar, and had thought they were in the Basque country. They took an instant liking to the region, and found the 'Basques' to be as friendly and open as the Irish. It was the beginning of July, but they knew nothing of the imminent festivities of the Sanfermines.

By a shaded stream on the outskirts of Echalar, Josie discovered the place she wanted to give birth to her first child with Derek. With branches and sheets of plastic they constructed what hippies and locals respectively described as a 'bender' or an 'igloo'. A healthy boy was born a few days later, and villagers came bearing gifts, as did journalists from Pamplona and Bilbao. The story of the birth by the stream became famous throughout the region.

But Derek and Josie did not stay long. They headed further south, carrying their new child on a donkey which soon proved useless and was traded in for a moped. They wintered in Andalusia, surviving at times by drinking boiled rainwater, and eating nuts and acorns, as well as tiny, tasteless fish they found in a nearby reservoir. With the arrival of spring they set off back north towards Echalar, but after reaching the capital of the Extremaduran Siberia, Josie discovered that she was pregnant again. They decided to settle in Herrera, and for almost nothing purchased the stable where I was sitting, talking with them in the candlelight.

'We've been desperate at times,' concluded Derek, 'but we've laughed more than we've cried, and have put up with hardships knowing that good times always follow. We want nothing else in life.'

They perceived Herrera very much as I did, as an unattractive village with an endearing personality. They had not a bad word for anyone here, not even for Enrique, who irritated them at times with all his talk of money and plans for the future.

I mentioned Enrique's theory about Siberia and the lost Atlantis to them.

'It's amazing,' Derek laughed, 'the things that intellectuals say, and the state they get into over nothing. They take themselves so seriously, and don't seem to realize that life's just a game to fill in time.'

Derek was a latent philosopher who was writing down in a childlike hand an account of his journey with Josie. He was indifferent to the possibility of publication, but should a publisher ever be interested in this account, he had already thought up a title. 'I'll call it', he said, *'Just Filling in Time till I Die.'*

CÉSAR, an Argentinian singer, came every Saturday night to Herrera from the faraway town of Don Benito. He was young and handsome, and had a large following among the teenagers and unmarried women of the village. He tried to seem fashionable, sophisticated, and worldly wise, but the slick and serious image he wanted to project was unfortunately belied by a taste for chewing-gum and pinball machines, and a musical talent limited to the strumming of songs by the Beatles, Bob Dylan, and Simon and Garfunkel. In Herrera he was an exotic.

Enrique, looking worse than ever, was listening to him when I entered the crowded bar shortly after midnight. The *concejal de cultura* had apparently stumbled across some friends just after leaving me, and had forsaken his rest in favour of what had been intended as a 'quick drink' before going home. It was now so late that he thought that he might as well wait until César had finished his last set. He was keen to introduce me to the Argentinian singer.

César, eyed by most of the people in the bar, came over to speak to us, thus considerably enhancing my kudos in the village.

Later, we all went on to a discotheque installed in what had been the only cinema in the Extremaduran Siberia. It was called 'Platoon', a homage to Oliver Stone's film about Vietnam.

Everyone I had met in Herrera seemed to be in Platoon that Saturday night, including the young policeman, who, straining his voice above the noise and music, asked me how long I was thinking of staying in Herrera. I was going, I shouted, to catch the Wednesday bus, a service that appeared to follow historical rather than commercial logic, and regularly plied between Herrera and the distant and obscure Córdoban village of Belalcázar. César overheard me, and insisted on taking me away from Herrera the very next day, and driving me instead to a 'real town', Don Benito, where the women were beautiful and the bars had live *salsa* music. In the excitement of the moment I agreed to go with him, and, in so doing, unwittingly condemned myself to spending my last moments in Extremadura in the ugliest of the region's towns, in a cold and sordid room that would dispel any notions I might have had about the glamour of César's life.

'THE DREAM was over,' concluded Gautier at the end of his Spanish tour, encapsulating in his final phrase the attitude towards Spain held by most of his fellow Romantics, people who preferred to think of Spain more as a state of mind than as a real country. Generally, they spent insufficient time here for their dreamlike impressions to be worn away by too much exposure to everyday reality, a reality that led at least one traveller to round off a book on Spain with the words, 'Thank God I'm an Englishman!'

Hemingway believed that 'if one has to write books on Spain', it would be best to 'write them as rapidly as possible after a first visit, as several visits could only confuse the first impressions and make conclusions much less easy to draw'.

The Spain which I have got to know over the years is certainly a country far more difficult to define than the Spain I first imagined, the Spain of the romantic stereotypes. It is also a different place from the Spain promoted for 1992, a Spain whose spirit of triumphalism rang hollow in a country fragmented by regional tensions, notorious for its individualism, and so lacking in self-confidence as to be unhealthily obsessed with the opinions of foreigners.

I have tried to look beyond the images Spain has presented to the world, but I can no longer be sure that the country I now see is any more 'real' than the 'romantic' or the 'new' Spains. I have travelled through a country that occupies an uncertain position between a future predicted as glorious and a past either forgotten or transformed into a pastiche. And I have made my way through a literature famed for its 'realism', and yet which has often presented 'reality' in such a distorted and fantastical light that it has provided a point of departure for the so-called 'magic realism' of contemporary Latin American writers.

Before leaving the Extremaduran Siberia, I searched for a final image with which to bring to an end a journey I would once have defined in spiritual terms. Other writers of today might have looked for an image to convey a sense of an inherently dynamic country enjoying a new dawn. But I was more interested now in the Spain of memories than in the Spain of hopes, which is why I asked César, on our drive to Don Benito, to make a detour to the half-submerged village of Peloche.

I wanted to see the ferryman, the last ferryman of the river Guadiana.

He had lived all his life in Peloche, which was once the liveliest village in Siberia and had even inspired a ditty, 'En Peloche, no hagas noche' ('At Peloche, don't bother to sleep'). The Guadiana had afterwards been expanded into a large reservoir, and the village reduced to a small group of simple, stone houses by the water's edge. The place was famous now for two reasons. One of these was its salad of tomatoes and fried fish known as an *escarapuche*; the other was its retired ferryman, Tío Vito.

Tío Vito was someone who had been variously described to me as a 'living legend of Siberia', 'a true personality', and 'a survivor from another era'. He had, I was told, remained proudly contemptuous of changing times, and was not only the district's last ferryman but also the last Siberian to wear traditional costume. His age was appropriately mythical and was reckoned to be somewhere between sixty and a hundred.

Pepa and Esther, two young women who were coming with us to Don Benito, had known Tío Vito since they were children, and instructed César to drive beyond the village and head to a waterside hut where the ferryman always spent his days fishing, mending tackle, and doing small carpentry jobs. I imagined that he would have a fund of stories from the old days of Siberia, and that his many years of ferrying passengers and cattle over the Guadiana would have given him the archetypal stature of some Charon conducting souls to the other world.

His appearance did not disappoint me. Hunchbacked from his years of bending with his oar, he had a black, wide-brimmed hat, black breeches, a black sash, and a once white shirt as grey and pitted as his long, lined face. But his expression was not one of tragedy or wisdom, but of smiling mischievousness.

He invited us inside to drink some wine, and apologized with a hoarse chuckle for the single glass we had to share, and for the lack of electricity or candles. It was an overcast late afternoon, and the light was rapidly failing, until eventually all I could see of Tío Vito was the sparkle in his eyes and the whiteness of his teeth. I had various questions to put to him about his life in Siberia, but his attention was entirely taken up by Esther and Pepa, whom he teased and joked with until they themselves were slapping their thighs with merriment, and tears were pouring from their eyes.

The responsiveness of his audience and the quantity of wine he was consuming encouraged Tío Vito to tell ever more salacious and outrageous stories, mainly about monks. Instead of tales of the old Spain, we began to hear jokes about castrated monks, masturbating monks, and monks with penises so large that their girdles had to be used to keep them in place. There was a short pause as he went outside and urinated against the wall of the hut so abundantly the whole structure seemed to quake. Then he resumed his anecdotes with the same vigour as before, and profited from the now total darkness to put his hand on Pepa's knee. 'Let's go off to the village,' he chortled once the wine had run out.

Tío Vito's granddaughter, who worked behind the village bar, threw a desperate glance up to the ceiling as her staggering grand-father, supported by Esther and Pepa, pushed his way through the swing doors. He ordered wine and *tapas* of *escarapuche*, oblivious of the severe, reprimanding stare of his granddaughter. She just shook her head as he briefly disappeared from our group to rattle furiously at one of the pinball machines.

The time finally came for us to go. He tried for a while to dissuade us, and reminded us of the ditty about Peloche. But one of his daughters soon appeared to tell him that he was making a spectacle of himself, and that he should come home immediately.

He raised his arm to say goodbye, and stared intently at me as if to relay at last some final message from the old Spain. Then, bursting into a large smile, he slapped his hand hard against mine, and winked. For a few moments I was gripped by a bony, callused hand: the hand of Tío Vito, the last ferryman of the river Guadiana.

ONE OF the most successful books on Spain in recent years has been John Hooper's *The Spaniards* (Harmondsworth, 1986; new edition in preparation) – an informative portrait of the 'new Spain' written by the *Guardian*'s long-standing correspondent in the country. *Fire in the Blood* (London, 1992), by the distinguished Irish Hispanist, Ian Gibson, is a less thorough and more controversial book on the same subject which none the less contains an especially lively description of the Spanish character. Two perennially popular books on an older Spain are V. S. Pritchett's subtle analysis, *The Spanish Temper* (London, 1954), and Jan Morris's slender and more straightforward *Spain* (London, 1964).

Some of the finest works on Spanish history have been by British historians and include J. H. Elliott, *Imperial Spain 1469–1716* (London, 1963); Raymond Carr, *Spain 1808–1975* (2nd edition, London, 1982); Hugh Thomas, *The Spanish Civil War* (London, 1961), and Paul Preston, *The Triumph of Democracy in Spain* (London, 1986). A more personal account of the background of the Civil War is provided by Gerald Brenan in *The Spanish Labyrinth* (Cambridge, 1943). The major ethnographic work on the Spanish peoples and their origins is Julio Caro Baroja, *Los Pueblos de Espana* (Madrid, 1946).

Few general works on the art and architecture of Spain can be recommended. José Gudiol, *The Arts of Spain* (London, 1964), is still the only introduction to the subject in English, but is useful largely for its illustrations. George Kubler and Martin Soria, *Art and Architecture in Spain and Portugal 1500–1800* (Pelican History of Art series, Harmondsworth, 1959), is much better on architecture than on art, but the general reader will probably get more out of Bernard Bevan, *The History of Spanish Architecture* (London, 1938), a good old-fashioned survey. Edward Street, *Gothic Architecture in Spain* (2 vols, London, 1865; reissued, 1969), is a pioneering account of the medieval period written by an architect heavily biased towards the French Gothic. John Harvey, *The Cathedrals of Spain* (1957) is another classic, as is Sacheverell Sitwell's

Spanish Baroque Art (1931), the first English work to treat this subject seriously, albeit in the most precious of prose. The leading historian of Spanish seventeenth-century painting is Jonathan Brown, the author of the stimulating *Images and Ideas in Seventeenth-Century Spanish Painting* (Princeton, 1978) and *The Golden Age of Painting in Spain* (London and New Haven, 1990).

Though regularly criticized by academics, Gerald Brenan's *The Literature of the Spanish People* (Cambridge, 1951) is surely one of the most exciting literary introductions to have been written to any country. A less personal and more scholarly history of Spanish literature is given in the series published by Ernest Benn, *A Literary History of Spain*, edited by R. O. Jones, which includes Donald L. Shaw's *The 19th Century* (London and New York, 1973). Donald Shaw is also the author of *The Generation of 1898 in Spain* (London and New York, 1975), a clear and thorough study of a subject that is treated in a more individual and challenging way in H. Ramsden's *The 1898 Movement in Spain* (Manchester, 1974). Philip Ward's *The Oxford Companion to Spanish Literature* (1978) is the best reference work.

A spate of books in English has recently appeared on the hitherto neglected subject of Spanish cooking, of which one of the most lavish is Alicia Ríos's *The Food of Spain* (London, 1992). The main historical works on this subject are Dionisio Perez (Post-Thebussem), *Guía del buen comer español* (1929) and Manuel Martínez Llopis, *Historia de la gastronomia española* (1989).

An enjoyable starting-point for those interested in the massive travel literature on Spain is David Mitchell's *Travellers in Spain: An Illustrated Anthology* (London, 1990). The earliest travel accounts have been brought together in García Mercedal's three-volume anthology, *Viajes de extranjeros por España y Portugal desde los tiempos más remotos hasta fines del siglo XV* (1952). The eighteen volumes of Antonio Ponz's *Viaje de España* (1784–94) have recently been reprinted by the publishers Aguilar in an attractive four-volume edition (Madrid, 1988). Of the hundreds of accounts by 'romantic travellers', the two most frequently reprinted are Théophile Gautier's *Voyage en Espagne* (Paris, 1843; translated into English as *A Romantic in Spain*, London, 1926) and George Borrow's delightfully perverse *The Bible in Spain* (London, 1843), which, like many of the finest travelogues, tells the reader more about the author than about the place. A paraphrase of the Spanish journeys undertaken by other foreigners in between 1760 and 1858 is given in Ian Robertson's *Los curiosos impertinentes* (Madrid, 1988). Among the more serious studies of this subject are Léon-François Hoffman's *L'Espagne Romantique, l'image de l'Espagne en France entre 1800 et 1850* (New Jersey, 1961); Hempel Lipschutz's *Spanish Painting and the French Romantics* (Cambridge, Massachusetts, 1972); Elena Fernández Herr's *Les origines de l'Espagne romantique, les récits de voyage, 1755–1823* (Paris, 1973); Gaspar Gómez de la Serna's *Los viajeros de la ilustración* (Madrid, 1974); *Imagen romántica de España*, edited by Martín de los Santos García Felguera (exhibition catalogue, Palacio de Velázquez, Madrid, 1981), and Ana Clara Guerrero's *Viajeros británicos en la España del siglo XVIII* (Madrid, 1990). The standard bibliography of the early travel literature is A. Farinelli's and R. Foulché-Delbosc's *Bibliographie des voyages en Espagne et Portugal* (Paris, 1896), which has a useful topographical index. Mario Praz's *Unromantic Spain* (London, 1928; originally entitled in Italian *Peninsola Pentagonale*) was the first serious attack on the tradition of romantic travel-writing.

The travel literature on Spain after the Romantic period has been relatively little studied. Of the accounts themselves, the best-known foreign ones of the late nineteenth and early twentieth centuries include Augustus Hare, *Wanderings in Spain* (London, 1886); Edmondo de Amicis's *Spain and the Spaniards* (London, 1881); Edward Hutton's *The Cities of Spain* (1906); Havelock Ellis's *The Soul of Spain* (1929), and Karel Čapek's *Letters from Spain* (London, 1931). Unamuno's philosophical travelogues on Spain were brought together in *Por tierras de Portugal y España* (Madrid, 1911) and *Andanzas y visiones españolas* (Madrid, 1922); among Azorín's collected travel essays are *Los Pueblos* (Madrid, 1905), *España, hombres y paisajes* (Madrid, 1909), and *El paisaje de España* (Madrid, 1917).

Of the more recent accounts of journeys through Spain, Laurie Lee's *As I Walked Out One Midsummer Morning* (London, 1971) has been unsurpassed as a poetic evocation of the country. Gerald Brenan's *The Face of Spain* (London, 1950) has celebrated passages – in particular the account of his search for Lorca's burial-place – but does not compare as a travel book with his *South from Granada* (London, 1957). The life of a Spanish coastal village has rarely been so well evoked as in Norman Lewis's *Voices of the Old Sea* (London, 1989). Rose Macaulay's *Fabled Shore* (London, 1949), an account of a solitary journey by car from the

Pyrenees to Portugal, views the Spanish coast from a more historical perspective, dwelling especially on its Classical past. Two other books better on history and culture than on people are Sacheverell Sitwell's *Spain* (London, 1950) and H. V. Morton's Anglocentric and aptly titled *A Stranger in Spain* (London, 1955); more ambitious than either of these works, but also mysteriously popular, is James Michener's *Iberia* (2 vols, New York 1968), a monument to self-indulgence. The many travel books on Spain brought out for 1992 include Robert Elms's *Spain: A Portrait after the General* – an attempt to portray the fashionable side to the 'new Spain' – and Adam Hopkins's *Spanish Journeys*, a cultural tour of Spain concentrating largely on mainstream aspects of art and architecture. David Gilmour's *The Cities of Spain* (London, 1992) is a broadly researched and eloquent work with an indeterminate status between history and guidebook.

The best general guidebook to Spain remains Richard Ford's witty, readable and highly opinionated *Handbook for Travellers in Spain* (London, 1845; reprinted in 3 vols in 1966), of which it was said at the time that 'so great a literary achievement had never before been performed under so unpretending an appellation'. Much more sober in tone, but also impressively thorough, is A. Germond de Lavigné's *Itinéraire général de l'Espagne et du Portugal* (Paris, 1881). Since then, however, remarkably few good guidebooks on Spain have appeared in any language. The most detailed of the cultural guides is Ian Robertson's *Blue Guide to Spain* (London, 1989), which draws extensively on nineteenth-century works and shows little interest in the modern aspects of the country. Better on practical information and more genial in approach are Mark Ellingham's and John Fisher's regularly updated *Rough Guide to Spain*, and *Spain, Everything Under the Sun* (1988), edited by Tom Burns. The most comprehensive of the Spanish guides is the excellent *Descubra España* (Selecciones del *Reader's Digest*, Madrid, 1984), which is beautifully illustrated and describes numerous little-known villages and beauty spots; the original hardback edition has been divided into six slim paperbacks, most of which are still available. The León-based publishers Ediciones Everest bring out glossy local guides covering most of the major tourist destinations of cultural or scenic interest, as well as a surprising number of little-visited sites and places, particularly in northern Spain. The gastronomically minded should purchase the *Guía gastronómica y turística de España*, which is published each year by *Gourmetour*. The only literary guide to Spain currently available is *Rutas literarias de España*, edited by Rubén Caba (Madrid, 1990), which comprises a collection of essays of variable quality, together with useful maps. Godfrey Goodwin's *Islamic Spain* (Harmondsworth, 1991), is a concise guide to the architectural monuments of the Islamic period; a comprehensive list of Roman sites is included in S. J. Keay's *Roman Spain* (London, 1988). The Barcelona-based publishers Ariel have brought out a fascinating series of guides on occult Spain, *Guías de la España Insólita* (series editor: Juan Capdevila), which includes Juan G. Atienza's very learned *Guía de las brujas en España* (1986).

ACKNOWLEDGEMENTS

MY TIME in Spain spent working on this book seems in retrospect like an endless *tertulia*, the participants of which continually buoyed my spirits with their conversation, good humour, energy, and generosity. I like to imagine that one day I'll be able to invite all my friends from different parts of Spain to a suitably long, lavish, and entertaining banquet. For the moment, however, I'll have to make do with adding their many names to the following list of those who have contributed to what might euphemistically be described as my 'field work':

Maria José Alcazar Aceituno, María José Alcaraz Mexia, María Luisa Alías, Paloma Alonso Fuentenebio, Carlos de Apazteguía, Inma Araito, Teresa Balsalobre, Enrique Benito, Annie Bennett, Mark Bitz, Maite Brik, Fernando Blanco Inglés, Berthus de Boer, Des Brennan, Antonio Buero Vallejo, Ignacio Cabano, Pablo Capilla, Diego Carrasco, Julio Caro Baroja, Camilo José Cela, William and Sonia Chislett, María Condor, Ángel Díaz, Juan Antonio Díaz, the staff of Equipo 28, Marifeli Etxeandia, Luis Fernández, Manuel Fernández Ongil, Anchi, Esperanza, Jesús and Lola Flores, Antonio and Perico Gadea Blanco, Carmen Gago, José Luis Gallo, Carmen María Garrido Alías, José Garrido, Ian and Carole Gibson, José Javier Gil Gómez-Lobo, Cuqui González de Caldas, Francisco Gonzalez Gómez, Alberto Gonzalez Morales, Stuart Goodsir, Gerardo Grau, Carmen de la Guardia, Gijs and Alexandra van Hensbergen, Jerónimo Hernández, Julio Mas Hernández, Elena Horas, Cyril and Mary Iles, Geraldine Kilpatrick, Sarah King, Javier Landa, Carmen, Pepe and Rafa Llanos, Paco and Pisco Lira, Manel Macià, Tomas Maeztu Echevarría, Maria José Manero, Carmen Martín Gaite, Lola Matalonga, Matilde and José Ignacio Mateo Sevilla, Bigoña Medina, Eli Mendez Alcarazo, Eusebio Moreno, María Ángeles Moreo, Adolfo Muñoz Martín, Paco Nieva, María Nieves Nuñez, Fernando Olmedo, Alfonso Ortega, Carlos Ortega, Fernando Ortiz, Alfonso Ormaetxea, Belinda, Deborah and Leslie Parris, Manuel Perrales, Javi Pascual, Ricardo Quintero Macías, Paco Pachón, Antonio Quijano, Nicolás Ramírez

Moreno, José Redondo, Mabel Regidor, José Rial Triñanes, Alicia Ríos, Juan Robles, Miguel Rodríguez Baeza, César Rodríguez Campos, Miryam Rodríguez Pasquín, María Ronan, Esther Rubio Jurado, Rosario Schlatter Navarro, Pepe Schwartz Mosco, Ricardo Solano, the staff of Sua Edizioak, Gonzalo Torrente Ballester, Magdalena Torres Hidalgo, Josefa Triñanes de Rial, Manuel Vázquez Montalbán, Oscar Villina, and Mariano Zorrilla Vera.

For help and support in Britain I am grateful to Mic Cheetham, Bob Goodwin, James Hughes, David and Mariagrazia Jacobs, Dámaso de Lario, Andi Stylianou, James Woodall, and the staff of London's Instituto Cervantes, in particular Matilde Javaloyes. My special thanks to Picador and to my dynamic and adventurous editor Peter Straus. And, of course, to Jackie.